Alcatraz
Island

S A N
F R A N C I S C O
B A Y

**Pacific Heights and
the Marina**
Pages 68–77

**Fisherman's Wharf and
North Beach**
Pages 78–95

Fisherman's Wharf and
North Beach

Pacific Heights and
the Marina

Chinatown
and Nob Hill

Financial District and
Union Square

Civic Center

**Chinatown and
Nob Hill**
Pages 96–107

Haight Ashbury and the
Mission

**Financial District and
Union Square**
Pages 108–123

0 kilometers   2

0 miles   1

D0278817

DK EYEWITNESS TRAVEL

San Francisco
& Northern California

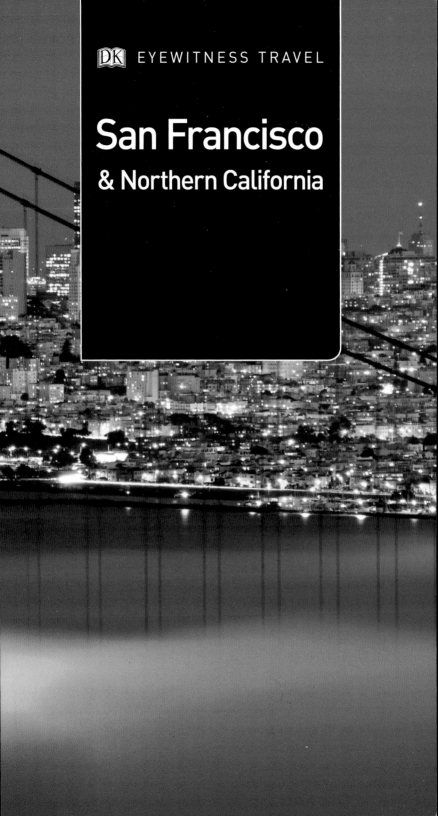

DK EYEWITNESS TRAVEL

San Francisco
& Northern California

Penguin
Random
House

Produced by Pardoe Blacker Publishing
Limited, Lingfield, Surrey
Project Editor Linda Williams
Art Editor Kelvin Barratt
Editors Jo Bourne, Irena Hoare, Esther Labi,
Molly Lodge
Designers Jon Eland, Nick Raven
Picture Research Jill Decet,
Lindsay Kefauvre
Consultant Don George

Main Contributors
Jamie Jensen, Barry Parr
Contributors
Dawn Douglas, Shirley Streshinsky

Photographers
Neil Lukas, Andrew Mckinney

Illustrators
Arcana Studios, Dean Entwhistle,
Nick Lipscombe

Printed and bound in Malaysia

First Published in the UK in 1994
By Dorling Kindersley Limited, 80 Strand,
London, WC2R 0RL

17 18 19 20 10 9 8 7 6 5 4 3 2 1

Reprinted with revisions 1995, 1996,
1997, 1999, 2000, 2002, 2003, 2004,
2005, 2006, 2008, 2009, 2010, 2011,
2013, 2014, 2015, 2016, 2017

Copyright 1994, 2017 © DK Limited, London
A Penguin Random House Company

All rights reserved. No part of this
publication may be reproduced,
stored in a retrieval system, or transmitted
in any form or by any means, electronic,
mechanical, photocopying, recording or
otherwise, without the prior written
permission of the copyright owner.
A CIP catalogue record is available
from the British Library.

ISBN 978-0-2413-0631-4

Throughout this book, floors are referred
to in accordance with American usage,
i.e., the "first floor" is the floor at
ground level.

MIX
Paper from
responsible sources
FSC
www.fsc.org   FSC™ C018179

Introducing San Francisco

Great Days in
San Francisco **10**

Putting San Francisco
on the Map **14**

San Francisco's
Earthquakes **20**

The History of
San Francisco **22**

San Francisco at
a Glance **36**

San Francisco Through
the Year **50**

One of San Francisco's famous cable cars
ascending a hill

San Francisco Area
By Area

The 49-Mile
Scenic Drive **56**

Presidio **58**

Pacific Heights and
the Marina **68**

Fisherman's Wharf and
North Beach **78**

Chinatown and
Nob Hill **96**

Financial District and
Union Square **108**

Civic Center **124**

Haight Ashbury and
the Mission **132**

Golden Gate Park
and Land's End **144**

Farther Afield **160**

Five Guided Walks **172**

The information in this
DK Eyewitness Travel Guide is checked regularly.
Every effort has been made to ensure that this book is as up-to-date as possible
at the time of going to press. Some details, however, such as telephone numbers,
opening hours, prices, gallery hanging arrangements and travel information are
liable to change. The publishers cannot accept responsibility for any consequences
arising from the use of this book, nor for any material on third party websites, and
cannot guarantee that any website address in this book will be a suitable source of
travel information. We value the views and suggestions of our readers very highly.
Please write to: Publisher, DK Eyewitness Travel Guides, Dorling Kindersley,
80 Strand, London, WC2R 0RL, UK, or email: travelguides@dk.com.

◀ **Title page** The magnicient Golden Gate Bridge at night   **Front cover image** The iconic Golden Gate Bridge
Back cover image The hairpin bends of Lombard Street in San Francisco

Contents

The colourful "painted ladies" on Steiner Street, near Alamo Square

The Conservatory of Flowers in Golden Gate Park

Alcatraz Island

HOW TO USE THIS GUIDE

This Eyewitness Travel Guide helps you get the most from your stay in San Francisco with the minimum of difficulty. The opening section, *Introducing San Francisco*, locates the city geographically, sets modern San Francisco in its historical context, and describes events through the entire year. *San Francisco at a Glance* is an overview of the city's main attractions. Section two, *San Francisco Area by Area*, covers the important city sights, with photographs, maps, and illustrations. The *Northern California* section features recommended places of interest in the region plus two suggested excursions. Tips for restaurants, shopping, hotels, entertainment, sports, and children's activities are found in the section on *Travelers' Needs*. The final section, *Survival Guide*, contains practical advice on everything from personal security to using public transportation.

Finding Your Way Around the Sightseeing Section

Each of the eight sightseeing areas in the city is color-coded for easy reference. Every chapter opens with an introduction to the part of San Francisco it covers, describing its history and character, followed by a Street-by-Street map illustrating the heart of the area. Finding your way around each chapter is made simple by the numbering system used throughout. The most important sights are covered in detail on two or more full pages.

Each area has color-coded thumb tabs.

A locator map shows where you are in relation to other areas in the city center.

A suggested route takes in the most interesting and attractive streets in the area.

1 Introduction to the Area
For easy reference, the sights in each area are numbered and plotted on an area map. To help the visitor, this map also shows BART and Muni stations, cable car turntables, and parking areas. Key sights are listed by category: Churches and Temples; Museums and Galleries; Historic Streets and Buildings; Shopping Streets; and Parks and Gardens.

2 Street-by-Street Map This gives a bird's-eye view of the most important parts of each sightseeing area. The numbering of the sights ties in with the area map and the fuller descriptions on the pages that follow.

The star indicates that this is a place that no visitor should miss.

San Francisco Area Map

The colored areas shown on this map *(see inside front cover)* are the eight main sightseeing areas – each covered by a full chapter in *San Francisco Area by Area* *(pp54–183)*. They are highlighted on other maps throughout the book. In *San Francisco at a Glance* *(pp36–49)*, for example, they help locate the top sights. The area map is also used to show some of the top shopping areas *(pp232–45)* and entertainment venues *(pp246–63)*.

Façades of important buildings are often shown to help you recognize them quickly.

Practical information lists all the information you need to visit every sight, including a map reference to the *Street Finder (pp290–99)*.

Numbers refer to each sight's position on the area map and its place in the chapter.

The Visitors' Checklist provides all the practical information needed to plan your visit.

3 Detailed Information on Each Sight
All the important sights in San Francisco are described individually. They are listed in order, following the numbering on the area map. Practical information on opening hours, telephone numbers, admission charges, and facilities available is given for each sight. The key to the symbols used can be found on the back flap.

4 San Francisco's Major Sights
Museums and galleries have color-coded floor plans to help you find important exhibits, and historic buildings are dissected to reveal their interiors.

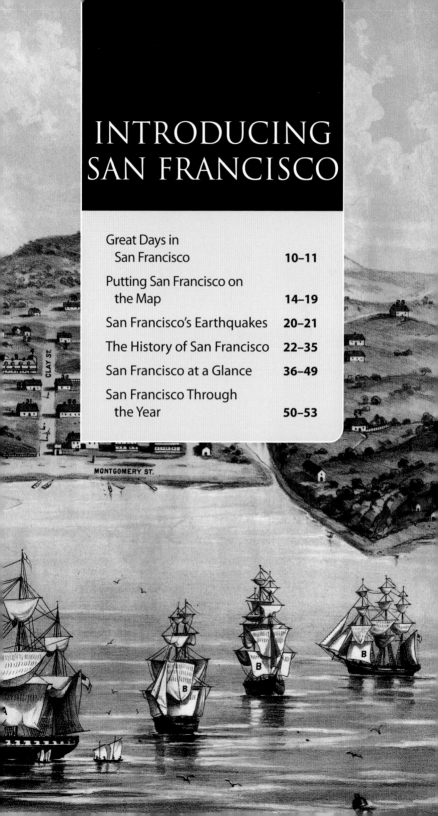

INTRODUCING SAN FRANCISCO

GREAT DAYS IN SAN FRANCISCO

Set on steep, wooded hills and almost surrounded by a vast bay, this jewel of a city is, above all, photogenic. Equip yourself with a camera, a map and good walking shoes, and set off to discover its historic sights, cultural treasures, and vibrant neighborhoods.

Here are itineraries for some of the best of the city's attractions, arranged first under themes and then by length of stay. Price guides on pages 10–11 include cost of travel, food, and admission charges for two adults, while family prices are for two adults and two children.

Rodin's *Thinker* at the Legion of Honor

Art, Old and New

Two adults allow at least $150

- See classic masterpieces at the Legion of Honor
- Contemporary art at SFMOMA
- Treasures and tea at the Asian Art Museum
- Shopping in Hayes Valley

Morning
Start the day with 4,000 years of ancient and European art at the **Legion of Honor** in Lincoln Park *(see pp158–9)*. From the wooded setting, enjoy the bay views, then take a Muni bus to the famous **Mission District** *(see p133)* to see flamboyant outdoor murals and browse avant-garde galleries and shops. For a quick lunch, munch on *tacos* at **La Corneta Taqueria** *(see p227)*.

Afternoon
Take Muni to Mario Botta-designed **SFMOMA** *(see pp120–23)* which reopened in May 2016 following extensive renovation, to commune with Warhol, Picasso, and more modern masters. Walk to Civic Center Plaza and the

Asian Art Museum *(see p128)*, one of the largest museums in the world devoted to Asian art. Relax in its café. Cross the plaza to the Beaux Arts-style, gilt rotunda of the **City Hall** *(see p129)*. Head to **Hayes Valley** *(see p130)*, admiring, as you walk by, the glass-walled **Louise M. Davies Symphony Hall** *(see p128)* and the **War Memorial Opera House** *(see p129)*. Enjoy shopping in fashion boutiques and book-stores around Hayes Valley and end with an apéritif at **Absinthe Brasserie and Bar** *(see p226)*.

Just for Kids

Family of four allow at least $130

- Playtime at Yerba Buena Gardens
- A picnic lunch
- Fun at Fisherman's Wharf
- Old ships at Hyde Street Pier

Morning
Start with pancakes and jukebox tunes at **Mel's Drive-In** *(see p227)*. Walk a half-block to **Yerba Buena Gardens**

(see pp116–17) and run up the ramps to the space-age Rooftop Playground and 360-degree city views. Watch skaters in the ice-skating rink or roll a few balls in the bowling center. Drop teenagers off at the Children's Creativity Museum for per-forming arts activities, explore exhibits with your younger ones, or take a spin on the 1906 Charles Looff carousel. Grab takeout at one of the outdoor cafés and relax in the gardens.

Afternoon
Walk to the **Embarcadero Center** *(see p112)* and along the waterfront, or take a cable car to **Fisherman's Wharf** *(see pp79–81)*. At Pier 45, feed quarters into the 200 antique arcade games at Musée Méchanique. Watch street performers at **PIER 39** *"(see p86)*, a sprawling seaside complex of shops, eateries, and entertainment. Enjoy the Venetian carousel, sharks in Underwater World, video games at Riptide Arcade, and the famous sea lions on K Dock. End up at Hyde Street Pier – board a schooner, then pop into the **Maritime Historical Park** *(see p87)*.

Colorful sailing boats lined up at Fisherman's Wharf

Vibrant red pagodas surrounded by Japanese and Chinese plants at the Japanese Tea Garden, Golden Gate Park

A Day Outdoors

Two adults allow at least $125

- **Sea views at Ocean Beach**
- **Golden Gate Park**
- **Walk Golden Gate Bridge**
- **Chocolate galore**
- **Cable-car ride to Nob Hill**

Morning

Start with breakfast at the **Beach Chalet** (1000 Great Highway), **Ocean Beach** (see p155). View the Depression-era murals, then set off into **Golden Gate Park** (see pp146–7), past gardens, lakes, meadows, and playing fields to the **Conservatory of Flowers** (see p154), a restored Victorian glasshouse filled with exotic flora. Stroll in the **Japanese Tea Garden** (see p149), rent a bike or a rowboat, or visit the **Strybing Arboretum** (see p154). Just outside the park, have a fresh sushi lunch at Japanese restaurant **Ebisu** (see p225).

Afternoon

Take Muni to San Francisco's landmark **Golden Gate Bridge** (see pp64–7) for a windy walk across and back. Walk under the bridge to pre-Civil War-era **Fort Point** (see p62) and follow the bayfront trail to **Crissy Field** (see p62), to watch boats and windsurfers. Have a hot drink here at the **Warming Hut Café**. Then take a stroll and enjoy the

beauty of the **Palace of Fine Arts** (see p62). Walk to **Ghirardelli Square** (see p87), where you'll find a range of shops, eateries, an old-fashioned soda fountain, and a chocolate factory. At the cable-car turn-around, hop onto a cable car and ride to the top of **Nob Hill** (see p103). After a wander here, amble down to the bustling streets of **Chinatown** (see pp96–103).

Along the Waterfront

Two adults allow at least $150

- **Home of the Giants**
- **Gourmet treats**
- **A walk in Levi's Plaza Park**
- **Sail around the bay or pay a visit to Alcatraz**

Morning

Start your expedition with a coffee at **Caffè Roma** (see p230), then head to **AT&T Park** (see p260), home of the San Francisco Giants. Stroll around the perimeter of the ball park for fabulous views. Proceed to the tall **Ferry Building** (see pp114–15), where you can buy artisan cheeses, rare teas, pastries, and locally grown produce in the bustling marketplace. Across the street, **Embarcadero Center** (see p112) is a six-block, high-rise complex of shops and restaurants topped by tree-lined, sky-high terraces.

From here, walk out onto the waterfront to hobnob with fishermen, perch on a bench, watch passing ships and snap the **Transamerica Pyramid** (see p113) on the skyline. Walk to **Levi's Plaza** (see p93), a grassy area with a backdrop of vintage houses on Telegraph Hill, topped by **Coit Tower** (see pp92–3). For lunch, try **Fog City** (see p224) for excellent gourmet sandwiches and a retro-chic atmosphere.

Afternoon

Jump onto a vintage streetcar, or walk to Pier 41 at **Fisherman's Wharf** (see pp80–81) and take an hour-long Blue and Gold Fleet sightseeing trip around the bay and under the bridge. You can also cruise to the notorious prison island **Alcatraz** (see pp82–5) for a guided tour – in summer months, be sure to book a few weeks ahead. Back at the wharf, look into **Madame Tussaud's** (see p86). Finally, amble to **Fort Mason** (see pp74–5) to watch the sun set over the harbor.

Fog City, a San Francisco landmark

The "Painted Ladies" on Steiner Street, near Alamo Square

2 Days in San Francisco

- Bicycle over the Golden Gate Bridge
- Explore the beatnik haunts of North Beach
- Discover the historic hippie neighborhood of Haight Ashbury

Day 1
Morning For some pedal-powered sightseeing, **rent a bike** *(p281)*. Start out from **Fisherman's Wharf** *(pp80–81)* and cycle through **Fort Mason** *(pp74–5)* and over the magnificent **Golden Gate Bridge** *(pp64–7)* to **Sausalito** *(p163)*. Explore this delightful fishing and sailing town, then catch a ferry back and have lunch at a café in the **Ferry Building** *(pp114–15)*.

Afternoon Visit **North Beach** *(pp88–9)*, stopping off at the **Beat Museum** *(p89)* to see some fascinating Beat Generation memorabilia. Climb the lovely **Vallejo Street Stairway** *(p89)* before making your way to **Coit Tower** *(pp92–3)* for some great North Bay views. Look out for the murals in the tower's lobby. End the day with an evening trip to **Alcatraz Island** *(pp82–5)*, the notorious, historic prison.

Day 2
Morning Start the day at **Civic Center** *(pp124–31)*, taking in the gilded **City Hall** *(p129)*, and **Hayes Valley** *(p130)*, one of the city's hippest shopping and dining districts. Continue on to **Alamo Square** *(p131)* to see the "Painted Ladies" – a unique downtown view, capturing rows of pretty Victorian houses and park. Walk through the **Golden Gate Park Panhandle** *(p136)* to the former "Flower Power" district **Haight Ashbury** *(pp134–5)* for lunch.

Afternoon Take in some of the spectacular attractions of **Golden Gate Park** *(pp144–59)*. The **California Academy of Sciences** *(pp152–3)* covers virtually every aspect of the natural world, and the **Japanese Tea Garden** *(p149)*, with its rock gardens and bonsai trees, is a serene haven. Spend the evening on Valencia Street, in the **Mission District** *(pp132–43)*.

3 Days in San Francisco

- Ride the vintage F line streetcar to MoMA
- Catch a ferry out to the old prison at Alcatraz Island
- Climb up the Vallejo Street Stairway to Coit Tower on Telegraph Hill

Day 1
Morning Have breakfast at **Fisherman's Wharf** *(pp80–81)* and see the sea lions sunbathing near **PIER 39** *(p86)*. Next, take the vintage **F line streetcar** *(pp282–3)* to **Union Square Shops** *(p118)*. The nearby Museum District, centered on the wonderful **San Francisco Museum of Modern Art** *(pp120–23)*, offers artistic gems from cartoons to works by Jeff Koons. Have lunch at the **Ferry Building** *(pp114–15)*.

Afternoon Catch a ferry out to **Alcatraz Island** *(pp82–5)* for a tour of the historic prison; the audioguide is a must. End the day by exploring bustling **Chinatown** *(pp98–9)*.

Day 2
Morning Many of the city's best sights can be reached by bicycle, which can be rented from **Fisherman's Wharf** *(pp80–81)*. Ride along the Bay through **Fort Mason** *(pp74–5)* and across Crissy Field, then over the iconic **Golden Gate Bridge** *(pp64–7)* to the pretty former fishing community of **Sausalito** *(p163)*. Enjoy the scenic ferry ride back to the city.

Coit Tower at the top of Telegraph Hill, one of the city's best viewpoints

Afternoon Head on foot into **North Beach** *(pp88–9)*. Explore the neighborhood's beatnik haunts, starting at the **Beat Museum** *(p89)*. Walk up the **Vallejo Street Stairway** *(p89)* and on to **Coit Tower** *(pp92–3)* for some stunning city and bay views. Continue to lovely **Washington Square** *(p92)* and visit nearby **Saints Peter and Paul Church** *(p92)*, once dubbed the "Marzipan Church" for the frothy stucco decoration on its spires.

Day 3
Morning Start your day near the grand **City Hall** *(p129)* at **Civic Center** *(pp124–31)*. Stroll along **Hayes Valley** *(p130)*, past shops and cafés, up to **Alamo Square** *(p131)* to see the pretty

Victorian houses known as the "Painted Ladies." Continue via the **Golden Gate Park Panhandle** *(p136)* to lively **Haight Ashbury** *(pp134–5)*. **Golden Gate Park** *(pp144–55)* is jam-packed with things to see and do, but be sure to visit the **California Academy of Sciences** *(pp152–3)* and the relaxing **Japanese Tea Garden** *(p149)*.

Afternoon The park ends at Ocean Beach. Head north to wild **Land's End** *(p159)* and visit **Cliff House** *(p159)* for a look at the Camera Obscura, and dinner in one of its restaurants.

5 Days in San Francisco

- Visit the myriad attractions of Golden Gate Park
- Take a cable car ride up Nob Hill
- Sample fine wine in Napa Wine Country

Day 1
Morning Rent a bicycle at **Fisherman's Wharf** *(pp80–81)* and head along the bike trail through **Fort Mason** *(pp74–5)* to **Golden Gate Bridge** *(pp64–7)*. Watch for dolphins as you cross into **Sausalito** *(p163)*. Spend some time exploring the town before taking the ferry back for lunch at the **Ferry Building** *(pp114–15)*.

Afternoon Take a walk up **Coit Tower** *(pp92–3)* to see the city from up high, before visiting Catholic **Saints Peter and Paul Church** *(p92)* near the pretty park at **Washington Square** *(p92)*. Walk to **North Beach** *(pp88–9)* and visit the **Beat Museum** *(p89)*, to learn about the artists and poets that gave this neighborhood its vibe.

Day 2
Morning Visit the Beaux-Arts-style **City Hall** *(p129)* at **Civic Center** *(pp124–31)*, then take a stroll along **Hayes Valley** *(p130)*, which has an interesting mix of boutiques and eateries. Stop off at **Alamo Square** *(p131)* to see the "Painted Ladies," a row

of quaint Victorian houses. Continue through the **Golden Gate Park Panhandle** *(p136)* to explore the historic hippie neighborhood of **Haight Ashbury** *(pp134–5)*.

Afternoon Head downtown to the **San Francisco Museum of Modern Art** *(pp120–23)*; enjoy stunning views from the top-floor terrace. End the day with some shopping around **Union Square** *(p118)*; be sure to visit **Gump's** *(p118)*, renowned for its inventive window displays.

Day 3
Morning Start early and head to **Golden Gate Park** *(pp144–55)*, which offers outdoor activities, botanical gardens, and museums galore. Visit the wonderful **California Academy of Sciences** *(pp152–3)* for its aquariums and the **de Young Museum** *(p149)* for an amazing art collection.

Afternoon Take a picnic to the broad sweep of **Ocean Beach** *(p155)*. Continuing north toward **Land's End** *(p159)*, stop off at **Cliff House** *(p159)* to see the fascinating Camera Obscura. In the evening, head to the sumptuous **Castro Theatre** *(p138)* in the city's historic gay district for a drink and a movie.

Day 4
Morning The Bay Area doesn't stop at the city limits, so take a day to get out and explore: **Napa Wine Country** *(pp192–5)* is just an hour away by car. Have breakfast in **Russian Hill** *(pp182–3)*, before heading out across the **Golden Gate Bridge** *(pp64–7)*

The grand dome of City Hall at Civic Center, San Francisco's main public space

toward Napa. Take a tour of the **Clos Pegase** winery *(p192)*, which specializes in Cabernet, Merlot, and Petite Syrah port.

Afternoon Continue north to the historic hot-springs town **Calistoga** *(p195)* and spend an indulgent afternoon in a spa.

Day 5
Morning Enjoy breakfast at **Fisherman's Wharf** *(pp80–81)* and watch the sea lions on fun-filled **PIER 39** *(p86)*. End the morning with a tour of the vintage submarine **USS Pampanito** *(p86)*.

Afternoon Take the ferry to historic **Alcatraz Island** *(pp82–5)*, making use of the informative audioguide. Afterward, explore **Chinatown** *(pp98–9)* and take a ride on San Francisco's famous moving landmark, a cable car, up to **Nob Hill** *(p103)*. See the majestic **Grace Cathedral** *(p105)* and finish the night with dinner at the Top of the Mark restaurant at the **Mark Hopkins InterContinental Hotel** *(p104)*.

Grapes ripening on the vine on a Napa Valley winery

Putting San Francisco on the Map

San Francisco is, after New York, the second most densely populated city in the United States, with over 830,000 residents crowded into an area of 47 sq miles (122 sq km). Its location at the tip of a hilly peninsula on the West Coast of North America, overlooking the Pacific Ocean, is one of the most beautiful in the world. Three airports in the Bay Area handle both international and domestic flights. There are also interstate highways and rail links serving the East Coast and other parts of the country, and Canada.

Key

≡ Freeway

≡ Major road

— Amtrak line

–·– International border

--- State line

The Bay Area

To the east, the cities of Oakland and Berkeley are reached via the Bay Bridge, while to the north, the Golden Gate Bridge links the peninsula to Marin County. These areas, together with the suburbs to the south, make up the Bay Area, which is served by Bay Area Rapid Transit (BART) lines, CalTrain, and freeways.

↑ *Santa Rosa*

Novato

SAN PABLO BAY

Fairfax

San Anselmo

San Rafael

Kent Lake

Larkspur

Richmond

Corte Madera

Bolinas

0 kilometers   10

0 miles   5

Tamalpais Valley

Tiburon

Stinson Beach

Sausalito

Angel Island

Muir Beach

Bay Bridge (Toll)

Golden Gate Bridge (Toll)

SAN FRANCISCO

Stonestown

Thornton Beach

Daly City

South San Francisco

Pacific Manor

Sharp Park Beach

San Franc Internatio

Pacifica

Millbrae

Pedro Valley

San Andreas Reservoir

Burlingame

Gray Whale Cove Beach

Montara

San Mateo

Montara Beach

Crystal Springs Lake

Moss Beach

Moss Beach

El Granada

Half Moon Bay

PACIFIC OCEAN

Half Moon Bay Beach

San Gregorio

San Gregorio Beach

Key

   Central San Francisco

   Urban area

═══ Freeway

▬▬▬ Major road

═══ Minor road

─── Railroad line

---- Ferry route

For keys to symbols *see back flap*

Central San Francisco

San Francisco is a compact city, and much of this vibrant metropolis can be explored on foot. The many hills mean a bit of climbing, but that will only whet your appetite for the city's famous gourmet food. Each neighborhood has its own charm, best explored by walking through it.

Victorian Houses
See pp76–7.

Golden Gate Bridge
Completed in May 1937, the bridge is as much a part of the landscape as the craggy Marin headlands and the idyllic bay *(see pp64–7)*.

Cliff House
One of the city's original tourist sights, Cliff House still attracts visitors who come to eat at the restaurant and admire the spectacular views of Seal Rocks and the Pacific surf *(see p159)*.

Lombard Street
Running across the tip of the peninsula, Lombard Street is famous for the short, steep section on Russian Hill. Known as the "crookedest street in the world," it stretches for only one block between Hyde and Leavenworth streets, yet has ten Z-bends *(see p88)*.

FISHERMAN'S WHARF

FORT MASON

MARINA

MARINA BOULEVARD

BAY STREET

LAGUNA STREET

BAY

LOMBARD STREET

VAN NESS

HYDE STREET

COLUMBUS AVENUE

POWELL STREET

STOCKTON

SANSOME STREET

THE EMBARCADERO

Exploratorium

NORTH BEACH

FILBERT STREET

LOMBARD

FILBERT STREET

WEBSTER STREET

GREEN STREET

TAYLOR STREET

GREEN STREET

BROADWAY

LOMBARD

GOUGH STREET

STREET

DIVISADERO STREET

BAKER STREET

BROADWAY STREET

JACKSON STREET

NOB HILL

CHINATOWN

Embarcadero

PACIFIC HEIGHTS

CLAY ST

STREET

CLAY STREET

AVENUE

CALIFORNIA STREET

Montgomery St

Greyhound Bus Depot

CALIFORNIA

BUSH STREET

TAYLOR STREET

Museum of Modern Art

PRESIDIO AVENUE

BUSH STREET

GEARY STREET

HYDE STREET

VAN NESS AVE.

STREET

Powell Street

3RD STREET

SOMA

Yerba Buena Gardens

BOULEVARD

GEARY

WESTERN ADDITION

GOUGH

EDDY STREET

TURK

MARKET ST

6TH ST

HARRISON STREET

JAMES LICK FREEWAY

MASONIC AVE

STREET

GOLDEN GATE STREET

FULTON STREET

AVENUE

ALAMO SQUARE

CIVIC CENTER

Civic Center

FELL STREET

OAK STREET

Van Ness

AIGHT HBURY

HAIGHT STREET

CLAYTON STREET

MASONIC AVE

BUENA VISTA PARK

ROOSEVELT WAY

DUBOCE AVE

CASTRO STREET

14TH STREET

CENTRAL FREEWAY

Church St

16TH St Mission

CORONA HEIGHTS PARK

STATES STREET

15TH STREET

16TH STREET

MARKET STREET

SOUTH VAN NESS AVENUE

STREET

Castro St

17TH STREET

18TH STREET

DOLORES STREET

MISSION STREET

MISSION

19TH STREET

DIAMOND STREET

9TH STREET

CHURCH STREET

STREET

TWIN PEAKS BOULEVARD

20TH STREET

21ST STREET

23RD STREET

24th St Mission

MARKET ST

DOUGLAS STREET

TWIN PEAKS

24TH STREET

JERSEY STREET

25TH STREET

0 kilometers 2

0 miles 1

San Francisco's Earthquakes

San Francisco lies west of the San Andreas Fault and experiences occasional earthquakes. The Loma Prieta earthquake of October 17, 1989, named after the hill close to its epicenter in the Santa Cruz Mountains, was the worst to hit the area since 1906 *(see pp30–31)*. Many buildings are now being strengthened to withstand tremors, and shelters like the one at the Moscone Center *(see pp116–17)* are stocked as emergency relief sites. In addition, most hotels have their own evacuation procedures, and the local telephone directory has four pages of advice.

The 1989 earthquake measured 7.1 on the Richter scale. It caused some of the houses that were built on landfill in the Marina District to shift off their foundations.

Berkeley

The San Andreas Fault is a major fracture in the Earth's crust. It extends almost the full length of California, some 600 miles (965 km).

San Francisco lies near the northern end of the fault.

Pacific Plate Meets North American Plate
The San Andreas Fault is the result of friction where two major plates of the Earth's crust meet – the eastern Pacific and the North American plates.

San Andreas Fault

North American plate

L (long) waves travel across the surface.

Epicenter (point on the surface above the focus of an earthquake)

Hypocenter (the focus of an earthquake)

S (secondary) waves travel through solid parts of the crust.

P waves   S waves   L waves

P (primary) waves travel through the Earth's core.

Pacific plate   Hypocenter

Earthquake energy vibrations travel like waves through the Earth's crust. The interval between the arrival of the P and S waves tells scientists how far away the epicenter of the earthquake is.

A seismograph printout shows the intensity of earthquake vibrations graphically. Inside the seismograph a pen traces P (primary), S (secondary), and L (long) waves on a rotating drum.

Scientists monitor the movement of the San Andreas Fault by bouncing laser beams off a network of reflectors. The system can pick up movements of less than 0.025 inch (0.6 mm) over a distance of 4 miles (6 km), enabling seismologists to predict when earthquakes are likely to occur.

The hills and coastal ranges of the Bay Area are pressure ridges formed by hundreds of fault movements compressing and uplifting the land.

Hayward Fault

In Oakland, 42 people were killed in 1989 when an elevated highway section collapsed and 44 slabs of concrete, each weighing 661 tons, fell onto the cars.

A Vibroseis truck produces artificial S (secondary) waves that probe the underlying rock structure to measure movement.

Calaveras Fault

1769 Members of Portolá's expedition are first Europeans to experience an earthquake in California

1872 Earthquake demolishes town of Lone Pine and Sierra Nevadas rise 13 ft (4 m)

1857 Strong earth tremor followed by smaller tremors in Bay Area

1890 Pronounced earth tremor

1989 Loma Prieta earthquake strikes city and Bay Area, killing 67 and making 1,800 homeless. Worst quake since 1906

1957 Strong tremor in Bay Area

1750	1800	1850	1900	1950

Don Gaspar de Portolá

1865 City suffers its first major earthquake on October 9, followed by second quake on October 23

1868 Strong tremor in Hayward Fault

1906 earthquake damage

1977 Eight earth tremors occur

1906 Strongest earthquake ever; 3-day fire destroys much of city leaving 3,000 dead and 250,000 homeless. 52 small tremors shake region over following two days

THE HISTORY OF SAN FRANCISCO

Even by the standards of the New World, San Francisco remained *terra incognita* for a surprisingly long time. A few early European explorers, including Portuguese-born João Cabrilho and England's Sir Francis Drake, sailed up and down the California coast in the 16th century, but they all sailed past the Golden Gate without noticing the bay that lay beyond it. It was not until 1769 that the first non-natives laid eyes on what is now San Francisco; thereafter the area was colonized swiftly by the Spanish, who established both missions and *presidios* (forts). In 1821, when Mexico declared independence from Spain, it became Mexican territory.

The Growing City

The first significant boost to growth occurred in 1848, when gold was discovered at Sutter's Mill in the Sierra Nevada foothills near Sacramento. Hundreds of thousands of prospectors were attracted to California from all over the world, leading to the Gold Rush of 1849 (the prospectors of this time were known as '49ers). This coincided with the United States' takeover of the West Coast and, by 1869, San Francisco had grown into an international city renowned both for its wild "Barbary Coast," stretching west from the waterfront, and for the fortunes that were made speculating on the newfound riches of the American frontier.

Earthquake and Recovery

As the population increased, the city grew westward to fill the narrow peninsula: cable cars were invented to conquer the steep hills, and blocks of ornate Victorian houses were built. The great earthquake and fire of 1906 destroyed much of the city but not its spirit, and reconstruction was soon underway. Throughout all of this, San Francisco retained its unique character and seemingly limitless energy. The following pages illustrate significant periods in the city's history.

Telegraph Hill and North Beach at the time of the Gold Rush

◀ An 1873 print of the city looking south, with Market Street running from the center of the waterfront

Early San Francisco

The first inhabitants of the area around San Francisco Bay were Native Americans, grouped into two main tribes, the Coast Miwok in the north and the Ohlone in the south. By the mid-1500s, European ships were exploring the California coast, but no contact was made with the Indians until Sir Francis Drake anchored off Point Reyes and claimed it for Queen Elizabeth I. The bay remained undiscovered until 1769, and in 1776 Spain established a small *presidio* (fort) and a mission, named in honor of the founder of the Franciscan order, San Francisco de Asis.

Extent of the City

☐ Today ☐ 1800
▨ Land reclaimed since 1800

Tcholovoni Indians
Various tribes, including these Tcholovoni Indians, hunted and settled in small villages on the shores of San Francisco Bay.

Missionaries from Spain tried to convert the Indians to Christianity, forcing them to live in barracks and to do forced labor.

Girdles were decorated with feathers and shells.

Drake Lands at Point Reyes (1579)
It is thought that Sir Francis Drake landed at what is now called Drake's Bay; he was greeted by Miwok Indians.

10,000 BC First Indians migrate to the Bay area

AD 1542 Portuguese-born explorer João Cabrilho sights the Farallon Islands off the coast of San Francisco

1602 Sebastian Vizcaino visits Point Reyes, but also fails to find the bay. His glowing reports encourage the later expedition that discovers San Francisco Bay

10,000 BC	AD 1550	1600	16

João Cabrilho (died 1543)

1579 Sir Francis Drake lands near Point Reyes for ship repairs

1595 Spanish trading ship *San Augustin* sinks off Point Reyes

1666 *Map showing California as an island*

Kule Loklo Indians

These early Bay Area inhabitants were depicted by Anton Refregier in his mural in the foyer of the Rincon Center Annex (see p115).

Where to See Early San Francisco

Early American Indian tools are at the California Academy of Sciences (pp152–3), while Mission Dolores (p139) and Oakland Museum of California (pp168–9) have Mission-era artifacts.

The Missions

Under the direction of Father Narciso Duran, the mission of San Jose was the largest and most prosperous in the Bay Area.

A spear was an important dance accessory.

Male dancers painted their bodies with red, black, and white pigments.

17th-century icon of St Peter, carved in Mexico and carried to California, is now in Oakland Museum of California (p168).

Dance at Mission Dolores

The Russian artist Ludovic Choris (1795–1828) drew this picture of Indians dancing outside Mission Dolores in 1816. They decorated their bodies, performing for the missionaries every Sunday.

1701 Father Kino crosses the Colorado River proving that Baja California is a peninsula, not an island

Portolá's 1769 expedition

1776 Juan De Anza leads the first party of settlers overland to San Francisco, arriving on March 28

1816 Russian traders arrive on the ship *Rurik* and are disturbed by the high mortality rate of American Indians

1700   **1750**   **1800**

1769 Don Gaspar de Portolá, leading a party of explorers overland, discovers the bay in November 1769

1775 Spanish ship *San Carlos*, captained by Lt Juan Manuel de Ayala, is the first to enter San Francisco Bay

1797 Mission San Jose founded

Indians gambling

The Gold Rush

Having broken away from Spain in 1821, Mexico opened California to foreign trade for the first time. Whaling vessels and traders anchored in San Francisco Bay, and a small village began to grow. In 1848, with the discovery of gold in the Sierra Nevada foothills, and the US annexation of California, everything changed. In two years, 100,000 prospectors poured into San Francisco transforming it into a wild frontier city.

Extent of the City

☐ Today   ☐ 1853

San Francisco Captured from Mexico
On July 9, 1846 the USS *Portsmouth* took control of the undefended bay, and 70 US sailors and marines marched ashore, raising the Stars and Stripes in the central plaza.

Vallejo's Goblet
This elegant goblet reveals the gracious way of life of General Vallejo, the last Mexican governor of California.

Sam Brannan set up the city's first newspaper in 1847.

Firemen pulling firefighting rig

Gambling
Fortunes and lives were won or lost on the turn of a card; gambling was a way of life.

1820 Whaling ships use Sausalito as main base of operations

1823 Mission San Francisco de Solano founded at Sonoma

1828 Fur trapper Jedediah Smith arrives at Presidio after making the first crossing of the rugged coastal mountains

1834 Missions close, and their assets are divided among Mexican landowners

1820

1830

1822 The Mexican Revolution ends Spanish rule over California

Richardson's hand-drawn map of Yerba Buena (San Francisco) in 1835

1835 William Richardson foun[ ] Yerba Buena, later renamed San Francisco

Where to See Gold Rush San Francisco

Little remains of the Gold Rush city, but you can get a feel for this era at the Wells Fargo History Museum *(see p112)*, the Oakland Museum of California *(see pp168–9)*, or the Jackson Square Historical District *(see p112)*.

Scales used by Wells Fargo

Ragged Gold Miner
A weary prospector endures the long trek to the gold fields; many returned empty-handed.

Burlesque theater
was a popular entertainment in the growing city.

Wells Fargo administrators

Tall ships brought gold seekers from all over the world.

News of Gold Reaches New York
Confirmed by President Polk on December 5, 1848, the gold find inspired thousands to head west.

Panning for Gold
In 1849, more than 90,000 "Forty-Niners" passed through San Francisco. They faced long, hard hours panning for gold in the streams of the Sacramento Valley and Sierra Nevadas.

Montgomery Street in 1852

This street was the business center. Here Wells Fargo, whose stagecoaches brought goods to the miners and carried back gold, built the city's first brick building.

1836 Juan Batista Alvarado marches on Monterey and declares California a "free sovereign state" within the Mexican republic

1840

John Fremont 1813–90

1846 Bear Flag Revolt is led by explorer John Fremont and settlers in May. US troops occupy state capital (Monterey) on July 7 and take Yerba Buena on July 9

1847 Village of Yerba Buena is officially renamed San Francisco. City now comprises 200 buildings with 800 inhabitants

1851 Clipper *Flying Cloud* takes 89 days to reach San Francisco from New York

1850

1848 Gold discovered by John Marshall in Sierra Nevada foothills, starting the Gold Rush of 1849

The Victorian Years

The city's real boom years occurred during the second half of the 19th century, when some San Franciscans made huge fortunes from the silver mines of Nevada's Comstock Lode, and from the transcontinental railroad, completed in 1869. Saloons and brothels abounded along the waterfront in the legendary Barbary Coast district, while the wealthy built palaces at the top of Nob Hill. As the city expanded, its streets were lined by ornate Victorian houses, and by the turn of the century the population topped 300,000, making it the largest city west of Chicago.

Extent of the City
▨ Today   ☐ 1870

Bathroom with original bathtub and tiles

The dining room was used for family meals and formal dinners.

Silver Urn
Presented to Senator Edward Baker in 1860, this urn celebrated future San Francisco business projects, particularly the transcontinental railroad.

Supper room in basement

Barbary Coast Saloon
Gambling and prostitution were rife in the Barbary Coast, and drunken men were often pressed into naval service.

The second parlor was a private sitting room for the family.

The front parlor was used only for entertaining.

1856 Increasing lawlessness: vigilantes hang four men

1862 First telegraph connection between New York and San Francisco

1869 Transcontinental railroad completed, making fortunes for the infamous "Big Four" *(see p104)*

1873 Levi Strauss patents process for making riveted jeans *(see p137)*

1850

1860

1870

Emperor Norton (died 1880)

1854 Local eccentric, Joshua Norton, proclaims himself Emperor of the United States and Protector of Mexico, issuing his own currency

1863 Ground is broken in Sacramento for the Central Pacific Railroad; thousands of Chinese are hired to build it

1873 First San Francisco cable car is tested on Clay Street

Union Pacific Railroad

In 1869, the Union Pacific met the San Francisco-based Central Pacific in Utah at Promontory Point to form the first trans-continental railroad.

Where to See the Victorian City

Well-preserved Victorian buildings can be seen all over San Francisco, but only Haas-Lilienthal House (see p72) and Octagon House (p75) are open to the public on a regular basis. Jackson Square Historical District (p112) is the best place to see what remains of the Barbary Coast.

Gothic Revival birdcage from the 19th century at Oakland Museum of California (pp168–9)

Haas-Lilienthal House

Wholesale grocer William Haas built this elaborate Queen Anne-style house in 1886, one of many in the Victorian-era suburbs. Today it is a museum and shows how a well-to-do family would have lived at the turn of the century.

Sutro Baths

These public baths, which stood until the 1960s, were built by philanthropist and one-time mayor Adolph Sutro in 1896.

The sitting room was originally the master bedroom.

Comstock Lode Silver

Between 1859 and the mid-1880s, $400 million was extracted from the mines.

Porch

Hall, with Victorian corner sofa

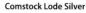

1886 10,000 trade unionists take part in the biggest labor parade to date in San Francisco

1896 Adolph Sutro opens the world's largest public baths north of Cliff House

1901 Power broker Abe Ruef runs San Francisco

1880

1900

1887 Scottish gardener John McLaren is hired to tend Golden Gate Park. He stays for 50 years (see p148)

1899 Frank Norris writes the classic novel *McTeague: A Story of San Francisco*

1900 Fisherman's Wharf is built

Adolph Sutro 1830–98

The 1906 Earthquake and Fire

The massive earthquake that hit San Francisco just after 5am on April 18, 1906, caused one of the worst disasters in US history. The tremor, many times more powerful than any other to hit the city before or since, instantly collapsed hundreds of buildings, and subsequent fires engulfed the city center. More than 6 sq miles (15 sq km) were reduced to rubble, and estimated death tolls ranged from an official 700 to a more credible 3,000, while as many as 250,000 people were made homeless. Since most property owners were insured against damage by fire, the city was able to rebuild quickly, and by the end of the decade business had returned to normal.

Extent of the City
▨ Today ☐ 1906

Powell Street cable cars were back in service within two years. The rest of the system, much reduced, was operational by 1915.

The House of Mirth
In the summer of 1906 more than 100,000 residents had to make their homes in refugee camps.

The Ferry Building was saved from destruction by fireboats spraying water from the bay.

Chinatown burned completely to the ground.

Spirit of San Francisco
Cartoonists were quick to see the funny side of their changed lives; scarcity of water provoked some ironic comment.

1905 Architect Daniel Burnham submits radical plans to improve the city center

1907 Fairmont Hotel reopens exactly one year after the earthquake

Fairmont Hotel

1909 Jack London writes *Martin Eden*, a thinly veiled autobiography

| 1905 | 1906 | 1907 | 1908 | 1909 |

Burnham Plan

1906 Earthquake, measuring 8.25 on the Richter scale, and 3-day fire, reduce the city to rubble; tremors continue for 2 days

1907 Abe "Boss" Ruef pleads guilty to extortion

Jack London 1876–1916

Feeding the Homeless in Union Square
The US Army took responsibility for providing food and shelter for the thousands of victims who lost members of their family, their homes and possessions.

Where to See Remnants of the 1906 Earthquake

Artifacts and exhibits pertaining to the 1906 disaster are found all over the city. Information on the quake can be viewed in the foyer of the Sheraton Palace Hotel and at www.sfmuseum.org.

Cups and saucers fused by the heat of the fire are among artifacts on display at the Oakland Museum of California *(pp168–9)*.

South of Market District, built on unstable soil, was one of the hardest-hit areas in the earthquake.

The Fairmont Hotel burned, but was rebuilt inside the original façade.

The Flood Mansion's stone frame survived the quake; it can be seen today as the Pacific-Union Club.

The Destruction

Traveling at 7,000 mph (11,265 km), the earthquake overwhelmed the city center. Flames erupted from burst gas mains and, in three days, destroyed 28,000 buildings: prime city property valued at $400 million.

The Homeless
Many people salvaged what they could and moved away for good.

Nob Hill's wooden mansions burned like kindling.

Clearing Up
As soon as the flames had abated, buildings were torn down and cleared for restoration.

Mayor "Sunny Jim" Rolph 1869–1948

Plans for San Francisco, the Exposition City

1913 Last horse-drawn streetcar withdrawn from service

1914 Stockton Street tunnel opens

1910	1911	1912	1913	1914

1911 "Sunny Jim" Rolph is elected mayor; serves until 1930

1912 San Francisco named as official site of 1915 Panama–Pacific Exposition

1913 Congress controversially approves dam that floods the Hetch Hetchy Valley, 150 miles (240 km) east of the city

The Golden Age

Neither World War I in Europe nor the beginning of Prohibition in the US could dampen the city's renewed energy after 1906. The 1920s saw the creation of major museums, theaters, and other civic buildings. Even the Great Depression was not as painful as it was elsewhere in the US – many of the city's monuments, including Coit Tower and both bay bridges, were built during these years. World War II brought industrial investment in the form of shipyards at Richmond and Sausalito. Fort Mason was the main supply base for the Pacific theater, and shipped out more than 1.5 million soldiers.

Extent of the City
- Today
- 1920

Tower of Jewels, decorated with 102,000 cut-glass "gems"

Palace of Fine Arts, the only building still standing today

Panama–Pacific Exposition of 1915

To celebrate the city's revival after 1906 and to mark the completion of the Panama Canal, San Francisco hosted the magical Exposition, which attracted 20 million visitors over 10 months (see p72).

Fountain of Energy by A. Stirling Calder, depicting victorious youth

Palace of Horticulture with plants from all over the world

Land of Plenty
California's farmland became the most productive in the US in the 1920s.

King Oliver's Creole Band
Catching the mood of the 1920s, King Oliver's jazz band became the hottest combo of the decade.

Panama–Pacific commemorative medal	**1921** de Young Museum opens		**1929** Stock exchange crash precipitates Depression
1917 Crissy Field Airfield at Presidio opens		**1924** California Palace of the Legion of Honor opens	
1915	**1920**	**1925**	**193**
1917 Main Public Library opens at Civic Center	**1920** Prohibition begins	**1924** First air-mail flight lands at Crissy Field	**1933** Prohibition ends
1915 Panama–Pacific Exposition runs from February 20 to December 4	**1923** President Warren G. Harding dies at the Palace Hotel	**1927** Mills Field airfield, now the site of San Francisco International Airport, opens	

Pan American Clippers Arrive
San Francisco Bay was the starting point for flights across the Pacific.

Defying Prohibition
Although Prohibition was not stringently enforced in the city, drinkers still had to be discreet.

Where to See the Golden Years

The only survivor of the 1915 Exposition is the landmark Palace of Fine Arts *(see pp62)*. The Old US Mint *(p119)* and the History Room of the Main Library *(p127)* both have extensive displays of objects from this era.

Ticket for Treasure Island World's Fair

Festival Hall, the musical center of the Exposition, seated 3,500.

McLaren's Hedge, a wall of grass

Longshoreman's Strike
On "Bloody Thursday," July 5, 1934, police opened fire on dockers striking for better conditions, killing two.

Sausalito Shipyard
Workers at this shipyard completed one ship a day during the World War II period.

Hetch Hetchy Dam

1934 Hetch Hetchy Dam project completed. Three-day general strike in sympathy with dockers

1936 Bay Bridge opens. Pan American Clippers arrive in the city

1937 Golden Gate Bridge opens

1939 World War II in Europe. Opening of World's Fair on Treasure Island

1941 Japan attacks US at Pearl Harbor

1942 Japanese-American internment begins

1945 End of World War II

1945 UN Peace Conference held at San Francisco April 25–June 25 to found the United Nations

1935 **1940** **1945**

Signing of the United Nations Charter in the city in 1945

Modern San Francisco

Since World War II, San Francisco has seen both good times and bad. Site of the founding of the United Nations in 1945, the city was home to the Beats of the 1950s and the scene of "Love-ins" and "Be-ins" in the Flower Power 1960s. At the same time, the Bay Area was the scene of angry antiwar and civil rights demonstrations. One of the wealthiest parts of the US, the area was hit hard by AIDS, homelessness, and a devastating earthquake in 1989.

1969 Indians of All Tribes occupy Alcatraz to publicize Indian grievances

1969 San Francisco blues and soul star Janis Joplin develops alcoholism and drug problems. She dies in 1970 from a heroin overdose

1970s Leader of the Oakland-based Black Panthers, Huey Newton (on the right) gains widespread sympathy on college campuses during the turbulent 1960s and 1970s

1978 Mayor George Moscone is assassinated at City Hall by former policeman Dan White, who also kills popular gay politician Harvey Milk

Neal Cassady and Jack Kerouac

1950s Jack Kerouac, Neal Cassady, Allen Ginsberg, and others strike chords of dissatisfaction and creativity to initiate the "Beat" movement and the "politics of dissent" and free love

George Moscone

1945	1950	1955	1960	1965	1970	1975	1980

1945	1950	1955	1960	1965	1970	1975	1980

August 15, 1945 Riotous celebrations break out across San Francisco at the end of World War II. Thousands of troops return to the US through the Golden Gate

1954 The San Francisco International Airport opens at former Mills Field airfield

1965 Ground is broken for the Dragon Gateway on Grant Avenue

1973 Transamerica Pyramid is completed and given mixed reviews by San Francisco critics

1978 Apple Computer, which grows into one of the Bay Area's largest businesses, designs and produces its first personal computer

1958 The New York Giants baseball team moves to San Francisco, bringing major league professional sport to the West Coast

1951 Six years after the fighting stopped between the US and Japan, the treaty ending the war was signed in the San Francisco War Memorial Opera House

1967 First Be-in attracts 25,000 hippies and others to Golden Gate Park for a day of music. The Monterey Pop Festival features such talents as Jimi Hendrix, Otis Redding, and The Who

San Francisco Giant Willie Mays

1992 Fires blaze across Oakland hills killing 26 people and burning 3,000 houses

1995 Candlestick Park renamed 3Com Park

2002 3Com Park naming rights expire, and stadium becomes Candlestick Park again

2007 Residents experience an earthquake measuring 4.2 on the Richter scale

2014 Michael Morse leads the San Francisco Giants to victory yet again in the World Series

2000 Opening game played at Pacific Bell Park (now AT&T Park)

2012 San Francisco Giants win the World Series for the eighth time

| | 1990 | 1995 | 2000 | 2005 | 2010 | 2015 | 2020 |

1994 Presidio Army Base turned over to the National Park Service

2010 San Francisco Giants win the World Series; the first win since the Giants relocated to San Francisco in 1958

2017 San Francisco celebrates the 50th anniversary of the Summer of Love with a variety of special events and exhibitions.

1989 Major earthquake hits San Francisco during World Series baseball game between Bay Area rivals: freeways collapse, killing dozens

2006 San Francisco congresswoman Nancy Pelosi is the first woman to become elected Speaker of the United States House of Representatives

2008 The Contemporary Jewish Museum, designed by Daniel Libeskind, opens

1999 After 15 years as the speaker of the California Assembly, Democrat Willie Brown is sworn in as San Francisco's first black mayor

SAN FRANCISCO AT A GLANCE

More than 200 places of interest are described in the *Area by Area* section of this book. They range from the bustling alleys, shops, and restaurants of Chinatown to the verdant expanses of Golden Gate Park, and from ornate Victorian houses to soaring city-center skyscrapers. The following 12 pages are a time-saving guide to the best San Francisco has to offer visitors. Museums and architecture each have a section, and there is a guide to the diverse cultures that have given the city its unique character. Below are the top attractions that no tourist should miss.

San Francisco's Top Tourist Attractions

California Academy of Sciences
See pp152–3

Ghirardelli Square
See p87

Coit Tower
See pp92–3

Golden Gate Bridge
See pp64–7

Golden Gate Park
See pp144–55

Grant Avenue
See p101

Cable Cars
See pp106–107

Union Square
See p118

Alcatraz Island
See pp82–5

Japan Center
See p130

◀ California Street's cable car running at night

San Francisco's Best: Museums and Galleries

Museums and galleries in the city range from the Legion of Honor and the de Young Museum to the contemporary art of the Museum of Modern Art and the Yerba Buena Center for the Arts. There are several excellent science museums, including the Exploratorium and the California Academy of Sciences. Other museums celebrate San Francisco's heritage and the people and events that made the city what it is today. More details on the area's museums and galleries can be found on pages 40–41.

de Young Museum
This landmark art museum showcases collections of art from the Americas, Africa, and the Pacific, as well as an astounding collection of textiles, photography, sculptures, crafts, and modern and contemporary art.

Legion of Honor
Sailboat on the Seine (c.1874) by Monet is part of a collection of 4,000 years of ancient and European art.

Presidio

Golden Gate Park and Land's End

Haight Ashbury and the Mission

0 kilometers 2
0 miles 1

California Academy of Sciences
Sensitively integrated into the environment of Golden Gate Park, the California Academy of Sciences includes an aquarium, planetarium, and natural history museum.

Fort Mason Museums
The Mexican Museum and the Museo Italo Americano display pieces such as *Muto* (1985).

Chinese Historical Society
This magnificent dragon's head belongs to the Society which administers one of the city's smallest museums. Within is a unique collection that tells the story of California's Chinese communities.

Wells Fargo History Museum
This bronze stagecoach (1984) is by M. Casper. The small gallery in which this is situated illustrates the colorful history of California, from the early days of the Gold Rush.

Fisherman's
Wharf and
North Beach

Pacific
eights and
e Marina

Chinatown and
Nob Hill

Financial
District and
Union Square

Civic Center

San Francisco Museum of Modern Art
Renovated in 2016, this museum boasts 45,000 sq ft (4,200 sq m) of free public space with selected artworks. The tickets allow entry into current exhibits and permanent collections.

Asian Art Museum
This museum is located in a lovely 1917 Beaux Arts building in the Civic Center.

Yerba Buena Center for the Arts
This gallery at Yerba Buena Gardens displays contemporary art in rotating exhibits; there is no permanent collection.

Exploring San Francisco's Museums and Galleries

San Francisco boasts a number of established and impressive collections of paintings, sculpture, photography, artifacts, and design. From the 12th century textiles at the De Young and Impressionist paintings at the Legion of Honor, to the modern art at MoMA and living rainforest at the California Academy of Sciences, the city is the US West Coast's center of art and culture. Other Bay Area gems are the many ethnic heritage and technology museums.

Saint John the Baptist Preaching (c.1660) by Mattia Preti at the Legion of Honor

Painting and Sculpture

Two renowned art museums, the **Legion of Honor** and the **de Young Museum** are impressive showcases for a comprehensive collection of European and American painting and sculpture. The Legion of Honor focuses on French art of the late 19th and early 20th centuries, with works by Renoir, Monet, and Degas, as well as more than 70 sculptures by Rodin. The famous collection of graphic works owned by the Achenback Foundation is also on display here.

The **Asian Art Museum** is located in its permanent home at the Old Main Library. It has Far Eastern paintings, sculpture, artifacts, and fine jade figurines.

With its vast array of 20th-century painting and sculpture, the most dynamic of the art museums in San Francisco is the **Museum of Modern Art**, which reopened in spring 2016 after

three years of expansion and renovation that have brought more vitality than ever. The SFMOMA holds works by Picasso and Matisse as well as an extensive holding of drawings and paintings by Paul Klee. Abstract Expressionists, particularly Mark Rothko and Clyfford Still, and California artists represented by Sam Francis and Richard Diebenkorn, are also included in this notable collection.

Another vibrant showcase for contemporary artists, the **Yerba Buena Center for the Arts** is well worth a visit. The same is true of the commercial **John Berggruen Gallery**, with its wide variety of works on display by both emerging artists and more mature, well-established artists.

Outside the city limits, the **Stanford University** Museum of Art has excellent sculptures by Rodin on display, while both the **UC Berkeley** Art Museum and the **Oakland Museum of California** boast valuable art collections.

Fletcher Benton's "M" sculpture outside the Oakland Museum of California

Design

Many of the larger, more prestigious museums in the San Francisco area have worthwhile holdings of design and applied art. Major collections of architectural models and drawings are held at the **Museum of Modern Art**.

You can see historical artifacts, ethnographic objects, and art pieces displayed at the **Oakland Museum of California**, as well as participate in the various programs they offer.

There is also a small, but interesting, collection of late 18th-century artifacts and furniture on display inside the **Octagon House**, itself a fine, and unique, example of Victorian architectural house design *(see pp76–7)*.

The **California Historical Society** *(see p115)* has an eclectic collection of fine and decorative arts as well as the largest single public collection of 19th century California prints and photography.

Photography and Prints

Photography is a field in which San Francisco's museums excel, with world-class examples of most periods and styles. The **Museum of Modern Art**'s collection ranges from the earliest form of daguerreo-types to classic images by modern masters such as Helen Levitt, Robert Frank, and Richard Avedon.

Oakland Museum of California displays rolling exhibitions by Bay Area-based photographers such as Ansel Adams and Imogen Cunningham and holds documentary collections including an impressive array of photographs by iconic American photographers such as Dorothea Lange.

The **Fraenkel** and **SF Camerawork** galleries are excellent, while for prints the Achenbach Foundation for Graphic Arts in the **Legion of Honor** has more than 100,000 works.

After the Earthquake (1906) photograph, Mission Dolores museum

History and Local Interest

No single museum is devoted to the city's entire history, although several collections cover different aspects of San Francisco's past. A small museum at **Mission Dolores** gives insight into the city's founding and early period. The **Wells Fargo History Museum** has a display on the Gold Rush, the small museum at the **Presidio Officers' Club** traces the area's military history, and the California Historical Society offers fertile ground for researchers and history buffs.

Also well worth a visit are the **Chinese Historical Society of America** and the African-American Historical and Cultural Society Museum at **Fort Mason**, which document the respective histories of the Chinese and African-American communities in San Francisco.

Science and Technology

One of the preeminent hands-on technological museums in the world, the **Exploratorium** has hundreds of interactive displays that explore the science behind everyday events. This is one of San Francisco's most popular museums, and it is especially fascinating for children.

Across the bay, the Lawrence Hall of Science at **UC Berkeley** plays an equally important role in promoting interest in science. South of the city, San Jose's growing **Tech Museum of Innovation** tells the inside story of computers, developed largely in surrounding Silicon Valley, and also has exciting hands-on displays.

Natural History

An extensive natural history collection is displayed at the **California Academy of Sciences**. This features such exhibitions as the evolution of species, plate tectonics (with a vibrating platform that simulates an earthquake), and gems and minerals. There is also a large planetarium, a four-story living rainforest, and one of the world's most diverse aquariums. The **Oakland Museum of California** has an entire floor devoted to the varied eco-systems of California, which are reconstructed through a series of realistic dioramas.

Octopus in the Oakland Museum of California

Art from Other Cultures

Art and artifacts from California's native cultures are on display in the Hearst Museum of Anthropology at **UC Berkeley**. Exhibitions are drawn from the museum's collection.

The **Contemporary Jewish Museum** explores Judaism through a range of art exhibits and installations.

Fort Mason has a wealth of art from other cultures: ethnic and American art can be seen at the Mexican Museum and the San Francisco Craft and Folk Art Museum; Italian-American works of the 20th century are displayed at the Museo Italo Americano.

Libraries

San Francisco has extensive general libraries including the **Main Library**, which has a special research collection comprising hundreds of books and thousands of photographs focusing on city history. The area's two main universities, **UC Berkeley** and **Stanford**, have extensive collections, including historical holdings.

Where to Find the Collections

Tile mural (1940–45) by Alfredo Ramos Martínez, Mexican Museum

Exploring San Francisco's Many Cultures

A substantial segment of San Francisco's population is either foreign-born or first-generation American. Spanish and Mexican pioneers who arrived in the 18th and early 19th centuries established the foundations of today's city, and the Gold Rush *(see pp26–7)* attracted fortune-seekers from all over the globe. Those who stayed built new communities and some, such as the Italians and the Chinese, have continued to maintain their own traditions.

Mission District mural commemorating the cease-fire in El Salvador

The Hispanic-Americans

You cannot go far in San Francisco without coming across signs of the Hispanic heritage of a city that was once the northernmost outpost of Spanish America, then Mexico. After the American takeover in 1846 *(see pp26–7)*, Mexican landowners were displaced by incoming prospectors and settlers, and most were left homeless. However, many stayed in the Bay Area and the Hispanic population has remained stable (about 10 per cent of the total) ever since.

Wandering among the *taquerias* (snack bars) and *mercados* (shops) of the Mission Street, it is easy to imagine you are somewhere far south of the border.

The Chinese

Since the Gold Rush days in the late 1840s, when an estimated 25,000 people fled from the chaos of China to work in the California mines, the Chinese have maintained a significant presence in San Francisco. A second wave of immigrants, almost exclusively from Canton, arrived to work on the transcontinental railroad in the 1860s. By the 1870s, the Chinese formed the largest of the city's minority groups, with 40,000 people living in poor conditions in and around Chinatown. At this time, Chinese men outnumbered Chinese women by 20 to one. In the decades that followed, the population of the Chinese community shrank due to the Exclusion Laws. In the 1960s, immigration controls were relaxed by President Kennedy, and opponents of the Mao regime living in Hong Kong were given permission to emigrate to the US. The population has now risen to over 100,000 – approximately one in five San Franciscans.

Chinatown *(see pp98–102)* is still the city's most populated sector, and the heart of the Chinese community. Banks, schools, and newspapers testify to its autonomy, which is as powerful today as it was when the first settlers arrived more than 150 years ago.

The Irish

In the late 1800s, thousands of Irish immigrants came to San Francisco and took what jobs they could find. Many worked as laborers on the huge steam shovels used to fill in the bayfront mudflats, while others joined the police and fire departments and rose to positions of authority. By the turn of the century, Irish labor leaders had become an effective force in the city. There is no readily identifiable Irish section of San Francisco, but Sunset and Richmond districts are packed with Irish bars, and the annual St. Patrick's Day parade *(see p50)* still draws a considerable crowd.

The Italians

The original Italians in San Francisco depended on fishing for their livelihood. Today's thriving North Beach is inhabited by descendants of the southern Italian fishermen who came to settle here in the late 1800s. The early immigrants to the area were mostly from the city of Genoa, the

A young San Franciscan woman wearing Chinese costume

birthplace of Christopher Columbus, after whom North Beach's main avenue is named.

By the turn of the century, the Sicilians had become the major force in the area. In the 1940s, Italians were the predominant foreign-born group in the city, with some 60,000 living and working in the lively North Beach area alone.

Descendants of the families who owned and operated the fleet at Fisherman's Wharf set up shops and small businesses here. The businesses prospered after World War II, and many families moved to the suburbs in the 1950s and 1960s. However, they often return to "Little Italy" to patronize the excellent Italian cafés and restaurants that still flourish in the area.

Little Italy illuminated by the vibrant café signboards, North Beach

An Afro-Caribbean street stall selling sweet potatoes and yams

The African-Americans

Although black communities have played an important role in San Francisco's culture, particularly in the Filmore District, the city's African-American population has declined in recent years. In the 1930s, fewer than 5,000 blacks lived in San Francisco. Thousands more came to work in the factories and shipyards during World War II, increasing the black population tenfold. Some settled in areas made available by the relocation of Japanese-Americans to internment camps, others in newer communities near the shipyards in Hunters Point.

The Russians

The first trappers and fur traders from Russia visited the bay during the early 1800s. Russian Hill is named after a party of Siberian sailors thought to be buried there. Russians established a successful though short-lived colony at Fort Ross (see pp190–91) 100 miles (160 km) north of the city, and many still live in San Francisco. Since 1921, five editions a week of the *Russian Times* have been published for the 25,000 Russians now concentrated in the Richmond District around the Orthodox Holy Virgin Cathedral (see p63).

The Japanese

Japanese businesses were active during the 1980s property boom, buying and building many prestigious city-center offices and hotels. Generally, however, the 15,000-strong Japanese community in San Francisco keeps a low profile. The exception is at the Japan Center (see p130), a prominent cultural and shopping complex on Geary Boulevard. In the late 1930s, this area extended over 40 blocks. During World War II, the Japanese along the US West Coast were relocated to internment camps in the nation's interior. After the war, they drifted back to the area, but now the community occupies only six blocks.

The Melting Pot

Other cultures are also represented in the city, but they are not as distinctly defined. Compared with New York or Los Angeles, the Jewish community in San Francisco is very small, but Jews have still wielded tremendous influence throughout the city's history.

Far Eastern cultures have also formed identifiable communities. Groups of Vietnamese and Cambodians live in the Tenderloin neighborhood, and significant populations of Koreans and Thais are scattered throughout the city.

Indians and Pakistanis have settled in the Bay Area of San Francisco, particularly in Berkeley and the Silicon Valley computer industry heartland of the South Bay.

A police *koban* (booth) in Japantown

Gay San Francisco: A History

The history of the Lesbian, Gay, Bisexual, and Transgender (LGBT) community in San Francisco is in some ways the story of the gay movement itself. The city has been a mecca for gay people for much of its existence, and social and political gains made here have had reverberations across the globe. The community is now more diverse than ever, spread out across the entire city, not just the Castro *(see p138)*, and same-sex partners walk hand-in-hand anywhere from the Financial District to the Sunset. This sense of freedom was a hard-won battle fought in the political arena of San Francisco.

The bohemian Black Cat Café, Montgomery Street, opened in 1933

The Early Days: 1849–1960

The California Gold Rush of 1849 drew scores of adventurers to the Bay Area, and its rough-and-tumble atmosphere helped establish its reputation for sexual license. Life along the Barbary Coast offered freedom from the conservative mores of the rest of the country, and by the beginning of the 20th century the city was already being called "Sodom by the Sea."

During World War II, the city's gay population positively exploded. San Francisco was a main point of deployment and re-entry for troops, and gay soldiers had numerous "off-limits" bars and private gatherings to choose from. Also, for the first time in the military's history, homosexuals were being sought out and dishonorably discharged, and many of these men chose to settle in San Francisco rather than risk stigmatization back home.

The 1950s, however, heralded the real beginnings of a gay social consciousness, with the founding of several "homophile" organizations, which emphasized emotional rather than sexual components of same-gender coupling and advised assimilation within heterosexual society. Foremost among these groups were the Mattachine Society, which first advanced the idea of gay people as an oppressed minority, and the Daughters of Bilitis, the first lesbian sociopolitical organization in the United States.

Getting Organized: 1960s–1970s

In the 1960s, police raids of gay gatherings were common, often resulting in public exposure of the arrested and affecting livelihoods. In 1961, José Sarria, a drag performer at the Black Cat Café, made history by running for the Board of Supervisors as an openly gay man. Although he wasn't elected, he proved there was a "gay vote" and inspired the founding of the Tavern Guild, the country's first gay business association.

Guests at the 1965 fundraising ball for the Council on Religion and the Homosexual (CRH) were harassed and photographed by police as they entered. The American Civil Liberties Union intervened, ultimately helping gays win legal support, including a community police liaison officer.

Another pivotal event was New York's Stonewall riots in 1969. Once gay people had stood up to police, they were no longer content with mere acceptance. "Liberation" and "pride" became the movement's watchwords. Gays wanted not just equal treatment but also

The colorful San Francisco Pride parade celebrates the city's gay history, culture and community

1930	1940	1950	1960	1970	1980	1990	2000	2010	2020

1955 Daughters of Bilitis, the nation's first lesbian group, is formed

1948 Alfred Kinsey's groundbreaking *Sexual Behaviour in the Human Male* is published

1974 First Castro Street Fair

1970 First San Francisco Gay Pride Parade, called "Gay-In"

2008 California Supreme Court overturns state's ban on same-sex marriage. This was soon invalidated by Proposition 8

2002 First purpose-built LGBT center opens

2015 1.8 million attend the 30th annual San Francisco Pride parade *(see p51)*

1930s First gay bars appear, including artists' hangout, the Black Cat Café, and Mona's, a lesbian bar

1964 *Life* magazine article "Homosexuality in America" names San Francisco "the capital of the gay world"

1981 First case of Kaposi's sarcoma (AIDS-related cancer)

1969 Police raid the Stonewall Inn in New York. Ensuing riots signal the start of the modern gay liberation movement

2004 Mayor Newsom allows same-sex marriages but these are later annulled

2013 California Court rules Proposition 8 unconstitutional gay events, businesses, and organizations to thrive.

With the establishment of the Castro as a gay area, the community gained political force. In 1977, local shop owner Harvey Milk was elected to the Board of Supervisors, becoming the nation's first openly gay elected official. His tenure was cut short in 1978 when he and Mayor George Moscone were shot at City Hall by Dan White. This further fueled the political movement – when White was found guilty only of manslaughter and given a light sentence, the city rioted in what became known as "White Night."

The Plague Years: 1980s

After all the hard-won political gains of the previous decades, the community was decimated by a new adversary. In 1981, the first incidence of a rare form of cancer was reported and within months, word spread of a disease dubbed "the gay cancer." The disease was later named AIDS (Auto-Immune Deficiency Syndrome), which is caused by the HIV virus (Human Immunodeficiency Virus). The city's gay community became one of the hardest hit, with as many as half of the city's gay men infected with HIV. It also became a model in developing a response. People rapidly mobilized to establish education and prevention efforts and community-based services to care for people with AIDS. San Francisco also leaped to the forefront of research, establishing the San Francisco AIDS Foundation and the Center for AIDS Prevention Studies at the UCSF Medical School.

The right to a same-sex wedding has been legal since 2013

Recovery: 1990–2010

The 1990s were perhaps most marked by the increase in political clout for gay people, with the passage of domestic partnership laws, more gay politicians being elected, military policies on gays being challenged, and much more.

The AIDS epidemic bred new forms of participation in San Francisco's gay community and to some degree made it more cohesive. But the sheer numbers of members lost meant that the community needed to redefine itself. As same-sex on-screen kissing and prom dating became more mainstream, gender roles became more fluid, and so the sense of urgency to sort out the "rules" of sexuality dwindled.

That said, the politics of being gay remained in the forefront, and were put famously on view by Mayor Gavin Newsom's attempt at legalizing same-sex marriage. Some 4,000 couples were wed at City Hall in February of 2004, a historic event broadcast around the world. The marriages were later invalidated by Proposition 8 in 2008, which eliminated the rights of same-sex couples to marry. This clearly became the

opening salvo of an ongoing battle as this Proposition was later ruled unconstitutional in 2010.

2010–Present

The Supreme Court's decision in 2010 to lift the ban introduced by Proposition 8 finally came into effect on June 28, 2013, and same-sex marriage resumed with great fanfare. The following month, more than 30,000 couples received marriage licenses in the state, a 35 per-cent increase from the prior year. Same-sex marriages are now relatively commonplace in California courts.

Fairs, Festivals, and Events

AIDS Candlelight Vigil
May, usually 3rd Sunday.

AIDS Walk San Francisco
July, date varies.
Tel 615-9255.

Castro Street Fair
October, usually first Sunday.

Folsom Street Fair
September, usually last Sunday.
Tel 777-3247.
Last and main event for popular Leather Week. Not only for the leather and fetish community.

Gay Pride Month
June, various events, including Dyke March (last Saturday of the month).

San Francisco Pride Parade and Celebration
June, last weekend of the month.
Tel 864-0831. **W** sfpride.org

Home for the Holidays
December 24. SF Gay Men's Chorus Christmas concert at the Castro Theatre (see p138).

Pink Saturday
June, Saturday evening before Pride parade (men and women). Women's alternate Pride parade and party in the Castro.

San Francisco International LGBT Film Festival
June, usually ten days before San Francisco Pride weekend.
Tel 703-8650.

Up Your Alley Fair
July, last Sunday.
Tel 777-3247.
SoMa's Dore Street fair.
Map 11 A2.

The San Francisco AIDS Fund, now AIDS Emergency Fund (AEF), established in 1982

San Francisco's Best: Architecture

Architectural highlights in San Francisco are mostly
small-scale; the overall fabric, rather than specific
buildings, lends the city its unique character. One
memorable aspect is the wide variety of house
styles, ranging from Arts and Crafts rustic chalets
to grand Victorian mansions. Commercial buildings
reflect a gamut of styles from Beaux Arts to
Postmodern. This map gives some highlights,
with a detailed overview on pages 48–9.

Octagon House
Octagonal houses were popular in the
mid-1800s because they allowed in more
sunlight than traditional Victorian designs.

Haas-Lilienthal House
This large Queen Anne-style house is
a typical upper-middle-class dwelling
of the late 1880s.

**Pacific Heights
and the Marina**

Presidio

Civic Center

**Golden Gate Park
and Land's End**

**Haight Ashbury
and the Mission**

City Hall
Many of the city's civic buildings
are examples of Classical Beaux
Arts style.

Goslinsky House
The charming Arts and Crafts
style was popular at the turn
of the century in San Francisco.

Coit Tower (1934)
The fluted column of
Coit Tower on Telegraph
Hill is one of the city's
best-known landmarks.

Hotaling Building (1866)
This Jackson Square edifice was the
largest of many neighboring Gold Rush
buildings to survive the 1906 earthquake.
It was a whisky distillery and warehouse.

**Old St. Mary's
Cathedral**
Standing among the
pagodas of Chinatown,
the brick walls of this
Gothic church date
back to the Gold Rush.

herman's
harf and
rth Beach

**Financial
District and
Union Square**

natown
Nob Hill

Hallidie Building
Built in 1917 by prolific
local architect Willis
Polk, this was the
world's first glass-
curtain-walled building.
It is topped with an
elaborate cast-iron
cornice.

Union Square
Before he built New York's
famous Guggenheim Museum
in 1959, architect Frank Lloyd
Wright experimented with the
use of ramps in the small Union
Square shop at 140 Maiden Lane.

SFMOMA
Built in 1995 at a cost of
$60 million, and extensively
renovated in 2014–16, the San
Francisco Museum of Modern
Art is one of the largest modern
art museums in the US.

Exploring San Francisco's Architecture

Few structures survive from the Mission or Gold Rush eras, and the 1906 earthquake and fire destroyed many major Victorian buildings. As a result, when the city was rebuilt, architecture became a focus of civic pride, and grand Neo-Classical edifices in the Beaux Arts style embodied the city's resurgence. By the 1930s, the Financial District's office towers proclaimed San Francisco's importance as the commercial center of the west. Engineering advances and soaring property values in the late 1960s gave rise to many of San Francisco's towering skyscrapers.

Mission

Between 1776 and 1823, Spanish missionaries employed American Indian laborers to construct seven missions and three fortresses, or "presidios," in the Bay Area. Known as the Mission style, this architecture is characterized by thick walls of rough adobe bricks, red tile roofs, and arcaded galleries surrounding courtyards. Fine examples of the style are **Mission Dolores**, San Francisco's oldest building, and the mission at **Carmel**.

Gold Rush

At the height of the Gold Rush, most buildings were only temporary, but as the population stabilized, fireproof brick was used. The best survivors from the time are preserved as part of **Jackson Square Historical District**. Particularly noteworthy examples include Hotaling's Warehouse and Distillery, which dates from the 1860s, with cast-iron pilasters and fireproof shutters, and three

1850s buildings on the 700 block of Montgomery Street.

Victorian

The most distinctive aspect of the city's architecture is its array of Victorian houses with their elaborate ornamentation *(see pp76–7)*. Examples of these timber-frame houses can be found throughout the city, but only two are open to the public: **Haas-Lilienthal House** and

Victorian mansion built for Mark Hopkins on Nob Hill, destroyed in the fire that followed the 1906 earthquake

Octagon House. Also worth a visit are the houses along the east side of **Alamo Square**, the group of well-preserved working-class cottages in **Cottage Row**, and **Clarke's Folly**, an elaborate 1892 Queen Anne-style "country house" now stranded in the cityscape.

Arts and Crafts

A more rustic, down-to-earth style was adopted after the turn of the century, inspired by the English Arts and Crafts movement. Architects used redwood and uncut stone, borrowing decorative Japanese motifs, to achieve a natural look. An entire block of Arts and Crafts houses surrounds Bernard Maybeck's **Goslinsky House** in Pacific Heights, and across the bay in Berkeley, his **Church of Christ, Scientist** is a particularly fine example.

Religious Architecture

The architectural diversity of the city is most apparent in its churches. Since the first simple, white-walled, and red-tile-roofed missions, the city's churches have been built in an array of styles from Gothic to Baroque, with numerous hybrids in between. Many prominent churches were built during the eclectic Victorian era of the late 19th century, and their architectural styles reflect the traditions of the countries from which their congregations came.

St. Stephen's Lutheran
German Renaissance

First Unitarian Church
Gothic Revival

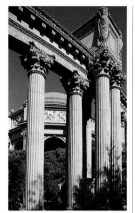

Beaux Arts-style Palace of Fine Arts

Beaux Arts

The rigorously Neo-Classical style of the Parisian Ecole des Beaux Arts was favored by designers in San Francisco for major buildings following the 1906 earthquake. Opulent colonnades, sculptures, and pediments are typical of this lavish style, which was readily adopted in a city eager to signal to the world its recovery from devastation.

The most perfect illustration of Beaux Arts style in the city is Bernard Maybeck's **Palace of Fine Arts**, built as the focus of the 1915 Panama–Pacific Exposition, and acclaimed as the city's most vibrant cele-bration of the art of architecture.

Other impressive examples surround Civic Center Plaza: the **City Hall** (Arthur Brown, 1915); the old **Main Library**, now the **Asian Art Museum** (George Kelham, 1915); the **War Memorial Opera House**

and the **Veterans Building** (both by Arthur Brown, 1932); and the oldest building in the Civic Center, the **Bill Graham Civic Auditorium** (John Galen Howard, 1915).

Commercial

Two early office buildings that are of architectural significance are Willis Polk's **Hallidie Building** (1917), the world's first glass-curtain-walled structure, and his stately **Merchant's Exchange** (1906).

Timothy Pflueger's building at **450 Sutter Street** (1929) is a shining example of Art Deco design. Its lobby is beautifully detailed with red marble and embossed aluminum.

The **Union Square Frank Lloyd Wright Building** (Xanadu Gallery) was designed in 1949 by Wright. The interior spirals up to a mezzanine, while the façade is broken by an arched, tunnel-like entrance. The 853 ft (256 m) **Transamerica Pyramid** (William Pereira, 1972) is also a notable piece of commercial architecture.

Highly ornate Art Deco entrance of 450 Sutter Street

Contemporary

Among the city's contemporary projects are the new **Transbay Terminal** (2017), the **MoMA expansion** (2016) by Snøhetta, and many new high-rise condos such as the **Lumina** (2016) and **100 Van Ness** (2015). In 2017, the contemporary **Millennium Tower** (2005) was discovered to be sinking, resulting in a tilted tower in San Francisco's skyline.

An aerial view of San Francisco's towering skyscrapers

Where to Find the Buildings

St. Paulus Gothic

St. Boniface Romanesque

Notre Dame des Victoires Roman and Byzantine

SAN FRANCISCO THROUGH THE YEAR

Springtime in San Francisco sees a city awakening from winter slumbers, with leaves returning to the trees, and the last gray whales migrating north along the coast. By May and June the air is often warm, and windsurfers can be seen on the bay. In August, afternoon fog rolls in from the sea, but summer weather returns in September. Cool daytime temperatures set in at the end of the year, with occasional snowfalls on Mount Diablo. The main annual events are listed below. For up-to-date information, the San Francisco Visitor Information Center *(see p266)* provides a free calendar of year-round city events.

Spring

Springtime is the season for long walks around San Francisco, wandering through the parks or along city center streets lined with blossoming trees. In March, bulbs come into bloom in the parks and gardens, and wildflowers cover the headlands on either side of the Golden Gate. In May, thousands of runners join the Bay to Breakers race.

March

CAAMFest *(Mar)*. Also celebrating Asian-American food and music, this is the largest showcase for new Asian-American and Asian films in North America.

St. Patrick's Day Parade *(Sun nearest Mar 17)*. Bars filled with merrymakers watch the parade down Market Street.

Easter
Easter Sunrise Services
Thousands of worshipers gather at dawn in front of the huge cross on Mount Davidson, the highest hill in the city.

April
Cherry Blossom Festival *(mid- to late Apr)*. This celebration of traditional Japanese arts and crafts attracts dancers, drummers, artists, and craftspeople from all around the Bay Area. It takes place at the Japan Center *(see p130)*, where there are lively performances and a colorful parade.

San Francisco International Film Festival *(late Apr–early May)*. For two weeks there are screenings every day at the Kabuki *(see p250)* and other theaters. American and international films are shown, many of them for the first time in the US.

Wildflower Walks *(Apr)*. Guided walks are offered at various San Francisco natural areas by volunteers. Commercial guided tours are offered in the Marin Headlands *(see pp176–7)*.

Opening Day of Baseball Season *(late Apr–early May)*. Sports fans turn out to see their baseball heroes perform at AT&T Park and O.co Coliseum.

Glittering Carnaval celebrations in the Mission District of San Francisco

May
Cinco de Mayo *(early May)*. Mexican cultural celebration, with a carnival in the Civic Center and special events in the Mission District.

Bay to Breakers *(late May)*. Partly a serious race, partly a mad dash in funny costumes, contenders run 7.5 miles (12.5 km) from the Ferry Building to Ocean Beach *(see p155)*.

Carnaval SF *(last weekend)*. Latin American and Caribbean festival in the Mission District, with salsa and reggae bands.

Colorful traditional costumes at the Japanese Cherry Blossom Festival Grand Parade

Runners in the Bay to Breakers race

Average Daily Hours of Sunshine

Days
25
20
15
10
5
0

Jan Feb Mar Apr May Jun Jul Aug Sep Oct Nov Dec

Days
25
20
15
10
5
0

Sunshine Chart
The sunniest months in San Francisco are September and October. In mid-summer almost everywhere else in the Bay Area is both warmer and sunnier. The Napa Valley *(see pp192–5)* and other inland valleys are baking hot and dry.

Summer

Mark Twain is said to have commented that the coldest winter he ever spent was a summer in San Francisco. June and July see the city besieged by tourists from all over the world, who often complain about the "cold" that can ruin their otherwise perfect days.

Golden Gate Bridge in fog

Foggy Days

Afternoon and evening fogs are common in San Francisco during the summer months. They form far out over the sea and roll in through the Golden Gate, shrouding parts of the city with a cold, damp cloud. These fogs are sometimes so dense that they can cause the temperature to fall by as much as 20° F (10° C) in a matter of hours.

June
San Francisco Jazz Festival
(early–mid-Jun). The best local and international jazz artists perform at various venues throughout the city.
North Beach Festival *(mid-Jun)*. Arts and crafts, bands and food stalls in the Italian district on Grant Avenue, Green Street, and Washington Square.
Juneteenth *(mid- to late Jun)*. African-American cultural celebration, with jazz and blues bands along Oakland's Lake Merritt *(see p166)*.
Haight Street Fair *(Sat or Sun in late Jun)*. Bands play, and

there are food stalls along Haight St *(see p136)*.
San Francisco Pride *(Sat & Sun in late Jun)*. The biggest show in San Francisco and the largest of its kind in the US – more than 1 million people every year attend the Market Street parade and Civic Center celebrations.

July
4th of July Fireworks *(Jul 4)*. On the waterfront at Crissy Field National Recreation Area *(see p62)* American Independence Day is celebrated with a

AT&T Park is home to the San Francisco Giants baseball team

spectacular pyrotechnic display at Golden Gate Bridge.
San Francisco Marathon *(late Jul)*. More than 25,000 athletes race around San Francisco, over the Golden Gate Bridge, into Marin and back again.
San Francisco Playwright's Festival *(late Jul)*. Fort Mason Center *(see pp74–5)*. Readings, workshops, and performances of new works. Audiences can talk to the artists at special sessions.

August
Baseball *(season Apr–Sep)*. The San Francisco Giants (AT&T Park) and Oakland Athletics (O.co Coliseum) play games throughout the summer *(see p260)*. Tickets are available on the day of play, although the best seats sell out in advance.

Participants in rainbow colored balloon costumes at the San Francisco Pride parade

Average Monthly Temperature

Temperature Chart
The chart shows the average minimum and maximum temperatures for each month. San Francisco and the Bay area enjoy mild weather all year round, with temperatures seldom rising above 70° F (21° C) or falling below 40° F (4° C).

Fall

San Franciscans reclaim their city from the visitors in September, just as the Bay Area summer begins. Many outdoor festivities and cultural events take place in the parks and on the streets, while the football, opera, and symphony seasons all open in the fall.

September
49ers and Raiders Football *(season begins Sep)*. Various arenas. To December, or January if teams are in the playoffs *(see p260)*.

49ers game season starts September

San Francisco's Opera Opening Night This glamorous gala event launches the San Francisco opera season which runs from September through December. It is a formal black-tie ball held at War Memorial Opera House, Van Ness Ave *(see p252)*.

Fringe Festival *(early to mid-Sep)*. The city celebrates its theater culture with a series of alternative performances ranging from the intensely dramatic to the mildly absurd.

Valley of the Moon Vintage Festival *(mid- to late Sep)*. California's oldest wine festival takes place at Sonoma Plaza, Sonoma.

Folsom Street Fair *(last Sun)*. Predominantly gay and lesbian event between 8th and 13th Streets. Music, comedy, crafts, dancing, and beer garden. Proceeds are donated to charity.

October
Castro Street Fair *(first Sun)*. One of the city's largest and longest-running street celebrations *(see p138)*.

Fleet Week *(early Oct)*. A celebration of the US Navy. Vessels gather near Golden Gate Bridge, and there are art displays, keynote speakers, and music.

SF Litquake *(early to mid-Oct)*. A week-long literary festival. Many of the Bay Area's finest writers take part in readings, talks, and performances.

Italian Heritage Parade *(2nd Sun in March)*. Pageant and procession down Columbus Ave in North Beach, finishing at Fisherman's Wharf.

Shakespeare in the Park *(Sats and Suns from Labor Day)*. Free performances on the Main Post Lawn in the Presidio. A temporary outdoor theater is erected especially for the event.

Italian Heritage Parade

Halloween *(Oct 31)*. The night is celebrated by thousands of revelers dressed in costume all converging on Market Street. and Castro Street. Though no longer sanctioned by the city, many die-hards still take part.

November
Dia de los Muertos/Day of the Dead *(Nov 2)*. Mexican celebration, marked by a night-time procession through the Mission District. Costumes, dances, festival food.

The Big Game *(third Sat)*. Major university football event when California Golden Bears play Stanford Cardinal, alternately at Stanford and UC Berkeley *(see p260)*.

Illuminate SF Festival of Light *(late Nov–early Jan)*. Over two dozen eco-friendly light art installations, both temporary and permanent, are put up throughout the city. Tours and events based on the installations are also held.

Day of the Dead procession in November

Average Monthly Rainfall

Rainfall Chart
The average annual rainfall for San Francisco is about 19 in (122 cm). Most rain falls from November to March, sometimes for days at a time, and there are often torrential storms. The driest months are May to September.

Winter

The Christmas shopping season starts the day after Thanksgiving with the lighting of the Union Square tree, while appealing pets appear in the windows of Macy's store *(see p118)*. Families of gray whales pass on their annual migration between Alaska and Mexico.

December

Christmas Displays in Union Square store windows *(see p118)* compete to be the best.
Holiday Lights Boat Parade *(mid-Dec)*. More than 100 boats with lights and holiday decorations parade along the waterfront.
The Nutcracker (3rd and 4th week) is performed by the San Francisco Ballet at the War Memorial Opera House *(see p252)*.
Sing for your Life *(Dec 30 & 31)*. 12 hours of singing at the First Congressional Church of Oakland.

Chinese New Year celebrations in Chinatown

January

New Year's Day Swim *(Jan 1)*. Sponsored swim at Aquatic Park *(see pp174–5)*.
Russian Orthodox Christmas *(Jan 7–8)*. Ceremony in Holy Virgin Cathedral *(see p63)*.
Gray Whale Migration *(Jan–Apr)*. Watch from the coast, or take a boat *(see p260)*.

February

Black History Month. African-American events take place throughout the city.
Chinese New Year Parade *(date varies, usually early Feb)*. Parade through Financial District and Chinatown featuring a colorful dragon *(see pp96–102 and 109–123)*.

Public Holidays

New Year's Day (Jan 1)
Martin Luther King Day (3rd Mon in Jan)
President's Day (3rd Mon in Feb)
Memorial Day (last Mon in May)
Independence Day (Jul 4)
Labor Day (1st Mon in Sep)
Columbus Day (2nd Mon in Oct)
Election Day (1st Tue in Nov)
Veterans Day (Nov 11)
Thanksgiving Day (4th Thu in Nov)
Christmas Day (Dec 25)

Christmas tree and decorations in Nieman Marcus department store

SAN FRANCISCO AREA BY AREA

The 49-Mile Scenic Drive

Linking the city's most intriguing neighborhoods, fascinating sights, and spectacular views, the 49-Mile Scenic Drive (79 km) provides a splendid overview of San Francisco for the determined motorist. Keeping to the well-marked route is simple enough – just follow the blue-and-white seagull signs. Some of these are hidden by overhanging vegetation or buildings, so you need to be alert. You should set aside a whole day for this trip; there are plenty of places to stop to take photographs or admire the views.

㉘ **Marina Green**
This is an excellent vantage point from which to view or photograph Golden Gate Bridge.

㉙ **Palace of Fine Arts** stands near the entrance to the wooded Presidio.

⑨ **Stow Lake**
There is a waterfall and a Chinese pavilion on the island in this picturesque lake. Boats are for rent.

⑧ **San Francisco Zoo and Gardens** is one of the best zoos in the US. Its attractions include Hearst Grizzly Gulch and the Primate Discovery Center.

⑬ **Twin Peaks**
From both summits, the views over the city and bay are magnificent and well worth the climb.

◀ The iconic San Francisco skyline at night

Tips for Motorists

Starting point: Anywhere. The circuit is designed to be followed in a counterclockwise direction starting and ending at any point.
When to go: Avoid driving during rush hours: 7–10am and 4–7pm. Most of the views are as spectacular by night as by day.
Parking: Use parking garages in Financial District, Civic Center, Nob Hill, Chinatown, North Beach, and Fisherman's Wharf. Elsewhere, street parking is usually available.
Stopping-off points: There are numerous cafés, bars, and restaurants (see pp216–31).

㉘ **Civic Center** is the stately official and administrative heart of San Francisco, where imposing Beaux Arts buildings surround a central plaza.

㉖ **Maritime National Historic Park Visitor Center** has a fine collection of ship models, photographs, and relics, with many historic ships moored nearby at Hyde Street Pier.

㉕ **Coit Tower**
Overlooking North Beach, Telegraph Hill is topped by this tower *(on the left)*, which has stunning murals and a viewing terrace.

⑮ **Ferry Building**
This building with its distinctive 230 ft (70 m) tower survived the 1906 earthquake intact.

Key

━━ 49-Mile Scenic Drive

❊ Viewing point

he Chinatown Gateway at the ntrance of Grant Avenue *(see p100)*

SAN FRANCISCO AREA BY AREA | 59

PRESIDIO

Once the nation's premier army post, the Presidio, located in a corner of the city bounded by beach, bluff, and stunning views, has been transformed into a new kind of National Park site. Thousands of people visit every year to enjoy a vibrant mix of museums, restaurants, events, trails, and recreational destinations. The Presidio offers experiences for everyone. Bike along the shoreline, glimpse rare birds and native wildflowers, learn about architecture and California history, take in a concert and great meal, spend the night in former officers' quarters at the Inn at the Presidio, picnic on the historic Main Parade Ground, or simply relax at one of the eight scenic overlooks.

Sights at a Glance

Historic Streets and Buildings
1 Palace of Fine Arts
3 Presidio Officers' Club
5 *Golden Gate Bridge pp64–7*
8 Clement Street

Museums and Galleries
2 The Walt Disney Family Museum
4 Fort Point and Crissy Field

Churches and Temples
7 Holy Virgin Cathedral
9 Temple Emanu-El

Parks and Gardens
6 Baker Beach

Restaurants
see p222

1 Aziza
2 Burma Superstar
3 Gaspare's Pizza House & Italian
4 King's Thai Cuisine
5 Pizzetta 211
6 The Presidio Social Club
7 The Tipsy Pig
8 The Warming Hut

See also Street Finder maps 1–3

◀ The stunning Palace of Fine Arts

For keys to symbols *see back flap*

A Tour of the Presidio

The Presidio's lush landscaping belies its long military history. This site has played a key role in San Francisco's growth, and has been occupied longer than any other part of the city. Remnants of its military past, including barracks, can be seen everywhere, and there are 24 miles (39 km) of hiking trails, cycle paths, and beaches. A free shuttle operates within the park, stopping at 40 destinations. Golden Gate Bridge crosses the bay from the northwest corner of the Presidio.

❹ Fort Point
This impressive brick fortress, now a national historic site, guarded the Golden Gate during the Civil War of 1861–5.

Golden Gate Bridge Visitor Gift Center

Gulf of the Farallones National Marine Sanctuary Visitor Center

❺ ★ Golden Gate Bridge
Opened in 1937, the bridge has a center span of 4,200 ft (1,280 m).

❻ Baker Beach
The Presidio's western edge harbors the surf and sand of Baker Beach, one of the best of the city's beaches.

Coastal Trail start

Marine Drive is a waterfront road, lined with palm trees.

Lobos Creek is a small stream that provides the Presidio with drinking water.

The Pet Cemetery has been going since 1945 and is the final resting place for many people's family pets.

Locator Map
See Street Finder map 1

4 Crissy Field, reclaimed from marshland for the 1915 Panama–Pacific Exposition. A restoration project started in 2017, but most of the area is still open.

San Francisco National Cemetery holds the remains of 30,000 soldiers killed in action.

William Penn Mott Jr. Presidio Visitor Center has high-tech interactive exhibits

Walt Disney Family Museum

Captured Cannon, a 19th-century cannon from the Spanish-American War, is still located on the grounds.

The Ecology Trail starts at Inspiration Point, inside the Arguello Gate.

Golf course

The main parade ground was first laid out in the mid-1890s. The buildings around it include Civil War officers' quarters and barracks from the Spanish-American War.

Mountain Lake is one of the few remaining natural lakes in San Francisco.

0 meters 500
0 yards 500

1 Palace of Fine Arts
Designed to resemble a Roman ruin for the 1915 Panama Pacific International Exposition.

3 Presidio Officers' Club
Built over the remains of the old Spanish El Presidio, the Officers' Club now houses two spectacular event spaces.

❶ Palace of Fine Arts

3301 Lyon St, Marina District. **Map** 3 C2. **Tel** (415) 563-6504. 22, 29, 30, 43, 45, 47, 49. **Open** for events only.

One of San Francisco's most prominent pieces of architecture, the Palace of Fine Arts is the sole survivor of the many grandiose monuments built as part of the 1915 Panama-Pacific Exposition *(see pp32–3)*. The building was not intended to last beyond the Exposition and subsequently suffered serious decay. Following restoration, it now functions as a space for a range of performing arts including theater, music, and dance.

❷ The Walt Disney Family Museum

104 Montgomery St. **Map** 3 A2. **Tel** 345-6800. 28L, 43. **Open** 10am–6pm Wed–Mon. **Closed** Jan 1, Thanksgiving, Dec 25. **W** waltdisney.org

Opened in 2009, this fascinating museum documents the life and achievements of Walt Disney (1901–66). A series of ten inter-active galleries incorporate film clips, storyboards, and scripts to tell the story of the man and his amazing career. Visitors will discover Hollywood's first feature-length animated film and early drawings of Mickey Mouse alongside exhibits dedicated to Disney's home life including photographs and movies.

❸ Presidio Officers' Club

50 Moraga Ave. **Map** 3 A2. **Tel** 561-4400. 29, 43.

The Officers' Club, situated in the southwest corner of the Plaza de Armas, overlooks the parade grounds of the Presidio and the 19th-century barracks. Built in the Spanish Mission style *(see p48)* in the 1930s, it incorporates the adobe (sun-dried brick) remains of the original 18th-century Spanish fort and hosts events and exhibits on California history.

An old Army shed, now the Crissy Field Warming Hut Bookstore and Café

❹ Fort Point and Crissy Field

Marine Drive. **Map** 2 E1. **Tel** 556-1693. **Open** 10am–5pm Thurs–Tues (winter: Fri–Sun only). partial.

Completed in the US Army in 1861, this fort was built partly to protect San Francisco Bay from any attack, and partly to defend ships carrying gold from California mines. It is the most prominent of the many fortifications constructed along the coast, and is a classic example of a pre-Civil War brick fortress. The building soon became obsolete, as its 10-ft- (3-m-) thick brick walls would not have stood up to powerful modern weaponry. It was closed in 1900, never having come under attack.

The brickwork vaulting is unusual for San Francisco, where the ready availability of good timber encouraged wood-frame constructions. This may have saved the fort from collapse in the 1906 earthquake *(see pp30–31)*. It was nearly demolished in the 1930s to make way for the Golden Gate Bridge, but it survived and is now a good place from which to view the bridge. National Park Service rangers in Civil War costume conduct guided tours. A tidal marsh once covered the area called Crissy Field. After two centuries of military use, the Field was transformed into a waterfront park for recreation and education. The Crissy Field Center offers a rich array of programs, including many geared toward kids, from wildlife treks to kite-flying.

❺ Golden Gate Bridge

See pp64–7.

❻ Baker Beach

Map 2 D4. **Open** dawn–dusk daily.

Baker Beach is the largest and most popular stretch of sand in the city and is often crowded with sunbathers. The chilly water and strong currents make it a dangerous place to swim, but it is a fine place to go for a walk. Fishing is also good here. There are forests of pine and cypress on the bluffs above the beach, where visitors can explore Battery Chamberlin, a gun emplacement from 1904. On the first weekend of each month rangers show the "disappearing gun," a heavy rifle that can be lowered behind a thick wall to protect it from enemy fire, and then raised again in order to be fired.

Golden Gate Bridge seen from Baker Beach

❼ Holy Virgin Cathedral

6210 Geary Blvd. **Map** 8 D1.
Tel 221-3255. 🚌 2, 29, 38, 38L.
🕐 8am, 6pm daily. 🌐 sfsobor.com

Shining gold onion-shaped domes crown the Russian Orthodox Holy Virgin Cathedral of the Russian Church in Exile, a startling landmark in the suburban Richmond District. Built in the early 1960s, it is generally open only during services. In contrast to those of many other Christian denominations, the services here are conducted with the congregation standing, so there are no pews or seats.

The cathedral and the many Russian-owned businesses nearby, such as the lively Russian Renaissance restaurant, are situated at the heart of San Francisco's extensive Russian community (see p43). This has flourished since the 1820s, but expanded greatly when more immigrants arrived after the Russian Revolution of 1917, and especially in the late 1950s and late 1980s.

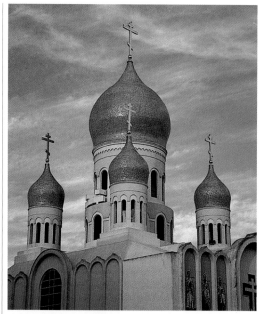

The Russian Orthodox Holy Virgin Cathedral

❽ Clement Street

Map 1 C5. 🚌 2, 29, 44.

This is the bustling main thoroughfare of the otherwise sleepy Richmond District. Bookstores and small boutiques flourish here, and the inhabitants of the neighborhood meet together in a lively mix of bars, fast-food cafés, and ethnic restaurants. Most of these are patronized more by locals than by tourists. Clement Street is surrounded by an area known as New Chinatown, home to more than one-third of the Chinese population of San Francisco. As a result, some of the city's best Chinese restaurants can be found here, and the emphasis in general is on East Asian cuisine. However, the area is known for the diversity of its restaurants, and Peruvian, Russian, and French establishments, among many others, also flourish here. The street stretches from Arguello Boulevard to the north–south cross-streets which are known as "The Avenues." It ends near the Legion of Honor (see pp158–9).

Interior of Temple Emanu-El, showing the Holy Ark

❾ Temple Emanu-El

Lake St and Arguello Blvd. **Map** 3 A4.
Tel 751-2535. 🚌 1, 1BX, 2, 33.
Open 🕐 by appointment only.
♿ 🌐 emanuelsf.org

After World War I hundreds of Jews from Russia and Eastern Europe moved into the Richmond District and built religious centers that are still major landmarks. Among these is the Temple Emanu-El, its dome inspired by that of the 6th-century Santa Sophia in Istanbul. The temple is a majestic piece of architecture. It was built in 1925 for the city's longest-established Jewish congregation (which was founded in 1850). The architect was Arthur Brown, who also designed San Francisco's City Hall (see p129). With its red-tiled dome, Emanu-El is a Californian architectural hybrid, combining the local Mission style (see p48) with Byzantine ornament and Romanesque arcades. Its interior, which holds nearly 2,000 worshipers, is especially fine when bright sunlight shines through the earth-toned stained-glass windows.

❺ Golden Gate Bridge

Named after the entrance to the Strait of San Francisco Bay called "Golden Gate" by John Fremont in 1846, the bridge opened in 1937, connecting San Francisco with Marin County. Breathtaking views are offered from this world-famous landmark, which has six lanes for vehicles, plus a pedestrian and bicycle path. It is the world's ninth-largest suspension bridge but it was the world's longest one when it was built.

Divers
To reach bedrock when building the south tower, divers used dynamite to smooth the surface of the ocean floor.

The Tower Piers

The foundations of the towers are a remarkable feat of engineering. The south tower, 1,125 ft (345 m) offshore, was sunk 100 ft (30 m) below the surface in open water.

KEY

① **The length** of the bridge is 1.7 miles (2.7 km), with a center span of 4,200 ft (1,280 m).

② **The roadway** is 220 ft (67 m) above water, 318 ft (97 m) deep at the midpoint.

Concrete Fender
During construction of the south (or San Francisco) tower, a ring or fender of concrete was first poured to form the base upon which the tower was built.

The Roadway
The roadway was constructed starting at the towers
and extending toward mid-span, so weight on the
suspension cables was evenly distributed.

Construction of the Towers
The two steel towers rise to a
height of 746 ft (227 m)
above the water.

Catching the Hot Rivets
Working in gangs of four, one man heated the
rivets and threw them to another, who caught
them in a bucket. The other two fastened
sections of steel with the hot rivets.

Joseph B. Strauss
Joseph B. Strauss is
officially credited as the
bridge's designer, though
his assistant Charles Ellis
has been given major
credit for the span's design.
Irving F. Morrow acted as
consulting architect.

1933	1934	1935	1936	1937
January Construction of the Golden Gate Bridge officially begins	**November** Work begins on the north tower	**June** Towers are complete		**June** Work ends on cables and starts on roadway
	January San Francisco pier is finished		**August** First cable across Golden Gate	**May** Opening Day
December Part of trestle is destroyed by a ship	**May** Marin Tower is topped off		**March** Last suspender rope in place	
	Marin Tower topping-off ceremony		**October** Spinning and compression begins on main cable	**April** Roadway is finished and last rivet is driven in
February Official ground-breaking				

The Opening of the Bridge

The bridge that most people said could never be built was completed on time and under budget in the midst of the Great Depression. Joseph B. Strauss finally won widespread support for the bridge, and a major bond issue financed its $35-million, four-year construction. When it opened, every siren and church bell in San Francisco and Marin sounded simultaneously as part of a huge celebration.

First Vehicles Cross
At noon on May 28, 1937, the roadway opened. An official convoy of Cadillacs and Packards were the first vehicles to cross the bridge.

Opening Day Crowd
On May 27, 1937, the bridge opened only for pedestrians. An estimated 200,000 people came to walk across the bridge.

The Bridge in Figures

- Every year approximately 40 million vehicles cross the bridge; every day about 112,000 vehicles use it.
- The original coat of paint lasted for 27 years, needing only touch-ups. From 1965 to 1995, a crew removed the old paint and applied a more durable coating.
- The two great 7,650 ft (2,332 m) main cables are more than 3 ft (1 m) thick, and contain 80,000 miles (128,744 km) of steel wire, enough to encircle the earth at the equator three times.
- The volume of concrete poured into the piers and anchorages during the bridge's construction would be enough to lay a 5 ft (1.5 m) wide sidewalk stretching from New York to San Francisco, a distance of more than 2,500 miles (4,000 km).
- The bridge was designed to withstand 100 mph (160 km/h) winds.
- Each pier has to withstand a tidal flow of more than 60 mph (97 km/h), while supporting a 22,000-ton steel tower above.

Original painting of the bridge

View from Vista Point
The best view of both the bridge and San Francisco is from the Marin side.

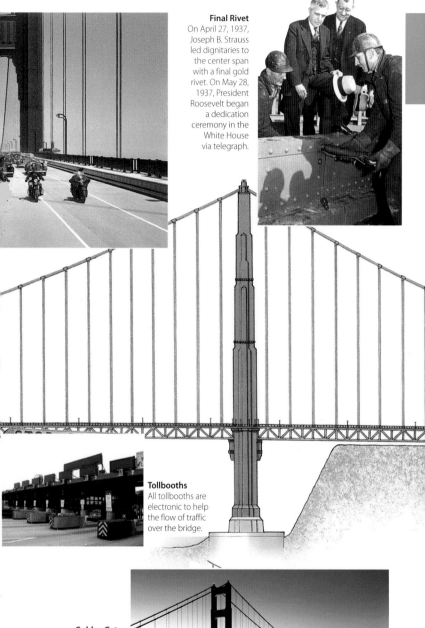

Final Rivet
On April 27, 1937, Joseph B. Strauss led dignitaries to the center span with a final gold rivet. On May 28, 1937, President Roosevelt began a dedication ceremony in the White House via telegraph.

Tollbooths
All tollbooths are electronic to help the flow of traffic over the bridge.

Golden Gate
The spectacular lighting display, originally envisaged by the architect, was not installed until 1987. The towers are designed to disappear into the darkness, which further accentuates their great height.

PACIFIC HEIGHTS AND THE MARINA

Pacific Heights is an exclusive neighborhood that clings to a hillside rising 300 ft (100 m) above the city. The area was developed in the 1880s, after cable cars linking it with the city center were introduced. With its magnificent views, it quickly became a desirable place to live, and elegant Victorian houses still line its tree-shaded streets. Most of these are privately owned, but the Queen Anne-style

Haas-Lilienthal House is open to the public. To the north of Broadway, the streets drop steeply to the Marina District, ending at San Francisco Bay. The houses here are built on a once-marshy site that was cleared and drained for the Panama–Pacific Exposition *(see p72)*, and the ambience is that of a seaside resort for the wealthy, with boutiques, lively cafés, and two prestigious yacht clubs.

Sights at a Glance

Historic Streets and Buildings
1. Haas-Lilienthal House
2. Spreckels Mansion
6. Convent of the Sacred Heart
7. Trinity+St. Peter's Episcopal Church
8. Cow Hollow
11. Octagon House
14. Wave Organ
15. Fort Mason

Parks and Gardens
3. Lafayette Park
4. Alta Plaza
13. Marina Green

Churches and Temples
9. Church of St. Mary the Virgin
10. Vedanta Temple

Shopping Streets
5. Fillmore Street
12. Chestnut Street

Restaurants *see p222*
1. Balboa Café
2. Belga
3. Brazen Head
4. Greens
5. La Mediterranee
6. Mel's Drive-In
7. Squat & Gobble

See also Street Finder maps 3 & 4

0 meters 500
0 yards 500

◄ Colorful sailboats on a dock at the Marina

For keys to map symbols *see back flap*

Street-by-Street: Pacific Heights

The blocks between Alta Plaza and Lafayette Park are at the heart of Pacific Heights. The streets here are quiet and tidy, lined with smart apartment blocks and palatial houses. Some date from the late 19th century, while others were built after the fire of 1906 *(see pp30–31)*. To the north of the area, the streets drop steeply toward the Marina District, affording outstanding views of the bay. Wander through the two large parks and past the luxuriant gardens of the mansions in between, then visit one of the numerous good bars, cafés, and restaurants on lively Fillmore Street.

Apartment blocks and palatial houses
surround Pacific Heights' Alta Plaza, a pleasant park area that features tennis courts and a playground.

Washington Street lies to the east of Alta Plaza. Here Victorian houses, in various architectural styles, fill an entire block.

❹ ★ Alta Plaza
Set aside as a public park in the 1850s, this hilltop green space offers splendid views of the Marina District and the bay beyond.

To bus nos.
3, 10, 24

WEBSTER STREET

FILLMORE STREET

STEINER STREET

Webster Street Row houses (terraced houses) have been declared an historic landmark. They were built for a middle-class clientele in 1878 and have since been restored.

0 meters 100
0 yards 100

Key

— Suggested route

2 ★ **Spreckels Mansion**
This impressive limestone building, constructed on the lines of a French Baroque palace, has been home to the family of best-selling novelist Danielle Steel since 1990.

Locator Map
See Street Finder maps 3 & 4

No. 2004 Gough Street, one of the more elaborate Victorian houses in Pacific Heights, was built in 1889.

To bus no. 10

3 Lafayette Park
This quiet park gives good views of the Victorian houses that surround it.

2151
SACRAMENTO STREET

This house, built
in 1881, was once
occupied by
SIR ARTHUR CONAN DOYLE

No. 2151 Sacramento Street
is an ornate French-style mansion. A plaque commemorates a visit by the author Sir Arthur Conan Doyle in 1923.

1 Haas-Lilienthal House
Furnished in Victorian style, this mansion is the headquarters of the Architectural Heritage Foundation.

❶ Haas-Lilienthal House

2007 Franklin St. **Map** 4 E3. **Tel** 441-3000. 🚌 3, 10, 24, 27, 30, 47, 49, 54, 70, 76X, 90, 93, 101. 🕐 noon–3pm Wed & Sat, 11am–4pm Sun. 🏛 📷 🌐 **sfheritage.org**

This exuberant Queen Anne-style mansion *(see p77)* was built for the rich merchant William Haas in 1886. Alice Lilienthal, his daughter, lived there until 1972, when it was given to the Foundation for San Francisco's Architectural

The Haas-Lilienthal House, a Queen Anne mansion from 1886

Heritage. It is the only intact private home of the period open as a museum, and is complete with authentic furniture. A fine example of an upper-middle-class Victorian dwelling, the house has elaborate gables, a circular corner tower, and luxuriant ornamentation.

A display of photographs describes the history of the building and reveals that this grandiose house was modest in comparison with some of those destroyed in the fire of 1906 *(see pp30–31)*.

❷ Spreckels Mansion

2080 Washington St. **Map** 4 E3. 🚌 1, 3, 10, 47, 49. **Closed** to the public.

Dominating the north side of Lafayette Park, this imposing Beaux Arts mansion *(see pp49)* is sometimes known as the "Parthenon of the West." It was built in 1912 for the flamboyant Alma de Bretteville Spreckels and her husband Adolph, who was heir to the sugar fortune of Claus Spreckels *(see pp136–7)*. Today the house is privately owned and occupies a block on Octavia Street, which is landscaped in the style of

Imposing façade of Spreckels Mansion at Lafayette Park

Lombard Street *(see p88)*. The mansion's architect was George Applegarth, who in 1916 designed the Legion of Honor *(see pp158–9)*. In 1924 the Spreckels donated the Palace to the city.

❸ Lafayette Park

Map 4 E3. 🚌 1, 10, 47, 49.

One of San Francisco's prettiest hilltop gardens, this is a leafy green haven of pine and eucalyptus trees, although its present tranquillity belies its turbulent history. Along with Alta Plaza and Alamo Square, the land was set aside in 1855 as city-owned open space, but squatters and others, including a former City

Panama–Pacific Exposition (1915)

San Francisco celebrated its recovery from the 1906 earthquake and fire with a monumental fair *(see pp32–3)*. Officially it was planned to celebrate the opening of the Panama Canal, and it was designed to be the most extravagant world's fair ever held. It was described by one highly enthusiastic visitor as "a miniature Constantinople."

The fair was held on land reclaimed from San Francisco Bay, on the site of today's Marina District. Its impressive pavilions were donated by all the states and by 25 foreign countries and lined a concourse 1 mile (1.6 km) long. Many of the buildings were based on such architectural gems as a Turkish mosque and a Buddhist temple in Kyoto. The lavish Tower of Jewels, at the center of the concourse, was encrusted with glass beads and lit by spotlights. To the west stood the Palace of Fine Arts *(see pp62)*, today the sole surviving structure from the fair, which visitors reached by gondola across a lagoon.

Ferry Building during Panama–Pacific Exposition

Panorama across the site of the Panama–Pacific Exposition

Attorney, laid claim to the land and built houses on it. The largest of the houses stood at the center of the hilltop park until 1936, as the squatter who had built it refused to move. It was finally torn down after the city authorities agreed to swap it for land on Gough Street. Steep stairways now lead to the park's summit and its delightful views. In the surrounding streets are scores of palatial buildings, with particularly ornate examples along Broadway, Jackson Street, and Pacific Avenue going east–west, and on Gough, Octavia, and Laguna streets going north–south.

❹ Alta Plaza

Map 4 D3. 🚌 1, 3, 10, 22, 24.

Situated in the center of Pacific Heights, Alta Plaza is a beautifully landscaped urban park, where San Francisco's elite come to relax. There are angular stone steps (offering great city views) rising up from Clay Street on the south side of the park. These steps may be familiar to you from films – Barbra Streisand drove down them in *What's Up, Doc?* The park has tennis courts and a playground, and from the north side of the park you can see splendid mansions, including the Gibbs House at 2622 Jackson Street, built by Willis Polk in 1894.

❺ Fillmore Street

Map 4 D4. 🚌 1, 2, 3, 22, 24.

Fillmore Street survived the devastating 1906 earthquake *(see pp30–31)* virtually intact, and for several years afterward served as the civic heart of the city. Government departments, as well as private businesses, were housed in the district's shops, homes, and even churches. Today the main commercial district of Pacific Heights is located here, from Jackson Street to Japantown around Bush Street. This area

Relaxing in Alta Plaza

boasts an abundance of bookstores, restaurants, and boutiques.

❻ Convent of the Sacred Heart

2222 Broadway. **Map** 4 D3. **Tel** 563-2900. 🚌 3, 10, 22, 24, 41, 45. **Closed** to the public. 🚻 🌐 **sacredsf.org**

This Neo-Classical villa was formerly known as the Flood Mansion. Designed by the architects Bliss and Faville for James Leary Flood, son of the Comstock Mine magnate *(see p104)*, it was completed in 1915. With harmonious proportions, impeccable detailing, and Tennessee marble façade, it is the most refined of the Pacific Heights mansions. In 1939 the building became home to one of the oldest private schools in California.

❼ Trinity + St Peter's Episcopal Church

1668 Bush St. **Map** 4 D4. **Tel** 775-1117. 🚌 1, 2, 3, 10, 19, 22, 38, 49, 70, 80, 90. 🌐 **trinity-stpeters.org**

This dramatic edifice is based on Durham Cathedral in northern England, arguably one of the finest examples of Norman architecture. The oldest Episcopal church on the Pacific Coast, it celebrated its 150th anniversary in 1999. Its colorful stained-glass windows were designed by a pupil of John LaFarge, a leading figure in the New York art scene during the late 19th century. The high altar displays the 1894 jewel-encrusted Trinity Cross, presented as a gift on Trinity Sunday by the women of the parish. The church is also home to the San Francisco Bach Choir.

❽ Cow Hollow

Map 4 D2. 🚌 28, 30, 30X, 41, 43, 45, 91.

Cow Hollow, a shopping district along Union Street, is so called because it was used as grazing land for the city's dairy cows up until the 1860s. It was then taken over for development as a residential neighborhood. In the 1950s the area became fashionable, and chic boutiques, antique shops, and art galleries took over the old neighborhood shops. Many of these are in restored 19th-century buildings, lending an old-fashioned air to the district, in stark contrast to the sophistication of the merchandise on display.

The view from Fillmore Street, overlooking Cow Hollow

ⓞ Church of St. Mary the Virgin

2325 Union St. **Map** 4 D3.
Tel 921-3665. 🚌 22, 41, 45.
Open 9am–5pm Mon–Fri.
🕇 8, 9, 11am Sun; 7am Wed.
🈲 during services. 🅆 smvsf.org

Evoking the more rural early 19th-century years of Cow Hollow (see p73), this rustic, wooden-shingled Episcopal church stands at the west end of what is now the busy Union Street shopping area.

One of the natural springs that provided water for the Cow Hollow dairy herds still bubbles up in the grounds, now largely hidden from the view of passersby on the church's original lych-gate and hedge.

The small, plain building is an early example of the Arts and Crafts style (see p48) later used in more prominent Bay Area churches. Below the steeply sloping roof, the walls are faced with "shingles," strips of redwood nailed in overlapping rows onto the building's

wooden frame. Part of the church was remodeled in the 1950s, when the entrance was moved from Steiner Street to the opposite end of the building, but the fabric has been well preserved.

ⓞ Vedanta Temple

2963 Webster St. **Map** 4 D2. **Tel** 922-2323. 🚌 22, 41, 45. **Closed** for renovation. 🕇 at the new temple: 2323 Vallejo St. 🈲 🅆 sfvedanta.org

One of the bay area's most unusual structures, the Vedanta Temple is an eclectic combination of a host of divergent decorative traditions. The roof is crowned by a rusty red onion-shaped dome similar to those seen on Russian Orthodox churches. It also has a tower resembling a crenellated European castle, and an octagonal Hindu temple cupola. Other architectural features

Ornate decoration on the Vedanta Temple

include highly decorated Moorish arches, medieval parapets and elements of Queen Anne (see p77) and Colonial styles. It was built in 1905 by the architect Joseph A. Leonard, working closely with the Northern California Vedanta Society minister, Swami Trigunatitananda.

Vedanta is the highest of the six schools of Hinduism, and the building symbolizes the Vedanta concept that every religion is just a different way of reaching one god. The Temple is now a monastery, but it is worth a visit just to marvel at this bizarre building from the outside.

⓰ Fort Mason

Map 4 E1. **Tel** 345-7500. 🚌 22, 28, 30, 43. ♿ partial. 🅆 fortmason.org
See Five Guided Walks pp174–5.

Fort Mason reflects the military history of San Francisco. The original buildings were private houses, erected in the late 1850s, which were confiscated by the US Government when the site was taken over by the US army during the Civil War (1861–5).

The Fort remained an army command post until the 1890s, and also housed refugees left homeless by 1906 earthquake (see pp30–31). In World War II, Fort Mason Army Base was the point of embarkation for around 1.6 million soldiers.

Fort Mason was converted to peaceful use in 1972. The original barracks, and the old hospital, which serves as a Visitor Center and headquarters of the Golden Gate National

Museo Italo Americano
Herbst Pavilion
The Mexican Museum
Festival Pavilion
Magic Theatre
Maritime Library
BATS Improv at the Bayfront Theater
Greens Restaurant
SFMOMA Artists Gallery
City College of San Francisco Art Campus
San Francisco Children's Art Center
Entrance
Young Performers Theatre
Great Meadow

⓫ Octagon House

2645 Gough St. **Map** 4 E2. **Tel** 441-7512. 🚌 24, 24X, 41, 45, 47, 49, 70, 90, 93, 97, 101, 101X. **Open** noon–3pm on second Sun and second and fourth Thu of the month, except Jan. Donation suggested. 🅿️ 🚹 limited. 🆆 nscda-ca.org/octagon-house

Built in 1861, the Octagon House is named for its eight-sided cupola. It houses a small, but engaging, collection of decorative arts and historic documents of the Colonial and Federal periods. Included are furniture, paintings, Revolutionary playing cards and signatures of 54 of the 56 signers of the Declaration of Independence.

⓬ Chestnut Street

Map 3 C2. 🚌 22, 28, 30, 43.

The main shopping and night-life center of the Marina District, Chestnut Street has a varied mix of movie theaters, markets, cafés, and restaurants. The commercial strip stretches just a few blocks from Fillmore Street west to Divisadero Street, after which the neighborhood becomes predominantly residential in character.

⓭ Marina Green

Map 4 D1. 🚌 22, 28, 30.

A long thin strip of lawn running the length of the Marina District, Marina Green is popular with kite-flyers and for picnics, especially on July 4, when the city's largest firework show can be seen from here *(see p51)*. Paths along the waterfront are the city's prime spots for bicyclists, joggers, and roller-skaters. Golden Gate Promenade leads from the west end of the green to Fort Point, or you can turn east to the Wave Organ at the harbor jetty.

⓮ Wave Organ

Map 4 D1. 🚌 30.

Sitting at the tip of the breakwater that protects the Marina is the world's most peculiar musical instrument. Built by scientists from the Exploratorium *(see pp94–5)*, the Wave Organ consists of a number of underwater pipes that echo and hum with the changing tides. Listening tubes are imbedded in a mini-amphi-theater that has views of Pacific Heights and the Presidio. The sounds you hear are more like gurgling plumbing than organ music.

Wave Organ at the end of the West Harbor jetty

International Youth Hostel

Fort Mason General's Residence

Chapel

Golden Gate National Recreation Area headquarters

Meta III (1985) by Italo Scanga at the Museo Italo Americano

Recreation Area (GGNRA) are both open to the public.

Fort Mason has some of the city's finest views, looking across the bay toward Golden Gate Bridge and Alcatraz.

Fort Mason Center

Part of the Fort is now occupied by one of San Francisco's prime art complexes. Fort Mason Center is home to over 25 cultural organizations, art galleries, museums, and theaters, including the Cowell Theater, BATS Improv at the Bayfront Theater, the Magic Theatre, and the Young Performers Theatre. The SFMOMA Artists Gallery offers art-works from Northern Californian artists for sale or rent, while Italian and Italian-American artists display their works at the Museo Italo Americano. The Mexican Museum has a unique collection of over 12,000 objects representing thousands of years of Mexican history. The Maritime Library has a wonderful mix of history books, oral histories, and ships' plans but its opening hours are limited. The Maritime Museum itself *(see p87)* is loc-ated near Fisherman's Wharf. Among the places to eat at Fort Mason Center is Greens *(see p226)*, one of the city's best vegetarian restaurants. Thousands of events occur at Fort Mason Center every year.

The SS *Balclutha*, at Hyde Street Pier, part of the Maritime Museum

Victorian Houses in San Francisco

Despite earthquakes, fires, and the inroads of modern life, thousands of ornate, late 19th-century houses still line the streets of San Francisco. In fact, in many neighborhoods they are by far the most common type of housing. Victorian houses are broadly similar, in that they all have wooden frames, elaborately decorated with mass-produced ornament. Most were constructed on narrow plots to a similar floor plan, but they differ in the features of the façade. Four main styles prevail in the city, although in practice many houses, especially those built in the 1880s and 1890s, combine aspects of two or more styles.

Detail of Queen Anne-style gateway at Chateau Tivoli

Gothic Revival (1850–80)

Gothic Revival houses are the easiest to identify, since they always have pointed arches over the windows and sometimes over the doors. Other features are pitched gabled roofs, decorated vergeboards (again, with pointed arch motifs) and porches that run the width of the building. The smaller, simpler houses of this type are usually painted white, rather than the vibrant colors often associated with later styles.

No. 1111 Oak Street is one of the city's oldest Gothic Revival buildings. Its front garden is unusually large.

The pitched roof over the main façade often runs lengthwise, allowing the use of dormer windows.

A gabled roof with decorated vergeboards is the clearest mark of Gothic Revival.

Gothic porch with cross bracing at 1978 Filbert Street

Wide porches can be reached by a central staircase.

Balustrades on the porch betray the origins of the style in the Deep South.

Italianate (1850–85)

Italianate houses were more popular in San Francisco than elsewhere in the US, perhaps because their compact form was suited to the city's high building density. The most distinctive feature of the Italianate style is the tall cornice, usually with a decorative bracket, which adds a palatial air even to modest homes. Elaborate decoration around doors and windows is another feature typical of the style.

No. 1913 Sacramento Street displays a typical formal Italianate façade, modeled on a Renaissance *palazzo*. The wooden exterior is made to look like stone.

Tall cornices, often with decorative brackets, conceal a pitched roof.

Imposing entrance with Italianate porch

Symmetrical windows are capped by decorative arches.

Neo-Classical doorways, sometimes with ornate pedimented porches, are a typical Italianate touch.

Stick (1860–90)

This architectural style, with its ungainly name, is perhaps the most prevalent among Victorian houses in the city. Sometimes also called "Stick-Eastlake" after London furniture designer Charles Eastlake, this style was intended to be architecturally "honest." Vertical lines are emphasized, both in the wood-frame structure and in ornamentation. Bay windows, false gabled cornices and square corners are key identifying features.

Gabled roof with Eastlake windows at 2931 Pierce Street

Wide bands of trim often form a decorative truss, emphasizing the underlying structure of Stick houses.

Decorative gables filled with "sunburst" motifs are used on porches and window frames.

Adjoining front doors can be protected by a single projecting porch.

No. 1715–1717 Capp Street is a fine example of the Stick-Eastlake style, with a plain façade enlivened by decorative flourishes.

Queen Anne (1875–1905)

The name "Queen Anne" does not refer to a historical period; it was coined by the English architect Richard Shaw. Queen Anne houses freely combine elements from many decorative traditions, but are marked by their turrets and towers and large, often decorative, panels on wall surfaces. Most houses also display intricate spindle-work on balustrades, porches, and roof trusses.

Palladian windows were used in gables to give the appearance of an extra floor.

Queen Anne gable filled with ornamental panels at 818 Steiner Street

Queen Anne turret topped by a finial at 1015 Steiner Street

Round, square, and polygonal turrets and towers are typical of Queen Anne-style houses.

Gable pediments hold ornamental windows and decorative panels.

The curved window frame is not itself characteristic of Queen Anne style, but many houses include features borrowed from other styles.

The asymmetrical façade of 850 Steiner Street, with its eclectic ornament, is typical of a Queen Anne house. Such features are often painted in various bright colors.

Where to Find Victorian Houses

1715–1717 Capp St. **Map** 10 F4
Chateau Tivoli, 1057 Steiner St. **Map** 4 D4
1978 Filbert St. **Map** 4 D2
1111 Oak St. **Map** 9 C1
2931 Pierce St. **Map** 4 D3
1913 Sacramento St. **Map** 4 E3
818 Steiner St. **Map** 4 D5
850 Steiner St. **Map** 4 D5
1015 Steiner St. **Map** 4 D5
2527–2531 Washington St. **Map** 4 D3
Alamo Square *p131*
Clarke's Folly *p141*
Haas-Lilienthal House *p72*
Liberty Street. **Map** 10 E3
Masonic Avenue. **Map** 3 C4
Octagon House *p75*
Spreckels Mansion *p72*

FISHERMAN'S WHARF AND NORTH BEACH

Fishermen from Genoa and Sicily first arrived in the Fisherman's Wharf area in the late 19th century, and founded here the San Francisco fishing industry. The district has slowly given way to tourism since the 1950s, but brightly painted boats still set out from the harbor on fishing trips early each morning. To the south of Fisherman's Wharf lies North Beach, sometimes known as "Little Italy." This lively part of the city has an abundance of aromatic delis, bakeries, and cafés, from which you can watch the crowds. It is home to Italian and Chinese families, with a sprinkling of writers and bohemians; Jack Kerouac (see p34), among others, found inspiration here.

Sights at a Glance

Historic Streets and Buildings
1. Alcatraz Island pp82–5
2. PIER 39
9. Lombard Street
11. Vallejo Street Stairway
18. Filbert Steps
19. Greenwich Steps
20. Upper Montgomery Street

Monuments
17. Coit Tower

Churches
15. Saints Peter and Paul Church

Restaurants and Bars
12. Club Fugazi

Parks and Gardens
14. Washington Square
16. Bocce Ball Courts
21. Levi's Plaza

Shopping Centers
6. The Cannery
7. Ghirardelli Square

Museums and Galleries
3. USS Pampanito
4. Madame Tussaud's
5. Ripley's Believe It Or Not! Museum
8. San Francisco Maritime National Historical Park Visitors' Center
10. San Francisco Art Institute
13. The Beat Museum
22. Exploratorium

Restaurants
see pp222–3
1. Buena Vista Café
2. Boudin
3. Caffé Greco
4. Caffé Sport
5. Fog City
6. Franchino
7. Gary Danko
8. The House
9. Scoma's
10. The Stinking Rose

See also Street Finder
maps 4–6

0 meters   500
0 yards   500

◀ Looking out to the city from the top of Lombard Street   **For keys to symbols** see back flap

Street-by-Street: Fisherman's Wharf

Italian seafood restaurants have replaced fishing as the primary focus of the Fisherman's Wharf local economy. Restaurants and outdoor crab stands serve San Francisco's celebrated Dungeness crab from November to June. Besides sampling the seafood, visitors can also take in the shops, museums, and attractions for which Fisherman's Wharf is noted. Tickets for Alcatraz can be purchased from Pier 33.

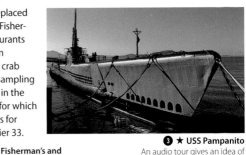

❸ ★ USS Pampanito
An audio tour gives an idea of the hardships endured by sailors in this World War II submarine.

Fisherman's and Seaman's Chapel
was built on the pier so that the devout could pray before they sailed and after they returned.

Pier 45

Fisherman's Wharf
is now a street lined with seafood restaurants and crab stands.

Fish Alley is where the morning's catch is landed and prepared.

❻ The Cannery
Once a fruit cannery, the building was converted to a mall, housing shops, restaurants, and a museum.

San Francisco Fire Engine Tours and Adventures
provides visitors with tours of the city on a big, shiny red Mack fire engine.

Historic Trolley Line offers colorful rides on restored, 1930s-vintage streetcars from US cities, on the E and F Muni Lines.

The Anchorage Shopping Center

To Powell – Hyde cable car turntable (1 block)

Key

— Suggested route

JEFFERSON

JONES STREET

LEAVENWORTH STREET

Sea lions sunbathing on PIER 39's boat docks are the delight of tourists, but a nuisance for boaters. The colony usually arrives around January.

Locator Map
See Street Finder, map 6

San Francisco Bay

FISHERMAN'S WHARF AND NORTH BEACH

CHINATOWN AND NOB HILL

FINANCIAL DISTRICT AND UNION SQUARE

Blue and Gold Fleet and bay cruise tickets *(p287)*

Boudin Sourdough Bakery produces the tangy bread for which San Francisco is famous. You can buy it fresh here then tour the museum *(p244)*.

Bus stop (No. 39, E, F)

Red and White Fleet tickets

E M B A R C A D E R O

To Pier 33 for tickets to Alcatraz

P O W E L L   S T R E E T

M A S O N   S T R E E T

T R E E T

❹ **Madame Tussaud's**
Almost 300 life-size wax figures of past and present-day personalities greet visitors to this museum.

❺ **Ripley's Believe It Or Not! Museum**
This is a selection of the famed cartoonist's strange collection of curiosities and odd facts.

0 meters 100
0 yards 100

❷ ★ **PIER 39**
A collection of restaurants, shops, and amusements, set against a backdrop of spectacular bay views, is one of the city's more popular tourist attractions.

For keys to symbols *see back flap*

● Alcatraz Island

Alcatraz means "pelican" in Spanish, a reference to the first inhabitants of this rocky, steep-sided island. Lying 3 miles (5 km) east of the Golden Gate, its location is both strategic and exposed to harsh ocean winds. In 1859, the US military established a fort here that guarded San Francisco Bay until 1907, when it became a military prison. From 1934 to 1963, it served as a maximum-security Federal Penitentiary. Unoccupied until 1969, the island was seized by Indians of All Tribes *(see p34)* laying claim to the island as their land. The group was expelled in 1971, and Alcatraz is now part of the Golden Gate National Recreation Area.

★ Cell Block
The cell house contains four free-standing cell blocks. No cell has an outside wall or ceiling. The dungeon-like foundation of the "Big House," as inmates called the main prison block, shares the original foundation of the old military fortress.

Lighthouse
The original Alcatraz lighthouse, the first on the Pacific coast of the United States, was activated in 1854 and replaced in 1909 by the present structure.

Warden's House
This house suffered extensive fire damage during the American Indian occupation of 1969–71.

KEY

① **Agave Trail** (open seasonally).

② **The officers' apartments** stood here.

③ **Military parade ground** (open seasonally).

④ **Metal detectors** checked prisoners on their way to and from the dining hall and exercise yards. The "machine" on display in the Cell House is a prop from the film *Escape from Alcatraz.*

⑤ **The Military Morgue** is tiny and cramped and not open to the public.

⑥ **Water tower**

⑦ **The Officer's Club**, also known as the Enlisted Men's Club, dates from the days of Fort Alcatraz. It served as the recreation center during the federal prison days.

⑧ **Electric maintenance shop**

⑨ **The Military Dorm** was built in 1933 for the military prison guards.

⑩ **Sally Port** dates from 1857. Equipped with drawbridge and dry moat, this guardhouse defended the approach to Fort Alcatraz.

⑪ **The Exhibit Area** is in the old barracks building behind the ferry jetty. It houses a bookstore, exhibits, multimedia show providing a historical overview of Alcatraz, and an information counter.

⑫ **Barracks buildings**

Alcatraz Island from the Ferry
"The Rock" has no natural soil. Earth was shipped
from Angel Island to make garden plots.

VISITORS' CHECKLIST

Practical Information
Map 6 F1. **Tel** 981-7625 for tickets
and schedules. Night Tours:
Thu–Mon. **Tel** 561-4900.
w **nps.gov/alcatraz**
w **alcatrazcruises.com**
Open daily. **Closed** Jan 1,
Thanksgiving, Dec 25.
in places. Visitor Center:
free film presentation.
Buy tickets for the tour in
advance, especially in summer.

Transport
from Pier 33.

★ **Exercise Yard**
Meals and walks around the exercise yard were
the highlights of a prisoner's day. The walled
yard featured in films made at the prison.

Alcatraz Pier
Visitors alight at this pier facing the Barracks. Most
prisoners took their first steps ashore nearby.

Key

— Suggested route

0 meters	75
0 yards	75

For keys to symbols *see back flap*

Inside Alcatraz

The maximum-security prison on Alcatraz, dubbed "The Rock" by the US Army, housed an average of 264 of the country's most incorrigible criminals, who were transferred here for disobedience while serving time in prisons elsewhere in the US. The strict discipline at Alcatraz was enforced by the threat of a stint in the isolation cells and by loss of privileges, including the chance at special jobs, time for recreation, use of the prison library, and visitation rights.

D Block
In the solitary confinement cells of D Block, prisoners had to endure hours of unrelieved boredom.

Broadway
The corridor that separates C and B blocks was nicknamed by prisoners after New York City's busiest thoroughfare.

Control Room
Reinforced to withstand a siege, this controlled the 24-hour electric security system.

Main cell house entrance

KEY

① **Warden's office**

② **Visiting area**

③ **Library** from which prisoners could order "approved" books

④ **Recreation yard**

⑤ **Kitchen**

⑥ **Hospital** above dining room

⑦ **Food preparation and store rooms**

⑧ **Barber shop**

Inside a Cell
Prisoners spent between 16 and 23 hours every day alone in stark cells, equipped with only a toilet and bunk. Many cells measured 5 ft by 9 ft (1.5 m by 2.7 m).

Gun Gallery

Guards armed with pistols and rifles patrolled along the caged walkways at the ends of the cell blocks.

Dining Room

Inmates were well fed, the better to quell rebellion. Note the sample menu on display at the kitchen entrance.

Famous Inmates

Al Capone

The notorious Prohibition-era gangster "Scarface" Capone was actually convicted, in 1934, for income tax evasion! He spent much of his 10-year sentence on Alcatraz in a hospital isolation cell, and finally left the prison mentally unbalanced after contracting syphilis.

Robert Stroud

Stroud spent all of his 17 years on The Rock in solitary confinement. Despite assertions to the contrary in the film *The Birdman of Alcatraz* (1962), Stroud was in fact prohibited from keeping birds in his prison cell.

Carnes, Thompson, and Shockley

In May 1946, prisoners led by Clarence Carnes, Marion Thompson, and Sam Shockley overpowered guards and captured their guns. The prisoners failed to break out of the cell house, but three inmates and two officers were killed in the "Battle of Alcatraz." Carnes received an additional life sentence, and Shockley and Thompson were executed at San Quentin prison, for their part as ringleaders of the insurrection.

Anglin Brothers

John and Clarence Anglin, along with Frank Morris, chipped through the back walls of their cells, hiding the holes with cardboard grates. They left dummy heads in their beds and made a raft to enable their escape. They were never caught. Their story was dramatized in the film *Escape from Alcatraz* (1979).

George Kelly

"Machine Gun" Kelly was one of The Rock's most infamous inmates. He served 17 years for kidnapping and extortion.

1775 Spanish explorer Juan Manuel de Ayala names Alcatraz after the "strange birds" that inhabit it

1859 Fort Alcatraz completed; equipped with 100 cannon and 300 troops

1909 Army prisoners begin construction on the cell house

1972 Alcatraz becomes a national park

1962 Frank Morris and the Anglin brothers escape

1750	1800	1850	1900	1950

John Fremont

1848 John Fremont buys Alcatraz

1850 Alcatraz declared a military reservation by President Fillmore

1857 Sally Port built

1854 First Pacific Coast lighthouse activated on Alcatraz

Sally Port

1963 Prison closed

1934 Federal Bureau of Prisons turns Alcatraz into a civilian prison

1969–71 Island occupied by Indians of All Tribes

❷ PIER 39

Map 5 B1. 🚌 4, 8, 39, 47. 🚋 E, F.
🚃 Powell–Hyde. ⛴ SF Bay Ferry.
See Shopping in San Francisco p233.

Refurbished in 1978 to
resemble a quaint wooden
fishing village, this 1905 cargo
pier now houses many tourist
shops and specialty stores
spread through two levels.

The pier's street performers
and amusements are popular
with families. You can try the
two-story carousel, play games
at the Riptide arcade, or brave
the Turbo Ride. The Aquarium
of the Bay houses 20,000 sea
creatures including sharks,
bat rays, and skates.

A multimedia show, the San
Francisco Experience, whisks
visitors through a historical
tour of the city, complete with
Chinese New Year celebrations,
fog, and an earthquake.

❸ USS Pampanito

Pier 45. **Map** 4 F1. **Tel** 775-1943.
🚌 4, 8, 39, 47. 🚋 E, F.
🚃 Powell–Hyde. ⛴ SF Bay Ferry.
Open 9am–6pm daily (to 8pm in
summer; call ahead for details). 🎫 🔊
🌐 **maritime.org/pamphome.htm**

This World War II submarine
fought in, and survived, several
bloody battles in the Pacific,
sinking six enemy ships and
severely damaging others.
Tragically for the allies, two of
its fatal targets were carrying
British and Australian POWs.
The *Pampanito* managed to
rescue 73 men and carry them
to safety in the US. A tour of the
ship takes visitors from stern to
bow to see the torpedo room,

Visitors at the popular PIER 39

the claustrophobic kitchen,
and officers' quarters. When
the *Pampanito* was in service,
it had a full crew of 10 officers
and 70 seamen.

❹ Madame Tussaud's

145 Jefferson St. **Map** 5 B1. 🚌 4, 8,
39 47. 🚋 E, F. 🚃 Powell–Hyde.
Open 10am–7pm Sun–Thu, 10am–
8pm Fri & Sat. 🎫 ♿ 🌐 **madame
tussauds.com/sanfrancisco**

Madame Tussaud's San
Francisco location is the brand's
17th wax museum in the world
and the second
one in California.
In addition to the
expected host
of historic lumi-
naries and figures
from the worlds
of entertainment
and sport, the
Tussaud's com-
plex features the
San Francisco
Dungeon, a
thrilling journey
through time

exploring some of the darker
aspects of the history of the
city, complete with live performers and special effects.

❺ Ripley's Believe It Or Not! Museum

175 Jefferson St. **Map** 4 F1. **Tel** 202–
9850. 🚌 4, 8, 39, 47. 🚋 E, F.
🚃 Powell–Hyde. **Open** 10am–10pm
Sun–Thu, 10am–11pm Fri & Sat (mid-
Jun–Labor Day: 9am–11pm Sun–Thu,
9am–midnight Fri & Sat). 🎫 ♿
🌐 **ripleysf.com**

California native Robert L.
Ripley was an illustrator with
a penchant for collecting
peculiar facts and artifacts.
He earned his fame and fortune
by syndicating his newspaper
cartoon strip, called "Ripley's
Believe It Or Not!" Among the
350 oddities on display are a
cable car built of 275,000 match-
sticks, a two-headed calf, and an
image of a man who had two
pupils in each eyeball. Get lost in
the Marvelous Mirror Maze and
sample some candy from the
factory. Some of Ripley's famous
cartoon strips are on display, too.

USS *Pampanito's* torpedo room

❻ The Cannery

2801 Leavenworth St. **Map** 4 F1.
🚌 4, 8, 39, 47. 🚋 E, F. 🚃 Powell–
Hyde. *See Shopping in San Francisco
p233.*

This 1909 fruit-canning plant
was refurbished in the 1960s
to incorporate footbridges,
sunny courtyards, and rambling
passages, with restaurants and
specialty shops selling clothes,
collector dolls, and American
Indian arts and crafts.

The Cannery also used to
house the Museum of the City
of San Francisco, but a fire
forced the premises to close.
However, the collection has
moved to the City Hall *(see p129)*,
where all the exhibits are now
on display. Among these is the
massive head of the statue that
capped City Hall before the
1906 earthquake *(see pp30–31)*.
The illuminated crown on the
head is an example of early
electric illumination. You can
also visit www.sfmuseum.org.

❼ Ghirardelli Square

900 North Point St. **Map** 4 F1. 🚌 4,
18, 19, 24, 27, 30, 38, 47, 49. 🚋 E, F.
🚃 Powell–Hyde. *See Shopping in San
Francisco p233.*

Once a chocolate factory and
woollen mill, this is the most
attractive of San Francisco's
refurbished factories, a mix
of old red-brick buildings and
modern shops and restaurants.
The shopping center retains the
famous Ghirardelli trademark
clock tower and the original
electric roof sign. Ghirardelli
Chocolate Manufactory on the
plaza beneath the tower still
houses vintage chocolate-

Ghirardelli Square

making machinery and sells
the confection, although the
chocolate bars are now made
in San Leandro, across the bay.

Fountain Plaza is a colorful
outdoor attraction for shoppers
day and evening.

❽ San Francisco Maritime National Historical Park Visitors' Center

900 Beach St. **Map** 4 F1. 🚌 4, 8, 19,
39, 47. 🚋 E, F. 🚃 Powell–Hyde.
Museum: **Tel** 561-7100. **Open** main
floor open 10am–4pm. Hyde Street
Pier: **Tel** 561–7169. **Open** 5:30am–
9pm daily (Jun–Aug: to 5:30pm).
Closed Jan 1, Thanksgiving, Dec 25.
🐾 Pier only. ♿ Pier and museum
only. 🐾 *See Five Guided Walks pp174–5.*
Visitor's Center: 499 Jefferson Street.
Tel 415-447-5000. **Open** 9:30am–
5pm daily. 🅦 maritime.org

Balclutha moored at Hyde Street Pier

Built in 1939, this building has
housed the Maritime Museum
from 1951. Visitors can still admire
the renovated Streamline Modern
building with its clean lines of an
ocean liner. Moored at nearby

Hyde Street Pier is one of the
world's largest collections of
old ships. Among the most
spectacular is the *CA Thayer*, a
three-masted schooner built in
1895 and retired in 1950. The
Thayer carried lumber along
the North California coast, and
later was used in Alaskan fishing.
Also at the pier is the 2,560-ton
side-wheel ferry-boat, *Eureka*, built
in 1890 to ferry trains between
the Hyde Street Pier and the
counties north of San Francisco
Bay. It carried 2,300 passengers
and 120 cars, and was the largest
passenger ferry of its day.

Balclutha

*This ship is the star of Hyde
Street Pier. Launched in
1886, she sailed twice a
year between Britain
and California,
trading wheat
for coal.*

Foremast

Mainmast

Mizzenmast

Quarterdeck

Bowsprit

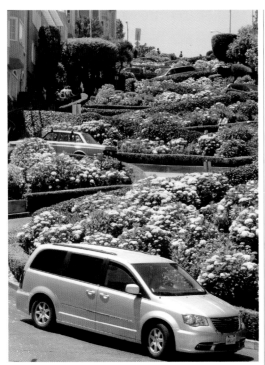
Cars negotiating the steep and crooked section of Lombard Street

❾ Lombard Street

Map 5 A2. 🚌 19, 41, 45. 🚋 Powell–Hyde.

Banked at a natural incline of 27°, this hill proved too steep for vehicles to climb. In the 1920s the section of Lombard Street close to the summit of Russian Hill was revamped, and the severity of its gradient lessened by the addition of eight curves.

Today it is known as "the crookedest street in the world." Cars can travel downhill only, while people take the steps or use the cable car.

❿ San Francisco Art Institute

800 Chestnut St. **Map** 4 F2. **Tel** 771-7020. 🚌 30, 41, 45, 91. 🚋 Powell–Hyde, Powell–Mason. Diego Rivera Gallery: **Open** 9am–7pm daily. **Closed** public hols. Walter and McBean Galleries: **Open** 11am–6pm Wed–Sat (to 7pm Tue). ♿ partial. 📷 🖥 🇼 sfai.edu

San Francisco's Art Institute dates from 1871 and once occupied the large wooden mansion built

A 30-Minute Walk through North Beach

Settlers from Chile, and later those from Italy, created the North Beach nightlife that earned this quarter its exuberant reputation. Its café-oriented atmosphere has long appealed to bohemians, particularly the 1950s Beat Generation (*see p34*).

Neighborhood of the Beats

Start from the southwest corner of Broadway and Columbus Avenue at City Lights Bookstore ①. Owned by Beat poet Lawrence Ferlinghetti, City Lights was the first bookshop in the US to sell only paperbacks. It was author Jack Kerouac, a friend of Ferlinghetti, who coined the word "Beat," later made popular as "Beatnik."

One of the most popular Beat haunts was Vesuvio ②, south of City Lights, across Jack Kerouac Alley. Welsh poet Dylan Thomas was a patron of this watering hole, which is still a favorite of poets and artists.

Jack Kerouac

From Vesuvio continue south to Pacific Avenue and cross to the opposite side of Columbus Avenue. Walk back toward Broadway, stopping first at Tosca ③. The walls of this old-world bar and café display evocative murals of rural Tuscany, and a jukebox plays selections from Italian opera. A few steps north bring you to Adler Alley. Specs ④, an exuberant, cozy bar filled with memorabilia of the Beat era, is at No. 12. Retrace the route to Columbus Avenue, then turn right into Broadway and walk as far as Kearny Street, taking in the hustle and bustle of Broadway.

Columbus Café ⑩

The Strip

This stretch of Broadway is known as The Strip ⑤, and is noted for its "adult entertainment." At the junction of Broadway and Grant Avenue is the former Condor Club ⑥, where the world's first topless stage show was performed in June 1964 by Carol Doda, a waitress at the club.

for Mark Hopkins' family on Nob Hill (see p104), which burned down in the 1906 fire (see pp30–31). Today it is housed in a 1926 Spanish Colonial-style building, with cloisters, bell tower, and courtyard fountain. The Diego Rivera Gallery, named after the Mexican muralist, is left of the main entrance. The Walter and McBean Galleries are the primary exhibition venues and feature changing shows from contemporary photography and film screenings to design and technology.

Entertainer from Club Fugazi

⓫ Vallejo Street Stairway

Vallejo St, between Mason St and Jones St. **Map** 5 B3. 🚌 10, 12, 41. 🚋 Powell–Mason.

The steep climb from Little Italy to the southernmost summit of Russian Hill reveals some of the city's best views of Telegraph Hill, North Beach, and the encompassing bay. The street gives way to steps at Mason Street, which climb up through the quiet and pretty Ina Coolbirth Park. Higher still, above Taylor Street, there is a warren of lanes, with several Victorian style wooden houses (see pp76–7). At the crest of the hill is one of the rare pockets of the city that was not destroyed in the earthquake and fire of 1906 (see pp30–31).

⓬ Club Fugazi

678 Green St. **Map** 5 B3. **Tel** 421-4222. 🚌 8, 8BX, 30, 39, 41, 45, 91. 🚋 Powell–Mason. **Open** Wed–Sun. See Entertainment p251.

Club Fugazi was originally built in 1912 as a community hall for Italians living in San Francisco in the wake of the 1906 earthquake. Club Fugazi is the home of the musical cabaret Beach Blanket Babylon (see p251). This lively show, famous for its topical and outrageous songs, has been running now for over two decades and has become a San Francisco institution.

⓭ The Beat Museum

540 Broadway. **Map** 5 B3. **Tel** (1-800) KER-OUAC (537-6822 or 399-9626). 🚌 8AX, 10, 12, 30, 39, 41, 45, 91. **Open** 10am–7pm daily. **Closed** public hols. 🖥️ 🌐 **kerouac.com**

This offbeat museum displays memorabilia related to the artists of the Beat Generation, who lived in San Francisco in the 1950s. Photographs, books, album covers, and letters line the walls and floors of the building. The museum hosts events related to Beat culture, while the shop sells a fascinating range of books, videos, T-shirts, and posters.

Upper Grant Avenue
Turn right into Grant Avenue where you will find The Saloon ⑦ with its original 1861 bar. On the corner of Vallejo Street is Caffè Trieste ⑧, the oldest coffeehouse in San Francisco and a genuine writers' and artists' rendezvous since 1956. Very much a part of Italian-American culture, it offers live opera on Saturday afternoons. Follow Grant Avenue north past Maggie McGarry's Pub ⑨, now an Irish Pub but formerly the Coffee Gallery, haunt of the Beats. Turn left at Green Street and look for Columbus Café ⑩ and its exterior murals. Go left at Columbus Avenue, and follow this main North Beach street south past many more Italian coffeehouses, to return to your starting point.

Vesuvio, a popular Beat bar ②

Tips for Walkers

Starting point: Corner of Broadway and Columbus Ave.
Length: 1 mile (1.5 km).
Getting there: Muni bus No. 41 runs along Columbus Ave.
Stopping-off points: All the bars and cafés mentioned are worth visiting for a drink and the atmosphere. Children are not usually allowed in bars.

Key

••• Walk route

0 meters   200
0 yards   200

Street-by-Street: Telegraph Hill

Telegraph Hill was named after the semaphore installed on its crest in 1850 to alert merchants of the arrival of ships. Today's hill falls away abruptly on its eastern side, where it was dynamited to provide rocks for landfill and paving. There are steep paths on this side of the hill, bordered by gardens. The western side slopes more gradually into "Little Italy," the area around Washington Square. In the past the hill has been home to immigrants and to artists who appreciated the panoramic views. These days the quaint pastel clapboard homes are much sought after and this is one of the city's prime residential areas.

Telegraph Hill is dominated by Coit Tower. At night the tower is bathed in yellow light and is visible from many parts of the city.

The Christopher Columbus Statue was erected in 1957.

The Statue of Benjamin Franklin stands above a time capsule planted in 1979, containing Levi's, a poem, and a recording of the Hoodoo Rhythm Devils.

🄲 Washington Square
This small park at the heart of Little Italy is dominated by Saints Peter and Paul Catholic Church, known as the "Italian Cathedral."

Bus stop (No. 39)

🄵 ★ Saints Peter and Paul Church
The Neo-Gothic church, consecrated in 1924, has an ornate interior with this fine image of Christ in the apse.

⓱ ★ Coit Tower
The frescoes inside were painted by local artists in 1933, as part of the Federal Art Project set up by President Roosevelt.

Bus stop (No. 39)

Locator Map
See Street Finder map 5

⓳ Greenwich Steps
These formally land-scaped steps contrast with the charmingly rustic Filbert Steps.

Napier Lane is a small lane lined with 19th-century cottages. It is the last of San Francisco's wooden plank streets and a tranquil retreat from the city.

Key

— Suggested route

| 0 meters | 100 |
| 0 yards | 100 |

⓲ ★ Filbert Steps
The descent through flower gardens down these steps gives fine views over the harbor to the East Bay.

No. 1360 Montgomery Street is decorated with an Art Deco figure of a modern Atlas.

The façade of Saints Peter and Paul Church

⓮ Washington Square

Map 5 B2. 🚌 8BX, 8X, 30, 39, 41, 45, 91. 🚋 Powell–Mason.

The square consists of a lawn surrounded by benches and trees, set against the twin towers of Saints Peter and Paul Church. It has an almost Mediterranean atmosphere, appropriate for the "town square" of Little Italy, although the Italian community is less evident in this neighborhood now than it was when the park was first laid out in 1955. Near the center of the square stands a statue of Benjamin Franklin. A time capsule was buried under this in 1979 and is scheduled to be reopened in 2079. It is said to contain some Levi jeans, a bottle of wine, and a poem by the famous Beat poet Lawrence Ferlinghetti *(see p88)*.

⓯ Saints Peter and Paul Church

666 Filbert St. **Map** 5 B2. **Tel** 421-0809. 🚌 8BX, 8X, 30, 39, 41, 45, 91. 🚋 Powell–Mason. **Open** 7:30am–4pm daily (to 1pm public hols). ✝ 7am, 8:45am, 1pm, 5pm Sun; Italian mass and choir 11:45am Sun. &♿ 🌐 salesiansspp.org

Known by many as the Italian Cathedral, this large church is

situated at the heart of North Beach, and many Italians find it a welcome haven when they first arrive in San Francisco. It was here that the local baseball hero, Joe Di Maggio, was photographed after his marriage to the actress Marilyn Monroe in 1957, although the actual wedding ceremony was held elsewhere. The building, designed by Charles Fantoni, has an Italianesque façade, with a complex interior notable for its many columns and ornate altar. There are also statues and mosaics illuminated by stained-glass windows. The concrete and steel structure of the church, with its twin spires, was completed in 1924.

Cecil B. DeMille filmed the workers laying the foundations of Saints Peter and Paul, and used the scene to show the building of the Temple of Jerusalem in his 1923 film *The Ten Commandments*.

The church is also known as the Fishermen's Church (many Italians once earned their living by fishing), and there is a Mass to celebrate the Blessing of the Fleet in October. Masses are held in Italian and Chinese, as well as English.

⓰ Bocce Ball Courts

Lombard St and Mason St, Joe Dimaggio Playground. **Map** 5 B2. **Tel** 831-5500. 🚌 8BX, 8X, 30, 39, 41, 45, 91. 🚋 Powell–Mason. **Open** dawn till dusk Mon–Sat. &♿

Italians have been influential in North Beach since the main wave of immigration from Italy in the late 19th and early 20th centuries. Along with their food, customs, and religion, they also brought games to their new home.

Among these was *bocce*, an Italian version of lawn bowling, played on a narrower and shorter court than the English version. In North Beach it is played most afternoons on the public court in a corner of the Joe Dimaggio Playground. There are four participants (or four teams), who roll a wooden ball at a smaller, target ball, at the opposite end of an earth court. The aim is for the balls to lightly "kiss" *(bocce)*, and the highest score goes to the player whose ball gets closest to this target.

⓱ Coit Tower

1 Telegraph Hill Blvd. **Map** 5 C2. **Tel** 249-0995. 🚌 8, 8BX, 8X, 30, 39, 41, 45, 91. **Open** 10am–6pm daily (to 5pm winter). 🎫 to tower. &♿ 📷

Coit Tower was built in 1933 at the top of 284 ft- (87 m-) high Telegraph Hill, with funds left to the city by Lillie Hitchcock Coit, an eccentric San Franciscan pioneer and philanthropist. The 210 ft (63 m) reinforced concrete tower was designed as a fluted column by the architect Arthur Brown. When floodlit at night it is an eerie white and can be seen from most parts of the eastern half of the city. The encircling view around the North Bay Area from the observation platform (reached by elevator) is spectacular.

Playing *bocce* at Joe Dimaggio Playground

The concrete Coit Tower at the top of Telegraph Hill

In the lobby of the tower are murals that are even more absorbing *(see p142)*. These were sponsored in 1934 by a government-funded program designed to keep artists employed during the Great Depression *(see pp32–3)*. Twenty-five artists joined efforts to paint a vivid portrait of life in modern California. Scenes range from the teeming streets of the city's Financial District (with a robbery in progress) to factories, dockyards, and Central Valley wheat fields.

There are many fascinating details, including a real light switch cleverly incorporated into a painting and a poor family of migrants encamped by a river, plus newspaper headlines, magazine covers, and book titles. The murals are effective social commentary and yet also whimsical in spirit. There are various political themes depicting labor problems and social injustice that run through them. Many of the faces in the paintings are those of the artists and their friends, along with local figures such as Colonel William Brady, care-taker of Coit Tower. The work's political content initially caused some public controversy.

⓲ Filbert Steps

Map 5 C2. 🚌 10, 19, 39, 41, 45, 47, 49, 54, 70, 990.

Telegraph Hill falls away sharply on its eastern side, and the streets here become steep steps. Descending from Telegraph Hill Boulevard, Filbert Street is a rambling stairway, made of wood, brick, and concrete, where fuchsia, rhododendron, bougainvillea, fennel, and blackberries thrive.

⓳ Greenwich Steps

Map 5 C2. 🚌 8X, 30, 39, 45, 91. 🚋 Powell–Mason.

Descending roughly parallel to Filbert Steps, the steps of Greenwich Street have splendid views, with luxuriant foliage from adjoining gardens overflowing onto them. Going up one set of steps and down the other makes a delightful walk around the eastern side of Telegraph Hill.

⓴ Upper Montgomery Street

Map 5 C2. 🚌 8, 8BX, 8X, 30, 39, 41, 45, 91.

Until it was paved in 1931, the Telegraph Hill end of Montgomery Street was mostly inhabited by working-class families. There was also a sprinkling of artists and writers. They were attracted by the

seclusion, the cheap rents, and the great views. It is now, however, a distinctly fashionable place to live, and visitors are drawn to it as a lovely area to take a leisurely stroll.

Steps at the bottom of Filbert Street leading up to Telegraph Hill

㉑ Levi's Plaza

1155 Battery St **Map** 5 C2. 🚌 39, 82X. 🚋 E, F.

This square is where the headquarters of Levi Strauss, the manufacturers of blue jeans *(see p137)*, can be found. It was landscaped by Lawrence Halprin in 1982, with the aim of recalling the company's history in California. The plaza is studded with granite rocks and cut by flowing water, thus evoking the Sierra Nevada canyon scenery in which the miners who first wore the jeans worked. Telegraph Hill in the background adds another mountainous element.

The headquarters of Levi Strauss & Co. on Levi's Plaza

⑳ Exploratorium

Since 1969 this renowned science museum and global learning center has been influencing people of all ages with its creative and interactive exhibits. The museum uses unique hands-on displays and encourages playful learning to inspire the curiosity of visitors and educate them about a wide range of scientific subjects. Learn how reflections work, how certain genes are passed on from parent to child, and examine local micro-organisms and their bay habitats. Using only the sense of touch, find your way out of the Tactile Dome, a pitch-dark network of chambers and mazes, and a star attraction. The all-glass Bay Observatory Gallery offers excellent views and exhibits of San Francisco Bay and the cityscape.

★ All Eyes on Me
This exhibit showcases a mosaic of tiny mirrors that reflect the viewer's own eyes.

Drip Chamber
Visitors can see unique shapes and patterns created by light rays passing through droplets of glycerine in a rotating chamber.

Bio Lab is a working laboratory. It is closed to the public, but visitors can see the work going on inside.

Water Drop
This quirky display, located in one of the connector galleries, provides hands-on experience in using the flash in high-speed photography.

Zebrafish
Developing zebrafish embryos are on display at the microscope imaging station located in the East Gallery.

Chaotic Pendulum
Twisting the knob at this exhibit reveals the pendulum's motion to be unpredictable and extremely complicated.

VISITORS' CHECKLIST

Practical Information
Pier 15. **Map** 6 D2. **Tel** 528-4444.
Open 10am–5pm Tue–Sun
(6–10pm Thu, adults only);
summer: also 10am–5pm Mon.
Some exhibits require reservation
exploratorium.edu/visit

Transport
8, 10, 12, 39, 82X.
Embarcadero. E, F, J, K, L,
M, T, N. Ferry Building (terminal)
10-min walking distance.

Tactile Dome
was originally
designed in 1971
by August Coppola

Entrance

Main Entrance

Your Father's Nose
Two people can view each other from opposite sides of a paneled mirror and see a composite image of their own face in this fun exhibit exploring perceptions and genetics.

Bay Windows
Spinning disks filled with samples of bay water, mud, and sand, show visitors more about the movement and settling characteristics of bay sediments.

Key to Floor Plan

- East Gallery
- Bay Observatory Gallery/Terrace
- Central Gallery
- West Gallery
- South Gallery
- Outdoor Gallery
- Public Plaza
- Intro Area

Gallery Guide

The main exhibit floor of the Exploratorium is anchored by four main galleries. The Central Gallery is themed around seeing and listening, the West Gallery focuses on human phenomena, and the East Gallery on living systems. The South Gallery, which contains the Tinkering Studio™, allows visitors to build their own exhibits. The Outdoor Gallery explores local weather and the Bay Observatory offers views of the bay and beyond. There are two dining areas: the plaza-side Seismic Joint Café on the west and the waterfront Seaglass Restaurant in the Bay Observatory.

CHINATOWN AND NOB HILL

The Chinese settled in the plaza on Stockton Street in the 1850s, and today the shops and markets recall the atmosphere of a typical southern Chinese town, although the architecture, customs, and public events are distinctly American variations on a Cantonese theme. This densely populated neighborhood with its colorful façades, teeming markets, temples, theaters, and unique restaurants and stores, is "a city" within the city and a place most visitors want to see.

Nob Hill is San Francisco's most celebrated hilltop. It is famous for its cable cars, plush hotels, and breathtaking views. In the late 19th century, the "Big Four," who built the first transcontinental railway, were among its richest tenants, in their large mansions on the hill. The earthquake and fire of 1906 *(see pp30–31)* leveled all but one of these, but today's hotels still recall the opulence of Victorian times.

Sights at a Glance

Historic Streets and Buildings
1 Chinatown Gateway
5 Golden Gate Fortune
  Cookie Company
6 Chinatown Alleys
7 Grant Avenue
8 East West Bank
14 The Pacific-Union Club

Historic Hotels
12 Mark Hopkins Inter-
  Continental Hotel
13 Fairmont Hotel

Galleries and Museums
10 Pacific Heritage Museum
11 Chinese Historical Society
  of America
15 Cable Car Museum

Churches and Temples
2 Old St. Mary's Cathedral
3 Kong Chow Temple
4 Tin How Temple
16 Grace Cathedral

Parks and Squares
9 Portsmouth Square

☐ Restaurants
see pp223–4

1 Acquerello
2 Golden Star Vietnamese
  Restaurant
3 Great Eastern
4 Henry's Hunan
5 House of Nanking
6 Nob Hill Café
7 R&G Lounge
8 Swan Oyster Depot

0 meters   500
0 yards   500

*See also Street Finder
maps 4–6*

◀ Colorful mural of a Chinese dragon in Chinatown

For keys to symbols *see back flap*

Street-by-Street: Chinatown

Grant Avenue is the tourist Chinatown of dragon
lampposts, upturned rooflines and neighborhood
hardware stores packed to the rafters with everything
from kites to cooking utensils. Locals shop up the hill
on Stockton Street, where the freshest vegetables,
produce, and fish spill over in boxes onto crowded
pavements. In the alleys in between, look for traditional
temples, shops, and family-run restaurants.

6 ★ Chinatown Alleys
Authentic sights and sounds of the
Far East echo in these busy alleys.

Ross Alley

JACKSON STREET

To bus nos. 8,
30, 45, 91

WASHINGTON STREET

**5 Golden Gate
Fortune Cookies**
Visitors can see San
Francisco cookies
being made.

**⑪ Chinese Historical
Society of America**

3 Kong Chow Temple
Fine Cantonese wood carvings
are a feature of this temple.

POWELL STREET

SACRAMENTO STREET

GRANT

4 Tin How Temple
This was founded in 1852
by Chinese people
grateful for their safe
arrival in San Francisco.

| 0 meters | 100 |
| 0 yards | 100 |

CALIFORNIA STREET

STOCKTON S

BUSH STR

8 East West Bank
Between 1909 and 1946 this
was home to Chinatown's
telephone exchange.

Cable cars run down two sides of
Chinatown and are an essential part
of the area's bustling atmosphere.
Any of the three lines will take you there.

9 Portsmouth Square
Laid out in 1839, this was the social center for the village of Yerba Buena. Today it is a gathering place for players of cards and mahjong.

7 ★ Grant Avenue
In the 1830s and early 1840s this was the main thoroughfare of Yerba Buena. It is now the busy commercial center of Chinatown.

Locator Map
See Street Finder map 5

Key

— Suggested route

The Chinese Cultural Center
contains an art gallery and a small crafts shop. It sponsors a lively series of lectures and seminars.

10 Pacific Heritage Museum
Housed in an elegant building below the Bank of Canton, this small museum has fine exhibitions of Asian art that are regularly changed.

KEARNY STREET

CLAY STREET

2 Old St. Mary's Cathedral
The clock tower of this church, built while the city was still in its infancy, bears an arresting inscription.

SON.OBSERVE THE TIME AND FLY FROM EVIL. Ecc. IV. 23.

PINE STREET

St. Mary's Square is a quiet haven in which to rest.

To bus nos. 8, 30, 45, 91

1 ★ Chinatown Gateway
Also known as the "Dragons' Gate," this marks Chinatown's southern entrance.

❶ Chinatown Gateway

Grant Ave at Bush St. **Map** 5 C4.
🚌 8, 30, 45.

This ornate portal, opened in 1970 and designed by Clayton Lee, spans the entrance to Chinatown's main tourist street, Grant Avenue. Inspired by the ceremonial entrances Zof traditional Chinese villages, the three-arched gateway is capped with green roof tiles and a host of propitiatory animals – including two dragons and two carp chasing a large, round pearl – all of glazed ceramic. Village gateways are often commissioned by wealthy clans to enhance their status, and the names of these benefactors are inscribed on the gates. This structure was erected by a peculiarly American institution, the Chinatown Cultural Development Committee, with materials that were donated by the Republic of China (Taiwan).

It is guarded by two stone lions suckling their cubs through their claws, in accordance with ancient lore. Once through the gate, you find yourself among some of the most elegant shops in Chinatown. Here you can buy antiques, silks, and gems, but sometimes at high prices, aimed at tourists.

❷ Old St. Mary's Cathedral

660 California St. **Map** 5 C4. **Tel** 288-3800. 🚌 8, 8X, 8BX, 30, 45,. 🚃 California St, Powell–Hyde, Powell–Mason. **Mass** 7:30am & 12:05pm Mon–Fri; 5pm Sat; 9am, 10:15am & 11:30am Sun. 🏠
🌐 oldsaintmarys.org

San Francisco's first Catholic cathedral, Old St. Mary's served a largely Irish congregation from 1854 to 1891, when a new St. Mary's Church was built on Van Ness Avenue. Due to the lack of suitable building materials in California, the bricks for the

Entrance to Old St. Mary's Cathedral below the clock tower

old church were imported from the East Coast, while the granite foundation stones came from China. The clock tower bears a large inscription, "Son, observe the time and fly from evil," said to have been directed at the brothels that stood across the street at the time it was built. Though twice damaged by fire, the church today retains its original foundations and walls. The interior,

with its stained-glass windows and balcony, was completed in 1909.

❸ Kong Chow Temple

4th floor, 855 Stockton St. **Map** 5 B4. **Tel** 788-1339. 🚌 1, 8, 8X, 8BX, 30, 45. 🚃 California St, Powell–Hyde, Powell–Mason. **Open** 9am–4pm daily. Donations appreciated. ✉ ♿

From the top floor above the post office, the Kong Chow Temple looks out over Chinatown and the Financial District. Although the building dates only from 1977, the temple altar and statuary are possibly the oldest Chinese religious shrine in North America. One altar was carved in Guangzhou (Canton), and shipped to San Francisco in the 19th century. The main shrine is presided over by a carved wooden statue of Kuan Di, also dating from the 19th century. He is the deity most often found in shrines in Cantonese cities.

Kuan Di is also frequently seen in Chinatown: his distinctive face looks down from Taoist shrines in many Chinatown restaurants. He is typically depicted with a large sword in one hand and a book in the other – symbols of his dedication to both the martial and the literary arts.

Carved statue of Kuan Di inside the Kong Chow Temple

Three-floor climb to the Tin How Temple, founded in 1852

❹ Tin How Temple

Top floor, 125 Waverly Pl. **Map** 5 C3. **Tel** 391-4841. 🚌 1, 8, 8X, 8BX, 30, 45. 🚋 California St, Powell–Hyde, Powell–Mason. **Open** 9:30am–3:30pm daily. Donation requested. ♿

This unusual temple, the longest-operating Chinese temple in the United States, is dedicated to Tin How (Tien Hau), Queen of Heaven and protector of seafarers and visitors. Originally founded by the Cantonese clan association in 1852, it is now situated at the top of three steep, wooden flights of stairs. The narrow space is smoky with incense and burned paper offerings, and hung with hundreds of gold and red lanterns. It is lit by red electric bulbs and burning wicks floating in oil. Gifts of fruit lie on the carved altar in front of the wooden statue of Tin How.

❺ Golden Gate Fortune Cookie Company

56 Ross Alley. **Map** 5 C3. **Tel** 781-3956. 🚌 1, 8, 8X, 8BX, 30, 45. 🚋 California St, Powell–Hyde, Powell–Mason. **Open** 8am–6pm daily.

Although the San Francisco Bay area has many fortune-cookie bakeries, the Golden Gate Fortune Cookie Company has been in business longer than most, since 1962.

The cookie-making machine nearly fills the tiny bakery, where dough is poured onto griddles and baked on a conveyor belt. An attendant inserts the "fortunes" (slips of paper bearing mostly positive predictions) before the cookies are folded.

Ironically, despite its association with Chinese culture, the fortune cookie is unknown in China. It was actually invented in 1909 in San Francisco's Japanese Tea Garden (*see p149*), by then chief gardener, Makota Hagiwara.

❻ Chinatown Alleys

Map 5 B3. 🚌 8, 8X, 8BX, 10, 12, 30, 45.

Contained within a busy neighborhood, the Chinatown Alleys are situated between Grant Avenue and Stockton Street. These four narrow lanes intersect Washington Street within half a block of each other. Of these, the largest is Waverly Place, known as the "Street of Painted Balconies," for reasons that are apparent to every passerby. The alleys contain many old buildings, as well as traditional shops and restaurants.

Effigy of the god of longevity on Grant Avenue

A woman making fortune cookies at the Golden Gate Fortune Cookie Company

There are also atmospheric, old-fashioned herbalist shops, displaying elk antlers, sea horses, snake wine, and other exotic wares in their windows. Small restaurants, both above and below street level, serve cheap, delicious, home-cooked food.

❼ Grant Avenue

Map 5 C4. 🚌 10, 12, 30, 45. 🚋 California St.

The main tourist street in Chinatown, Grant Avenue is also distinguished for being the first street of Yerba Buena, the village that preceded San Francisco. A plaque at No. 823 Grant Avenue marks the block where William A. Richardson and his Mexican wife erected Yerba Buena's first edifice, a canvas tent, on June 25, 1835. By October, they had replaced this with a wooden house, and the following year with a yet more permanent adobe (sun-dried brick) home, called Casa Grande. The street in which the Richardsons' house stood was named Calle de la Fundación, the "Street of the Founding." It was renamed Grant Avenue in 1885 in memory of Ulysses S. Grant, the US president and Civil War general who died that year.

8 East West Bank

743 Washington St. **Map** 5 C3.
Tel 421-5215. 🚌 1, 8, 8X, 8BX, 30, 45.
Open 9am–5pm Mon–Thu, 9am–
6pm Fri, 10am–5pm Sat.

Before being turned into
a bank in the 1950s, this
building housed the Chinese
Telephone Exchange. It was
built in 1909 on the site where
Sam Brannan printed California's
first newspaper. The three-
tiered tower is like a pagoda,
with upward-curving eaves
and a ceramic tiled roof, and
is the most distinctive work
of architectural chinoiserie
in the neighborhood.

The telephone operators
worked on the main floor and
lived on the second floor. They
were multilingual, speaking
Cantonese and four other
Chinese dialects. One of their
original telephone books can be
seen on display in the Chinese
Historical Society on Clay Street.

East West Bank entrance

9 Portsmouth Square

Map 5 C3. 🚌 1, 8, 8X, 8BX, 30, 45.

San Francisco's original town
square was laid out in 1839. Also
lesser known as the Portsmouth
Plaza, it was once the social
center for the small village of
Yerba Buena. On July 9, 1846,
less than a month after American
rebels in Sonoma declared
California's independence from

Portsmouth Square

Mexico, a party of marines rowed
ashore. They raised the American
flag above the plaza, officially
seizing the port as part of the
United States (see pp26–7). Two
years later, on May 12, 1848, it
was here that Sam Brannan
announced the discovery of
gold in the Sierra Nevada (see
pp26–7). Over the next two
decades, the square became
the hub of an increasingly
dynamic city. In the 1860s
the business district shifted
southeast to flatlands reclaimed
from the bay, and the plaza
declined in civic importance.

Portsmouth Square today is
the social center of Chinatown.
In the morning, people practice
t'ai chi, and from midday to evening others gather to play
checkers and cards.

10 Pacific Heritage Museum

608 Commercial St. **Map** 5 C3.
Tel 399-1124. 🚌 1, 8, 8X, 8BX, 30X, 41.
Open 10am–4pm Thu–Sat, except
public hols. ♿

As elegant as the frequently
changing collections of Asian
arts displayed within, this is
actually a synthesis of two
distinct buildings. The US
Sub-Treasury was built
here in 1875–7 by William
Appleton Potter, on the
site of San Francisco's original mint. You can look into
the old coin vaults through a
cutaway section on the
ground floor, or descend in
the elevator for closer inspection. In 1984 architects
Skidmore, Owings, and
Merrill designed the 17-story
headquarters of the Bank of

Canton (now East West Bank)
above the existing building,
incorporating the original street-
level façade and basement.

11 Chinese Historical Society of America

965 Clay St. **Map** 5 B3. **Tel** 391-1188.
🚋 Powell–Clay. 🚌 1, 8, 8X, 8BX, 30, 45.
Open noon–5pm Tue–Fri, 11am–4pm
Sat. **Closed** public hols. 📷 except first
Thu of month. 🏛 📶 🌐 **chsa.org**

Founded in 1963, this is the
oldest and largest organization
dedicated to the study, docu-
mentation, and dissemination
of Chinese American history.
Exhibits include the Daniel
Ching collection, the original
hand-written Chinatown
telephone book, a ceremonial
dragon costume, and a "tiger
fork." This triton was wielded
in one of the battles during
the reign of terror known
as the Tong Wars. Many objects,
documents, and photographs
illuminate the daily life of
Chinese immigrants in San
Francisco in the late 19th
and early 20th centuries.

The Chinese contribution
to California's development
was extensive. Chinese helped
build the western half of the
first transcontinental railroad
and constructed dikes throughout the Sacramento River delta.
The CHSA sponsors oral history
projects, an "In Search of Roots"
program, and a monthly
speakers forum.

Dragon's head, Chinese
Historical Society of America

Street-by-Street: Nob Hill

Nob Hill is the highest summit of the city center, rising 338 ft (103 m) above the bay. Its steep slopes were treacherous for carriages and kept prominent citizens away until the opening of the California Street cable car line in 1878. After that, the wealthy "nobs" soon built new homes on the peak of the hill. Though the grandiose mansions were burned down in the great fire of 1906 *(see pp30–31)*, Nob Hill still attracts the affluent to its splendid hotels.

Locator Map
See Street Finder map 5

⑬ Fairmont Hotel
This luxurious hotel is known for its marble lobby and elegant dining.

⑭ The Pacific-Union Club
Now an exclusive men's club, this was once the mansion of Comstock millionaire James Flood.

The Stanford Court, a Renaissance hotel, occupies the site of Stanford's mansion; the original boundary walls remain.

⑯ ★ Grace Cathedral
The cathedral is a replica of Notre Dame in Paris.

SACRAMENTO STREET

TAYLOR STREET

CALIFORNIA STREET

MASON STREET

JONES STREET

PINE STREET

Huntington Park
is on the site of Collis P. Huntington's great mansion.

Huntington Hotel
with its Big Four Bar and Restaurant exudes the opulent urbane atmosphere of the Victorian era on Nob Hill.

The Nob Hill Masonic Auditorium honors Freemasons who died in American wars.

⑫ ★ Mark Hopkins InterContinental Hotel
The hotel's Top of the Mark penthouse bar is celebrated for its spectacular views.

| 0 meters | 150 |
| 0 yards | 150 |

Key

━ Suggested route

⓬ Mark Hopkins InterContinental Hotel

999 California St. **Map** 5 B4. **Tel** 392-3434. 🚌 1. 🚋 California St, Powell–Mason, Powell–Hyde. *See Where to Stay p215.* 🅦 **intercontinental markhopkins.com**

At the behest of his wife Mary, Mark Hopkins *(see below)* arranged for a fantastic wooden mansion, surpassing every other for ostentatious ornamentation, to be built on Nob Hill *(see below)*. When Mrs. Hopkins died, the house became home to the fledgling San Francisco Art Institute. It burned in the fire of 1906 *(see pp30–31)*, and only the granite retaining walls remain. The present 25-story tower, capped by a flag visible from all over the city, was built in 1925 by architects Weeks and Day. Top of the Mark *(see p259)*, the glass-walled bar on the 19th floor, is one of the city's most celebrated drinking establishments. World War II servicemen customarily drank a farewell toast to the city here before leaving for overseas.

Forecourt of the Mark Hopkins InterContinental Hotel

⓭ Fairmont Hotel

950 Mason St. **Map** 5 B4. **Tel** 772-5000. 🚌 1. 🚋 California St, Powell–Mason, Powell–Hyde. *See Where to Stay p215.* 🅦 **fairmont.com/san-francisco**

Built by Tessie Fair Oelrichs *(see below)*, this Beaux Arts building was completed on the eve of the 1906 earthquake *(see pp30–31)*, and stood for two days before it was burned down. Rebuilt by Julia Morgan within the original white terra-cotta façade, it opened for business one year later. After World War II it was the scene of meetings that led to the founding of the United Nations. For stunning views, ride the elevator to the city's highest observation point, the Fairmont Crown; or, enjoy a cocktail at the hotel's famed Tonga Room and Hurricane Bar.

⓮ The Pacific-Union Club

1000 California St. **Map** 5 B4. **Tel** 775-1234. 🚌 1. 🚋 California St, Powell–Mason, Powell–Hyde. **Closed** to the public.

Augustus Laver built this town house for the "Bonanza King" James Flood *(see below)* in 1885. Its Italianate, brown sandstone façade survived the 1906 fire *(see pp30–31)*, though the other mansions, built of wood, were destroyed. The gutted building was bought by the Pacific-Union Club, an exclusive gentlemen's club that had its origins in Gold Rush San Francisco *(see pp26–7)*.

The Nobs of Nob Hill

"Nob" was one of the kinder names reserved for the unscrupulous entrepreneurs who amassed vast fortunes during the development of the American West. Many of the nobs who lived on Nob Hill acquired other nicknames that hint at the wild stories behind their vast wealth. "Bonanza King" James Flood joined in a partnership with Irish immigrants James Fair, John Mackay, and

Bonanza Jim

Mark Hopkins 1814–78

William O'Brien. In 1872, the four men bought controlling interests in some dwindling Comstock mines, sinking new shafts and striking a "bonanza" – a rich pocket of high-grade silver ore. Flood returned to San Francisco as a millionaire and bought a parcel of land on the summit of Nob Hill, across the street from a plot owned by James Fair. The Flood Mansion (now the Pacific-Union Club) still stands. The monument on Fair's property, the Fairmont Hotel, was built by his daughter, Tessie, after his death *(see above)*.

The Big Four

Other distinguished residents of Nob Hill were the "Big Four," Leland Stanford, Mark Hopkins, Charles Crocker, and Collis P. Huntington. This shrewd quartet made up the principal investors behind the first transcontinental railway. Their biggest enterprise, the Central Pacific Railroad (it was later renamed Southern Pacific) was an influential corporation in the burgeoning West. It acquired great wealth and influence as a result of the generous land grants bestowed by the US Congress to encourage railroad construction. Bribery and corruption made the Big Four among the most hated men of 19th-century America. In this capacity, they were characterized by yet another popular nickname: the "Robber Barons." All four built big mansions on Nob Hill, but these did not survive the devastation of the 1906 earthquake and fire.

⓯ Cable Car Museum

1201 Mason St. **Map** 5 B3.
Tel 474-1887. 🚌 1, 10, 12.
🚋 Powell–Mason, Powell–Hyde.
Open 10am–6pm daily (Oct–Mar:
to 5pm). **Closed** Jan 1, Thanksgiving,
Dec 25. ♿ mezzanine only. 📷
🌐 cablecarmuseum.org

This is both a museum and the powerhouse of the cable car system (*see pp106–7*).

Anchored to the ground floor are the engines and wheels that wind the cables through the system of channels and pulleys beneath the streets. Observe them from the mezzanine, then walk downstairs to see under the street. The museum houses an early cable car and specimens of the mechanisms that control the individual cars. The system is the last of its kind in the world.

Entrance to San Francisco's Cable Car Museum

⓰ Grace Cathedral

1100 California St. **Map** 5 B4. **Tel** 749-6300. 🚌 1, 27. 🚋 California St. **Open** 8am–6pm daily (to 7pm Sun). ✝ 8:30am & 6pm Sun; choral evensong 5:15pm Thu, 3pm Sun; choral Eucharist 11am Sun. ♿ 📷 daily; see website for times. 📷 🌐 gracecathedral.org

Grace Cathedral is the mother church of the Episcopal Diocese of California and the third-largest Episcopal cathedral in the US. Designed by Lewis P. Hobart, it stands on the site of the two Charles and William H. Crocker mansions (*see p104*). Although building started in

September 1928, the cathedral was not completed until 1964, and the interior vaulting remains unfinished to this day. Notre Dame in Paris was one of several inspirations for the building, which incorporates traditional elements such as a rose window.

The interior is replete with marble and stained glass. Its leaded-glass windows were designed by Charles Connick, inspired by the

blue glass of Chartres. The rose window, made with 1-inch- (2.5-cm-) thick faceted glass, is illuminated from inside at night.

Other windows, by Henry Willet and Gabriel Loire, include depictions of modern heroes such as Albert Einstein. Objects in the cathedral include a 13th-century Catalonian crucifix and a 16th-century silk and gold Brussels tapestry. The doors of the main entrance are cast from molds of Lorenzo Ghiberti's "Doors of Paradise," made for the Baptistry in Florence.

Stained-glass detail

The New Testament Window, made in 1931 by Charles Connick, is placed on the south side of the church.

The Rose Window was made in Chartres by Gabriel Loire in 1964.

The Carillon Tower houses 44 bells made in England in 1938.

Entrance

The Chapel of Grace, funded by the Crocker family, has a 15th-century French altarpiece.

The Doors of Paradise are decorated with scenes from the Bible and portraits of Ghiberti and contemporaries.

Entrances

San Francisco's Cable Cars

The cable car system was launched in 1873, with its inventor Andrew Hallidie riding in the first car. He was inspired to tackle the problem of transporting people up the city's steep slopes after seeing a horrible accident: a horse-drawn tram slipped down a hill, dragging the horses with it. His system was a success, and by 1889 cars were running on eight lines. Before the 1906 earthquake (see pp30–31), more than 600 cars were in use. With the advent of the internal combustion engine, cable cars became obsolete, and in 1947 attempts were made to replace them with buses. After a public outcry the present three lines, using 17 miles (25 km) of track, were retained.

The Cable Car Barn garages the cars at night and is a repair shop, museum, and powerhouse for the entire cable-car system (see p105).

KEY

1. Bell
2. Sandbox
3. Grip handle
4. Center plate and jaws grip the cable
5. Emergency brake
6. Wheel brake
7. Cable
8. Brake block
9. Brake shoe

How Cable Cars Work

Engines in the central powerhouse wind a looped cable under the city streets, guided by a system of grooved pulleys. When the gripman in the cable car applies the grip handle, the grip reaches through a slot in the street and grabs the cable. This pulls the car along at a steady speed of 9.5 mph (15.5 km/h). To stop, the gripman releases the grip and applies the brake. Great skill is needed at corners where the cable passes over a pulley. The gripman must release the grip to allow the car to coast over the pulley.

Cable-car grip mechanism

Grip handle

Destination board

Wooden beams

Grip crotch

Brake lever

Side seating

Cable-car floor

Paving stones

Yoke

Hatch House is the name given to a four-story house that needed moving in its entirety in 1913. Herbert Hatch used a system of jacks and hoists to maneuver the house across the cable car line without causing any cessation of the service.

A cable-car celebration was held in 1984 after a two-year renovation of the system. Each car was restored, and all lines were replaced with reinforced tracks. The system should now work safely for 100 years.

A cable-car bell-ringing contest is held in Union Square every July, when conductors ring out their most spirited rhythms. On the street, the bell signals a warning to other traffic.

The original San Francisco cable car, tested by Hallidie on Clay Street on August 2, 1873, is on display in the Cable Car Barn *(see p105)*. The cable car system has remained essentially unchanged since its invention.

Rebuilding the cable cars is done with attention to historical detail because they are designated historic monuments.

Andrew Smith Hallidie

Andrew Smith was born in London in 1836 and later adopted his uncle's surname. He trained as a mechanic, moving in 1852 to San Francisco, where he formed a company that made wire rope. In 1873 he tested the first cable car, which soon became profitable and opened the hills of the city to development.

FINANCIAL DISTRICT AND UNION SQUARE

Montgomery Street, now in the heart of the Financial District, was once a street of small shops, where miners came to weigh their gold dust. It roughly marks the old shoreline of the shallow Yerba Buena Cove, which was filled in during the Gold Rush years (see pp26–7) to

create more land. Today, old-style banking halls from the early 20th century stand in the shadow of glass and steel skyscrapers, and crowds of office workers throng the streets. Union Square is at the center of the city's main shopping district, and has a wealth of fine department stores.

Sights at a Glance

Historic Streets and Buildings
2 Jackson Square Historical District
6 Bank of California
7 Merchant's Exchange
8 Pacific Coast Stock Exchange
10 Ferry Building
11 California Historical Society
23 Powell Street Cable Car Turntable
25 The San Francisco Mint

Museums and Galleries
3 Wells Fargo History Museum
12 Museum of the African Diaspora
14 Contemporary Jewish Museum
16 Museum of Modern Art pp120–23

Modern Architecture
1 Embarcadero Center
4 555 California
5 Transamerica Pyramid
13 Rincon Center
15 Yerba Buena Gardens pp116–17

Hotels
17 Palace Hotel

Visitor Information
26 San Francisco Visitor Information Center

Shops
18 Crocker Galleria
19 Gump's
22 Union Square Shops
24 Westfield San Francisco Centre

Theaters
21 Theater District

Parks and Squares
9 Justin Herman Plaza
20 Union Square

☐ **Restaurants** see pp224–5
1 5A5 Streak Lounge
2 21st Amendment
3 54 Mint
4 Anchor & Hope
5 Bouche
6 Chutney
7 Le Colonial
8 Delancey Street Restaurant
9 Farallon
10 The Grove

11 Hidive
12 Kokkari Estiatorio
13 Lao Table
14 Michael Mina
15 Old Ship Saloon
16 One Market
17 PABU
18 Press Club
19 Salt House
20 Sam's Grill and Seafood Restaurant
21 South Park Café
22 Tadich Grill
23 Yank Sing

See also Street Finder maps 6 & 11

0 meters   300
0 yards   300

◀ Downtown San Francisco at dusk

For keys to symbols see back flap

Street-by-Street: Financial District

San Francisco's economic engine is fueled largely by the Financial District, one of the chief commercial centers in the US. It reaches from the imposing modern towers and plazas of the Embarcadero Center to staid Montgomery Street, sometimes known as the "Wall Street of the West." All the principal banks, brokers, exchanges, and law offices are situated within this compact area. The Jackson Square Historical District, north of Washington Street, was once the heart of the business community.

❶ ★ Embarcadero Center
The center houses both commercial outlets and offices. A shopping arcade occupies the first three tiers of the towers.

Hotaling Place, a narrow alley leading to the Jackson Square Historical District, has several good antiques shops.

❷ Jackson Square Historical District
This district recalls the Gold Rush era more than any other.

The Golden Era Building, was built during the Gold Rush. It was the home of the paper *Golden Era*, for which Mark Twain wrote.

Bus stop (no. 41)

WASHINGTON STREET

BATTERY STREET

SANSOME STREET

MONTGOMERY STREET

❺ ★ Transamerica Pyramid
Since 1972, this 853 ft (256 m) skyscraper has been the tallest on the city's skyline.

❻ Bank of California
The grand banking hall is guarded by fierce stone lions carved by sculptor Arthur Putnam.

❸ Wells Fargo History Museum
An original stagecoach, evoking the wilder days of the old West, is one of the many exhibits in this recently renovated transportation and banking museum.

❹ 555 California
The former world headquarters of Bank of America was the city's tallest skyscraper until 1972.

❼ Merchant's Exchange
Epic paintings of local shipping scenes line the walls.

California Street, busy with clanging cable cars, sweeps to the top of Nob Hill.

9 Justin Herman Plaza
On sunny days lunchtime crowds fill the plaza.

Bus stop (nos. 2, 9)

FISHERMAN'S WHARF AND NORTH BEACH

CHINATOWN AND NOB HILL

FINANCIAL DISTRICT AND UNION SQUARE

Locator Map
See Street Finder maps 5 & 6

The Gandhi Monument (1988), on the east side of the Ferry Building, facing the Bay Bridge, was designed by K.B. Patel and sculpted by Z. Pounov and S. Lowe. It bears an inscription of Gandhi's words.

DAVIS STREET

SACRAMENTO STREET

FRONT STREET

DRUMM STREET

CALIFORNIA STREET

MARKET STREET

PINE STREET

8 Pacific Coast Stock Exchange
Now converted to a health club, this was once the focal point of city's trade.

First Interstate Center, home of the Mandarin Oriental Hotel.

10 Ferry Building
This building houses more than 40 gourmet shops and eateries.

Key

— Suggested route

0 meters 100
0 yards 100

❶ Embarcadero Center

Map 6 D3. 🚌 1, 6, 7X, 9, 14, 21, 30, 31, 38,, 41. 🚎 E, F, J, K, L, M, N, T. 🚋 California St. *See Shopping in San Francisco p233.*

The Embarcadero Center was completed in 1981 after a decade of construction. It is San Francisco's largest redevelopment project and reaches from Justin Herman Plaza to Battery Street. Four separate high-rise towers reach upward 35 to 40 stories above the landscaped plazas and elevated walkways.

Embarcadero Center's most spectacular interior is the lobby of the Hyatt Regency Hotel. Its 17-story atrium contains an immense sculptured globe by Charles Perry, entitled *Eclipse* (1973). Glass elevators glide up and down one wall, carrying visitors to and from their rooms. Also housed in the center are an array of shops and a movie theater screening an impressive number of independent and foreign films.

Lobby of the Hyatt Regency Hotel at the Embarcadero Center

Hotaling Place in Jackson Square

❷ Jackson Square Historical District

Map 5 C3. 🚌 8AX, 8BX, 10, 41.

Renovated in the early 1950s, this low-rise neighborhood contains many historic brick, cast-iron, and granite façades dating from the Gold Rush era. From 1850 to 1910, it was notorious for its squalor and the crudeness of its inhabitants and was known as the Barbary Coast

(see pp28–9). The Hippodrome at 555 Pacific Street used to be a theater; the bawdy relief sculptures in the recessed front recall the risqué shows that were performed there. Today the buildings are used as showrooms, law offices, and antique shops; the best can be seen on Jackson Street, Gold Street, Hotaling Place, and Montgomery Street.

❸ Wells Fargo History Museum

420 Montgomery St. **Map** 5 C4. **Tel** 396-2619. 🚌 3, 8, 30X, 41. 🚋 California St. 🚇 Montgomery. **Open** 9am–5pm Mon–Fri. **Closed** public hols. ♿ 📷 🌐 wellsfargohistory.com/museums/san-francisco

Founded in 1852, Wells Fargo & Co. became the greatest banking and transport company in the West and was influential in the development of the American frontier. The company moved people and goods from the East to the West Coast, and between California mining camps and towns. It also

transported gold from the West Coast to the East and delivered mail. Wells Fargo put mail boxes in convenient locations and messengers sorted the letters en route. Wells Fargo played a major role in the mail service venture, Pony Express.

The stagecoaches *(see p110)*, like the one on display in the museum, are famous for the legends of heroic drivers and the bandits who robbed them. The best-known bandit was Black Bart, who left poems at the scene of his crimes. He stalked the roads from Calaveras County to the Oregon border between 1875 and 1883, holding up stagecoaches. In one holdup he mistakenly left a handkerchief with a distinctive laundry mark, revealing him to be a mining engineer named Charles Boles. Visitors to the recently renovated museum can experience how it felt to sit for days in a jostling stagecoach, listen to the recordings of Francis Brocklehurst, an immigrant, and view exhibits that include Pony Express mail, a working telegraph, weaponry, and gold nuggets.

Black Bart, the poet bandit

❹ 555 California

555 California St. **Map** 5 C4. **Tel** 392-1697. 8, 8AX, 8BX. California St. Montgomery.

Formerly the global head-quarters of Bank of America, this red granite-clad building symbolized the importance and power of the banking industry. Completed in 1969, its 52 stories made it at one time the tallest skyscraper in San Francisco. There are incredible views of the city from the 52nd floor.

The Bank of America was originally the Bank of Italy, founded by A. P. Giannini in San Jose, California. It built up a huge clientele early in the 20th century by catering to immigrants and by investing in the booming farmlands and small towns. In the great fire of 1906 *(see pp30–31)* Giannini personally rescued his bank's deposits, carting them to safety hidden in fruit crates, so there were sufficient funds for the bank to invest in the rebuilding of the city.

Transcendence (1967) by Masayuki Nagare outside 555 California

❺ Transamerica Pyramid

600 Montgomery St. **Map** 5 C3. 1, 8AX, 8BX, 10, 41. **Closed** to the public. **transamerica.com**

Capped with a pointed spire on top of its 48 stories, the pyramid reaches 853 ft (256 m) above sea level. It is the tallest and most recognized building in the city and, although San Franciscans disliked it when it opened in 1972, they have since accepted it as part of their city's skyline. Since September 11, 2001, the pyramid has been closed to the public, though there is a visitor's center in the lobby.

Designed by William Pereira & Associates, the pyramid houses 1,500 office workers on a historically rich site. The Montgomery Block, which contained many important offices and was the largest building west of the Mississippi, was built here in 1853. In the basement was the Exchange Saloon, which was frequented by Mark Twain. In the 1860s artists and writers took up residence in the Montgomery Block. The Pony Express terminus, marked by a plaque, was at Merchant Street opposite the pyramid.

The spire is hollow, rising 212 ft (64 m) above the top floor. Lit from inside, it casts a warm yellow glow at night. Its purpose is purely decorative.

Vertical Wings
The wings of the building rise vertically from the middle of the ground floor and extend beyond the frame, which tapers inward. The east wing houses 18 elevator shafts; the west wing houses a smoke tower and stairs.

Earthquake Protection
The exterior is covered with white precast quartz aggregate, interlaced with reinforcing rods on each floor. Clearance between the panels allows lateral movement in case of an earthquake.

The 3,678 windows take cleaners one month to wash.

City Views
Workers in the upper-floor offices have stupendous 360° views of the entire city, and right across San Francisco Bay.

The Shape
The building tapers so that it casts a smaller shadow than a conventional design.

The foundation rests on a steel-and-concrete block, sunk 52 ft (15.5 m) into the ground, and designed to move with earth tremors.

Classical façade of the Bank of California

❻ Bank of California

400 California St. **Map** 5 C4.
Tel 765-0400. 🚌 30X, 41.
🚊 California St. ♿ 🚻

William Ralston and Darius Mills founded this bank in 1864. Ralston, known as "the man who built San Francisco," invested profitably in Comstock mines *(see p29)*. He, in turn, used the bank and his personal fortune to finance many civic projects in San Francisco. These included the city's water company, a theater, and the Palace Hotel *(see p115)*. However, when economic depression struck in the 1870s, Ralston's empire also collapsed.

The present colonnaded building was completed in 1908. In the basement there is a pleasant arcade of shops, restaurants, and small art and photography exhibits.

❼ Merchant's Exchange

465 California St. **Map** 5 C4.
Tel 591-1833. 🚌 3, 8, 30X, 41.
🚊 Montgomery. **Open** 9am–5pm Mon–Fri, Sat & Sun by appt only.
Closed public hols. ♿ 🚻
🌐 mxbuilding.com

The exchange, designed by Willis Polk in 1903, survived the great fire of 1906 with little damage. Inside, fine seascapes by the Irish painter William Coulter line the walls. These depict epic maritime scenes from the age of steam and sail. The building was the focal point of San Francisco's commodities exchange in the early 20th century, when lookouts in the tower relayed news of ships arriving from abroad.

❽ Pacific Coast Stock Exchange

301 Pine St. **Map** 5 C4. 🚌 30X, 41.
Closed to the public.

This was once America's largest stock exchange outside New York. Founded in 1882, it occupied these buildings, which were remodeled by Miller and Pflueger in 1930 from the existing US Treasury. The monumental granite statues that flank the Pine Street entrance to the building were made by the renowned San Francisco sculptor, painter, and muralist Ralph Stackpole, also in 1930. Due to changing trading methods, the building is no longer a stock exchange and has been converted into a fitness club.

❾ Justin Herman Plaza

Map 6 D3. 🚌 many buses.
🚋 J, K, L, M, N. 🚊 California St.

Popular with lunchtime crowds from the nearby Embarcadero Center and other offices, this plaza is mostly known for its avant-garde Vaillancourt Fountain, made in 1971 by Canadian artist Armand Vaillancourt. The fountain is modeled from huge concrete blocks, and some find it ugly, especially when allowed to run dry in times of drought. However, you can climb on and through it, and its pools and columns of falling water make it an intriguing public work of art when it is functioning as intended.

The Vaillancourt Fountain in Justin Herman Plaza

The clock tower on the Ferry Building

❿ Ferry Building

Embarcadero at Market St. **Map** 6 E3.
🚌 many buses. 🚋 E, F, J, K, L, M, N.
🚊 California St. 🌐 **ferrybuilding marketplace.com**

Constructed between 1896 and 1903, the Ferry Building survived the great fire of 1906 *(see pp30–31)* through the intercession of fireboats pumping water from the bay. The clock tower is 235 ft (71 m) high, and was inspired by the Moorish bell tower of Seville Cathedral. In the early 1930s more than 50 million passengers a year passed through the building. The Ferry Building now houses many gourmet shops selling a huge variety of fresh produce, as well as several restaurants and eateries. On Tuesdays and Saturdays, a Farmers' Market is held around the outside of the building.

With the opening of the Bay Bridge in 1936, the Ferry Building ceased to be the city's main point of entry. Today, ferries still cross the bay to Larkspur and Sausalito in Marin County *(see p163)*, and Alameda and Oakland in the East Bay *(see pp166–9)*.

⓫ California Historical Society

678 Mission St. **Map** 6 D5. **Tel** 357-1848. 8, 14, 30, 45, 81X. J, K, L, M, N, T. Montgomery. **Open** Library: 1–5pm Wed–Fri; Gallery: 11am–5pm Tue–Sun. ⓦ californiahistoricalsociety.org

The society provides research libraries, museum galleries, and a bookstore. There is a photographic collection, more than 900 paintings and water-colors by American artists, a decorative arts exhibit, and a unique costume collection.

⓬ Museum of the African Diaspora

685 Mission St. **Map** 5 C5. **Tel** 358-7200. 8, 14, 30, 45, 81X. J, K, L, M, N, T. **Open** 11am–6pm Wed–Sat, noon–5pm Sun. **Closed** major hols. ⓦ moadsf.org

This museum's central idea is that we all share a com-mon African past. Its varied exhibits cover African music, culinary traditions, and the slave trade. There are interactive displays, guest speakers, contemporary art galleries, private tours, and workshops. The museum has emerged as an important destination within the Yerba Buena Center for the Arts campus.

Rincon Annex mural depicting the Spanish discovery of San Francisco

⓭ Rincon Center

Map 6 B4. 14. *See Shopping in San Francisco p233.*

This shopping center, with its soaring atrium, was added on to the old Rincon Annex Post Office Building in 1989. The Rincon Annex is known for Anton Refregier's murals, showing aspects of the city's history.

⓮ Contemporary Jewish Museum

736 Mission St. **Map** 5 C5. **Tel** 655-7800. 8, 14, 30, 45, 81X. J, K, L, M, N, T. **Open** 11am–5pm Fri–Tue, 11am–8pm Thu. **Closed** major Jewish holidays, Jan 1, Jul 4, Thanksgiving. ⓦ thecjm.org

This museum partners with national and international cultural institutions to present a variety of art, photography, and installations celebrating and exploring Judaism.

The museum is housed in an early 20th-century Pacific Gas & Electric (PG&E) Power Substation, which was adapted and redesigned by architect Daniel Libeskind and unveiled in 2005. The reimagined space features more than 10,000 sq ft (930 sq m) of exhibition space and an impressive education center.

⓯ Yerba Buena Gardens

See pp116–17.

⓰ Museum of Modern Art

See pp120–23.

⓱ Palace Hotel

2 New Montgomery St. **Map** 5 C4. **Tel** 512-1111. 8, 12, 14, 30, 45, 81X. J, K, L, M, N, T. *See Where to Stay p215.*

The original Palace Hotel was opened by William Ralston, one of San Francisco's best-known financiers, in 1875. It was the most luxurious of San Francisco's early hotels and was regularly frequented by the rich and famous. Among its patrons were Sarah Bernhardt, Oscar Wilde, and Rudyard Kipling. The celebrated tenor Enrico Caruso was a guest at the time of the earthquake of 1906 *(see pp30–31)*, when the hotel caught fire. It was rebuilt by the architect George Kelham, and reopened in 1909.

The magnificent Garden Court at the Palace Hotel

⑮ Yerba Buena Gardens

The construction of the Moscone Center, San Francisco's largest venue for conventions, was just the first in a series of ambitious development plans for Yerba Buena Gardens. Housing, hotels, museums, shops, galleries, restaurants, and gardens have followed. This area is a vibrant hub of activity. World-class art events take place as part of the Yerba Buena Gardens Festival between May and October.

★ Yerba Buena Center for the Arts
Galleries, Forum, and a screening room featuring contemporary films and videos are the highlights.

Esplanade Gardens
Visitors can wander along the paths or, in the summer, catch a free event.

KEY

① **Children's Creativity Museum** is a top destination for children of all ages. Combining imagination with art and technology tools, visitors can create animations, music videos, digital art, and more.

② **The Martin Luther King Jr. Memorial** has words of peace in several languages.

③ **North entrance to Moscone Center**

④ **South entrance to Moscone Center**

⑤ **East Garden**

⑥ **Esplanade Ballroom** is part of San Francisco's extensive convention facilities. It is available for large conferences and symposia.

⑦ **Ice-skating rink**

⑧ **The children's center** has imaginative play equipment in a pleasant outdoor setting.

Moscone Center

Engineer T.Y. Lin found an ingenious way to support the children's center above this huge underground hall without a single interior column. The bases of the eight steel arches are linked, like an archer's bowstrings, by cables under the floor. By tightening the cables, the arches exert enormous upward thrust.

Lam Research Theater at Yerba Buena Center for the Arts
Performing arts reflecting the cultural diversity of San Francisco are presented in the 755-seat indoor theater.

★ **San Francisco Museum of Modern Art**
This privately funded museum is opposite Yerba Buena Gardens.

Entrance foyer
Ballroom
Exhibition hall
Ground-level rooftop
Base of supporting arch

VISITORS' CHECKLIST

Practical Information
Mission, 3rd, Folsom & 4th Streets.
Map 5 C5. **Tel** 820-3550.
W yerbabuenagardens.com

Children's Creativity Museum:
Tel 820-3320. **Open** 10am–4pm
Wed–Sun. **Closed** Jul 4, Dec 25.

Yerba Buena Center for the Arts:
Tel 978-2787. **Open** 11am–6pm
Tue–Sun (to 8pm Thu; also noon–
8pm 1st Tue of month).
Closed public holidays.
(free 1st Tue of month).

Transport
8, 14, 30, 45, 81X.
J, K, L, M, N, T.

Central plaza of the Crocker Galleria

⑱ Crocker Galleria

Between Post, Kearny, Sutter, and Montgomery Sts. **Map** 5 C4. **Tel** 393-1500. 🚌 3, 5, 6, 8, 21, 30, 38, 45. 🚃 J, K, L, M, N, T. 🚇 Montgomery. *See Shopping in San Francisco p233.*

The Crocker Galleria was built in 1982, by architects Skidmore, Owings, and Merrill. Inspired by the Galleria Vittorio Emmanuelle in Milan, this building features a central plaza under a vaulting sky-light roof. A rooftop garden, farmers' market, food court, and dozens of shops are housed here on three floors.

⑲ Gump's

135 Post St. **Map** 5 C4. **Tel** 982-1616. 🚌 3, 5, 6, 8, 9, 21, 30, 38, 45. 🚃 J, K, L, M, N, T. 🚇 Powell–Mason, Powell–Hyde. **Open** 10am–6pm Mon–Sat, noon–5pm Sun. ♿ *See Shopping in San Francisco p237.*

Founded in 1861 by German immigrants who were former mirror and frame merchants, this homegrown San Francisco depart-ment store is an institution. Many local couples register their wedding present list with the store.

Victory monument in Union Square

Gump's has the largest collection in the US of fine china and crystal, which includes famous names such as Baccarat, Steuben, and Lalique.

The store is also celebrated for its Oriental treasures, furniture, and the rare works of art in the art depart-ment. The Asian art is particularly fine, especially the remarkable jade collection, which enjoys a worldwide reputation. In 1949 Gump's imported the great bronze Buddha and presented it to the Japanese Tea Garden (*see p149*). Gump's has an exclusive, refined atmosphere and is frequented by the rich and famous. It is renowned for its colorful and extravagant window displays.

⑳ Union Square

Map 5 C5. 🚌 3, 5, 6, 8, 9, 21, 30, 38, 45. 🚃 J, K, L, M, N, T. 🚇 Powell–Mason, Powell–Hyde.

Union Square was named for the big, pro-Union rallies held there during the Civil War of 1861–5. The rallies galvanized popular support in San Francisco for the Northern cause, and this was instrumental in bringing California into the war on the side of the Union. The square is at the heart of the city's shopping district and marks the edge of the Theater District. It is bordered on the west side by the famous Westin St. Francis Hotel, and at the center there is a statue of *Victory* at the top of a 90 ft (27 m) column. This monu-ment commemorates Admiral Dewey's victory at Manila Bay during the Spanish-American War of 1898.

㉑ Theater District

Map 5 B5. 🚌 2, 3, 27, 38, 45. 🚃 Powell–Mason, Powell–Hyde. 🚃 J, K, L, M, N, T. *See Entertainment pp250–51.*

Several theaters are located near Union Square, all within a six-block area. The two biggest are on Geary Boulevard, two blocks west of the square. These are the Curran Theater, built in 1922, and the Geary Theater, built in 1909 and now home to the American Conservatory Theater (ACT). Drama has flourished in San Francisco since the days of the Gold Rush (*see pp26–7*), and great actors and opera stars have been attracted to the city. Isadora Duncan, the famous, innovative 1920s dancer, was born in the Theater District at 501 Taylor Street.

San Francisco's famous stores overlooking Union Square

㉒ Union Square Shops

Map 5 C5. 🚌 3, 5, 6, 8, 9, 21, 30, 38, 45. 🚃 Powell–Mason, Powell–Hyde. 🚃 J, K, L, M, N, T. *See Shopping p233.*

Many of San Francisco's largest department stores can be found here, including Macy's, Sak's Fifth Avenue and Neiman Marcus (*see pp232–3*), as well as grand hotels, bookstores, and major flagship stores, such as Nike and Apple.. The Union Square Frank Lloyd Wright Building, at 140 Maiden Lane, is the precursor to New York's Guggenheim Museum.

㉓ Powell Street Cable Car Turntable

Hallidie Plaza, Powell St at Market St. **Map** 5 C5. 🚌 many buses. 🚋 J, K, L, M, N, T. 🚋 Powell–Mason, Powell–Hyde.

The Powell–Hyde and the Powell–Mason cable car lines are the most spectacular routes in San Francisco. They start and end their journeys to Nob Hill, Chinatown, and Fisherman's Wharf at the corner of Powell Street and Market Street. Unlike the double-ended cable cars on the California Street line, the Powell Street cable cars were built to move in one direction only – hence the need for a turntable at every terminus.

After the car's passengers have disembarked, it is pushed onto the turntable and rotated manually by the conductor and gripman. Prospective customers for the return journey wait amid an ever-moving procession of street musicians, shoppers, tourists, and office workers.

㉔ Westfield San Francisco Centre

Market St and Powell St. **Map** 5 C5. **Tel** 512-6776. 🚌 many buses. 🚋 J, K, L, M, N. 🚋 Powell–Mason, Powell–Hyde. 🚇 Powell. **Open** 10am–8:30pm Mon–Sat; 11am–7pm Sun. 🆆 westfield.com *See Shopping in San Francisco p233.*

Shoppers are carried upward on semi-spiral escalators through this mall, which consists of a soaring, central atrium with nine floors of elegant shops. It is topped by a dome, 150 ft (45 m) above the ground floor. The basement levels provide access to the Powell Street Station. Nordstrom's department store is on the top five levels and is the mall's main tenant. Entrances to Bloomingdale's, famed

Rotating a cable car on the Powell Street turntable

for its Neo-Classical rotunda, can be found on the lower-level floors.

㉕ The San Francisco Mint

Fifth St and Mission St. **Map** 5 C5. 🚌 many buses. 🚋 J, K, L, M, N, T. Occasional public events, see website. 🆆 thesanfranciscomint.com

One of San Francisco's three mints, the Old Mint operated as a museum from 1973 to 1994; its last coins were produced in 1937. Designed in a Classical style, the building is constructed of sturdy granite, hence its nickname, "Granite Lady." It was built by A.B. Mullet between 1869 and 1874, its

The impregnable "Granite Lady" Old Mint

windows fortified by iron shutters and its basement vaults impregnable. While plans are underway to convert the Mint into a community cultural center, it is currently often hired out for weddings and private events.

㉖ San Francisco Visitor Information Center

Powell St at Market St under Hallidie Plaza. **Map** 5 B5. **Tel** 391-2000 or 391-2001. 🚌 many buses: J, K, L, M, N, T. 🚋 Powell–Mason, Powell–Hyde. **Open** 9am–5pm Mon–Fri, 9am–3pm Sat & Sun. 🚻 limited. 🆆 sftravel.com

Inquire here for information on tours of the city and surrounding areas, festivals, special events, restaurants, accommodations, nightlife, sightseeing, and shopping. Maps and a wide range of brochures are available in English and other languages, while a multilingual staff is on hand to answer any questions. You can make inquiries by telephone, or use their 24-hour information recording.

⑯ San Francisco Museum of Modern Art

This museum forms the nucleus of San Francisco's reputation as a leading center of modern art. Created in 1935, it moved into its current quarters in 1995, and in Spring 2016 reopened after a major three-year $365 million expansion that doubled its capacity. Designed by the international architecture firm Snøhetta, the new 235,000-square-foot expansion is seamlessly integrated with Swiss architect Mario Botta's 1995 modernist building. The museum offers a dynamic schedule of special exhibitions and permanent collection presentations in its 170,000 sq ft (15,790 sq m) gallery space.

Expansion
The eastern facade of the new expansion, designed by Snøhetta, is inspired in part by the waters of the San Francisco Bay. Its ground level features free exhibition spaces.

Museum Guide

The ground floor welcomes visitors with free art-filled public spaces and galleries. The Koret Education Center and works from the permanent collection of painting and sculpture are on the second floor, as is a new gallery for works on paper and galleries dedicated to California art. The new 15,000 square-foot Pritzker Center for Photography is on the third floor. The Doris and Donald Fisher Collection, comprising more than 1,100 works, begins on the third floor with a gallery of works by Alexander Calder, and continues in the Fisher Galleries on the fourth, fifth, and sixth floors. The sixth floor also features spaces dedicated to architecture and design, while the seventh floor showcases contemporary works as well as galleries dedicated to media arts, and a two-story conservation lab and artist's studio.

★ No. 14, 1960
This oil on canvas was painted by Mark Rothko, a leading Abstract Expressionist. It is one of the artist's most beautiful and hypnotic works.

Second floor

First floor

Atrium

Theatre

Third Street entrance

Key to Floor Plan

- Painting and sculpture
- Architecture and design
- Photography
- Media arts
- Koret Education Center
- Special exhibitions
- Roberts Family Gallery
- Sculpture Garden
- Contemporary Galleries
- Non-exhibition space

Seventh floor
and Terrace

Sixth floor

Fifth floor

Fourth
floor

Third floor

★ **Lesende (Reader)**
This 1994 work is by the
German artist Gerhard
Richter, whose oeuvre
encompasses gestural
abstraction, landscape,
portraiture, and photo-
based painting.

Koret Education Center
The reimagined Koret
Education Center houses
a resource library and
classrooms, serving
students, teachers,
and lifelong learners.

★ **California Art**
Richard Shaw's sculpted
figure *Melodious Double
Stops* (1980) is a highlight
of the collection.

Country Dog Gentlemen
Bay Area artist Roy De Forest
painted this fantasy of a universe
guarded by animals in 1972.

Exploring the San Francisco Museum of Modern Art

SFMOMA is both an outstanding repository of modern and contemporary art and a powerhouse of inspiration and encouragement to the local art scene. With more than 30,000 works of art in the museum's permanent collection, its strengths lie in US and Latin American modernism, Fauvism, Surrealism, American Abstract Expressionism, Minimalism and post-Minimalism, Pop art, postwar German art, the art of California and contemporary art from around the globe. The 2016 expansion has brought a notable addition: the 15,000 square-foot Pritzker Center for Photography, the largest space dedicated to photography in any art museum in the country.

Georgia O'Keeffe, Rufino Tamayo, and Joaquin Torres-Garcia. One of the museum's most powerful images is *The Flower Carrier*, a 1935 oil painting by Mexican artist Diego Rivera, who is celebrated for his murals *(see p142)*. Another exhibition area permanently shows works by Jasper Johns, Robert Rauschenberg, and Andy Warhol, among others, from the Anderson Collection of American Pop Art.

There is a good collection of the European Modernists, including notable paintings by Jean Arp, Max Beckmann, Constantin Brancusi, Georges Braque, André Derain, Franz Marc, and Pablo Picasso.

A large collection of works by Swiss-born Paul Klee are accommodated in an individual gallery, with works by the famous French painter of the Fauvist school, Henri Matisse, nearby on the second floor. Henri Matisse's *Femme au Chapeau (Woman with a Hat)* is perhaps the museum's best known painting.

Women of Algiers (1955) by Pablo Picasso

Paintings and Sculpture

Included in the museum's permanent holdings are over 8,000 paintings, sculptures, and works on paper. Paintings and sculpture from 1900 through to present day are in the second-floor galleries, while postwar painting and sculpture are displayed throughout the top four floors.

American Abstract Expressionism is well represented at the museum by Philip Guston, Willem de Kooning, Franz Kline, Joan Mitchell, and Jackson Pollock, whose *Guardians of the Secret* is a masterpiece of the genre.

Separate galleries have been allocated for paintings by Clyfford Still, who in the mid-20th century served on the faculty of the California School of Fine Arts, now the San Francisco Art Institute *(see p88)*.

Clyfford Still donated 28 of his paintings to the museum in 1975.

Other prominent North and Latin American artists whose works are displayed in the museum collections include Stuart Davis, Marsden Hartley, Frida Kahlo, Wilfredo Lam,

Architecture and Design

The Department of Architecture and Design was founded in 1983. Its function is to procure and maintain a collection of historical and contemporary architectural drawings, models, and design objects, and to examine and illuminate their influences on modern art. Its current holding of over 6,000 items focuses on

92 Chaise (1992) by Holt Hinshaw Pfau Jones

architecture, furniture, product design, and graphic design. and is widely considered one of the most significant in the United States. The new sixth-floor galleries offer rotating exhibitions.

Among items included in the permanent collection are models, drawings, prints, and prototypes by well-known and emerging designers. These include the famous architect Bernard Maybeck, who was responsible for some of the most beautiful buildings in the Bay Area, including the Palace of Fine Arts *(see p62)*. Other noted San Francisco Bay Area architects represented are Timothy Pflueger, William Wurster, William Turnbull and Willis Polk, known for his design of the glass and steel Halladie Building *(see p47)*, as well as the California design team of Charles and Ray Eames.

The permanent collection also includes works by Frank Lloyd Wright, Frank Gehry, and Fumihiko Maki.

Graphite to Taste (1989) by Gail Fredell

Media Arts

Established in 1988, the Department of Media Arts collects, conserves, documents, and exhibits art of the moving image, including works in video, film, projected image, electronic arts, and time-based media. The seventh-floor galleries have state-of-the-art equipment to present photo-graphic, multi-image and multimedia works, film, video, and selected programs of interactive media artwork.

The museum's growing permanent collection includes pieces by accomplished artists such as Nam June Paik, Don Graham, Peter Campus, Joan Jonas, Lynn Hershman Leeson, Bill Viola, Doug Hall, and Mary Lucier.

Michael Jackson and Bubbles (1988) by Jeff Koons

Photography

Drawing on its enormous permanent collection of over 17,800 photographs, the museum presents exhibitions of the photographic arts in the Pritzker Center for Photography, located on the third-floor.

The collection of Modernist American masters includes Berenice Abbott, Walker Evans, Edward Steichen, and Alfred Stieglitz, with special attention paid to California photographers including Edward Weston, John Gutmann, Imogen Cunningham and Ansel Adams. It has the finest collection of Japanese photography outside of Japan, as well as extensive collections from Latin America and Europe, including German avant-garde photographers of the 1920s, and European Surrealists of the 1930s.

California Arts

On the second floor there are galleries dedicated to works by California artists. These painters and sculptors have drawn their inspiration from local materials and scenes to create an influential body of art that is unique to the West Coast. Important Bay Area Figurative painters include Elmer Bishoff, Joan Brown and David Park, and there is a significant collection by Richard Diebenkorn.

Collage and assemblage artists exhibited from the museum's collection include Bruce Connor, William T. Wiley and Mission District resident Jess. Their use of everyday materials such as felt-tip pens, junkyard scrap and old paintings has produced art with a distinctive West Coast flavor.

Contemporary Art and Special Exhibitions

The fourth floor features special exhibition galleries. An actively changing schedule of contemporary art exhibits supplements the museum's historical collection and does much to encourage today's art scene.

Cave, Tsankawee, Mexico (1988), photographed by Linda Connor

CIVIC CENTER

The administrative center of San Francisco has as its focal point the Civic Center Plaza. This includes some of the best architecture in the city. Its grand government buildings and palatial performing arts complex are the source of great local pride. The former City Hall was destroyed in the earthquake of 1906 (see pp30–31), creating an opportunity to build a civic center more in keeping with San Francisco's fast-emerging role as a major port. The challenge was taken up by "Sunny Jim" Rolph (see p31) after he became mayor

in 1911. He made the building of a new Civic Center a top priority, and the funding for the project was found in 1912. The buildings provide an outstanding example of the Beaux Arts style (see p49), and in 1987 the whole area was declared an historic site. It is perhaps the most ambitious and elaborate city center complex in the US and well worth an extended visit. Fulton Street climbs gently to nearby Alamo Square, where there are several fine late Victorian houses.

Sights at a Glance

Historic Streets and Buildings
- ② Bill Graham Civic Auditorium
- ⑥ Veterans Building
- ⑦ City Hall
- ⑪ Cottage Row
- ⑬ Alamo Square
- ⑭ University of San Francisco

Shopping Area
- ⑫ Hayes Valley

Modern Architecture
- ⑩ Japan Center

Theaters and Concert Halls
- ④ Louise M. Davies Symphony Hall
- ⑤ War Memorial Opera House
- ⑧ Great American Music Hall

Museums and Galleries
- ① Asian Art Museum
- ③ San Francisco Arts Commission Gallery

Churches
- ⑨ St. Mary's Cathedral

☐ **Restaurants** see pp225–6
1. 1300 on Fillmore
2. Absinthe Brasserie & Bar
3. Ananda Fuara
4. Boxing Room
5. Dosa
6. Hinodeya Ramen Bar
7. Jardinière
8. Lers Ros Thai
9. Little Star Pizza
10. NOPA
11. Saigon Sandwich
12. Stacks
13. Tommy's Joynt

See also Street Finder
maps 3–5 & 9–11

0 meters 500
0 yards 500

Street-by-Street: Civic Center

San Francisco's main public space is a triumph of planning and design. Its well-balanced Beaux Arts architecture *(see p49)*, with the impressive dome of City Hall, is a tribute to San Francisco's energy in the years after the 1906 earthquake *(see pp30–31)*. Construction started with the Civic Auditorium, completed in 1915 for the Pan-Pacific Exposition *(see p72)*. This was followed by the City Hall, Library, and War Memorial Arts complex.

The State Building, completed in 1986, was designed by Skidmore, Owings and Merrill. The building mirrors the curves of the Davies Symphony Hall, one block away.

❸ San Francisco Art Commission Gallery is also here.

❻ Veterans Building
Home to the Herbst Theater and various veterans' associations.

❺ ★ War Memorial Opera House
The distinguished San Francisco Opera and Ballet companies both perform in this elegant spot.

❹ Louise M. Davies The San Francisco Symphony Orchestra, founded in 1911, is based here. Completed in 1981, to a design by Skidmore, Owings and Merrill, the hall has a grand lush interior.

MCALLISTER STREET

VAN NESS AVENUE

HAYES STREET

Key

— Suggested route

❼ ★ City Hall
This building is the city's most imposing structure, with a vast rotunda inside containing a wealth of architectural detail.

The Civic Center Plaza is a formally landscaped square where political protests are often held.

Locator Map
See Street Finder maps 4–5

The Federal Building houses US government offices, including the post office.

To bus no. 5

Civic Center Station

United Nations Plaza commemorates the signing of the United Nations Charter in 1945. There is a Farmer's Market on Wednesdays and Sundays.

San Francisco New Main Library, across from the Asian Art Museum, combines Beaux Arts and modern architectural styles.

0 meters 100
0 yards 100

❷ Bill Graham Civic Auditorium
This hall was constructed in 1915 to meet the city's need for a public meeting place.

❶ ★ Asian Art Museum
The building, designed by George Kelham, dates from 1917. It was once the Old Main Library, but now houses the Asian Art Museum.

Locator map labels: PACIFIC HEIGHTS AND THE MARINA, PRESIDIO, CIVIC CENTER, HAIGHT ASHBURY AND THE MISSION

Street labels: HYDE STREET, LARKIN STREET, GROVE STREET, POLK STREET, MARKET STREET

❶ Asian Art Museum

200 Larkin St. **Map** 4 F5. **Tel** 581-3500.
🚌 5, 7X, 9, 19, 21, 31. 🚋 F, J, K, L, M, N,
T. 🚇 Civic Center. **Open** 10am–5pm
Tue–Sun (to 9pm Thu). **Closed** public
hols. 🐾 except 1st Tue of month.
♿ 🎫 🏛 📷 🌐 asianart.org

The Asian Art Museum is
located on Civic Center Plaza
across from City Hall in a building that was the crown jewel
of the Beaux Arts movement
in San Francisco. The former
Main Library, built in 1917,
underwent major renovation
in 2001 to create the largest
museum outside Asia devoted
exclusively to Asian art.
   The museum's holdings
include more than 17,000 art
objects spanning 6,000 years of
history and representing cultures
and countries throughout Asia.
Among the exhibits is a gilt
bronze Buddha, one of the oldest
Chinese Buddhas in the world.
There are also venues for performances and festivals, a library, a
hands-on discovery center where
families can explore Asian art
and culture, and classrooms
for educational programs.
   The café's beautiful outdoor
terrace overlooks the Civic
Center and Fulton Street mall.

Grand staircase in the Asian Art Museum

Interior of San Francisco Art
Commission Gallery

❷ Bill Graham Civic Auditorium

99 Grove St. **Map** 4 F5. **Tel** 624-8900.
🚌 5, 7X, 9, 19, 21, 31, 47, 49. 🚋 J, K,
L, M, N, T. 🚇 Civic Center. **Open** for
performances. 🌐 billgraham
civicauditorium.com

Designed in Beaux Arts
style (see p49) by architect
John Galen Howard to
form a major part of
the Panama-Pacific
Exposition (see pp32–3),
San Francisco's Civic
Auditorium was opened
in 1915, and since then
has been one of the
city's most prominent
performance venues. It was
inaugurated by the French
pianist and composer Camille
Saint-Saens. The building was
completed along with City Hall,
in the course of the
massive architectural
renaissance that
followed the disasters
of 1906 (see pp30–31).
It was built, together
with the adjoining
Brooks Exhibit Hall,
beneath the Civic
Center Plaza. The
Civic Auditorium
now serves as the
city's main conference
center, and has the
capacity to seat 7,000
people. In 1992 its
name was changed in
honor of Bill Graham
(see p131), the local
rock music impresario
who was a pivotal
figure in both the
development and
promotion of the
city's trademark
psychedelic sound.

❸ San Francisco Arts Commission Gallery

401 Van Ness Ave. **Map** 4 F5. **Tel** 252-
2100. 🚌 5, 7X, 9, 19, 21, 47, 49. 🚋 J, K,
L, M, N, T. **Open** 11am–6pm Tue–Sat.
♿ 🌐 sfartscommission.org/gallery

Located in the Veterans Building
(see p129), this dynamic gallery
shows paintings, sculptures, and
multimedia works made by local
artists. The gallery's previous
location is now View 155, an
annex gallery southeast of the
main gallery at 155 Grove Street.
Some photography exhibitions
are on display at City Hall.

Louise M. Davies Symphony Hall

❹ Louise M. Davies Symphony Hall

201 Van Ness Ave. **Map** 4 F5. **Tel** 864-
6000. 🚌 7X, 19, 21, 47, 49. 🚋 J, K, L,
M, N, T. 🚇 Civic Center. ♿ 🎫
🌐 sfsymphony.org
See Entertainment p252.

Loved and loathed in equal
measure by the citizens of
San Francisco, this curving,
glass-fronted concert hall
was constructed in 1980 – the
creation of architects Skidmore,
Owings, and Merrill. The ultramodern hall is named for the
prominent philanthropist who
donated $5 million of the $35
million construction cost. It is
home to the San Francisco
Symphony Orchestra and also
welcomes many visiting artists.
   The acoustics of the building
were disappointing when it first
opened, but after many years of
negotiations a new sound system
was installed. The interior was
also redesigned, and the walls
were resculptured to reflect
sound better. These measures
improved the acoustics.

Front entrance of War Memorial Opera House, built in 1932

❺ War Memorial Opera House

301 Van Ness Ave. **Map** 4 F5.
Tel 552-8338. 🚌 5, 7X, 9, 19, 21, 47, 49.
🚃 J, K, L, M, N, T. 🚇 Civic Center. ♿
✉ Call ahead 🌐 **sfwmpac.org**

Opened in 1932, the War Memorial Opera House, designed by Arthur Brown, was dedicated to the memory of World War I soldiers. In 1951 it was used for the signing of the peace treaty between the US and Japan, marking the formal end of World War II. The building is now home to the San Francisco Opera and San Francisco Ballet *(see p252)*.

❻ Veterans Building

401 Van Ness Ave. **Map** 4 F5.
Tel 621-6600; Herbst Theater 392-4400.
🚌 5, 7X, 9, 19, 21. 🚃 J, K, L, M, N, T.
♿ limited. ✉ call 552-8338.
🌐 **sfwmpac.org**

Like its almost identical twin, the War Memorial Opera House, the Veterans Building was designed by Arthur Brown and built in 1932 to honor World War I soldiers. It was rededicated in 2015 after the opening of a 3,000 sq ft art gallery. In addition to displays of historic weapons, there are showcases of military memorabilia. The building is also home to the Herbst Theater, a 928-seat concert hall. Because of its good

acoustics, many classical music recitals are held here. The theater was the site of the signing of the United Nations Charter in 1945.

❼ City Hall

400 Van Ness Ave. **Map** 4 F5.
Tel 554-6139. 🚌 5, 7X, 9, 19, 21, 47, 49.
🚃 J, K, L, M, N, T. **Open** 8am–8pm
Mon–Fri. ♿ ✉ call 554-6023.
🌐 **sfciviccenter.org/visit**

City Hall, completed in 1915, just in time for the Panama-Pacific Exposition *(see pp32–3)*, was designed by Arthur Brown when he was at the height of his career. The original building was completely destroyed in the 1906 earthquake. Its Grand Baroque dome was modeled on St. Peter's Church in Rome and is higher

than the US Capitol in Washington, DC. The upper levels of the dome are accessible to the public.

The restored building is at the center of the Civic Center complex and is a magnificent example of the Beaux Arts style *(see p49)*. There are allegorical figures evoking the city's Gold Rush past in the pediment above the main Polk Street entrance. This entrance leads into the marble-floored Rotunda.

❽ Great American Music Hall

859 O'Farrell St. **Map** 4 F4.
Tel 885-0750. 🚌 19, 31, 38, 47, 49.

Built in 1907 as a place for bawdy comedy shows, the Great American Music Hall was soon in use as a brothel. Since then, it has become an excellent performance space, with a rich interior containing tall marble columns and elaborate balconies, adorned with ornate gilt plasterwork.

The venue is intimate, stylish, and known throughout the US, and famous artists such as Carmen McCrae, B. B. King, Duke Ellington, the Grateful Dead, Van Morrison, and Tom Paxton have played every kind of music here, from blues, jazz, and folk to rock 'n' roll. The views here are good from almost every table.

The imposing façade of the Beaux Arts-style City Hall in the heart of the Civic Center of San Francisco

The altar in St. Mary's Cathedral

❾ St. Mary's Cathedral

1111 Gough St. **Map** 4 E4.
Tel 567-2020. 🚌 2, 3, 31, 38.
Open 8:30am–4:30pm Mon–Fri,
9am–6:30pm Sat & Sun. 🕐 7:30am,
12:10pm Mon–Fri; 8am, 5:30pm Sat;
7:30am, 9am, 11am, 1pm (in Spanish)
Sun. 🈳 during services. ◪ ⬗
🅦 stmarycathedralsf.org

Situated at the top of Cathedral
Hill, the ultramodern St. Mary's
is the city's principal Roman
Catholic church and one of
its most prominent landmarks.
Designed by architect Pietro
Belluschi and engineer Pier Luigi
Nervi, it was completed in 1971.
The four-part arching
paraboloid roof stands out
like a white-sailed ship on
the horizon. The 200-ft- (60-m-)
high concrete structure, which
supports a cross-shaped
stained-glass ceiling, seems
to hover effortlessly over the
2,500-seat nave. A sunburst
canopy made of aluminum
rods sparkles above the
plain stone altar.

❿ Japan Center

Post St and Buchanan St.
Map 4 E4. **Tel** 440-1171. 🚌 2, 3, 22,
31, 38. **Open** 10am–7pm Wed–Mon
(restaurants open till later). **Closed** Jan
1, Thanksgiving, Dec 25.
🅦 sfjapantown.org

The Japan Center was built in
the 1960s as part of a scheme
to revitalize the Fillmore District.
Blocks of aging Victorian houses
were demolished and replaced
by the Geary Expressway and
the large Japan Center shopping
complex. At the heart of the complex, and centered upon a five-

tiered, 75-ft
(22-m) concrete
pagoda, is the
remodeled Peace
Pagoda Garden.
Taiko drummers
and others perform
here at the Cherry
Blossom Festival
(see p50) each April.
Both sides of the
Garden are lined
with Japanese
restaurants, shops, and the eight-
screen AMC Kabuki *(see p250)*.
This area has been the heart
of the Japanese community for
over 80 years. More authentic
Japanese shops are on Post
Street, where there are twin steel
sculptures by Ruth Asawa.

⓫ Cottage Row

Map 4 D4. 🚌 2, 3, 8AX, 8BX, 22, 38.

One of the few surviving remnants of working-class Victorian
San Francisco, this short stretch
of flat-fronted cottages was
built in 1882, at the end of the
Pacific Heights building boom.
Unusual for San Francisco, the
cottages share dividing walls,
like terraced houses in Europe
or on the East Coast of America.
Their utter lack of ornament,
and their siting on what was
a dark and crowded back
alley, emphasize their lower-

class status. The Cottage Row
houses were saved from
destruction during the process
of slum clearance in the 1960s.
A program organized by Justin
Herman awarded grants to
help people restore their
existing houses, rather than
replace them. All but one of
the houses have now been
restored, and they face a
small attractive city park.

Flat-fronted houses on Cottage Row

⓬ Hayes Valley

Map 4 E5. 🚌 6, 7, 21, 22.

Just west of City Hall, these few
blocks of Hayes Street became
one of San Francisco's trendier
shopping districts after US 101
highway was badly damaged
in the Loma Prieta earthquake
of 1989 *(see p20)*.
The road was then
torn down, having
previously cut Hayes
Valley off from the
wealthy power
brokers and theater-
goers of the Civic
Center. A few
of the local cafés
and restaurants, like
Hayes Street Grill,
had already mixed
in with the Hayes
Street secondhand
furniture and thrift
shops. The influx
of expensive art
galleries, interior
design shops, and
clothing boutiques
has made the Hayes
Valley area noticeably
more upscale.

The Japan Center pagoda by night

⑬ Alamo Square

Map 4 D5. 🚌 5, 21, 22, 24.

San Francisco's most photo-graphed row of colorful Victorian houses lines the eastern side of this sloping green square, which is some 225 ft (68 m) above the Civic Center, giving grand views of City Hall backed by the Financial District skyscrapers. The square was laid out at the same time as the pair of Pacific Heights squares *(see pp72–3)*, but it developed later and much more quickly, with speculators building large numbers of nearly identical houses.

The "Six Sisters" Queen Anne-style houses *(see p77)* built in 1895 at 710–20 Steiner Street are good examples. They appear on many San Francisco postcards. So many grand old Victorian houses line the streets around Alamo Square that the area has been declared an historic district.

St. Ignatius Church on the University of San Francisco campus

⑭ University of San Francisco

2130 Fulton St. **Map** 3 B5. **Tel** 422-5555. 🚌 5, 21, 33, 43. 🕇 8am & 12:05pm Mon–Fri; 5pm Sat; 8am, 9:30am, 11am & 5pm Sun 🆆 usfca.edu

Founded in 1855 as St. Ignatius College, the University of San Francisco (USF) is still a Jesuit-run institution, though classes are now coeducational and non-denominational. The landmark of the campus is the striking St. Ignatius Church, completed in 1914. Its buff-colored twin towers are visible from all over the western half of San Francisco, especially when lit up at night. The university campus and residential neigh-borhood that surrounds it occupy land that historically formed San Francisco's main cemetery district, on and around Lone Mountain.

The Sounds of 1960s San Francisco

During the Flower Power years of the late 1960s, and most notably during the 1967 Summer of Love *(see p34)*, young people from all over the US flocked to San Francisco. They came not just to "turn on, tune in and drop out," but also to listen to music. Janis Joplin, Jimi Hendrix, and the Grateful Dead all emerged out of a thriving music scene.

In 2017, a variety of special events and exhibitions were

Hippies lounging on a psychedelic bus

held throughout San Francisco to celebrate the 50th anniversary of the Summer of Love.

Premier Music Venues

The Avalon Ballroom, now the Regency II theater on Van Ness Avenue, was the first and most significant rock venue. Run by Chet Helms and the Family Dog collective, the Avalon pioneered the use of colorful psychedelic posters by designers such as Stanley Mouse and Alton Kelly.

Fillmore Auditorium, facing the Japan Center *(see p130)*, used to be a church hall. In 1965

Janis Joplin (1943–70), hard-edged blues singer

it was taken over by rock impresario Bill Graham, after whom the Civic Auditorium *(see p128)* is named. Graham put such unlikely pairs as Miles Davis and the Grateful Dead on the same bill, and brought in big-name performers from Jimi Hendrix to The Who. The Fillmore was damaged in the 1989 earthquake but reopened in 1994.

Bill Graham also opened the Winterland and the Fillmore East, and by the time he died in 1992 he became one of the most successful rock music promoters in the US.

HAIGHT ASHBURY AND THE MISSION

To the north of Twin Peaks – two windswept hills rising 900 ft (274 m) above the city – lies Haight Ashbury. With its rows of beautiful late Victorian houses *(see pp76–7)*, it is mostly inhabited by the wealthy middle classes, although this is where thousands of hippies lived in the 1960s *(see p131)*. The Castro District,

to the east, is the center of San Francisco's gay community. Well-known for its wild hedonism in the 1970s, the area is quieter these days, although its cafés and shops are still lively. The Mission District, farther east still, was originally settled by Spanish monks *(see p24)* and is home to many Hispanics.

Sights at a Glance

Historic Streets and Buildings
② Haight Ashbury
③ (Richard) Spreckels Mansion
⑤ Lower Haight Neighborhood
⑨ Castro Street
⑪ Dolores Street
⑮ Noe Valley
⑯ Clarke's Folly

Churches
⑩ Mission Dolores

Landmarks
⑲ Sutro Tower

Parks and Gardens
① Golden Gate Park Panhandle
④ Buena Vista Park
⑥ Corona Heights and Randall Museum
⑫ Dolores Park

⑰ Twin Peaks
⑱ Vulcan Street Steps

Museums and Galleries
⑧ GLBT History Museum
⑬ Mission Cultural Center for the Latino Arts
⑭ Carnaval Mural

Theaters
⑦ Castro Theatre

☐ **Restaurants** *see pp226–8*

1 Alembic
2 Amasia Hide's Sushi Bar
3 Axum Café
4 El Castillito
5 Cha Cha Cha
6 Chow
7 La Corneta Taqueria
8 Delfina
9 Farina
10 Foreign Cinema
11 Gracias Madre
12 Indian Oven

13 Limon Rotisserie
14 Lovejoy's Tea Room
15 Magnolia Gastropub & Brewery
16 Memphis Minnie's BBQ Joint
17 Mission Cheese
18 Mission Chinese Food
19 The Monk's Kettle
20 Nopalito
21 Pancho Villa Taqueria
22 Pork Store Café
23 Regazza
24 Rhea's Deli and Market
25 Rosamunde Sausage Grill
26 Schmidt's
27 SoMa StrEat Food Park
28 Sunflower
29 La Taqueria
30 Tartine Bakery
31 Thep Phanom Thai Cuisine
32 Truly Mediterranean
33 Zazie
34 Zuni Café

See also Street Finder maps 9 & 10

◀ Giant stockinged legs sticking out of Piedmont Boutique *(see p239)* in Haight Ashbury   For keys to symbols *see back flap*

Street-by-Street: Haight Ashbury

Stretching from the hilly Buena Vista Park to the flat expanses of Golden Gate Park, Haight Ashbury was a place to escape to from the city center in the 1880s. It developed into a residential area, but between the 1930s and 1960s it changed dramatically from middle-class suburb to center of the "Flower Power" world, with a free clinic to treat hippies. It is now one of the liveliest and most unconventional places in San Francisco, with an eclectic mix of people, excellent book and record stores, and good cafés.

2 Haight Ashbury
In the 1960s, hippies congregated at this major intersection, from which the area takes its name.

Wasteland, at 1660 Haight Street, is an anarchic used-clothing, curio, and furniture emporium housed in a colorful painted Art Nouveau building. Bargain hunters will find plenty to delight them in this unconventional store.

1 Golden Gate Park Panhandle
This thin green strip runs west into the heart of Golden Gate Park.

To bus nos. 7, 33

Cha Cha Cha is one of the liveliest places to eat in San Francisco, serving Latin American food in a variety of small dishes (see p225).

The Red Victorian Bed and Breakfast, a relic of the hippie 1960s, caters to a New Age clientele with health food and rooms with transcendental themes (see p214).

No. 1220 Masonic Avenue is one of many ornate Victorian mansions built on a steep hill to the south of Haight Street.

Locator Map
See Street Finder map 9

❸ ★ (Richard) Spreckels Mansion
This grand home at No. 737 Buena Vista Avenue was built in 1897.

| 0 meters | | 100 |
| 0 yards | | 100 |

❹ ★ Buena Vista Park
Through its mass of twisting trees growing closely together, this dramatic park offers magnificent views over the city.

Key

— Suggested route

To bus no. 37

❶ Golden Gate Park Panhandle

Map 9 C1. 5, 6, 7, 21, 24, 31, 33, 43. N.

This one-block-wide, eight-block-long stretch of parkland forms the narrow "Panhandle" to the giant rectangular pan that is Golden Gate Park (see pp144–59). It was the first part of the park to be reclaimed from the sand dunes that rolled across west San Francisco, and its stately eucalyptus trees are among the oldest and largest in the city. The Panhandle's winding carriage roads and bridle paths were first laid out in the 1870s, and the upper classes came here to walk and ride. They built large mansions on the outskirts of the park; many can still be seen today. In 1906 the Panhandle was a refuge for families made homeless by the earthquake (see pp30–31). Today the old roads and paths are used regularly by large crowds of joggers and bicyclists.

The Panhandle is still remembered for its "Flower Power" heyday of the 1960s (see p131), when bands gave impromptu concerts here.

Haight Ashbury and the Panhandle

❷ Haight Ashbury

Map 9 C1. 5, 6, 7, 24, 31, 33, 37, 43. N.

Taking its name from the junction of two main streets, Haight and Ashbury, this district contains independent bookstores, large Victorian houses, cafés, and hip clothing boutiques. Following the

reclamation of Golden Gate Park (see p148) and the opening of a large amusement park called The Chutes, the area was rapidly built up in the 1890s as a middle-class suburb – hence the dozens of elaborate Queen Anne-style houses (see p77) lining its streets. The Haight survived the 1906 earthquake and fire (see pp30–31), and experienced a brief boom, followed by a long period of decline.

After the streetcar tunnel under Buena Vista Park was completed in 1928, the middle classes began their exodus to the suburbs in the Sunset. The area reached its lowest ebb in the years after World War II. The big Victorian houses were divided into apartments and the low rents attracted a mixed population. By the 1960s the Haight had become host to a bohemian community that was a hotbed of anarchy. A component of this "hippie scene" was the music of rock bands such as the Grateful Dead, but the area stayed quiet until 1967. Then the media-fueled "Summer of Love" (see p131) brought some 75,000 young people in search of free love, music, and drugs, and the area became the focus

Mansion built for Richard Spreckels

of a worldwide youth culture. Today, the Haight retains its anti-establishment atmosphere, but there are problems of crime, drug abuse, and homelessness. However, from the congenial cafés to the secondhand clothing shops, you will still find the aura of the past here.

❸ (Richard) Spreckels Mansion

737 Buena Vista West. **Map** 9 C2. 5, 6, 7, 24, 31, 33, 37, 43. **Closed** to the public.

This house should not be confused with the larger and grander Spreckels Mansion on Washington Street (see p72). It was, however, also built by the millionaire "Sugar King" Claus Spreckels, for his nephew Richard. The elaborate Queen Anne-style house (see p77), built in 1897, is a typical late-Victorian Haight Ashbury home. It was once a recording studio, and later a guesthouse, but is now in private hands. Guests have included the acerbic journalist and ghost-story writer Ambrose Bierce, and the adventure writer Jack London, who wrote White Fang here in 1906.

The mansion is situated on a hill near Buena Vista Park. Rows of Victorian houses, many of them well preserved and some palatial, are nearby.

The Cha Cha Cha restaurant on Haight Street

One of these, a block away at 1450 Masonic Street, is an onion-domed house, one of the most unusual of the many eccentric mansions built in the Haight since the 1890s.

❹ Buena Vista Park

Map 9 C1. 🚌 5, 6, 7, 24, 31, 33, 37, 43.

Buena Vista Park rises steeply, 569 ft (18 m) above the geographical center of San Francisco. First landscaped in 1894, it is a pocket of land left to nature. A network of paths winds up from Haight Street to the crest, where densely planted trees frame views of the Bay Area. Many of the trails are overgrown and eroded, but there is a paved route up to the summit from Buena Vista Avenue. It is best to avoid the park at night.

❺ Lower Haight Neighborhood

Map 10 D1. 🚌 6, 22, 66, 71.
🚃 K, L, M, N, T.

Halfway between City Hall and Haight Ashbury, and marking the southern border of the Fillmore District, the Lower Haight is an area in transition. New markers of gentrification line the streets, such as hip art galleries, salons, eclectic boutiques, and shops, including Rooky Ricardo's Records, which sells rare and unusual records. These are in addition to the inexpensive

Levi Strauss and his Jeans

First manufactured in San Francisco in the days of the Gold Rush *(see pp26–7)*, denim jeans have had a great impact on popular culture. One of the leading producers of jeans is Levi Strauss & Co., founded in

Two miners wearing Levi's at the Last Chance Mine in 1882

the city in the 1860s. The company's story started in 1853, when Levi Strauss left New York to set up a branch of his family's cloth firm in San Francisco.

In the 1860s, though still primarily a seller of cloth, he pioneered the use of durable blue canvas to make workpants, sold directly to miners. In the 1870s his company began to use metal rivets to strengthen stress points in the garments, and demand increased. The company expanded, and early in the 20th century moved to 250 Valencia Street in the Mission District, where it remained until 2002. Levi's jeans are now produced and worn all over the world, and the company that was founded by Levi Strauss is still owned by his descendants.

cafés, bars, and restaurants serving a bohemian clientèle that were already in business in the area. This combination has created one of the most lively districts in San Francisco.

As in nearby Alamo Square *(see p131)*, the Lower Haight holds dozens of houses known as "Victorians" *(see pp76–7)*, built from the 1850s to the early 1900s. These include many picturesque cottages such as the Nightingale House at 201 Buchanan Street, built in the 1880s.

Populated with bars and restaurants, this artsy neighborhood has great nightlife options.

Though it is safer now, elements of its somewhat seedy past can still be encountered.

❻ Corona Heights and Randall Museum

Map 9 D2. **Tel** 554-9600. 🚌 24, 37.
Randall Museum, 199 Museum Way:
Open 10am–5pm Tue–Sat. **Closed** public hols. ♿ limited.
🌐 randallmuseum.org

Corona Heights Park is a dusty and undeveloped rocky peak. Clinging to its side is an unusual museum for children. The Randall Museum has an extensive menagerie of raccoons, owls, snakes, and other animals. The emphasis of the museum is on participation. It also offers hands-on experiences with woodworking, pottery, painting, theater, photography, model railroads, storytelling, and more.

Corona Heights was gouged out by brick-making operations in the 19th century. It was never planted with trees, so its bare red-rock peak offers a panoramic view over the city and East Bay, including the winding streets of Twin Peaks.

Panoramic view of the city from Corona Heights

The historic Castro Theatre

❼ Castro Theatre

429 Castro St. **Map** 10 D2. **Tel** 621-6120. 🚌 24, 33, 35, 37. 🚃 F, K, L, M, T. *See Entertainment p250.*
🆆 **castrotheatre.com**

Completed in 1922, this brightly lit neon marquee is a Castro Street landmark. It is the most sumptuous and best preserved of San Francisco's neighborhood film palaces, and one of the first commissions of the architect Timothy Pflueger. With its lavish, *Arabian Nights* interior, complete with a glorious Wurlitzer organ that rises from the floor between screenings, it is well worth the price of admission. The ceiling of the auditorium is particularly noteworthy: it is cast in plaster and resembles the interior of a large tent, with imitation swathes of material, rope, and tassels. The theater seats 1,400 and shows mainly revival classics. It also hosts the San Francisco International LGBT Film Festival, held each June.

❽ GLBT History Museum

4127 18th St. **Map** 10 D3. **Tel** 621-1107. 🚌 24, 33, 35, 37. 🚃 KT, F, L, M, S. **Open** 11am–6pm Mon–Sat, noon–5pm Sun. **Closed** Tue in fall and winter months. 🆆 **glbthistory.org**

This is the first full-scale, stand-alone museum devoted to the evolution of the liberation of the gay, lesbian, bisexual, and transgender community in the United States. Though fairly small, the museum packs a punch, celebrating

the city's vast queer past through dynamic and surprising exhibitions and programming. Discover treasures from the archives of the GLBT Historical Society that reflect the fascinating stories of this vibrant community.

GLBT History Museum

❾ Castro Street

Map 10 D2. 🚌 24, 33, 35, 37. 🚃 F, K, L, M, T.

The hilly neighborhood around Castro Street between Twin Peaks and the Mission District is the heart of San Francisco's

high-profile gay and lesbian community. Focused on the intersection of Castro Street and 18th Street, the self-proclaimed "Gayest Four Corners of the World" emerged as a homosexual nexus during the 1970s. Gays of the Flower Power generation moved into this predominantly working-class district and began restoring Victorian houses and setting up such businesses. They also opened gay bars including the Twin Peaks on the corner of Castro Street and 17th Street, and Flore at Market Street and Noe Street. Unlike earlier bars, where lesbians and gays hid in dark corners out of public view, the Twin Peaks installed large windows. Though the many shops and restaurants attract all kinds of people, the Castro's openly homosexual identity has made it a place of pilgrimage for gays and lesbians. It symbolizes for this minority group a freedom not generally found in cities elsewhere.

In the 1970s, a man named Harvey Milk championed the rights of the gay community in the Castro district, earning the title Mayor of Castro Street. He went on to become the first elected openly gay politician in California but was assassinated on November 28, 1978. He and Mayor George Moscone were killed by an ex-policeman, whose lenient sentence caused riots in the city. Milk is remembered by a memorial plaque outside the station on Market Street, and by an annual candlelit procession from Castro Street to City Hall.

Rainbow flags lining Castro Street

⑩ Mission Dolores

16th St and Dolores St. **Map** 10 E2.
Tel 621-8203. 🚌 22. 🚃 J. **Open** 9am–4pm daily (May–Oct: to 4:30pm).
Closed Easter Sunday, Thanksgiving, Dec 25.
📷 ♿ 🏛 **w** missiondolores.org

Preserved intact since it was completed in 1791, Mission Dolores is the oldest building in the city and an embodiment of San Francisco's religious Spanish colonial roots *(see pp24–5)*. The mission was founded by a Franciscan friar, Father Junipero Serra, and is formally known as the Mission of San Francisco de Asis. The name Dolores reflects its proximity to Laguna de los Dolores (Lake of Our Lady of Sorrows). The building is modest by mission standards, but its 4 ft (1.2 m) thick walls have survived the years without serious decay. Paintings by American Indians adorn the ceiling, which has been preserved. There is a fine Baroque altar and reredos, as well as a display of historical artifacts in the small museum *(see p41)*. Most services are held in the basilica, which was built next to the original mission in 1918. The white-walled cemetery contains graves

Figure of saint in the Mission Dolores

of prominent San Franciscans from the Gold Rush days. A statue honoring the graves of 5,000 Indians, most of whom died in the great measles epidemics of 1806 and 1826, was stolen and returned in 1993. It stands on a pedestal reading, "In Prayerful Memory of our Faithful Indians." The famous graveyard scene in Hitchcock's *Vertigo* was filmed here in 1957.

The painted and gilded altarpiece was imported from Mexico in 1797.

The Statue of Father Junipero Serra, founder of the mission, is a copy of the work of local sculptor Arthur Putnam.

The ceramic mural was created by Guillermo Granizo, a native San Francisco artist.

Museum and display

The ceiling paintings are based on original Ohlone designs using vegetable dyes.

Entrance for the disabled

The mission cemetery originally extended across many streets. The earliest wooden grave markers have disintegrated, but a more recent marker honors two Indians who were baptized, married, and buried here.

Statue of St. Rita

The front of the mission has four columns that support niches for three bells. The bells are inscribed with their names and dates.

Entrance and gift shop

⓫ Dolores Street

Map 10 E2. 🚌 22, 33, 48. 🚋 J.

Lined by lovingly maintained late Victorian houses *(see pp76–7)* and divided by an island of palm trees, Dolores Street is one of San Francisco's most attractive public spaces. The broad straight boulevard runs for 24 blocks, parallel to Mission Street, forming the western border of the Mission District. It starts at Market Street, where a statue in honor of Spanish–American War soldiers is overwhelmed by the hulking US Mint.

The Mission High School, with the characteristic white walls and red-tile roof of Mission-style architecture, is on Dolores Street, as is the historic Mission Dolores *(see p139)*. The street ends near prosperous Noe Valley.

Sculpture commemorating soldiers in the Spanish–American War

⓬ Dolores Park

Map 10 E3. 🚌 22, 33. 🚋 J.

Originally the site of the city's main Jewish cemetery, Dolores Park transformed in 1905 into one of the Mission District's few large open spaces. Bounded by Dolores, Church, 18th, and 20th

People enjoying the sunshine at the lush Dolores Park

streets, it is situated high on a hill with a good view of the city center.

Dolores Park is popular during the day with tennis players, sunbathers, and dog walkers, but after dark can draw drug dealers. Above the park to the south and west, the streets rise so steeply that many turn into pedestrian-only stairways. Here are some of the city's finest Victorian houses, especially on Liberty Street.

⓭ Mission Cultural Center for the Latino Arts

2868 Mission St. **Map** 10 F4. **Tel** 821-1155; Box Office: 643-2785). 🚌 12, 14, 27, 36, 49. 🚋 J. 🚇 24th St. Gallery: **Open** 10am–5pm Tue–Sat. ♿ 🌐 missionculturalcenter.org

This dynamic arts center displays and promotes Latino culture through its art. It offers classes and workshops and stages theatrical events and exhibitions. Chief among these is the parade held in November to celebrate the Day of the Dead *(see p52)*.

⓮ Carnaval Mural

24th St and South Van Ness Ave. **Map** 10 F4. 🚌 12, 27, 48, 67. 🚋 J. 🚇 24th St.

One of the many brightly painted murals to be seen on walls in the Mission District, the *Carnaval Mural* celebrates the diverse people who come together for the Carnaval festival *(see p50)*. This event, held annually in late spring, is the high spot of the year.

Guided tours of other murals, some with political themes, are given by civic organizations. There is also an outdoor gallery with murals in Balmy Alley *(see pp142–3)*, near Treat and Harrison streets.

⓯ Noe Valley

🚌 24, 35, 48. 🚋 J.

Noe Valley is known as "Noewhere Valley" by its residents, who are intent on keeping it off the tourist map. It is a comfortable neighborhood mainly inhabited by young families. Named after its original land-grant owner, José Noe, the last *alcalde* (mayor) of Mexican Yerba Buena, the area was first developed in the 1880s following the completion of a cable-car line over the steep Castro Street hill. Like many other areas of San Francisco, this once working-class district underwent wholesale gentrification in the 1970s, resulting in today's engaging mix of boutiques, bars, and restaurants. The Noe

Detail from the *Carnaval Mural*

Valley Ministry, at 1021 Sanchez Street, is a late 1880s Presbyterian church in the "Stick Style" *(see p77)*, with emphasis on vertical lines. It was converted into a community center in the 1970s.

⑯ Clarke's Folly

250 Douglass St. **Map** 10 D3. 🚌 24, 35, 37. **Closed** to the public.

This resplendent white manor house was originally surrounded by extensive grounds. It was built in 1892 by Alfred Clarke, known as Nobby, who worked in the San Francisco Police Department at the time of the Committee of Vigilance. The house is said to have cost $100,000, a huge sum in the 1890s. Now divided into private apartments, its turrets and other features make it an evocative example of Victorian-era domestic architecture.

⑰ Twin Peaks

Map 9 C4. 🚌 36, 37.

These two hills were first known in Spanish as El Pecho de la Chola, "the Bosom of the Indian Girl." At the top there is an area of parkland with steep and grassy slopes, from which you can enjoy incomparable views of the whole of San Francisco.
Twin Peaks Boulevard circles both hills near

Motorists enjoying the breathtaking panoramic views on the Twin Peaks Boulevard

their summits, and there is a parking and viewing point from which to look out over the city. Those who are prepared to climb up the steep footpath to the very top can leave the crowds behind and get a 360° view. The residential districts on the slopes lower down have curving streets that wind around the contours of the slopes, rather than the formal grid that is more common in San Francisco.

⑱ Vulcan Street Steps

Vulcan St. **Map** 9 C2. 🚌 37.

Apart from a tiny figure of Spock standing on a mailbox, there is no connection between the popular television program *Star Trek* and this block of almost rural houses climbing between Ord Street and Levant Street. Like the Filbert Steps on Telegraph Hill *(see pp92–3)*, however, Vulcan Steps does feel light years away from the busy streets of the Castro District below. The small vegetable and flower gardens of the houses spill out and soften the edges of the steps, and a canopy of pines muffles the city sounds. There are grand views of the Mission District and beyond.

⑲ Sutro Tower

Map 9 B3. 🚌 36, 37. **Closed** to the public.

Marking the skyline like an invading robot, Sutro Tower is 970 ft (290 m) high. It was named after local landowner and philanthropist Adolph Sutro, and it carries antennae for the signals of most of the city's TV and radio stations. Built in 1973, it is still much used, despite the rise of cable networks. The tower is visible from all over the Bay Area, and sometimes seems to float above the summer fogs that roll in from the sea. On the north side of the tower there are dense eucalyptus groves, first planted in the 1880s by Adolph Sutro. They drop down to the medical center campus of the University of California San Francisco (UCSF), one of the most highly rated teaching hospitals in the United States.

The magnificent facade of Nobby Clarke's Folly

San Francisco's Murals

San Francisco is proud of its reputation as a culturally rich and cosmopolitan city, qualities evident in the vivid elaborate murals that decorate walls and fences in several areas of the city. Many were painted in the 1930s, and many more in the 1970s, with some appearing spontaneously while others were commissioned. One of the best is the *Carnaval Mural* on 24th Street in the Mission District *(see p140)*; further examples are shown here.

503 Law Office at Dolores and 18th streets

Past and Present

Some of the best examples of San Francisco's historical mural art can be found inside Coit Tower, where a series of panels, funded during the Great Depression of the 1930s by President Roosevelt's New Deal program, is typical of the period. Many local artists participated in creating the work, and themes include the struggles of the working class and the rich resources of California. The city has since been decorated with a number of modern murals, most notably by the Precita Eyes Mural Arts Studio.

Detail from Coit Tower mural focuses on California's rich resources

Coit Tower mural showing life during the Depression years

Precita Eyes Mural Arts Studio is a community-based organization that seeks to promote the mural arts through collaborative projects. They also sponsor new murals by established artists and run lively mural tours around San Francisco.

Mosaic mural (2007) by Precita Eyes, Hillcrest school

Balloon Journey, Precita Eyes

This mural was designed and painted by AYPAL (Asian Pacific Islander Youth Promoting Advocacy and Leadership) students in 2007, in association with Precita Eyes. The organization runs a number of community and youth workshops, which produce between 15 and 30 new murals every year. Visitors can see examples of these throughout the Bay Area.

Stop the Violence at 1212 Broadway #400, Oakland

Life Today

Life in the modern metropolis is one of the major themes of mural art in San Francisco, as much now as it was in the 1930s. In the Mission District particularly, every aspect of daily life is illustrated on the walls of banks, schools, and restaurants, with lively scenes of the family, community, political activity, and people at work and play. The Mission District contains around 200 murals, many painted in the 1970s, as part of a city program that paid young people to create works of art in public places. The San Francisco Arts Commission continues to foster this art form.

Golden Gate Bridge

Palace of Fine Arts

Cable car

BART

Tourists

This Balmy Alley mural is a view of the city as tourists see it. The alley, in the Mission District, is decorated with numerous vivid murals, first painted by local children, artists, and community workers in the 1970s. The works are now a major attraction.

The Learning Wall, Franklin St, depicts education and art

Positively Fourth Street, a weathered mural at Fort Mason

The Multicultural City

San Francisco's heritage of diversity and tolerance comes alive in the murals that enliven its ethnic neighborhoods. In Chinatown, Chinese-American artists evoke memories of the "old country." The Mission District is filled with art, some of it politically inspired, celebrating the struggles and achievements of its Mexican and Latin American population.

Mexican American dancer

American Indian drummer

Caucasian bass player

African American maracas player

Multicultural San Francisco is celebrated at Park Branch Library in Haight Ashbury.

Mural in Washington Street encapsulating life in China

Where to Find the Murals

Balmy Alley. **Map** 11 A5
Clarion Alley. **Map** 10 F2
Coit Tower pp92–3
Dolores and 18th St. **Map** 10 E3
Fort Mason pp74–5
Franklin Street. **Map** 4 E1
Oakland p166
Park Branch Library
1833 Page St. **Map** 9 B1
Precita Eyes Mural Arts Studio
348 Precita Ave. **Map** 10 F5
Washington Street. **Map** 11 A2

GOLDEN GATE PARK AND LAND'S END

Lying to the south of the Richmond District is the spectacular Golden Gate Park, a masterpiece of landscape gardening, created in the 1890s out of a sandy wasteland. Little grows here by chance, and trees have been planted where they will best deflect the prevailing winds. All shrubs and bushes are carefully chosen to ensure there is color at every season. Among the many attractions of the park are meandering paths, sports facilities ranging from archery to golf, and three major museums. More parklands lie to the north and west of the Richmond District, linked by the Coastal Trail. This is where rugged Land's End, the scene of so many shipwrecks, meets the sea. Nearby Lincoln Park, with its manicured golf course, makes a dramatic contrast.

Sights at a Glance

See also Street Finder
maps 1, 3 & 7–9

0 meters | 1,000
0 yards | 1,000

Bright red pagoda in the Japanese Garden, Golden Gate Park

Street-by-Street: Golden Gate Park

Golden Gate Park is one of the largest urban parks in the world.
It stretches from the Pacific Ocean to the center of San Francisco,
forming an oasis of greenery and calm in which to escape from the
bustle of city life. Within the park an amazing number of activities
are possible, both sporting and cultural. The landscaped area
around the Music Concourse, with its fountains, plane trees, and
benches, is the most popular and developed section. Here you
can enjoy free Sunday concerts at the Spreckels Temple of Music.
Two museums stand on either side of the Concourse, and the
Japanese and Shakespeare gardens are in walking distance.

❹ ★ de Young Museum
This state-of-the-art, landmark
museum showcases collections
from around the world. Exhibits
include this mahogany chest,
made in Philadelphia in 1780.

The Great Buddha, nearly
11 ft (3 m) high, is probably
the largest statue of its kind
outside Asia.

❸ Japanese Tea Garden
This exquisite garden, with its well-
tended plants, is one of the most
attractive parts of the park.

HAGIAWARA

The bust of Verdi
reflects the city's
passion for opera.

**The Spreckels Temple of
Music** is an ornate band
shell, the site for free Sunday
summer concerts since 1899.

MARTIN LUTHER KING D

The bridge in the Japanese
Tea Garden is known as the
Moon Bridge. It arches steeply,
and its reflection in the water
below forms a perfect circle.

| 0 meters | | 80 |
| 0 yards | | 80 |

The bust of Miguel de Cervantes, the Spanish author, was sculpted by Jo Mora. He is depicted with his two fictional creations, Don Quixote and Sancho Panza.

Locator Map
See Street Finder map 8

The statue of the *Apple Cider Press*, by sculptor Thomas Shields-Clarke, is one of the few monuments to survive from the California Midwinter Fair of 1894.

The John McLaren Rhododendron Dell is planted in memory of the superintendent (see p148) of Golden Gate Park.

❷ ★ **California Academy of Sciences**
This complex combines an aquarium, a planetarium, a museum, and a research facility (see pp152–3).

The Music Concourse, a formally landscaped area with fountains and benches, is where the Golden Gate Park Band performs on Sundays (Apr–Oct).

❶ **Shakespeare Garden**
This tiny garden holds more than 150 species of plants, all mentioned in Shakespeare's poetry or plays.

KEY

— Suggested route

The Creation of Golden Gate Park

As San Francisco prospered and matured in the 1860s, its citizens demanded the same amenities as other great cities. Prominent among these was a large city park, for which they petitioned in 1865. New York had just finished building its trendsetting Central Park, created largely by landscape designer Frederick Law Olmsted. San Francisco's mayor, HP Coon, sought Olmsted's advice on a piece of land that the city had recently secured for a park. This vast, undeveloped wasteland to the west of the city by the Pacific Ocean was known as the "Outside Lands."

John McLaren

Reclaiming the Land

The city planners turned to a surveyor and engineer named William Hammond Hall. He had already achieved some success in dune reclamation in the Outside Lands, and in 1870 he applied his methods to Golden Gate Park. Hall was appointed the park's first superintendent in 1871. He started work at the east end, laying out meandering roads and trying to create a seemingly natural landscape. The developing park soon proved popular. Families came to picnic and young dandies raced their carriages.

Cyclists in Golden Gate Park

The Plan Falters

Despite the popularity of the park, it was nearly prevented from reaching maturity by public corruption.

Throughout the 1870s city officials siphoned off funds and the budget was repeatedly cut. In 1876 Hall was falsely accused of corruption and resigned in protest. The park fell into a period of decline, but after a decade of decay, Hall was asked to resume the task of managing it. The remarkable man he chose as superintendent in 1890 was a Scotsman named John McLaren, who agreed with Hall that a park should be a natural environment. He planted thousands of trees, bulbs, flowers, and shrubs, chosen so blooms would appear each month.

He also imported exotic plants from around the world. These thrived in his care, despite the poor soil and foggy climate of San Francisco. McLaren devoted his whole life to the park, personally fighting the developers who threatened encroachment. He died at the age of 93, after 53 years in office.

The Changing Park

The park still reflects the vision of McLaren and Hall, but contrary to their plans, the park today is scattered with buildings, and McLaren's most prominent defeat became a popular attraction. In what is now the Music Concourse, the California Midwinter Fair opened in 1894, despite his protests. Urban encroachment continued to press upon the park in the 20th century, but for most San Franciscans the park remains what it was intended to be – a place in which to escape from city life.

1894 California Midwinter Fair

Plaques in the Shakespeare Garden

❶ Shakespeare Garden

Music Concourse, Golden Gate Park. **Map** 8 F2. 6, 7, 43, 44.

Gardeners here have tried to cultivate all the plants mentioned in William Shakespeare's works. The relevant quotes are written on plaques set in a wall at the back of the garden.

❷ California Academy of Sciences

See pp152–3.

❸ Japanese Tea Garden

Music Concourse, Golden Gate Park. **Map** 8 F2. **Tel** 752-1171. 44. **Open** 9am–5:45pm daily (Nov–Feb: to 4:45pm).
W japaneseteagardensf.com

Established by the art dealer George Turner Marsh for the California Midwinter Fair of 1894 *(see p148),* this garden is a popular attraction. The best time to visit is when the cherry trees bloom in April. Paths wind through the carefully manicured Japanese trees, shrubs, and flowers. The steeply arched Moon Bridge forms a dramatic circular reflection in the pond below. The largest bronze Buddha to be found outside Asia, which was cast in Japan in 1790, is seated at the top of the garden stairs.

❹ de Young Museum

50 Hagiwara Tea Garden Drive, Golden Gate Park. **Map** 8 F2. **Tel** 750-3600. 5, 44. N. **Open** 9:30am–5:15pm Tue–Sun (Jun–Nov: to 8pm Fri). **Closed** Thanksgiving, Dec 25. (free first Tue of month).
W deyoung.famsf.org

Founded in 1895, the de Young Museum houses one of the city's finest art collections. In 1989 the building was too damaged by an earthquake to be saved. However, an exciting state-of-the-art facility opened in 2005. The museum now contains a broad range of American art, with more than 1,000 paintings on view, as well as extensive pre-Columbian-American, African, and Oceanic works.

❺ McLaren Lodge

Near junction of Stanyan St and Fell St on the park's east side. **Map** 9 B1. **Tel** 831-2700. **Open** 8am–5pm Mon–Fri. **Closed** major holidays. 7, 21.

This sandstone villa, designed by Edward Swain, was built in 1896. As superintendent of the park, John McLaren lived here with his family until his death in 1943. His portrait hangs on the wall, and every December the cypress tree outside is lit with colored lights in his memory. The lodge is now a park office that also dispenses maps and information.

Gateway in the Japanese Tea Garden

❻ Children's Playground

Kezar Drive, near First Ave. **Map** 9 A1. 5, 71. N. No adults allowed unless accompanied by children.

This is the oldest public children's playground in the United States, and it set the style for many later ones. In 1978 it was redesigned with sandboxes, swings, sprawling slides, and a climbing "fortress." On the Herschell-Spillman merry-go-round, housed in a Greek-inspired structure that dates from 1892, children ride on brightly painted beasts.

Inside the Columbarium

❼ Columbarium

1 Loraine Court. **Map** 3 B5. **Tel** 771-0717. 33, 38. **Open** 8am–5pm Mon–Fri, 10am–3pm Sat & Sun. **Closed** Jan 1, Thanksgiving, Dec 25. ground floor only.

The San Francisco Columbarium is the sole survivor of the old Lone Mountain Cemetery, which once covered sizable tracts of the Richmond District. Most of the remains were disinterred and moved to Colma in 1914. This Neo-Classical rotunda houses the remains of 6,000 people in elaborate decorated urns. Unused for several decades, it was rescued and restored by the Neptune Society in 1979. The ornate, bright interior under the dome has lovely stained-glass windows. The narrow passages encircling the dome are remarkable for their acoustics.

❷ California Academy of Sciences

The California Academy of Sciences has been located in Golden Gate Park since 1916, settling into a new building in late 2008. It houses the Steinhart Aquarium, Morrison Planetarium, and the Kimball Natural History Museum, and combines innovative green architecture with flexible exhibition spaces. A lovely piazza is at the heart of the building. Filled with native plant species, the 2.5-acre (1-ha) living roof, which can be seen from the rooftop deck, is designed to make the museum blend in with the surrounding parkland.

Discovery Tidepool
Located in the main level, this exhibit allows visitors to touch sea creatures that live in the local coast's rock pools.

Museum Guide

Steinhart Aquarium displays are spread throughout the museum, but most of the tanks can be found in the lower level beneath the Piazza. An auditorium above the café hosts traveling exhibits as well as special performances and programs. The back of the building holds the museum's collection of over 28 million scientific specimens along with staff offices and research laboratories.

The Swamp

Philippine Coral Reef Tank
(Lower Level)

Sharks and Rays
(Lower Level)

Planetarium
Visitors leave planet Earth behind as they fly through space and time inside the world's largest all-digital planetarium.

Key to Floor Plan

- African Hall
- Kimball Natural History Museum
- Morrison Planetarium
- Rainforests of the World
- Building Green
- Steinhart Aquarium
- Science in Action
- Islands of Evolution
- Early Explorers Cove
- Non-exhibition space

African Hall
Preserved animals from Africa's jungles and savannas are displayed here, in lifelike dioramas.

California Coast Tank
Critters that live in the cold waters of California, such as this hermit crab, can be found in this section on the lower level.

Piazza (more Steinhart Aquarium exhibits one floor below)

★ Steinhart Aquarium
A collection of the world's deepest living coral reef display, a two-story Swamp, Discovery Tidepool, and hundreds of "jewel" tanks showcase the stunning diversity of aquatic life.

Entrance

Level 1

Tyrannosaurus Rex Skeleton
This gigantic predator was the most powerful carnivore ever to walk the earth.

★ Rainforests of the World
This four-story exhibit offers a vertical journey through four different rainforest habitats. Free flying butterflies and birds, snakes, and lizards live in this exhibit.

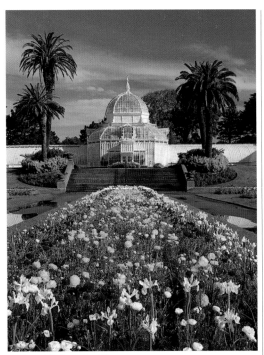

Glass-house at the Conservatory of Flowers

Central America. Surprisingly, all these gardens thrive in the coastal fog. The Arboretum has a shop, selling seeds and books, and it also houses the Helen Crocker Russell Library of Horticulture, which is open to the public. A flower show is held in the summer.

❿ Stow Lake

50 Stow Lake Drive, Golden Gate Park. **Map** 8 E2. 📟 28, 29, 44. **Open** summer: 10am–5pm Mon–Thu, 10am–6pm Fri & Sat; fall and winter: 10am–4pm daily. 🛥 Boat rental: 386-2531. 🆆 **stowlakeboathouse.com**

This artificial lake created in 1895 encircles Strawberry Hill such that the summit of the hill now forms an island, linked to the mainland by two stone-clad bridges. Stow Lake's circular stream is ideal for rowing laps from the boathouse, though leisurely drifting seems more appropriate. The Chinese moon-watching pavilion on the island's shore was a gift from San Francisco's sister city Taipei, in Taiwan. The red and green pavilion was shipped to San Francisco in 6,000 pieces and then assembled on the island.

The millionaire Collis P. Huntington (*see p104*) donated the money to create the reservoir and the waterfall that cascades into Stow Lake and is one of the park's most attractive features.

❽ Conservatory of Flowers

John F. Kennedy Drive, Golden Gate Park. **Map** 9 A1. **Tel** 831-2090. 📟 5, 21, 33, 44. 🚃 N. **Open** 10am–4pm Tue–Sun. 🏛 (free 1st Tue of the month.) 🆗 🆆 **conservatoryofflowers.org**

This ornate glasshouse was the oldest building in Golden Gate Park. A jungle of orchids, ferns, and palms thrived here but a strong storm hit the city in December 1995, and it was largely destroyed. A campaign for its repair was launched, and it reopened in 2003.

❾ Strybing Arboretum

9th Ave at Lincoln Way, Golden Gate Park. **Map** 8 F2. **Tel** 661-1316. 📟 5, 7, 44. 🚃 N. **Open** Mar–Sep: 7:30am–6pm daily (Oct: to 5pm; Nov–Jan: to 4pm).. 🆗 📷 1:30pm daily. 📷 🆆 **sfbotanicalgarden.org**

On display are 7,500 species of plants, trees, and shrubs from many different countries.

There are Mexican, African, South American, and Australian gardens, and one devoted to native California plants.

Well worth a visit is the enchanting Moon-Viewing Garden. It exhibits East Asian plants in a setting that, unlike that of the Japanese Tea Garden (*see p148–9*), is naturalistic rather than formal. Both medicinal and culinary plants grow in the Garden of Fragrance, which is designed for blind plant-lovers. Here the emphasis is on the senses of taste, touch, and smell, and the plants are identified in Braille. Another area is planted with indigenous California redwood trees, with a small stream winding through. This re-creates the flora and atmosphere of a northern California coastal forest. There is also a New World Cloud Forest, with flora from the mountains of

Moon-watching pavilion on Stow Lake

Queen Wilhelmina Tulip Garden and the Dutch Windmill

⓫ Polo Fields

John F. Kennedy Drive, Golden Gate Park. **Map** 7 C2. 🚌 5, 29.

You are increasingly likely to see joggers and soccer teams rather than polo ponies using the Polo Fields stadium in the more open western half of Golden Gate Park. Horses, on which to explore the park's equestrian trails and the Bercut Equitation Field, are available by the hour at the adjacent riding stables. For anglers, there is a fly-casting pool nearby.

To the east of the stadium, in the green expanse of Old Speedway Meadows, many celebrations were held during the late 1960s, including some notable rock concerts. The Grateful Dead and Jefferson Airplane, among others, played here. Here, in the spring of 1967, thousands attended a huge "Be-in," one of many events that led to the "Summer of Love" *(see p34)*.

⓬ Buffalo Paddock

John F. Kennedy Drive, Golden Gate Park. **Map** 7 C2. 🚌 5, 29.

The shaggy buffalo that graze in this paddock are the largest of North American land animals. With its short horns and humped back, the buffalo is the symbol of the American plains and is more properly known as the American bison. This paddock was opened in 1892, at a time when the buffalo was on the verge of extinction. In 1902

William Cody, alias "Buffalo Bill," traded one of his bulls for one from the Golden Gate Park herd. Both parties thought that they had rid themselves of an aggressive beast, but Cody's newly purchased bull jumped a high fence once back at his encampment and escaped. According to one newspaper of the day, the *San Francisco Call*, it took a total of 80 men to recapture it.

⓭ Queen Wilhelmina Tulip Garden

Map 7 A2. 🚌 5, 18, 31, 31AX. Windmill ♿

The Dutch windmill was built near the northwest corner of Golden Gate Park in 1903. Its original purpose was to pump water from an underground source for irrigating the park, but now it is

no longer in use. Its companion, the Murphy Windmill, was erected in the park's southwest corner in 1905. The garden was named after the Dutch Queen Wilhelmina, and tulip bulbs are donated each year by the Dutch Bulb Growers' Association.

⓮ Ocean Beach

Map 7 A1–5. 🚌 5, 7X, 18, 31, 31AX, 48. 🚋 L, N.

Most of San Francisco's western boundary is defined by this broad sweep of sand. Though sublime when viewed from Cliff House or Sutro Heights, the beach is dangerous for swimming because of its icy waters and a strong undertow. Surfers in wet suits are a common sight, but there is often a stiff wind, or fog. On rare hot days, it is also a popular spot for sunbathers and picnickers.

⓯ Seal Rocks

Map 7 A1. Not accessible to visitors. View from Ocean Beach, Cliff House, or Sutro Heights Park. 🚌 18, 38.

Bring binoculars to watch the sea lions and birds in their natural setting. At night, from the beach or Cliff House promenade, the barking of the sea lions is both reassuring and eerie, especially when it is foggy. On a clear day you can see the Farallon Islands 32 miles (51 km) off the coast. These are also inhabited by sea lions and contain a rookery that has been protected by the state since 1907.

Looking out toward Seal Rocks from Ocean Beach

⓰ Legion of Honor

Inspired by the Palais de la Légion d'Honneur in Paris, Alma de Bretteville Spreckels built this museum in the 1920s to promote French art in California and to commemorate the state's casualties in World War I. Designed by the architect George Applegarth, it contains European art from the last eight centuries, with paintings by Monet, Rubens, and Rembrandt, as well as over 70 sculptures by Rodin. The Achenbach Foundation, a famous collection of graphic works, is also part of the gallery.

★ **The Thinker**
This original bronze casting of Rodin's *Le Penseur* (1904) is in the colonnaded Court of Honor.

★ **Waterlilies**
Claude Monet's famous work (c.1914–17) is one of a series depicting his lily pond.

Florence Gould Theater

St. Wenceslaus
Figurine, made around 1732, after a model by Johann Gottlieb Kirchner.

Stairs down from first floor

Gallery Guide

The museum's permanent collection is displayed in 19 galleries on the first floor. Beginning at the left of the entrance, works are arranged chronologically from the medieval period to the 20th century. Current exhibitions are on the lower level.

Key to Floor Plan

- ■ Permanent displays
- ■ Achenbach Foundation Library
- ■ Porcelain gallery
- ■ Theater storage
- ☐ Temporary displays
- ☐ Non-exhibition space

Old Woman
Georges de la Tour
painted this study
in about 1618.

Entrance

The Impresario
In this portrait (c.1877), artist
Edgar Degas emphasizes the
subject's size by making him
appear too large for the frame.

Lincoln Park Golf Course with views of the Golden Gate Bridge

⑰ Lincoln Park

Map 1 B5. 🚌 1, 1AX, 18, 38.

This splendid park, located
above the Golden Gate Park,
is the setting for the Legion of
Honor. The land was originally
allocated to Golden Gate
Cemetery, where graves were
segregated according to the
nationality of their occupants.
When these graves were
cleared in the first decade of
the 20th century, the park was
established and landscaped
by John McLaren (see p148).

The park now boasts an
18-hole golf course and scenic
walks. City views from the
hilltop course are superb.

⑱ Land's End

Map 1 B5. 🚌 1, 1AX, 18, 38.

A rugged seascape of rock,
cliff, and matted cypress woods,
Land's End is the wildest part
of San Francisco. It is reached
by foot along the Coastal Trail,
which can be accessed by stairs
from the Legion of Honor, or
from the Point Lobos parking
area near Sutro Heights Park.
The Coastal Trail is safe, ending
in a spectacular viewing point
overlooking the Golden Gate.
Do not leave the trail. Those
who do risk being stranded by
incoming tides or swept away
by high waves. Call the National
Parks Service Visitors Center
(tel: 556-8642) for tide information. Mile Rock Lighthouse
can be seen offshore from here.

⑲ Cliff House

1090 Point Lobos. **Map** 7 A1.
Tel 386-3330 (Visitor Center). 🚌 38AX.
Open daily. Camera Obscura:
Tel 750-0415. **Open** 11am–5pm daily.
📷 ♿ 🏛 🎬 W **cliffhouse.com**
W **giantcamera.com**

Built in 1909, the present
building, which was renovated
in 2004, is the third on this site.
Its predecessor, an elaborate
eight-story Gothic structure
that burned down in 1907,
was built by the flamboyant
entrepreneur Adolph Sutro.
His estate on the hill overlooking Cliff House is now
Sutro Heights Park. There are
several restaurants on the upper
levels, live jazz on Friday nights,
and three observation decks
with panoramic views. A
camera obscura is located
on the lower level.

The cliffs of Land's End and Mile Rock
Lighthouse offshore

FARTHER AFIELD

San Francisco is the smallest in size of the seven counties that encircle the bay. To the north of Golden Gate Bridge, Marin County has a wild, windswept coastline, forests of redwoods, and Mount Tamalpais, which offers magnificent views of the Bay Area. Marin's settlements, such as Sausalito and Tiburon, have retained their village atmosphere, and the county is the perfect escape for visitors who want an afternoon away from the metropolis.

In the East Bay, popular destinations are the Museum of California, Jack London Square and hip restaurants of Oakland, and the famous university, Gourmet Ghetto and botanical gardens of Berkley. Near the southwest corner of the city, San Francisco Zoo has thousands of exotic, endangered, or rescued species. Beyond the city to the south lies the beach town of Pacifica and suburbs stretching down to Silicon Valley.

Sights at a Glance

Museums and Galleries
13 Lawrence Hall of Science
16 Magnes Collection of Jewish Art and Life
23 Oakland Museum of California pp168–9

Parks and Gardens
1 San Francisco Zoo and Gardens
4 Muir Woods and Beach
5 Mount Tamalpais
8 Angel Island
9 Tilden Park
14 University Botanical Garden

Churches and Temples
19 Mormon Temple

Shops, Markets, and Restaurants
10 Fourth Street
11 Gourmet Ghetto
15 Telegraph Avenue
18 Rockridge

22 Jack London Square
25 Oakland Chinatown

Historic Streets and Buildings
12 University of California at Berkeley
17 Claremont Resort and Spa
20 Bay Bridge
24 Old Oakland

Historic Towns
6 Sausalito
7 Tiburon

Lakes
21 Lake Merritt

Beaches
2 Point Reyes National Seashore
3 Stinson Beach

Key
▨ Main sightseeing areas
☐ Urban areas
═ Freeway
━ Major road
═ Minor road

0 kilometers   10

0 miles   10

◀ Sunlight shining through the trees, Muir Woods

For keys to symbols see back flap

Orangutan at San Francisco Zoo and Gardens

❶ San Francisco Zoo and Gardens

Sloat Blvd and 45th Ave.
Tel 753-7080. 🚌 18, 23, 28, 57.
🚃 L. **Open** 10am–5pm daily.
🅿 (free first Wed of every month for SF residents.) **W** sfzoo.org

San Francisco Zoo is at the far southwest corner of the city, between the Pacific Ocean and Lake Merced. The complex houses more than 2,000 species of birds and mammals, among which 30 are considered to be endangered, including snow leopards, a Bengal tiger, and a jaguar. At the innovative Primate Discovery Center there are 15 different species of primates, including monkeys, langurs, and macaques.

One of the zoo's highlights is the Koala Crossing, which is designed like an Australian outback station. Grizzly Gulch features an expansive habitat where large bears can romp, play, and explore. The Gorilla Preserve is one of the world's largest naturalistic exhibits.

Dairy farm at picturesque Point Reyes

At 2pm every day except Monday, the big cats are fed at the Lion House. Nearby is the Children's Zoo, where animals can be petted.

❷ Point Reyes National Seashore

US Highway 1 to Olema; once past town, follow signs for Point Reyes National Seashore. 🚌 Golden Gate Transit buses 70 & 101 to San Rafael Center, then West Marin Stage 68.

Point Reyes peninsula is wild and windswept, and a haven for wildlife, including a herd of tule elk. There are cattle and dairy ranches, and three small towns: Olema, Point Reyes Station, and Inverness.

The peninsula is due west of the San Andreas Fault, which caused the 1906 earthquake *(see pp30–31)*. A displaced fence on the Earthquake Trail near Bear Valley Visitor Center shows how the Fault caused the peninsula to move a full 20 ft (6 m) north of the mainland.

In 1579 the British explorer Sir Francis Drake is said to have landed in Drake's Bay *(see p24)*, named the land Nova Albion, and claimed it for England.

The Visitor Center has tide tables and trail maps. From December to mid-March, whales can be seen offshore.

❸ Stinson Beach

US 101 N to Highway 1, continue to Stinson Beach. Stinson Beach Park: **Tel** 868-0942. 🚌 Golden Gate Transit bus 70, then West Marin Stage 61. **Open** 7am–one hour after sunset daily.

Since the early days of the 20th century this has been a popular vacation spot; the first visitors came on ferries from San Francisco and were met by horse-drawn carriages. Stinson remains the preferred swimming beach for the whole area. It is a stretch of soft white sand, where surfers mingle with swimmers and sunbathers. The village nearby has good bookstores, a few restaurants, and a small grocery store.

Giant redwoods in Muir Woods

❹ Muir Woods and Beach

US 101 N, exit for Highway 1; then either turn onto Panoramic Highway and follow signs to Muir Woods, or stay on Highway 1 to Muir Beach turnoff. No public transportation. **Tel** Gray Line Tours 401-1860.

Nestling at the foot of Mount Tamalpais is Muir Woods National Monument, one of the few remaining stands of first-growth coast redwoods. These giant trees (the oldest is at least 1,000 years old) once covered the coastal area of California. The woods were named in honor of John Muir, a 19th-century naturalist who was one of the first to

The attractive main street of Tiburon

persuade Americans of the need for conservation.

Redwood Creek bubbles out of Muir Woods and makes its way down to the sea at Muir Beach, a wide expanse of sand popular with beachcombers and picnickers. The road to the beach passes the Pelican Inn. This 16th-century-style English inn is extremely proud of its English menu, and its welcoming hospitality.

The beach is likely to be crowded on weekends, but visitors who are prepared to walk a mile or more are usually rewarded with solitude.

❺ Mount Tamalpais

US 101 N, exit for Highway 1, turn on to Panoramic Highway. Mount Tamalpais State Park: **Tel** 388-2070. 🚌 Golden Gate Transit bus 70 to Marin City, then West Marin Stage 61. **Open** 7am–sunset. Mountain Theater East Ridgecrest: performances May & Jun: 2pm Sun except Memorial Day. Reservations: **Tel** 383-1100. Ⓦ **mountainplay.org**

Mount Tamalpais State Park is a wilderness nature preserve with trails that wind through redwoods and alongside creeks. There are picnic areas, campsites, and meadows for kite flying. Mount Tamalpais, at 2,571 ft (784 m), is one of the highest peaks in the Bay Area; the rough tracks gave rise to the invention of the mountain bike. Near the summit, the Mountain Theater is a natural amphitheater where musicals and plays are performed.

❻ Sausalito

US 101 N, first exit after Golden Gate Bridge, to Bridgeway. 🚌 Golden Gate Transit buses 10, 70, 80. 🚢 from Ferry Building or Pier 43½. Bay Model Visitor Center: **Tel** 332-3871. **Open** 9am–4pm Tue–Sat. **Closed** Jul 4 & public hols.

In this small town that was once a fishing community, Victorian bungalows cling to steep hills rising from the bay. Parallel to the waterfront, Bridgeway Avenue serves as a promenade for the weekend crowds that come to patronize the restaurants and boutiques and enjoy the views. Ship's Store offers an eclectic array of vintage maps, knick knacks, and local fishermen stories. At 2100 Bridgeway, the Bay Model simulates the movement of the bay's tides and currents.

Floating homes in Sausalito

❼ Tiburon

US 101 N, Tiburon Blvd exit. 🚌 Golden Gate Transit bus 8. 🚢 from Ferry Building or Pier 43.

The main street in this chic waterfront town is lined with shops and restaurants housed in "arks." These are turn-of-the-century houseboats that have been pulled ashore, lined up, and refurbished. They now stand in what is called "Ark Row."

Less hectic than Sausalito, Tiburon is a good town for walking, with parks along the scenic waterfront that offer a place for contemplation.

Angel Island and the waterfront town of Tiburon

❽ Angel Island

🚢 from Pier 41 and Tiburon. **Tel** State Park 435-3972. Ⓦ **angelisland.org**

Angel Island is reached by ferry from Tiburon and San Francisco. Boats dock at Ayala Cove with its sweeping lawn and picnic tables. Hiking trails loop the wooded island, rising to 776 ft (237 m) above sea level, and past an old military garrison that once housed Asian immigrants. During World War II, prisoners of war were detained here. No motor vehicles are allowed here, except for a few park service vans. Most visitors prefer to cycle or walk on the island.

Berkeley

Carousel in Tilden Park

❾ Tilden Park

Tel (510) 544-2747. 🚇 Downtown Berkeley, then AC Transit 67 bus. Park: **Open** 5am– 10pm daily. Steam trains: **Tel** (510) 548-6100. **Open** summer: 11am–5pm daily; winter: 11am–6pm Sat & Sun. Carousel: **Tel** (510) 559-1004. **Open** 11am–5pm daily in summer. 🅿 🚻 Botanical Garden: **Tel** (510) 643-2755. **Open** 9am–5pm daily (Jun–Sep: to 5:30pm). ♿ limited. 🌐 **ebparks.org/parks/tilden.html**

Though preserved for the most part in a natural wild condition, Tilden Park offers a variety of attractions. It is noted for the enchantingly landscaped Botanical Garden, specializing in California plants. Visitors can enjoy a leisurely stroll from alpine meadows to desert cactus gardens by way of a lovely redwood glen, and there are also guided nature walks. If you have children, don't miss the carousel, the miniature farmyard, and the model steam train.

❿ Fourth Street

🚌 AC Transit Z. 🚇 Ashby, then AC Transit 51B, Z bus.

This gentrified enclave north of University Avenue is characteristic of Berkeley's climate of fine craftsmanship and exquisite taste. Here you can buy everything from handmade paper, stained-glass windows, and furniture, to organically grown lettuce and designer garden tools. There is also a handful of renowned restaurants *(see p229)*.

⓫ Gourmet Ghetto

Upper Shattuck Ave. 🚇 Downtown Berkeley, then AC Transit 7, 18, 67 bus. 🌐 **gourmetghetto.org**

This north Berkeley neighborhood acquired fame as a gourmet's ghetto when Alice Waters opened Chez Panisse here in 1971. The restaurant is acclaimed for its use of fresh local ingredients in a French-inspired style that gave rise to what is known as California cuisine. In its original house on Shattuck Avenue, Chez Panisse has influenced many worthy imitators. There are also many specialty markets and coffeehouses in the surrounding neighborhood – hence its salubrious nickname.

⓬ University of California at Berkeley

Sather Tower, built in 1914

Tel (510) 642-6000. 🚇 Downtown Berkeley. 🚌 AC Transit 1, 12, 18, 25, 49, 51B, 52, 65, 67, F. Hearst Museum of Anthropology: **Tel** (510) 642-3682. **Open** 11am–5pm Sun, Wed–Fri (to 8pm Thu); 10am–6pm Sat. Berkeley Art Museum: **Tel** (510) 642-0808. **Open** 11am–7pm Wed–Sun (to 9pm Fri & Sat). **Closed** public hols. ♿ ♿ 🅿 🚻 🌐 **berkeley.edu**

Some would argue that UC Berkeley's reputation for countercultural movements sometimes eclipses its reputation for academic excellence. Yet, it remains one of the most prestigious universities in the world.

Founded as a utopian "Athens of the Pacific" in 1868, Berkeley has more than 10 Nobel Laureates among its fellows and staff.

The campus *(see pp178–9)* was laid out by Frederick Law Olmsted on the twin forks of Strawberry Creek; changes by San Francisco architect David Farquharson were later adopted. Today there are over 30,000 students and a wide range of museums, cultural amenities, and buildings of note. These include the Berkeley Art Museum *(see p40)*, the Hearst Museum of Anthropology, and Sather Tower, also known as the Campanile.

⓭ Lawrence Hall of Science

Centennial Drive, Berkeley. **Tel** (510) 642-5132. 🚇 Downtown Berkeley, then AC Transit 65 bus. 🚌 from Mining Circle, UC Berkeley (except Sat, Sun). **Open** 10am–5pm Wed–Sun. **Closed** public hols. ♿ 🅿 🏠 🚻 🌐 **lawrencehall ofscience.org**

At this fascinating museum, workshops and classes make science fun. Hands-on exhibits encourage younger visitors to study the effects of mirrors on lasers or manipulate a hologram. They can also plot stars in the planetarium, build a dinosaur skeleton, calculate odds by rolling dice, or feed a snake. Along with a resident mechanical dinosaur are changing exhibitions, popular with families and children. The stunning view from the outdoor plaza includes much of the northern Bay Area, as far west as the Farallon Islands. By night, the lights around the bay are an extraordinary sight.

The fountain outside the Lawrence Hall of Science

⓮ University Botanical Garden

200 Centennial Dr, Berkeley. **Tel** (510) 643-2755. 🚌 from Mining Circle, UC Berkeley Hills (except Sat, Sun & hols). **Open** 9am–5pm daily. **Closed** public hols & first Tue of month. 🅿 (free first Thu of month.) ♿ limited. 📷

More than 12,000 species from all over the world thrive at Berkeley's Strawberry Canyon. Collections are arranged in thematic gardens linked by paths. Particularly noteworthy are the Asian, African, South American, European, and California gardens. The Chinese medicinal herb garden, orchid display, cactus garden, and the carnivorous plants are also well worth a visit.

⓯ Telegraph Avenue

🚇 Downtown Berkeley. 🚌 AC Transit 1, 1R, 800.

From Downtown Oakland to UC Berkeley, this is the most stimulating street in the East Bay. The blocks near the UC Berkeley have one of the highest concentrations of bookstores in the country, in addition to the coffee houses and eateries. This district was the center of student protest in the 1960s. Today it swarms with students from dawn to dusk, along with street vendors, musicians, protesters, and eccentrics.

⓰ Magnes Collection of Jewish Art and Life

Bancroft Library, University of CA Berkeley, 2121 Allston Way, Berkeley. **Tel** (510) 643-2526. 🚇 Downtown Berkeley, 🚌 AC Transit 1, 12, 18, 25, 49, 51B, 52, 65, 67, F. **Open** 11am–4pm Tue–Fri, events only on Sat & Sun. **Closed** Jewish and federal hols. 📷 ♿ arrange in advance. 🎧 by arrangement. 🌐 **magnes.org**

This is one of California's largest collection of historical artifacts pertaining to Jewish culture, from ancient times to today. Among them are fine art

Jewish ceremonial dress, Magnes Collection of Jewish Art and Life

treasures from Europe and India, paintings by Marc Chagall and Max Liebermann, and Nazi Germany mementos, such as a burned Torah scroll rescued from a synagogue. Lectures, films, and traveling exhibits periodically enliven the halls. The Blumenthal Library has permanent resources for scholars.

⓱ Claremont Resort and Spa

41 Tunnel Rd (Ashby & Domingo Aves), Berkeley. **Tel** (510) 843-3000. 🚇 Rockridge, then AC Transit E, 49 bus. ♿ 📷 ✒ 🌐 **claremontresort.com**

The Berkeley Hills form a backdrop to this half-timbered fairytale castle. Construction began in 1906, and ended in 1915. In the early years the hotel failed to prosper, due partly to a law that forbade the sale of alcohol within a 1-mile (1.6-km) radius of the Berkeley university campus. An enterprising student actually measured the distance in 1937, and found that the radius line passed through the *center* of the building. This revelation led to the founding of the Terrace Bar, which is now known as The Paragon, beyond the radius line.

As well as being one of the Bay Area's plushest hotels, this is a good place to have a drink and enjoy the views.

View of the Claremont Resort and Spa at Berkeley

Central ziggurat of the Mormon Temple

Oakland

⑱ Rockridge

🚇 Rockridge.

A leafy residential area with large houses and flower gardens, Rockridge also attracts shoppers to College Avenue. The streets are lined with posh markets, boutiques, and restaurants with al fresco dining.

⑲ Mormon Temple

4770 Lincoln Ave, Oakland.
Tel (510) 531-1475 (Visitor Center).
🚍 Fruitvale, then AC Transit 54 bus.
Open 9am–9pm daily. Temple: call the Visitor Center for times.
📵 (except Visitor Center.)
♿ 🎥 of Visitor Center.

Designed in 1963 and built on a hilltop, this is one of only two Mormon temples in

Northern California. Its full name is the Oakland Temple of the Church of Jesus Christ of the Latter Day Saints. At night the temple is floodlit and can be seen from Oakland and San Francisco. The central ziggurat is surrounded by four shorter towers, all terraced and clad with white granite and capped by glistening golden pyramids.

From the temple there are magnificent views over the entire Bay Area. The Visitor Center offers guided tours by missionaries, who explain the tenets of the faith with a series of multimedia presentations.

⑳ Bay Bridge

Map 6 E4.

The compound, high-level San Francisco–Oakland Bay Bridge was designed by Charles H. Purcell. It has two distinct structures, joining at Yerba Buena Island in the middle of the Bay, and reaches 4.5 miles (7.2 km) from shore to shore. Its completion in 1936 heralded the end of the age of ferryboats on San Francisco Bay by linking the peninsular city at Rincon

Hill to the Oakland "mainland" with road and rail. The tracks were removed in the 1950s, leaving the bridge for use by more than 250,000 vehicles

Construction of the east span of the Bay Bridge

㉑ Lake Merritt

🚇 Lake Merritt or 19th Street.

Formed when a saltwater tidal estuary was dredged, embanked, and partly dammed, Lake Merritt and its surrounding park form an oasis of rich blue and green in the urban heart of Oakland. Designated in 1870 as the first state game refuge in the United States, Lake Merritt still attracts migrating flocks of birds. Rowers can rent boats from two boathouses on the west and north shores, and joggers and bicyclists can circle the lake on a 3 mile (5 km) path. The north shore at Lakeside Park has flower gardens, an aviary, and a

Lake Merritt, Oakland

a day. Five traffic lanes wide, it has two levels: westbound traffic into San Francisco uses the top deck; eastbound to Oakland, the lower.

The eastern cantilever section is raised on more than 20 piers. It climbs up from the toll plaza causeway in Oakland to 191 ft (58 m) above the bay at Yerba Buena Island. In 1989 a 50 ft (15 m) segment of

10 miles (16 km) of cable holding up the bridge

2,310 ft (704 m)

The West Bay Crossing section of Bay Bridge

Children's Fairyland where young visitors can enjoy pony rides, puppet shows, and nursery rhyme scenes.

㉒ Jack London Square

🚋 to Oakland. 🚇 12th Street, then AC Transit 31, 58, 72, 88 bus.

Jack London, author of *The Call of the Wild* and *White Fang*, grew up in Oakland in the 1880s, and was a frequent visitor to the Oakland Estuary waterfront. You can drive or catch the ferry to its cheerful, bright promenade of shops and restaurants, which have outdoor tables in fine weather. There are also pleasure boats offering trips along the estuary.

Little of the waterfront that London knew remains. However, the writer's footsteps can be traced to Heinold's First and Last Chance Saloon, which has now sunken with age into the street. The Yukon cabin that was purportedly occupied by London during the Gold Rush of 1898 has also been erected at the dockside.

㉓ Oakland Museum of California

See pp168–9.

The nautical-themed Waterfront Hotel at Jack London Square

㉔ Old Oakland

🚇 12th Street. Farmers' Market:
Tel (510) 238-1630. **Open** 8am–2pm
Fri. 🌐 old-oakland.com

Also known as Victorian Row, these two square blocks of wood and brick commercial buildings were erected between the 1860s and 1880s, but they were thoroughly renovated in the 1980s and now contain an array of shops, restaurants, and art galleries. Fridays bring crowds of shoppers to the Farmers' Market, where stalls sell fresh produce and prepared foods. By night, the crowds move to the Pacific Coast Brewing Company on Washington Street. Don't miss 103-year-old Rattos, at 827 Washington Street, an Italian delicatessen famed for

its Friday and Saturday night "Pasta Operas," when the management and visiting singers serenade the clientele.

㉕ Oakland Chinatown

🚇 12th Street or Lake Merritt.

The bay area's second-largest Chinatown should perhaps be called "Asiatown." Its Cantonese majority is augmented by immigrants from Korea, Vietnam, and other parts of Southeast Asia. The neighborhood receives far fewer tourists than San Francisco's Chinatown. Its restaurants have a reputation for hearty, dependable, and reasonably priced food.

---

the bridge collapsed during the Loma Prieta earthquake *(see p21)*. The East Bay crossing was rebuilt between 2002 and 2013 to make it more earthquake resistant. The new suspension bridge features a single tower across the shipping channel, which gives way to a graceful skyway.

Boring through the island in a tunnel 76 ft (23 m) high and 58 ft (17 m) wide, the roadway emerges at the West Bay section of the bridge. Two

suspension spans join at the concrete central anchorage, which is deeper in the water than that of any other bridge.

The World's Fair (1939 to 1940) was held on Treasure Island, part of Yerba Buena Island, to celebrate the bridge's completion *(see pp32–3)*. Now this small island is home to small parks and fine residences.

Plan of the 1939–40 World's Fair on Treasure Island

Central anchorage   5-lane double-level highway   Pylons supporting both road decks

400 ft (122 m)   2,310 ft (704 m)

㉓ Oakland Museum of California

California's only museum exclusively dedicated to documenting the state's art, history, and natural sciences opened in 1969. The building and the handsomely terraced gardens, designed by architect Kevin Roche and landscape architect Dan Kiley respectively, are features that mark this museum as an important architectural icon. The Natural Sciences Gallery showcases more than 2,000 Californian species. The Gallery of California History has a large collection of Californian artifacts, while the Gallery of California Art boasts early oil paintings of Yosemite and San Francisco. Check the museum website for details of the latest exhibitions.

Coming to California
The Gallery of California History explores the past and present of the state.

Roof and gardens

Gallery of California Art
The modern art in this collection includes the painting *Ocean Park No: 107* (1978) by Richard Diebenkorn.

The Great Hall
is used for special changing exhibitions.

Level 2

Level 3

Iconic Exhibits
This customized Harley-Davidson is just one of the arresting exhibits on display in the Gallery of California Art.

Key to the Oakland Museum Levels

☐ Gallery of California Art   ☐ Gallery of California History
☐ Gallery of California Natural Sciences

VISITORS' CHECKLIST

Practical Information
1000 Oak St, Oakland.
Tel (510) 318-8400.
Open 11am–5pm Wed & Thu,
11am–10pm Fri, 10am–6pm
Sat & Sun. **Closed** Jan 1, Jul 4,
Thanksgiving, Dec 25. P 🅿️
(free 1st Sun.) 🏛️ 🖼️ 🅿️ ♿
W **museumca.org**

Transport
🚌 Lake Merritt

California Mud Wagon
Developed for rural life
during the mid-19th
century, this multi-
purpose vehicle could
be converted easily
from a field wagon
to a stylish carriage.

Forces of Change
Dioramas present a variety
of Californian perspectives
on the tumultuous social
and political change of the
1960s and 1970s.

Level 1

Sculpture Gardens
host the popular Friday
Nights @ OMCA from
5 to 9pm every Friday,
with food trucks,
cocktails and half-
price admission.

Museum Guide

*The main entrance to the museum
is on Oak Street. Ticketing is on
Level 2, where you will also find the
Gallery of California History,
the Blue Oak café, the OMCA Store,
and the Great Hall, for special
exhibitions. The Gallery of
California Art is on Level 3.*

★ Gallery of Natural Sciences
Explore California's conservation
with more than 2,000 different
native species and 7
major habitats.

Day Trips South of the City

South of San Francisco Bay, Santa Clara County became famous in the late 1960s for its Silicon Valley. It is well worth exploring on day trips. San José has a variety of fascinating museums, while Filoli estate offers a mansion and garden tour. Stanford University and Pescadero are interesting for their fine architecture and history.

The Winchester Mystery House

Sights at a Glance

Museums
1 The Winchester Mystery House
2 Rosicrucian Egyptian Museum and Planetarium
3 Tech Museum of Innovation
4 Children's Discovery Museum
5 History Park at Kelley Park
8 Stanford University

Historic Places
6 Filoli   7 Pescadero

Key
- Central San Francisco
- Urban area
- Freeway
- Major road
- Minor road
- Railroad line

1 The Winchester Mystery House

525 South Winchester Blvd, between Stevens Creek Blvd and I-280, San José. **Tel** (408) 247-2101. Caltrain to San Jose Diridon Station, then Santa Clara Transportation Agency bus 323. **Open** 9am–7pm daily. **Closed** Dec 25. required. winchestermysteryhouse.com

In 1884 Sarah Winchester, heiress of the rifle fortune, was grieving over the loss of her child and husband. She consulted a medium who advised her to build a house that would never be completed, in order to silence the evil spirits that haunted her. She employed carpenters for 38 years and built 160 rooms set in beautiful gardens. The stairways that lead nowhere and windows set into the floor are just a few of the oddities within. Book a Flashlight Tour to see it at its creepiest.

Forecourt of the Rosicrucian Egyptian Museum

2 Rosicrucian Egyptian Museum and Planetarium

1660 Park Ave, San José. **Tel** (408) 947-3635. Caltrain to Santa Clara Station, then Santa Clara Transportation Agency bus 22. **Open** 9am–5pm Wed–Fri, 10am–6pm Sat & Sun. **Closed** public holidays. egyptianmuseum.org

Inspired by the Temple of Amon at Karnak, Egypt, this museum houses ancient Egyptian, Babylonian, Assyrian, and Sumerian artifacts. Funerary boats and models, human and animal mummies, Coptic textiles, pottery, jewelry, and a full-size tomb are on display.

3 The Tech Museum of Innovation

201 South Market St (at Park Ave), San José. **Tel** (408) 294-8324. Fremont, then Santa Clara Transportation Agency bus 181. **Open** 10am–5pm daily. **Closed** Dec 25. thetech.org

The Tech is a colorful technological museum divided into several themed galleries, including life sciences, energy, and communication. Many of the exhibits have a "hands-on" element, such as making your own film, or discovering the latest tricks in animation. There is also an Imax® Dome Theater, which is open for screenings on Friday and Saturday nights.

❹ Children's Discovery Museum

180 Woz Way, San José. **Tel** (408) 298-5437. 🚉 Fremont, then Santa Clara Transportation Agency bus 181. **Open** 10am–5pm Tue–Sat, noon–5pm Sun. 🎁 ♿ 🅦 cdm.org

A short walk leads from San José Convention Center to this museum, where children can play in a real red fire engine or in an ambulance with flashing lights. The more adventurous can crawl through a multi-level maze to experience 3-D space or step into dedicated environments to explore the phenomenon of rhythm. At the Waterways exhibit, children can discover the special properties of water by creating unique fountains from magnetic half-pipes.

❺ History Park at Kelley Park

1650 Senter Rd, San José. **Tel** (408) 287-2290. 🚃 Caltrain to Tamien Station, then Santa Clara Transportation Agency bus 25t. **Open** noon–5pm Mon–Fri; 11am–5pm Sat & Sun. **Closed** major public holidays. 🎁 🅦 historysanjose.org

This charming museum in Kelley Park re-creates San José as it was in the early 20th century. More than 21 original houses and businesses have been restored and set around a town square. They include a fire station, an ice-cream parlor with

A popular exhibit in the Children's Discovery Museum

working soda fountain, a gas station, and a historic trolley that travels around the grounds.

❻ Filoli

86 Cañada Rd, near Edgewood Rd, Woodside. **Tel** (650) 364-8300. 🎁 **Open** 10am–5pm Tue–Sun (last admission 4:30pm). **Closed** federal hols. 🅦 filoli.org

The lavish 43-room Filoli mansion was built in 1915 for William Bourne II, owner of the Empire Gold Mine. Gold from the mine was used in its opulent decoration. The elegant house is surrounded by a large garden and an estate where guided nature walks can be arranged. "Filoli" is an acronym for "Fight, love, live," which refers to Bourne's love for the Irish and their struggle.

❼ Pescadero

🚌 Daly City, then SamTrans routes 17, IC, or IL to Half Moon Bay, then 96C (weekdays only).

This quaint village with its many two-story wooden buildings has antique stores, gift shops, and one of the southern peninsula's best restaurants, Duarte's Tavern. Families will enjoy Swanton Berry Farm which has a barn-yard and "pick your own" fruit. Pigeon Point Lighthouse lies 8 miles (12 km) to the south.

❽ Stanford University

Palo Alto. **Tel** (650) 723-2560. 🚃 Caltrain to Palo Alto station. 🎁 phone for details. 🅦 stanford.edu

One of the country's most prestigious private universities, with 15,000 students, Stanford was built by railroad mogul Leland Stanford (see p104) in memory of his son, and opened in 1891. The heart of the campus is the Main Quad, in Romanesque style with some Mission architecture characteristics. Main landmarks are the Hoover Tower, the Memorial Church, and the Stanford University Museum of Art, where you can see the Golden Spike that completed the trans-continental railroad in 1869. The Museum of Art owns an impressive collection of Rodins.

Memorial Church at Stanford University, Palo Alto

FIVE GUIDED WALKS

These five walks take in much of the Bay Area's intriguing cultural and geographical diversity and sweeping views. The Aquatic Park walk along the northern waterfront covers the area from Hyde Street Pier *(see p87)*, with its historic sailing ships and echoes of the past, to Fort Mason Center *(see pp74–5)*, a military relic transformed into a lively community with theaters, museums, and arts activities. Less than an hour's drive away, the Marin Headlands walk is into another world, of rolling hills with cliffs

that drop dramatically into the sea. The third walk moves to Berkeley *(see pp164–5)* in the East Bay to explore the groves of academe. The city walk through Russian Hill takes you through a warren of hidden parks and gardens, or take in the atmosphere on a walk around the SoMa District, with its trendy galleries, shops, cafés, and glitzy hotels. In addition to these walks, each of the eight areas of San Francisco described in the *Area by Area* section of this book has a walk on its *Street-by-Street* map.

California Hall
(pp178–9)

University of California Campus, Berkeley *(pp178–9)*

Marin Headlands
(pp176–7)

Aquatic Park *(pp174–5)*

SoMa
(pp180–81)

Russian Hill
(pp182–3)

Cable car traveling on Hyde Street *(pp174–5)*

0 kilometers 5

0 miles 3

Key

• • • Walk Route

◀ *Balclutha*, built in 1886, at Hyde Street Pier

A 90-Minute Walk around Aquatic Park

Side by side on San Francisco's northern waterfront, Aquatic Park and Fort Mason offer some fascinating glimpses into the city's past, especially its colorful history as a seaport. There are no cars here, just walkers, cyclists, and skaters sharing lushly overgrown paths. The route winds past historic ships moored in the bay, Depression-era swim clubs, Gold Rush cottages, and military installations dating from Spanish colonial times to World War II. You can swim if you don't mind the chilly bay water, fish for crabs, paddle off a small beach, or just stop to admire the view and picnic in one of the many grassy spots. For more details see pages 74–5 and 87.

Marina Green and Fort Mason

Ships moored in Aquatic Park

Hyde Street Pier

Begin at the seaward end of Hyde Street Pier ①. Until 1938, when the opening of the Golden Gate Bridge made it obsolete, this pier was the center of activity on the city's northern waterfront. It is now part of the San Francisco Maritime National Historical Park, used as a mooring for a collection of historic ships (see p87). Among these is a handsome steam-powered ferry boat, the *Eureka* ②, built in 1890. The ship is full of old cars and ephemera from 1941, the last year it was in service. From the landward end of the pier, where there is a bookstore ③ operated by the National Park Service, walk west along the waterfront past

the Hyde Street cable-car turntable on your left. In flower-filled Victorian Park ④ street musicians perform. There is a pair of whitewashed clapboard buildings ⑤ on the sandy beach to your right, which house the South End and Dolphin swimming and rowing clubs.

Aquatic Park

Continue westward to the broad Golden Gate Promenade, popular with joggers, cyclists, and skaters. This right of way follows the old Belt Line railroad, which once ran along the Embarcadero from the wharves and warehouses of China Basin and Potrero Hill to Fort Mason and the Presidio.

On the left is a large building known as the Casino ⑥, built in 1939 as a public bathing club. Since 1951 it has been the West Coast home of the Maritime National Historical Park Visitors' Center (see p87), which has been renovated and expanded. Look out for the exhibit showcasing the city's historic waterfront.

West of the Casino is a topiary sign spelling out "Aquatic Park." Behind this are red-and-white plastic-roofed *bocce* ball courts. The old dock and boathouse ⑦ to your right are used on weekends by sea scouts learning seamanship. Continue along the waterfront to the

Fort Mason (13)
Center

Great
Meado

Great
Meado

LAGUNA STREET

(12)

BAY STREE

Boat building in progress on Hyde Street Pier ①

curving concrete pier ⑧ that marks the western end of Aquatic Park. People fish here at all hours, mostly for crabs. The Mission-style building at

Key

••• Walk route

0 meters   250
0 yards   250

The Maritime National Historical Park

Municipal Pier

⑧

AQUATIC COVE

①
Hyde Street Pier ②
③

⑤ JEFFERSON STREET
④

⑦

Aquatic Park

⑥ BEACH STREET

FRANKLIN

HYDE STREET

LARKIN STREET

Officers' Club

POLK STREET

NORTH POINT STREET

STREET

⑪

VAN NESS AVE

BAY STREET

STREET

ℹ

as homes. Follow Funston Street along the length of the hostel, and then turn right at Franklin Street. Here there are several interesting buildings, including the exclusive Fort Mason General's residence on the left. Turn right by the chapel to arrive at the headquarters of the Golden Gate National Recreation Area (GGNRA) ⑪.

The grassy knolls of Great Meadow ⑫ extend westward from here. This was where refugees from the 1906 earthquake camped until they could be rehoused. A statue of Congressman Phillip Burton, the inspiration behind the formation of the GGNRA, has been erected in the middle of the field. From the Great Meadow, take the narrow steps down the hill to Fort Mason Center (see pp74–5). Continue north toward the piers ⑬ and stop in Building D to visit the Mexican Museum, or view the Outdoor Exploratorium, which illustrates the history of the shoreline in that part of the Bay and the area's natural environment.

the foot of the pier is an emergency pumping station.

Fort Mason
West of Aquatic Park, the Golden Gate Promenade climbs upward, rounding Black Point and giving excellent views of Alcatraz and Angel Island. Above the pathway, cypress trees cover the headland, and a series of terraces ⑨ hold the

Phillip Burton in Great Meadow ⑫

remains of artillery emplacements from the late 1800s.

Follow the Golden Gate Promenade to the top of the slope, then turn left and go around to the front of the Youth Hostel ⑩. This is one of the few ornate wooden houses open to the public. Most of the buildings date from the 1850s and today serve

Tips for Walkers

Starting point: The seaward end of Hyde Street Pier.
Length: 1.5 miles (2.5 km).
Getting there: The Powell–Hyde cable car's northern terminus and turntable at Beach Street is a short walk from Hyde Street Pier. Muni bus no. 19, 28, and 49 take you to the Van Ness Avenue–Beach Street.
Stopping-off points: The Buena Vista Café, opposite the cable-car turntable, is always packed with customers who come for the good breakfasts and strong coffee (including a famous Irish Coffee). Greens restaurant (see p226) in Building A at Fort Mason Center, considered to be San Francisco's finest vegetarian restaurant, is run by disciples of Zen Buddhism. At the south end of Building C, there is the Reader's Café Bookstore featuring a Thursday poetry series.

A 90-Minute Walk through the Marin Headlands

At its northern end, the Golden Gate Bridge is anchored in the rolling green hills of the Marin Headlands. This is an unspoiled wild area of windswept ridges, sheltered valleys, and deserted beaches, once used as a military defense post and now part of the vast Golden Gate National Recreation Area. From several vantage points there are spectacular views of San Francisco and the sea and, on autumn days, you can see migrating eagles and ospreys gliding past Hawk Hill.

Schoolchildren on a trip to the Marin Headlands

③ Rodeo Beach

Visitor Center to Rodeo Beach

Before starting this walk, pause a while at the steeled Visitor Center ①, which was once the interdenominational chapel for Fort Barry. It has since been refurbished and is now a museum and information center, with a natural history bookstore that specializes in books on birds. Here you can discover the history of the Marin Headlands and see a Coast Miwok Indian shelter. The walk, which will take you around Rodeo Lagoon ②, begins at the gate on the west, ocean side, of the parking area. Take the path to the left that leads to the sea. This part of the trail is thick with trees and shrubs, including the poison oak, of which visitors should be aware. The songs of birds fill the air, and around the edges of the lagoon you will see brown pelicans, snowy egrets, and mallards. A 15-minute walk will bring you to the sandy, windblown Rodeo Beach ③, and from here you can see Bird Island ④ lying offshore to

MARIN HEADLANDS
(GOLDEN GATE NATIONAL
RECREATION AREA)

MITCHELL ROAD

⑥

⑤

Rode

②

COAST

③
Rodeo
Beach

Battery
Smith-Guthr

PACIFIC
OCEAN

④
Bird
Island

MENDELL RO

Battery
Mendel

Key

••• Walk route

② The serene Rodeo Lagoon

(7) Seal at the Marine Mammal Center

path, then turn left at the road that climbs a hill to the Marine Mammal Center (7). This was used as a missile defense site during the Cold War, but is now run by volunteers who rescue and care for sick or injured marine mammals. Sea lions and seals, including elephant seals, are examined and treated here, in specially designed pens, then put back

(1) Visitor Center

ends, a path (9) plunges down to the right into the dense shrubbery.

Take this, and then continue up the hill again, via a series of steps that will return you to the path at the end of the Visitor Center parking area. Walk across the lot and cross Field Road going up the hill to a three-story wooden building, constructed at the turn of the century. This is listed on the National Historic Registry and has been officers' headquarters, a hospital, and a missile command center. It is now the Golden Gate Hostel (10) for travelers. The Marin Headlands also offer a wide range of longer, more challenging wilderness walks. Wolf Ridge and Bobcat Trail are two popular routes to try.

Rodeo Lake

0 meters 250
0 yards 250

the south. Fishing boats may be seen bobbing out at sea, but the beach is mostly empty of people, although sometimes you might see groups of children studying the coastal ecology: educational programs are run by the Headlands Institute, based in the nearby former army barracks.

Barracks to the California Marine Mammal Center
From the beach, turn inland again as you approach the tip of the lagoon, crossing a wooden footbridge (5). Here there are barracks (6) housing various offices, among them the Headlands District Office, the Golden Gate Raptor Observatory, and an energy and resources center. Walking past the barracks, continue along the

in the sea when they have recovered. You can watch the vets at work and get a close view of the mammals, many of which are orphaned pups. There are also displays on the marine ecosystem.

Lagoon to the Golden Gate Hostel
Make your way back down the hill and return to the paved road that runs past the lagoon (8). There is a separate roadside pathway for hikers, but occasionally there may be a guard rail that you will need to climb over. Just before the road crosses a bridge, you can stop to watch the water birds. There are plenty of these to be seen in this brackish lagoon with its tall grasses. Stay on the path as you cross the bridge. Before the guard rail

Horse Trail

Bike Trail

Sign marking a trail

Tips for Walkers

Starting point: The Visitor Center at Fort Barry.
Length: 2 miles (3 km).
Getting there: San Francisco Muni bus 76X leaves from the intersection of Sutter Street and Sansome Street on Sundays and major holidays. **Tel** (415) 673-6864 (Muni). By car, drive across the Golden Gate Bridge, taking the Alexander Avenue exit. Turn under the freeway, following signs for the Headlands and Fort Barry.
Stopping-off points: Water is available, but there are no refreshment facilities in the Marin Headlands. You will need to bring your own picnic lunch, which can be enjoyed at any number of tables dotted along the trails and on the beaches.

A 90-Minute Walk around the University of California Campus in Berkeley

This walk concentrates on a distinct area of Berkeley, the campus of the University of California, allowing a stimulating glimpse into the intellectual, cultural, and social life of this vibrant university town *(see pp164–5)*.

University students outside Wheeler Hall

⑤ Esplanade near Sather Tower

the Hearst Mining Building ⑨, built by Howard in 1907. Inside are ore samples and pictures of old mining operations. Return to University Drive, turn left and out of the East Gate to the Hearst Greek Theater ⑩.

West Entrance to Sather Tower

From University Avenue ①, cross Oxford Street and follow University Drive past the Valley Life Sciences Building ②. Wellman Hall can be seen on the north fork of Strawberry Creek as you follow the road to the right, keeping California Hall ③ on your right. Turn left on the Cross Campus Road ④. Wheeler Hall lies to the right and ahead is the main campus landmark, the 307 ft- (94 m-) tall Sather Tower ⑤, commonly referred to as "The Campanile." Built by John Galen Howard in 1914, it was based on the campanile in the Piazza San Marco in Venice. Before going there, visit the Doe Library ⑥ and the A. F. Morrison Memorial Library ⑦ in the north wing. The adjacent Bancroft Library houses the plate supposedly left by Sir Francis Drake, claiming California for Queen Elizabeth I *(see p24)*. Return to Sather Tower, which is open 10am to 3:30pm Monday to Saturday and offers fine views from the top. Across the way lies South Hall ⑧, the oldest building on campus.

Hearst Mining Building to the Greek Theatre

Continuing north, pass LeConte Hall, then cross University Drive to the Mining Circle. Here is

Wellman Hall on the University of California Campus

e Cal Straw Hat Band at UC Berkeley

look at Hertz Hall ⑬, then go down the diagonal walk that passes Wurster Hall to Kroeber Hall. Here you can visit the Hearst Museum of Anthropology. Cross Bancroft Way to the Caffè Strada ⑭, and then proceed to the wildly modern Berkeley Art Museum ⑮. Continue along Bancroft Way to Telegraph Avenue ⑯, famous for the student activism of the 1960s and 1970s. The entrance to the university opposite Telegraph Avenue opens onto Sproul Plaza ⑰. Step into the

⑤ Sather Tower, a campus landmark

lower courtyard with its modern Zellerbach Hall ⑱, then pass Alumni House, noting the state-of-the-art Haas Pavilion, and turn right. Cross over the south fork of Strawberry Creek at Bay Tree Bridge, and bear left for the nature area, with its eucalyptus trees, some of the tallest in the world ⑲. The path ends near the start of the walk.

| 0 meters | | 250 |
| 0 yards | | 250 |

Key

••• Walk route

Tips for Walkers

Starting point: The West Gate at University Ave and Oxford St.
Length: 2.5 miles (4 km).
Getting there: San Francisco–Oakland Bay Bridge, Interstate 80 east, University Avenue exit. By BART, Downtown Berkeley stop.
Stopping-off points: The Caffè Strada, on Bancroft Way, is always crowded with students. A few steps down the street, in the Berkeley Art Museum, is Babette Café, which looks out on to the sculpture garden. You may want to browse in the bookstores on Telegraph Avenue, or sample food from one of the many carts at the entrance to Sproul Plaza. Here you can find everything from smoothies to Mexican and Greek food. In the lower Sproul Plaza of the University there are several cafés. Log on to **www.visitberkeley.com** for more information.

Faculty Club to the Eucalyptus Grove

Follow Gayley Road, which straddles a major earthquake fault, and turn right down the first path past Lewis Hall and Hildebrand Hall, then left over a footbridge. The path winds between a log house and the Faculty Club ⑪. This rambling, rustic building, partly designed by Bernard Maybeck, dates from 1903. Faculty Glade ⑫ in front of the club is a favorite picnic spot.

The path now swings to the right, then sharply left. Take a

⑮ *Within* (1969) by A. Lieberman at UCB Art Museum

A 90-Minute Walk around South of Market

Once a grubby warehouse district, SoMa is a model of urban revitalization. The name SoMa is derived from the contraction of "South of Market." This was once the "wrong side" of the Market Street cable-car track when Gold Rush-era immigrants worked in the factories here. Today, a four-block square area surrounding the Moscone Convention Center is packed with major art and history museums, high-rise hotels, trendy galleries, and shops. On this walk you will encounter vestiges of the city's lively past among its dazzling 21st-century architecture, as well as trendy cafés and bars.

The SoMa skyline with its mix of old and new architecture

Mission Street
Begin at St. Patrick's Church ①, a soaring brick landmark built in 1851. Notice the green open space of Yerba Buena Gardens across the street, and the variety of vintage and contemporary buildings that characterize this diverse district. Walking in a northeasterly direction will take you past the Contemporary Jewish Museum ② *(see p115)*, housed in a former power substation. The museum's breathtaking interior was designed by the architect Daniel Libeskind. Continue on to the California Historical Society ③ *(see p115)*, where the colorful story of the Golden State is told through art and photography. You might like to return here another time to delve into manuscripts in the library, or to sign up for narrated history walks. Step into the Cartoon Art Museum ④ to see exhibitions of comic book superheroes, great women cartoonists, or the work of Charles Schultz, the Peanuts creator – it depends on what is on display at the time. Stroll up to Second Street and turn left to find the Alexander Book Company ⑤, an old favorite,

that is unassuming on the outside, with three floors of treasures inside.

SFMOMA
Retrace your steps to Mission Street and walk south two blocks to Third Street. Across from Yerba Buena Gardens, admire the cylinder of the San Francisco Museum of Modern Art ⑥ *(see pp120–23)*, one of the architectural wonders of the city. The architect, Mario Botta, described the tilting skylight as

"the eye for the city." Browse in the museum store for art books, jewelry, and children's games. Plan to return for a full tour of the displays of contemporary art. On either side of SFMOMA are skyscraper hotels, the St. Regis Museum Tower and W San Francisco. At the base of the St. Regis, a turn-of-the-century building houses the Museum of the African Diaspora (MoAD), where

multimedia displays present such subjects as celebrations, slavery, art, and origins. At the sleek W Hotel, take a look into the "Living Room," the octagonal, three-story lobby that's walled with glass and flowing drapes. Here, you can rest with a drink or a coffee.

Yerba Buena Gardens to the San Francisco Mint
Cross Third Street to enter Yerba Buena Gardens ⑦ *(see p116–17)*. Take a stroll beneath the sycamores and around the flower gardens, and walk

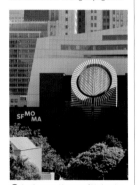
⑥ San Francisco Museum of Modern Art, a stunning work of architecture

MARKET STREET
4TH STREET
YERBA BUENA

🚇🚃 Powell Street Station

5TH STREET
STEVENSON ST
MINT STREET
JESSIE ST
MARY STREET
NATOMA STREET
HOWARD STREET
TEHAMA STREET
STEVENSON ST
MISSION STREET
MINNA STREET
NATOMA STREET
5TH STREET
⑩

Ⓜ️ Montgomery
St Station

St Regis

W San Francisco

⑦ Yerba Buena Gardens

Moscone Convention Center

0 meters 200
0 yards 200

⑩ Façade of the Old Mint on Mission Street

you around. Look for the nine-story-tall mural rising above a riot of roses, lettuce, and daisies. Now head for the Society of California Pioneers Museum ⑨ on Fourth Street, which was founded in 1850 and is now home to both a museum and library. Here you will find many fine paintings of 19th-century Yosemite National Park *(see pp202–5)*, the Sierra Nevada, and other early landscapes, featured along with Gold Rush artifacts and hundreds of daguerreotypes and photos. Turn left on Howard Street, then take a right on Fifth Street. On the corner of Mission Street, you will see the magnificent façade of the "Granite Lady," the Greek Revival-style San Francisco Mint ⑩ *(see p119)*, erected in 1869–74 to make coins from California gold and Nevada silver.

Tips for Walkers

Starting point: St. Patrick's Church on Mission Street between 3rd and 4th streets.
Distance: 0.5 mile (0.8 km).
Getting there: On BART, and on MUNI Metro lines F, J, K, L, M, N, and T exit at Powell Street Station.
Stopping-off points: Food and drink are nearly as expensive here as they are in Union Square and on the waterfront In the glitzy hotels (W, the St. Regis, and the Marriott) expect to pay $5 for a cup of coffee. Enjoy a great sandwich at The Grove in Yerba Buena or have a picnic in Yerba Buena Gardens. Alternatively, head over to the Metreon *(see pp250–51)*, which has a good range of eateries and cafés.

Key

····· Walk route

behind the Martin Luther King Memorial Waterfall to read passages from King's "I Have a Dream" speech. Leaving the gardens, walk down Third Street and turn right into Harrison Street and right again toward the intersection with Bonifacio Street, where the Alice Street Community Gardens ⑧ make for another fascinating urban experience. The proud senior and disabled people from the neighborhood who keep the patch in bloom will be glad to show

⑦ Yerba Buena Gardens, an elegant and restful space

A 90-Minute Walk around Russian Hill

A hilltop warren of parks and rare pre-earthquake architecture are the rewards for this scramble up the steep stairways and leafy alleyways of Russian Hill. Here, you will encounter few cars and fewer people as you wander among carefully preserved buildings from the city's lively and notorious past, and enjoy the dazzling views, the birdsong, and the luxuriant hillside gardens that are the pride of the neighborhood. At the end of your walk, descend to indulge in the European-style cafés and boutiques at the foot of the hill.

Russian Hill, fabulous views and pre-quake houses

Russian Hill Place

Start the walk from the corner of Jones and Vallejo streets on the whimsical, Beaux Arts balustrade ①, designed in 1915 by Willis Polk, one of the architects of the post-1906 earthquake reconstruction (see pp30–31). Before climbing the stone stairway, notice the Spanish-tile-roofed, Mission Revival-style houses, with their fanciful balconies and arched windows on either side. Then take the stairs and walk into the short alleyway of Russian Hill Place ② to see the backs of those homes and their gardens. No. 6 is a turn-of-the-century Bay Area Tradition-style house. Vallejo Street has a variety of homes and apartments built between 1888 and the 1940s.

Florence Street to Coolbrith Park

Turn right into short Florence Street ③ and, at the end, look across the rooftops to Nob Hill. Once called Snob Hill, it is sprinkled with 19th-century mansions and grand hotels – look for the towers of Grace Cathedral (see p105). No. 40, one of the oldest houses on the hill, built in 1850, is hidden within additions from later

decades. Peek through the fence to see an 8-ft- (2-m-) tall rabbit, and a contemporary mobile sculpture. Note the Pueblo Mission Revival-style homes along this street.

Back on Vallejo Street, the gems of Russian Hill are two steep-roofed, gabled houses in the Bay Area Tradition-style at Nos. 1013–19 ④. Here, leading a move away from the gingerbread-house design of the Victorian era, Polk designed a home (at 1019) in 1892 for a wealthy client (who hosted, among others, Robert Louis Stevenson and Laura Ingalls

Wilder) and, next door, his own house (at 1013), which is a shingle-sided, six-story arrangement reminiscent of the English Arts and Crafts movement. After the quake, Polk was appointed supervising architect of the 1915 Panama-Pacific International Exposition, a world fair that celebrated the building of the Panama Canal and the rebuilding of San Francisco (see p72). Below his house, he created the zigzagging, Beaux Arts-style Vallejo Street steps, known as

④ Part of the rambling Vallejo Street steps or "the ramps"

0 meters 100
0 yards 100

Key

····· Walk route

"the ramps." All along the extensive, three-part stairway are gardens overflowing with blue hydrangeas, azaleas, palms, magnolias, and overarching pines and cypress trees. There is also a bench where tired walkers can rest. At the bottom of the steps at Taylor and Vallejo, stroll across the street to enjoy the sun at tiny Coolbrith Park ⑤. From here you can see islands in the bay, North Beach, the Bay Bridge, and the lower Financial District. On July 4th, locals

At Nos. 5–17, plaster garlands drape over the doorways of this rare earthquake survivor. Turn left on Leavenworth Street, then right onto Green Street. The block between Hyde and Leavenworth streets is also called "the Paris Block" ⑦, a reference to the house at No. 1050, which is reminiscent of those in Paris. A number of buildings on the block are on the National Register of Historic Places, including the last

⑥ A local relaxing in Macondray Lane, scene of TV's *Tales of the City*

Hyde Street

Continue west on Green Street to Hyde Street where cafés and shops cluster between Jackson and Union streets ⑧. Lovers of all things French will like Cocotte (at No. 1521), the boutiques, and charming antiques shops. After browsing here, catch a bus directly from Hyde Street to various points across the city.

Tips for Walkers

Starting point: The stone stairway at Jones and Vallejo streets.
Distance: 0.75 miles (1.2 km).
Getting there: Take the Hyde–Powell cable car or the 45 Muni line to Vallejo Street and walk east two blocks.
Stopping-off points: On Hyde Street, Frascati (at 1901) caters to neighborhood regulars with a pan-European menu of paella, and coq au vin in a cozy setting. The young and the hip hang out on leather love seats in the window of Bacchus Wine & Sake Bar (at 1954).

gather here to watch the fireworks display.

Macondray Lane to Green Street

Proceed north on Taylor Street to Macondray Lane ⑥ on the left, which is accessed by a creaky stairway winding through dense vegetation. Along the two-block walkway are shingled "Edwardian" cottages, ballast stones from sailing ships, and rustic country houses set in flower gardens. This was the setting for Barbary Lane in Armistead Maupin's *Tales of the City* book and television series.

firehouse built for horse-drawn vehicles, and, across the street, the flamboyant 1857 Freusier Octagon House, with its mansard roof and cupola.

Hyde Street, with its French-style boutiques, cafés, and antique shops

Scenic Yosemite Valley, Yosemite National Park ▶

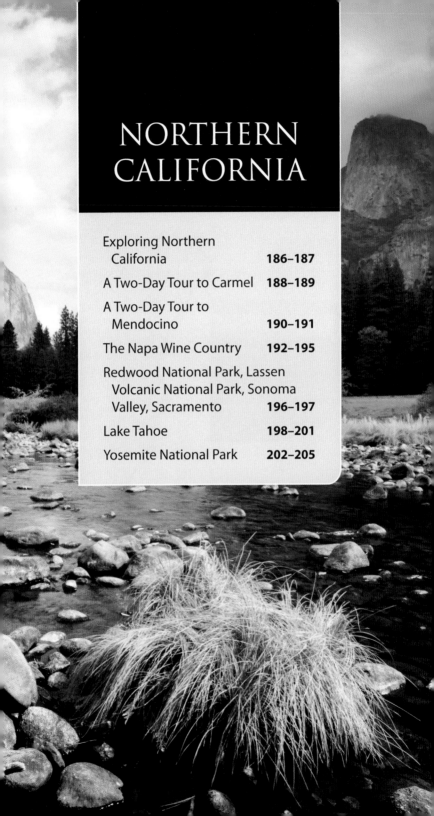

NORTHERN CALIFORNIA

Exploring Northern California

San Francisco sits at the apex of a beautiful, varied, and historic region of California. The sheltered valleys of the coastal ranges, perfect for vineyards, have given visitors a rich array of wineries to explore, and the extensive coastline is ideal for relaxing on pristine beaches or birdwatching. There are scores of old, fascinating towns, and visitors can ski or hike among the lofty summits of the Sierra Nevada, all within a few hours of the city. The excursions described on pages 188–205 have been selected to give visitors a sample of what is on offer beyond San Francisco.

Lake Tahoe in winter

Sights at a Glance

1. Carmel
2. Mendocino
3. Napa Valley Wine Country
4. Redwood National Park
5. Lassen Volcanic National Park
6. Sonoma Valley
7. Sacramento
8. Lake Tahoe
9. Yosemite National Park

Oak trees in Yosemite Valley in the fall

0 kilometers 50

0 miles 50

Picturesque houses in the rural town of Mendocino

Getting Around

Most visitors will want to explore the region by car. Roads are good, and service stations and accommodations are plentiful. All destinations are also accessible by Greyhound bus *(see pp278–9)*. Organized bus tours *(see p281)* can be arranged from San Francisco to the Wine Country, allowing visitors to take advantage of the many wine-tasting opportunities. Gambler Specials are an inexpensive way of getting to Lake Tahoe by bus, and most offer special package deals on hotels as well. A quicker, but more expensive, alternative is to fly to Reno, Nevada, or South Lake Tahoe. Yosemite is accessible by train from Oakland to Merced, with bus connections included.

Key

= Highway

= Major road

- Secondary road

- Other road

Scenic route

Main railroad

- Other railroad

- State border

- Summit

✕ Pass

Rows of grapevines in a California Vineyard

For keys to symbols *see back flap*

❶ A Two-Day Tour to Carmel

Skirting cliffs and coves, pocket beaches, lighthouses, parks, and old historic towns, coastal Hwy 1 is a highly scenic route from San Francisco to Carmel. The region has a colorful history, particularly in old Monterey, the original capital of Spanish California. Carmel itself, a pretty seaside town, has been a haven for artists and writers since the early 20th century. Here you can visit the Carmel Mission, burial place of Father Junipero Serra *(see p139)*.

San Francisco to Santa Cruz
Leaving the city at Pacifica, Hwy 1 narrows to a two-lane road. At Sharp Park, you can hike to Sweeny Ridge ①, a distance of 1.5 miles (2 km). From here, in 1769, Gaspar de Portolá's party of Spanish explorers became the first Europeans to see the Bay of San Francisco *(see pp24–5)*.

The strong currents and cold waters of the Pacific discourage most swimmers at the state-owned beaches at Gray Whale Cove ② and Montara. At low tide, the exposed rock pools reach from Fitzgerald Marine Preserve south to Pillar Point, the most extensive along the San Mateo County coast.

The fishing fleet still docks at nearby Princeton ③, while the big event of the year at Half Moon Bay ④ is the Pumpkin Festival in October. Princeton's main street retains the flavor of an old coastal town, and many Portuguese and Italian immigrants have settled here. To the south, the countryside quickly becomes much less populated. At Pigeon Point ⑤, just south of Pescadero *(see p171)*, is a lighthouse built in 1872. Though the tower has been closed for renovation, the

exterior buildings and grounds remain open. From here, side roads climb into the Santa Cruz Mountains. The spectacular Ano Nuevo State Park ⑥ lies 20 miles (32 km) north of

④ Child at the Pumpkin Festival in Half Moon Bay

Santa Cruz, along Hwy 1. You can make a reservation with a ranger to hike a 3 mile (5 km) roundtrip to the beach to see the colony of elephant seals.

Santa Cruz to Monterey
At Monterey Bay's northern end, Santa Cruz offers some excellent swimming beaches. Though the sandstone bridge of the Natural Bridges State Beach ⑦ disappeared long ago into the waves, the beach here is protected and provides a safe harbor for swimmers.

Santa Cruz is famous for the Boardwalk ⑧, an amusement park that stretches for 0.5 mile (1 km) along the beach. The Big Dipper roller coaster has thrilled riders since 1923.

From Santa Cruz the highway curves around the bay to Monterey, 28 miles (45 km) away. Midway between them is the University of California's marine science station at Moss Landing ⑨, where visitors can watch birds and learn about the area's flora and fauna.

Monterey to Pacific Grove
The first capital of California, Monterey ⑩ was established by the Spanish in 1770. Many Spanish, Mexican, and early American buildings still stand in the central part of the city.

⑤ Pigeon Point lighthouse

For keys to symbols *see back flap*

⑩ Fisherman's Wharf, Monterey

A free walking map, produced by the Chamber of Commerce, is readily available. This map indicates sights such as Robert Louis Stevenson's home and Colton Hall, where California's first Constitution was written.

In the 1940s John Steinbeck, author of *Cannery Row* and *Tortilla Flat*, wrote about Monterey, describing it as a collection of sardine canneries and whorehouses. The spectacular Monterey Bay Aquarium stands on the 3.3 acre (1 ha) site of the largest of the old canneries. The galleries and exhibits at the Aquarium utilize the unique marine habitats of the Bay itself. On the edge of the Monterey Peninsula is Pacific Grove ⑪, where in the autumn thousands of butterflies cluster in the trees. The 17 Mile Drive ⑫ starts here, following a scenic route past the world-famous golf courses of Pebble Beach and Spyglass Hill.

The drive ends at Carmel ⑬, with its quaint streets and eccentric houses. This hillside town was founded as an artists'

colony in the early 20th century, and there are more than 80 art galleries where visitors can browse. Many of the houses were designed by artists, inspired perhaps by romanticized impressions of old France. The quaint streets, quiet courtyards, and shops encourage strollers. Father Junipero Serra, founder of the missions, is buried in Mission Carmel, which is one of the most beautiful churches in California.

Tips for Travelers

Distance from San Francisco: 137 miles (220 km).

Duration of journey: About 4 hours, excluding stops.

Getting back to San Francisco: Monterey Peninsula is linked to US 101. It takes 2.5 hours to reach San Francisco via San José.

When to go: The best weather is in September and October, when skies are clear and temperatures average 70° F (21° C).

Where to stay and eat: Santa Cruz, Monterey, Carmel, Pacific Grove, and Pebble Beach have a wide selection of hotels, motels, and B&Bs, while Municipal Wharf in Santa Cruz has numerous snack bars. Restaurants abound in Monterey on Cannery Row and Fisherman's Wharf and Carmel has a variety of eateries.

Visitor information: Monterey Peninsula Chamber of Commerce, 243 El Dorado St, Monterey. **Tel** (831) 648-5350.

Ⓦ **montereychamber.com** Monterey County Convention and Visitors Bureau, 787 Munras Ave, Suite 110, Monterey. **Tel** (831) 657-6400. Ⓦ **seemonterey.com** Carmel Chamber of Commerce, **Tel** (831) 624-2522 Ⓦ **carmelcalifornia.org**

⑬ The Mission at Carmel, dating from 1771

Key

— Tour route

— Main road

— River

San Jose

Monterey Bay Aquarium

Salinas

⑬ Carmel

❷ A Two-Day Tour to Mendocino

A trip to Mendocino will take you along the rugged coastline of northern California, through wild and unspoiled country, to a small picturesque town that was once a logging village. It became a haven for artists in the 1950s, and was so well restored that it was declared an historical monument. Inland there are valleys with forests of redwood trees, best seen from the "Skunk Train" out of Fort Bragg, 10 miles (16 km) north of Mendocino.

Coastal redwoods

Western Marin to Bodega Bay

Start the trip north by crossing Golden Gate Bridge and then continue on US 101 through southern Marin County (see pp162–3). At Mill Valley take a turn west on to Hwy 1, which climbs up the 1,500 ft- (450 m-) high coastal hills then hugs the coast through Stinson Beach. At the town of Point Reyes Station ①, you can detour left and follow the road leading to Point Reyes National Seashore (see p162), which takes about two hours. Hwy 1 continues along the edge of Tomales Bay ②,

one of California's prime oyster growing estuaries. Beyond the bay the road winds inland for 30 miles (48 km) through the dairy farms of west Marin County, returning to the coast at Bodega Bay ③, where Alfred Hitchcock filmed *The Birds* in 1962.

Russian River and Fort Ross

North of Bodega Bay, Hwy 1 continues along the Pacific coastline, reaching the wide mouth of the Russian River at Jenner ④, where there is a broad beach. Guerneville, the area's main town, lies up the river. The road climbs up the steep switchback of the Jenner Grade high above the Pacific, where you can stop to admire the views. On a windswept headland 12 miles (19 km) north of Jenner you will find the Fort Ross State Historic Park ⑤, a restored Russian fur trading outpost that stood from 1812 until it was closed in 1841. The original house of the fort's last manager, Alexander Rotchev, is

Johnson's Beach at Guerneville, on the Russian River

For keys to symbols see back flap

Key

▬ Tour route

═ Other road

⌇ River

0 meters   20

0 yards   10

A "Skunk Train" on its way through the redwood forest

still intact, and other buildings have been carefully reconstructed within a wooden palisade. The highlight is the Russian Orthodox chapel, built from local redwood in 1824. The park, which has a visitor center, is open from 10am to 4:30pm. Beyond Fort Ross, Hwy 1 snakes along the coast, passing through several coastal state parks, including the Kruse Rhododendron Reserve ⑥. The best time to visit is during April and May, when the flowers are in bloom. This stretch of coast is ruggedly beautiful, with windswept headlands and hidden coves.

Point Arena and Manchester State Beach

The drive continues through open meadows and cypress groves to Point Arena ⑦. Here visitors can climb up the 147 steps in the old lighthouse for a spectacular view of the coast.

Manchester State Beach ⑧ hugs the coastline for the next 5 miles (8 km), and from here you can take a detour of about three hours to visit northern California's breweries. Among the best brews are Red Tail Ale from Mendocino Brewing in Hopland ⑨ on US 101, and Boont Amber, made in Boonville ⑩ in the heart of the Anderson Valley. Both have pubs on the premises.

Three miles (5 km) south of Mendocino on Hwy 1 is Van Damme State Park ⑪, a redwood forest with several good hiking trails. Mendocino Headlands State Park ⑫ is a bit farther along the highway – a greenbelt area where no development is allowed. Mendocino ⑬ itself is tucked away west of the highway, on a rocky promontory above

the Pacific. The town has retained much of the picturesque charm of its logging days, and although tourism is now its main industry, it remains unspoiled by commercialism, and is a thriving center for the arts, ideal for a stroll around.

⑬ 19th-century buildings in Mendocino

❸ Napa Valley Wine Country

The narrow Napa Valley, with its rolling hillsides and fertile valley floor, is the heart and soul of the California wine industry. It supports over 450 wineries, some dating from the 19th century, with one or two down every country lane. Many welcome visitors for tours and tastings, and each part of the valley has its own distinctive wines *(see pp220–21)*. The rural beauty of the valley is striking at every season, and can be viewed from a balloon, a bike, or a train. Other attractions include museums, galleries, and the hot springs in Calistoga.

Napa Valley Sign
This sign cheerfully welcomes visitors to the valley's lush vineyards. Make reservations for wine tasting and expect a fee.

Clos Pegase Winery
With its free tours, this winery actively encourages visitors. It is housed in an award-winning Postmodern building.

KEY

① **Silverado Vineyards**

② **Trefethen Vineyards**

③ **Hess Collection** has both distinctive wines and fine works of art.

④ **Domain Chandon** produces elegant sparkling wines.

⑤ **Robert Mondavi Winery** is known for its innovative tour and tasting programs.

⑥ **Inglenook Estate** dates back to 1879. Tours start from the original winery, now the tasting room.

⑦ **Beaulieu Vineyard** surrounds a château-style building.

⑧ **Beringer Vineyards** has operated continuously since 1876.

⑨ **Schramsberg Vineyards**

⑩ **Old Faithful**, a geyser, discharges hot water and steam every 30 minutes or so.

⑪ **Frog's Leap Winery**

⑫ **Duckhorn Vineyards**

⑬ **Mumm Napa Valley** is known for its classic sparkling wines.

⑭ **Clos du Val**, despite its small size, has a reputation for high-quality wines.

⑮ **The Silverado Trail** is a quiet road that offers fine views overlooking the vineyards.

Napa Valley Wine Train
Gourmet meals and excellent wines are served on this luxury train as it makes its 3-hour trip along the valley, but some passengers come just for the ride.

Key

━━ Road

〜 River

▨ Vineyard

▨ Railroad

••• Silverado Trail

For keys to symbols *see back flap*

Sterling Vineyard
Perched on a rocky knoll overlooking the vineyards below, this unusual Greek style winery is reached via an overhead gondola. The tour is marked by signs, allowing visitors to set their own pace.

V. Sattui Winery
French oak barrels are used for aging the wine in some wineries.

Joseph Phelps Vineyard
Grape-pickers harvest the year's crop in one of California's most prestigious wineries. Tours are by appointment.

Tips for Travelers

Distance from San Francisco: 55 miles (120 km).
Duration of journey: About 1 hour to Napa.
Getting there: Take US 101 north, then Hwy 37 to Vallejo, then Hwy 29 to Napa. Hwy 29 runs along the valley to Calistoga. Several bus companies offer tours, often including lunch.
When to go: In early spring the fields are carpeted with bright yellow mustard. Grapes begin to ripen in the summer heat. In September and October grapes are harvested and pressed, and vine leaves turn gold and red. Winter is when the pace slows, the vines are pruned in preparation, and new wine is bottled.
Where to stay and eat: For information, visit
W visitnapavalley.com
Visitor information: Napa Valley Welcome Center, 600 Main St, Napa. **Tel** (707) 251-5895 or (1-855) 847-NAPA.

Focus on Sustainable Farming

In order to ensure best agricultural practices in the area, the Napa Valley Vintners formed a voluntary program called Napa Green. So far, more than 70,000 acres are enrolled in the program, with 40,000 acres already certified. The certification is carried out by an independent third party and is awarded when all best land and production practice criteria are met.

Healthy vines in the carefully monitored Napa Valley region

Exploring Napa Valley Wine Country

Napa Valley specializes in rich, distinctive wines, designer winery buildings, modern art collections, spas, Michelin-rated restaurants, and artisan crafts. Indulging in a few wine tastings with a picnic and some shopping can easily consume one day. A dawn balloon ride, mud-bath treatment, and visits to art galleries will fill another. Before the 1970s, the phylloxera louse, Prohibition, and dull flavors haunted Napa winemakers. In 1976, Chateau Montelena Chardonnay and Stag's Leap Cabernet Sauvignon won a blind tasting competition in Paris, and with a fresh marketing approach led by Robert Mondavi, the Napa Valley emerged as a competitive wine region with trellised vines stretching across the valley floor and rolling hills.

Wine tasting at one of Napa Valley's many wineries

Wine Tasting

W napavintners.com/wineries

Most wineries have tasting rooms for the sampling of new releases. Employees are knowledgable about vintages, the characteristics of a vineyard's soil, and the influence of the climate on the wine's flavor. Some wineries offer tours with a tasting, and allow picnics in their beautiful gardens. The increasing tourism and popularity of this region has inspired many wineries to charge for tastings and tours. These require reservations, especially for large groups. Robert Mondavi Winery and Cakebread Cellars are just two of several that bustle with tastings, tours, and cooking demonstrations. Grgich Hills Cellars, Chateau Montelena Winery, Duckhorn Vineyards, Franciscan Oakville Estates, V. Sattui Winery, and Beaulieu Vineyard are among dozens that have wines with distinctive styles to taste. Sparkling

wine fans should head to Mumm Napa, Domaine Chandon, and Domaine Carneros.

Art Museums and Galleries

Wineries are a superb venue for art exhibits, adding cultural cachet to the experience.

The Hess Collection gallery has the contemporary European and US painting and sculpture collection of owner Donald Hess and includes artists Robert Motherwell and Frank Stella.

Artesa Winery's visitor center features artist-in-residence Gordon Huether's glass, metal, and canvas art. Clos Pegase has a famed modern-era sculpture garden, and Peju Province's contemporary art collection is on display in its Liana Gallery. Mumm Napa's Fine Art photography galleries offer changing exhibitions, while the Private Collection Gallery includes images by famed photographers such as Ansel

Adams. Evolved beyond a winery to a nature and art setting, di Rosa Preserve features a lake, a glass chapel, the Gatehouse Gallery, and gardens to showcase artists' work from California and the San Francisco Bay Area.

The Napa Valley Museum features regular exhibitions showcasing the work of local and national artists. Other art galleries and public art walks throughout the valley add to the ample opportunities for cultural exploration.

Architecture

There are many buildings of architectural note in the valley. The hospitality center at St. Helena's Beringer Vineyards, the oldest continuously operating winery in the area, is the Rhine House, dating from 1883, with wooden paneling, a long bar, and stained-glass windows.

Whitewashed, Mykonos-style Sterling Vineyards perches prettily on a Calistoga hill, while Robert Mondavi Winery adopted a California Mission style, with statues of animals and St. Francis by renowned sculptor Beniamino Bufano.

Architect Michael Graves was commissioned to design the Clos Pegase Winery, with its spare, Post-Modern lines. Some wineries, like Domaine Carneros by Taittinger, acknowledge French winemaking roots with grand chateau structures. In 2004, in deference to his origins, Darioush Khaledi gave the Silverado Trail a row of columns leading to his golden

The Rhine House at Beringer Vineyards

NAPA VALLEY WINE COUNTRY | 195

Hot-air balloon rides over Napa Valley Wine Country vineyards

Darioush winery building built to look like Persepolis, Persia's ancient capital city.

Balloon, Bicycle, and Train Travel

Napa Valley Wine Train, 1275 McKinstry St, Napa, CA 94559. Reservations **Tel** (707) 253-2111. **W** winetrain.com

Pre-dawn Napa Valley skies reveal a parade of colorful hot-air balloons ascending above vineyards or descending to almost touch the tops of vines. Prevailing winds coming north from San Francisco Bay dictate the early launch. Morning fog makes the journey surreal and chilly, warmed by the balloon burner's flame. Floating above the orderly rows of vineyards and springtime fields of yellow mustard is rewarded upon landing with a traditional toast of sparkling wine, often accompanied by a gourmet breakfast.

Cyclists find the long, generally flat valley a delight, and take to the Silverado Trail on the valley's east side to visit some of the more than 30 wineries on the route between Napa and Calistoga. Summer heat is most intense in the afternoon. Savvy cyclists start early to avoid traffic that can be congested on weekends and holidays.

The Napa Valley Wine Train trip from Napa to St. Helena and back lasts 3 hours. Tours include lunch or dinner prepared on board, and served in restored 1915–17 Pullman Dining and Lounge Cars. Special itineraries stop for tours of Domaine Chandon, Castello di Amorosa, or Grgich Hills Winery. Informal wine tasting seminars are conducted in the Napa Valley Wine Train's McKinstry station before passengers board the sleek gold and maroon train.

Themed events are organized in the glass-topped dining car including a five-course Moonlight Escape Dinner held each full moon, and 1915 is recreated on Murder Mystery Theatre Gourmet Dinner trips.

Spas

See **W** visitnapavalley.com for information on the local spas.

Calistoga, at Napa Valley's north end, is literally a hotbed of geothermal activity. Natural hot springs and local volcanic mud from an ancient eruption of Mount St. Helena created an industry here today that was started thousands of years ago. Many of the spas are located on Calistoga's main streets, but there are also numerous other places to visit scattered throughout the valley.

Mud-bath treatments are a return to a natural form of relaxation, and for some, detoxification and rejuvenation. Guests immerse their bodies in a tub filled with brown mud consisting of peat, clay, and mineral water from the local hot springs. An array of other therapeutic treatments have been developed that integrate locally produced oils, herbs, and honey. Some spas overlook vineyards or are located in caves similar to those used to age the area's wines.

Shopping

A winery tasting room may be the only place to taste and buy a delightful wine that is in limited production, and veteran winecountry shoppers advise visitors to taste and buy on the spot. Wineries will check legal restrictions on shipping to other states or internationally. Winery gift shops stock everything from cookbooks to corkscrews, embellished with the establishment's name. Comestibles, convenient for picnics, are also often on sale.

At the Oakville Grocery on Highway 29 you can buy local wines, condiments, and olive oils, or order a sandwich piled with local cheese and meats. Alternatively, visit Oxbow Public Market in downtown Napa to find an emporium of artisan food producers.

St. Helena's Main Street is a boutique lover's paradise. There is also an outpost of Dean & DeLuca – New York's famed artisan food temple. It is a great place to shop for fresh local Napa-area produce and 1,400 California wines. The V Marketplace has clothing and wine shops, a wine-tasting room, and several art galleries.

The luxurious Napa Valley Wine Train

❹ Redwood National Park

Information Center 1111 Second St, Crescent City. **Tel** (707) 465-7335. Arcata to Crescent City is 78 miles (125 km). Best route is US Hwy 101. **W** nps.gov/redw

Some of the largest original redwood forests in the world are preserved in this national park. Stretching along the coastline, the 91 sq mile (235 sq km) park includes many smaller state parks and can be explored along a day-long drive. A two-day trip, however, allows time to walk away from the roads and experience the tranquility of the stately groves, or spot one of the world's last remaining herds of Roosevelt elk.

The park's headquarters are in **Crescent City**, a few miles north of which lies the 14 sq mile (37 sq km) Jedediah Smith Redwoods State Park, with the most awe-inspiring coastal redwoods. Named after the fur trapper Jedediah Smith, the first white man who walked across the US, it has excellent campground facilities. South from Crescent City, the **Trees of Mystery** grove features remarkable-looking giant fiberglass statues.

The park's main attraction is the world's tallest tree, a 368 ft (112 m) giant, standing in the **Tall Trees Grove**. Farther south is Big Lagoon, a freshwater lake stretching for 3 miles (5 km) and two other estuaries. Together, they form **Humboldt Lagoons State Park**. The headlands at Patrick's Point State Park, at the

Lassen Volcanic National Park

southern end, are great for spotting migrating gray whales in winter. Rock pools abound with smaller marine life.

❺ Lassen Volcanic National Park

⊞ Chester, Red Bluff. **Visitor Center Tel** (530) 595-4480. **Open** daily. **W** nps.gov/lavo

Before the eruption of Mount St. Helens in Washington in 1980, the 10,457 ft- (3,187 m-) high Lassen Peak was the last volcano to erupt on mainland US. In nearly 300 eruptions between 1914 and 1917, it laid 156 sq miles (405 sq km) of the surrounding land to waste.

Lassen Peak is considered to be still active. Numerous areas on its flanks show clear signs of the geological processes. The boardwalk trail of Bumpass Hell (named for an early guide, who lost his leg in a boiling mudpot in 1865) leads past a series of steaming sulfurous pools of boiling water, heated by molten rock deep underground. In summer, visitors can take the winding road through the park, climbing more than 8,500 ft (2,590 m) to Summit Lake. The road continues winding its way through the so-called Devastated Area, a bleak gray landscape of rough volcanic mudflows, which terminates at the Manzanita Lake, and the **Loomis Museum**.

🏛 Loomis Museum
Lassen Park Rd, N Entrance. **Tel** (530) 595-6140. **Open** late May– late Oct only; call for times.

❻ Sonoma Valley

⛰ 8,600. 🚆 🚌 90 Broadway & W Napa Sts, Sonoma Plaza. **ℹ** 453 1st St E, (707) 996-1090. 🍇 Valley of the Moon Vintage Festival (late Sep).

Nestling picturesquely in the crescent-shaped Sonoma Valley are 9 sq miles (24 sq km) of beautiful vineyards. At the foot of the valley lies the tiny town of Sonoma. This town has had a colorful past, as it was here on June 14, 1846 that about 30 armed American farmers captured Mexican General Mariano Vallejo and his men, to protest the fact that land ownership was reserved for Mexican citizens. They seized control of Sonoma, declared California an independent republic, and flew their own flag, with a crude drawing of a grizzly bear. Although the republic was annulled 25 days later when the United States annexed California, the Bear Flag design was adopted as the official state flag in 1911.

Sonoma's main attractions are its world-famous wineries and meticulously preserved historical sites around the Spanish-style plaza. Many of the adobe buildings house wine shops, boutiques, and restaurants serving excellent local cuisine. East of the plaza is the restored **Mission San Francisco Solano de Sonoma**, the last of California's 21 historic Franciscan missions (founded by Father José Altimira of Spain in 1823). Today, all that survives of the original building is the corridor of his quarters. The adobe chapel was built

Coastal redwood trees

by General Vallejo in 1840. A short drive northward leads to the **Jack London State Historic Park**. In the early 1900s, London, author of *The Call of the Wild and The Sea Wolf*, abandoned his hectic lifestyle to live in this 1 sq mile (3 sq km) expanse of oaks, madrones, and redwoods. The park retains eerie ruins of London's dream home, the Wolf House, mysteriously destroyed by fire just before completion. After London's death, his widow, Charmian Kittredge, built a magnificent home on the ranch, called the House of Happy Walls. Today it is a museum, worth a visit for its display of London memorabilia.

Mission San Francisco Solano de Sonoma
114 E Spain St. **Tel** (707) 938-9560. **Open** 10am–5pm daily.

Jack London State Historic Park
2400 London Ranch Rd, Glen Ellen. **Tel** (707) 938-5216. Park & Museum: **Open** Mar–Nov: 9:30am–5pm daily. museum only. **W** jacklondonpark.com

❼ Sacramento

30, 31, 32. Old Sacramento Visitor Center: 1002 2nd St, Old Sacramento. **Tel** (916) 970-5226. **Open** 10am–5pm daily. **W** oldsacramento.com

Founded by John Sutter in 1839, California's capital city has many historic buildings along the waterfront in Old Sacramento. Most date from the 1850s, when it became the supply point for miners. Both the transcontinental

Sonoma Valley Wineries

The arms of the Sebastiani Vineyards

The Sonoma Valley has a rare combination of soil, sun, and rain perfect for growing superior wine grapes. In 1824, Father José Altimira planted Sonoma's first grapevines to produce sacramental wine for mass at the Mission San Francisco Solano de Sonoma. In 1834, General Vallejo replanted the vines and sold the wine he made to San Francisco merchants. In 1857, Hungarian Count Agoston Haraszthy planted the nation's first European varietals at Sonoma's Buena Vista Winery, now the oldest premium winery in the state.

The Sonoma Valley includes the Sonoma Valley, Carneros, and Sonoma Mountain wine-growing regions. The climate varies slightly creating different environments suitable for particular grape varieties, including Pinot Noir and Zinfandel. Today, Sonoma has more than 425 wineries, which produce millions of cases of wine a year. Some of the most notable wineries in the area are Sebastiani Vineyards, St. Francis Winery, Gundlach-Bundschu Winery, and Château St. Jean. Most wineries have picnic areas, free wine tastings, and tours.

Vineyards in the Sonoma Valley

railroad and Pony Express had their western terminus here, with riverboats providing passage to San Francisco. The **California State Railroad Museum** houses some fine, old locomotives. A little away from the old city, the State Capitol stands in a landscaped park.

To its east, Sutter's Fort is the town's restored original settlement.

California State Railroad Museum
125 I St. **Tel** (916) 445-7387. **Open** 10am–5pm daily. **Closed** Jan 1, Thanksgiving, Dec 25. **W** csrmf.org

California State Capitol

Designed in 1860 in grand Renaissance Revival style, this building was completed in 1874. Housing the office of the governor and the state senate chambers, the Capitol also serves as a museum of the state's political and cultural history.

The Capitol Rotunda was restored to its original 19th-century splendor in 1975.

Original 1860 statuary

Entrance

The Historic Offices on the first floor contain a few government offices restored to their turn-of-the-century appearance.

❽ Lake Tahoe

One of the most beautiful bodies of water in the world, Lake Tahoe lies in an alpine bowl on the border between Nevada and California. Surrounded by forested peaks, its shoreline measures 72 miles (116 km). The spectacular setting led Mark Twain, who spent a summer here in the 1860s, to coin it "surely the fairest picture the earth affords." Calling itself a year-round playground, Tahoe today has ski resorts, gambling, hiking trails, lakeside cabins, historic architecture, and special summer events including the Lake Tahoe Shakespeare Festival.

Hellman-Ehrman Mansion and Visitor Center
This Queen Anne-style summer home was built in 1903. It opens for tours in summer.

Rubicon Bay   *Meeks Bay*

Marla Bay

KEY

① **Cave Rock**

② **Stateline** is Lake Tahoe's main gambling center, with many casinos.

③ **Heavenly Aerial Tram**

④ **South Lake Tahoe**

⑤ **Tahoe Keys**

⑥ **Vikingsholm Castle**, built in 1929, is a replica of a Scandinavian Castle now open to visitors in summer.

⑦ **Emerald Bay State Park**, one of the natural wonders of California, is a wooded, isolated wilderness with granite crags and waterfalls.

⑧ **US Forest Service Visitor Center**

⑨ **DL Bliss State Park**

⑩ **Homewood** is a popular ski resort in winter, with spectacular views all year.

⑪ **Kaspian picnic area**

⑫ **Tahoe City** is the focal point for shopping and nightlife in North Tahoe.

⑬ **Stateline Point**

⑭ **Incline Village** is a small, sophisticated ski town.

⑮ **Lake Tahoe State Park**

Zephyr Cove and MS Dixie
Many visitors enjoy touring the lake on a stern-wheeler paddle boat. The MS *Dixie* makes regular trips from Zephyr Cove.

For keys to symbols *see back flap*

Skiing Around Lake Tahoe

The peaks surrounding Lake Tahoe, particularly those on the California side, are famous for their many ski resorts. These include the world-class Alpine Meadows and Squaw Valley, where the Winter Olympics were held in 1960. The area is a sunny paradise for both downhill and cross-country skiers, with miles of runs through pine forests and open meadows, and down ridges

Ski slopes near Lake Tahoe

with splendid views of the lake. Skiing offers something for everyone, with powder areas

and challenging slopes for advanced skiers, as well as gentle snow bowls for beginners.

McKinney Bay

Agate Bay

Crystal Bay

Incline Beach

Sand Harbor

Glenbrook Bay

Chimney Beach

Nevada Shore during Summer
Lake Tahoe's wild, unspoiled Nevada shoreline is popular with cyclists and hikers and has some fine sandy beaches.

Tips for Travelers

Distance from San Francisco: 200 miles (320 km).
Duration of journey: About 4 hours to reach Tahoe.
Getting there: At Sacramento, either take I-80 to the north shore, or US 50 to the south shore. Amtrak trains go to Truckee, where you can rent a car. Greyhound buses and limited flights from the Bay Area serve South Lake Tahoe.
When to go: Peak seasons are July and August, and December, when ski resorts are open. Spring and fall are less crowded, but some facilities may be closed.
Where to stay and eat: For ideas and suggestions, contact the visitor information centers.
Visitor information: Lake Tahoe Visitors Authority, South Lake Tahoe: **W** tahoesouth.com **Tel** (530) 541-5255. North Lake Tahoe Visitors Bureau: **Tel** (1-888) 434-1262. **W** gotahoenorth.com

Exploring Lake Tahoe

Beauty, size, and a unique alpine setting distinguish Lake Tahoe from other lakes in the US. It is sometimes compared to Russia's Lake Baikal despite much more lakeshore development. Lake Tahoe offers outstanding pedestrian and bike-accessible views from a loop trail, which took some 20 years to build, as well as a variety of water-based sports. There are distinctive historic mansions built as summer getaways for the rich; and a choice of California or Nevada views from casino rooms at Stateline and the Crystal Bay Corridor.

Winter Olympic Games, Squaw Valley, 1960

Hiking along one of Lake Tahoe's many trails

Tahoe Rim Trail

Tel (775) 298-4485
W tahoerimtrail.org

Hikers, equestrians, and mountain bikes can travel on most stretches of the eight segments that complete the Tahoe Rim Trail's (TRT) 165 mile (266 km) loop. The TRT is open from snowmelt, usually in June, until the first major snowfall, normally in October. Some of Lake Tahoe's most scenic vistas are accessible on this trail, which features beautiful pine and aspen forests, huge grey granite boulders, alpine meadow wildflowers, and streams. Alpine elevations range from 6,300 ft (1,920 m) to 10,300 ft (3,150 m).

Moderate trails, with an average ten percent grade, are indicated with light blue triangular trailhead signs, though the TRT can be accessed almost anywhere along its well-constructed dirt path. The pedestrian-only 1.3 mile (2 km) Tahoe Meadows Interpretive Trail at the north end is a quick introduction to TRT scenery

and terrain. The most rugged segment is on the western side of the lake.

Sports on the Lake

Fishing trips are a popular form of recreation on Lake Tahoe. Visitors may prefer a challenging search for one of the large Mackinaw trout that swim up to 400 ft (122 m) below the surface, or angling for rainbow or brown trout or Kokanee salmon.

Motorboats, some with water-skiers or wakeboarders in tow, speed across the lake, and those in search of a further adrenaline rush can also rent waverunners. Sailors and kitesurfers are challenged by winds coming down from the Sierra peaks. Hang- and paragliders enjoy views of the blue waters from above, while canoes and kayaks are a silent way to explore hidden coves and shorelines. Scuba divers seeking underwater forests or monster trout can enter the 100 ft (30 m) visibility freshwater lake from sloping beaches or kayaks.

Squaw Valley

8 miles northwest of Tahoe City.
Tel (800) 403-0206. **W** squaw.com

Squaw Valley landed on the international ski map as host of the VIII Winter Olympic Games in 1960. This was the site of the first televised Olympics and an opening-ceremony snowfall arrived just in time to ensure a sufficient base for downhill events.

Today, the Olympic Flame and original Tower of Nations still remain at the valley's entrance. This all-season resort includes more than 30 lifts, shopping and restaurants facilities, and accommodation. Winter skiers and snowboarders can expect an average of 450 inches of annual snowfall. High Camp, at 8,200 ft (4,500 m) above sea level, has magnificent views of Lake Tahoe. There is also a 1960 Olympic Winter Games Museum, a year-round ice pavilion for skating, an indoor climbing wall, a swimming pool, guided hikes through slopes of wildflowers, and full-moon night walks to the valley floor.

Kayaking on the clear waters of Lake Tahoe

Emerald Bay and the Eagle Falls trail

Stateline

Situated on the border of California and the more liberal state of Nevada, Stateline is the main gambling town of the Lake Tahoe region. In the 1860s, Comstock Silver prospectors journeyed to Virginia City through Lakeside and Edgewood, and Pony Express riders made this their last stop in Nevada. In 1873, a formal state border was established along the southern end of Lake Tahoe.

There are rooms in the hotel-casinos here where your feet can straddle both states. Views of either state are fine, but the west has prized California views of the lake, shore, forests, and mountains.

Emerald Bay

22 miles (35 km) south of Tahoe City. **Tel** (530) 541-3030.

The most famous postcard view of Lake Tahoe depicts the deep blue green waters of Emerald Bay, with tiny Fannette Island in the middle. The granite rock of Fannette Island is thought to have been resistant to the glacial ice, and the surviving stone ruins here were once a private teahouse.

Emerald Bay, 3 miles (4.8 km) long, is the best-known feature of the state park that adopts its name. The three-tiered Eagle Falls cascades through the park 500 ft (152 m) down to Vikingsholm, and visitors can walk the trail.

The glacier-sculpted bay became a National Natural Landmark in 1969 and draws kayakers to explore its calm waters. Emerald Bay is also a protected Underwater Park, where scuba divers can explore an ancient underwater forest, and wrecked dorries and barges.

Vikingsholm Castle

Emerald Bay St Pk. **Tel** (530) 583-9911. **Open** Memorial Day–Sep 30. 💲 $10 (adults); $10 (parking fee). 🌐 **vikingsholm.org**

Mrs. Lora Josephine Knight's summerhouse, completed in 1929, is a fine example of 11th- century Scandinavian architec-ture, complete with turrets, sod roofs, and carved dragons. Mrs. Knight visited Scandinavia with her architect in 1928 to gather ideas for the castle's design. Using local wood and granite, 200 artisans handmade, planed, carved, stained, and painted Vikingsholm's outer walls and interiors. The gaily-painted furniture and textiles are also replicated, down to hand-forged hinges and latches.

Hellman-Ehrman Mansion

Sugar Point Pine St Pk. **Tel** (530) 525-7982 (Tour information: (530) 583-9911). **Open** Jul–Labor Day. 🎟 Memorial Day–Sep 30. Call for park times. 💲 $10 (adults).

Banker Isaias W. Hellman joined other wealthy landowners building summer homes – around Lake Tahoe in 1903. Hellman engaged architect William Danforth Bliss to design a Queen Anne-style residence in the most sophisticated rustic style. The Hellman-Ehrman Mansion is three stories high, consisting of redwood-paneled walls and bright, large windows. A palatial veranda with rustic chairs for rocking and lounging looks down over Lake Tahoe. A wood-burning steam generator produced electric lighting, the latest in modern technology, until the arrival of commercial energy in 1927, and there was also a modern plumbing system.

Lake Tahoe Facts

More than two million years ago, rain and snow formed a lake at the south end of this valley, between two parallel sections of Earth crust. Ice Age glaciers shaped the lake into a round bowl that averages a depth of 990 ft (300 m) but plunges to 1,685 ft (515 m) below the surface at one point. North America's third-deepest lake, Lake Tahoe is 22 miles (35 km) long by 12 miles (19 km) wide. It lies 6,300 ft (1,920 m) above sea level and extends over 193 sq miles (99 sq km). The deep, fresh, and clear emerald green and dark sapphire blue water of this seemingly endless lake is estimated to be 99.7 percent pure – the quality of distilled water.

The surrounding peaks of Lake Tahoe

🟠 Yosemite National Park

Proclaimed protected by President Abraham Lincoln, the Yosemite Valley has long been cherished for its unique ecosystem. Over 4 million visitors delight in the natural majesty of evergreen forests, alpine meadows, and sheer walls of granite every year. The valley floor is accessible by vehicle along 200 miles (320 km) of paved roads. The soaring cliffs of Half Dome and El Capitán along with the plunging waterfalls, gigantic sequoias, rugged ravines and babbling streams give Yosemite its incomparable beauty.

Upper Yosemite Fall
In two mighty leaps linked by a cascade, Yosemite Creek drops 2,425 ft (739 m).

Yosemite Chapel (1879)
This wooden church is all that is left of the Old Village.

KEY

① **Sentinel Dome** is reachable from Glacier Point Road.

② **Sentinel Rock**

③ **Bicycle rental**

④ **Lower Yosemite Fall**

⑤ **Yosemite Village**

⑥ **Yosemite Museum**

⑦ **The Valley Visitor Center**
Behind this, an American Indian village can be explored.

⑧ **The Majestic Yosemite Hotel** is renowned for its rustic architecture, elegant decor, and beautiful views.

⑨ **North Dome**

⑩ **Washington Column**

⑪ **Quarter Domes**

⑫ **Tenaya Canyon**

⑬ **Mirror Lake**

⑭ **Tenaya Creek**

⑮ **Liberty Cap**

⑯ **Nevada Fall**

⑰ **Merced River**

⑱ **Half Dome Village** (formerly known as Camp Curry)

⑲ **Winter ice skating**

⑳ **Staircase Falls**

View from Glacier Point
The 3,200 ft (975 m) brink of Glacier Point provides a fine view down Tenaya Canyon.

Beyond the Valley

From May to October, shuttle buses carry visitors to Mariposa Grove, 35 miles (56 km) south of Yosemite Valley, where the Grizzly Giant is the largest and oldest sequoia tree in the Park. Northeast, Tuolumne Meadows is the largest Sierra alpine meadow and a good place to see deer and bears.

Giant sequoia tree

Half Dome in Autumn
A formidable trail climbs to the top of this polished cliff jutting above the wooded valley floor.

| 0 meters | | 1,500 |
| 0 yards | | 1,500 |

Key

≡≡≡ Road
∘∘∘ Bicycle route
●●● Suggested walk
⌁ Paths and trails
≈≈≈ Rivers

Vernal Fall
The Merced River pours into its canyon over the 317 ft (97 m) lip of this waterfall.

Tips for Travelers

Distance from San Francisco: 170 miles (274 km).
Duration of journey: About 4 hours to reach Yosemite.
Getting there: From Stockton, Hwy 120 is the fastest route; Hwy 140, the All-Weather Highway, is prettier and preferable in winter. Bus tours operate to Yosemite Valley (*see p281*), but a rental car is advisable for other parts.
When to go: Waterfalls are fullest May & Jun. Peak season is Jun–Aug. Crowds diminish Sep & Oct. Snow can close many roads: tire chains are required between Nov–Apr (weather-dependent).
Where to stay and eat: Accommodation ranges from rustic tent shelters to lodges. All hotels have good restaurants.
Visitor information: Valley Visitor Center, Yosemite Village.
Tel (209) 372-0200 (also, 24-hour park, weather, and traffic info).
Ⓦ **nps.gov/yose**.

Exploring Yosemite National Park

Some of the world's most beautiful mountain terrain is protected within the 1,170 sq miles (3,030 sq km) of Yosemite National Park. Hordes of visitors descend upon the park each year to admire its breathtaking views, formed by millions of years of glacial activity. Each season offers a different experience, from the swelling waterfalls in spring to the rustic colors of autumn. The summer months are the most crowded, but during the snowbound winter months several roads are inaccessible. Fall is the best time to visit, when temperatures are mild and crowds are reduced. Bus tours, cycle paths, hiking trails, and roads are all aimed at leading visitors from one awe-inspiring panoramic scene to another.

Upper Yosemite Falls, swollen with ice-melt in the spring

🏞 Half Dome
Eastern end of Yosemite Valley.
Open daily (weather permitting).
At nearly 1 mile (1.6 km) above the valley floor, the silhouette of Half Dome has become a symbol of Yosemite. Its curved back rises to a peak, before dropping vertically down to the valley. Geologists believe that Half Dome is not half, but three-quarters of its original size. It is thought that as recently as 15,000 years ago glacial ice floes moved through the valley from the Sierra crest, scything off rock and depositing it downstream. The 8,840 ft (2,695 m) summit of Half Dome offers an amazing view of the valley. The 9-mile (14 km) trail from Happy Isles trailhead to the peak can be strenuous and long, taking around 10 to 12 hours.

🏞 Yosemite Falls
North Yosemite Valley. **Open** daily.
Yosemite Falls are the highest waterfalls in North America and tumble from a height of 2,425 ft (740 m) in three great drops: Upper Yosemite, Middle Cascade, and Lower Yosemite Falls. One of the most recognizable features of the park, the cascades are visible all over the valley.

The top of Upper Yosemite Fall, by far the longer and more elegant of the pair, can be reached via a strenuous 7 mile (11 km) round-trip trail. The Lower Fall is easier to visit, via a short trail that starts next to Yosemite Valley Lodge and frames an unforgettable view of both falls.

As with all the park's waterfalls, the Yosemite Falls are at their peak in May and June, when the winter snows melt and fill the creek to capacity. Conversely, by September the falls often dry up and disappear altogether, their presence marked only by a dark stain on the granite wall.

🏞 Vernal and Nevada Falls
Eastern end of Yosemite Valley.
Open daily.
A popular half-day hike in Yosemite National Park is the Mist Trail, which visits these two waterfalls. The first fall on the 7 mile (11 km) round trip is Vernal Fall, which plunges 320 ft (95 m) and spreads its spray across the trail (carry a poncho or rain jacket in spring.) The trail can be strenuous for the 2 miles (3 km) to the top of Nevada Fall, which drops an impressive 595 ft (180 m). Here, the Mist Trail joins the John Muir Trail, which runs around the back of Half Dome all the way south to the summit of Mount Whitney.

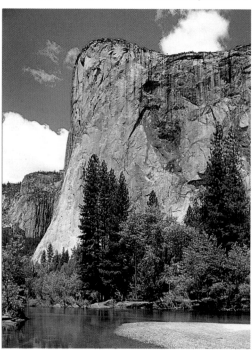

Sheer drop of El Capitán

🌄 Glacier Point

Glacier Point Rd. **Open** May–Oct: daily.

The great Yosemite panorama can be experienced from Glacier Point, which rests on a rocky ledge 3,215 ft (980 m) above the valley floor. Most of the waterfalls and other features of Yosemite Valley are visible from here, but the dominant feature is Half Dome. The panorama also includes much of the surrounding landscape, a beautiful area of alpine peaks and meadows.

Glacier Point can be reached only during the summer. The road is blocked by snow during winter at Badger Pass, which was developed in 1935 as California's first commercial ski resort. Another summer route is the Four-Mile Trail, which begins at the western side of the valley. Summer bus services also allow hikers to ride up to Glacier Point then hike down to the valley.

🌄 Mariposa Grove

Visitor Center Hwy 41, South Entrance. **Open** mid-May–Oct: daily.

At the southern end of Yosemite, this beautiful grove was one of the main reasons the park was established. More than 500 giant sequoia trees can be seen here, some of which are more than 3,000

Tunnel View, looking across Yosemite Valley

years old, 250 ft (75 m) tall and more than 30 ft (9 m) in diameter at their base. A series of hiking trails winds through the grove.

🌄 Tunnel View

Hwy 41 overlooking Yosemite Valley. **Open** daily.

One of the most photographed views of Yosemite can be seen from this lookout on Hwy 41 at the western end of the valley. Despite the name, which is taken from the highway tunnel that leads to Glacier Point Road, the view is incredible, with El Capitán on the left, Bridalveil Fall on the right, and Half Dome at the center.

🌄 El Capitán

Northwestern end of Yosemite Valley. **Open** daily.

Standing guard at the western entrance to Yosemite Valley, the granite wall of El Capitán rises more than 3,500 ft (1,070 m) above the valley floor. One of the largest granite monoliths in the world, El Capitán is a magnet to rock climbers, who spend days on its sheer face to reach the top. The less adventurous congregate in the meadow below, watching the rock climbers through binoculars.

Named by US soldiers, who in 1851 were the first white Americans to visit the valley, *El Capitán* is the Spanish phrase for "captain."

🌄 Tuolumne Meadows

Hwy 120, Tioga Rd. **Open** May–Nov daily.

In summer, when the snows have melted and the wildflowers are in full bloom, the best place to experience the striking beauty of the Yosemite landscape are these sub-alpine meadows along the Tuolumne River. Located 55 miles (88 km) from Yosemite Valley via Tioga Road, Tuolumne Meadows are also a base for hikers setting off to explore the area's many granite peaks and trails.

A pair of mule deer roaming Yosemite's meadows

🏨 The Majestic Yosemite Hotel

Yosemite Valley. **Tel** (888) 413-8869. **Open** daily.

A building that comes close to Yosemite's natural beauty is the Majestic Yosemite Hotel (formerly the Ahwahnee), built in 1927 at a cost of $1.5 million. It was designed by Gilbert Stanley Underwood, who used granite boulders and wood timbers to create a rustic elegance in tune with its surroundings. The interior of the hotel also emulates the natural setting, decorated in a Native American style. Examples of Native American arts and crafts are on display in the lobbies. The hotel is also noted for its high-quality restaurant.

Giant sequoia trees in Mariposa Grove

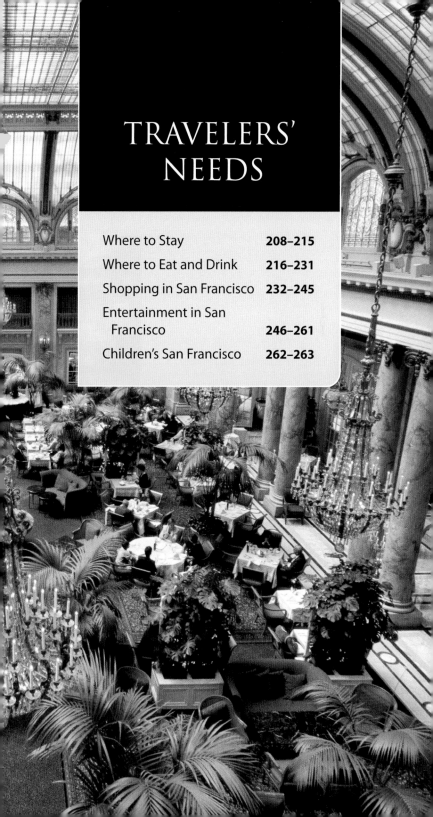

TRAVELERS' NEEDS

WHERE TO STAY

San Francisco offers a wide choice of places to stay, from spartan youth hostels to the most elegant and luxurious of hotels. There are more than 33,000 rooms available in the city, providing accommodations to suit every budget and taste. The top hotels are good value by international standards and have long been rated among the best in the world. For the traveler on a budget, there are many cheap and comfortable youth hostels and motels.

Another option is to stay somewhere offering bed-and-breakfast facilities. Bed and breakfasts are usually smaller than hotels, and sometimes quite opulent. Or, you could opt to stay in a unique boutique hotel. For the eco-conscious traveler, green hotels are becoming increasingly popular. The following selection of places to stay represents the best of their kind, covering all price ranges. For more details on each hotel, turn to the listings on pages 212–15.

Where to Look

Many of San Francisco's hotels are located in and around bustling Union Square, within easy walking distance of the Financial District and the Moscone Convention Center. Nearby Nob Hill, where many of the finer hotels are situated, is more tranquil, while the Fisherman's Wharf area has a number of hotels and motels suitable for families.

Away from the center, on the fringes of the Financial District and along Lombard Street in the Marina District, are a tremendous number of moderately priced motels. Bed-and-breakfast rooms are scattered throughout the city, often in quiet neighborhoods.

Hotel Prices

Considering the comfort and high level of service, hotel prices in San Francisco are generally quite reasonable, particularly in comparison with Europe or New York. Average room rates are $200–225 a night, though this depends on when and where you stay. See *Special Rates (p210)* for details of any discounts or packages that might be available. Larger hotels often charge more for additional amenities, such as parking, Internet access, or breakfast. It is worth checking with the hotel before booking.

Single travelers receive only a small discount, if any, and many hotels charge visitors $10 to $15 a night for each additional person (in addition to the standard two) in the same room. For details on traveling with children, *see page 210*.

Chain Hotels

You can count on good service, moderate prices, and comfortable surroundings at a chain hotel. The popular chains include the Westin, Hilton, Sheraton, Marriott, Ramada, Hyatt, and Holiday Inn. Some of these chains operate more than one hotel and designate one location as the flagship facility. All chain

Opulent furnishings at Chateau Tivoli
(see p212)

hotels have websites, or you can call the hotel's toll-free number to ask about rates and availability.

Bed and Breakfasts

A notable alternative to the large city-center hotels are the many fine establishments that offer bed-and-breakfast accommodations. These are often found in some of the city's extensive stock of well-preserved 19th-century houses. In San Francisco they are often referred to as bed-and-breakfast "inns"; they are unique to the city, varying from quaint, country-style cottages to converted hilltop mansions. They should not be confused with the European tradition of bed-and-breakfast accommodations, where you rent a room from a private individual in their own home and are also given breakfast. Some inns are very luxurious, and rival the city's best hotels for comfort. They vary in size, from a few to no more than 30 rooms, and are generally cozier in atmosphere and decor than a normal hotel.

The Room of the Dons at the Mark Hopkins InterContinental Hotel *(see p215)*

◄ The Garden Court at the Palace Hotel *(see p215)*

All rates include breakfast, and usually a glass of wine and light snacks in the afternoon.

Hidden Extras

Room rates are generally quoted exclusive of room tax, which adds an additional 14 to 15 percent to the bill. No sales tax is levied. However, added fees are often charged for phone calls. Local calls, including access calls to toll-free services, can cost up to $1 each. Long-distance calls can cost as much as five times more than they would from a private phone. Wi-Fi access can also carry a fee, generally from $15 a day, so be sure to inquire before using the Internet. The sending or receiving of faxes costs around $2 to $3 a page, plus any phone charges.

Parking at a city-center hotel can add at least $25 a day to the bill, plus a tip for the attendant, but motels will usually have free parking. Some rooms come with stocked minibars but you will be charged substantially for anything you eat or drink – as much as $5 for a candy bar. Prices for these will be prominently displayed.

A tip of $1 for each bag is usually paid to porters for carrying luggage to or from rooms. Room-service waiters expect a tip of 15 percent of the bill, rounded up to the next full dollar and paid in cash. Visitors who stay more than a day or two may also want to leave the housekeeping staff a $5 to $10 tip next to the bed.

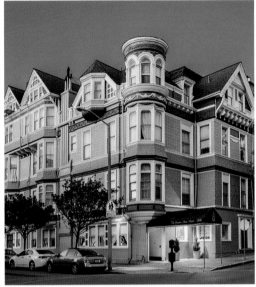

The elegant exterior of Queen Anne Hotel *(see p213)*

Facilities

It is usually possible to gauge a hotel's ambience simply by setting foot in the lobby. Some of the luxury hotels, such as the Hyatt Regency, with its impressive 20-story atrium, or the plushly appointed Fairmont *(see p215)*, are famous landmarks, which adds to the glamour of your stay in them. Also, most of the better establishments have excellent restaurants where hotel guests are often given preferential treatment. Some hotels have a piano bar or nightclub on the premises, enabling visitors to enjoy a night on the town without having to set foot outside. In San Francisco, "boutique" hotels are often older properties and rooms tend to be smaller. Review websites and ask reservation agents for details. See *Entertainment* on pages 256–7 for details. Many hotels offer discounted access at nearby gyms, if they don't have their own facilities. At most of the hotels in the city, guests can expect complimentary assorted toiletries and often a morning newspaper, in addition to free cable TV, and a minibar.

King Terrace at the Orchard Garden Hotel *(see p214)*

How to Book

Travelers should reserve rooms at least one month in advance (if not more) during peak season, which runs from June through October. Telephone and online bookings are accepted with a credit card, but a deposit of one night's room rate will usually be required. Remember to give advance notice if you think you will be arriving later than 6pm. There is no official reservation agency, but hotels may be booked via the website of the Visitor Information Center (see p266) (www.sfvisitor.org). Many hotels are listed in the center's free *Visitor Planning Guide*. Some agencies will book rooms for visitors. They do not charge for this, and can often get you discount rates.

Special Rates

It is always worthwhile to check hotel websites or ask reservation agents about any special discounts that might be available, in particular during the off-peak months between November and March. It is also useful to ask for discounts when booking weekend visits, as many hotels that usually cater to the business traveler will cut their rates for families. Some may also provide special offers, such as a free bottle of wine or lower-price meals, with the aim to gain the patronage of those who travel for pleasure.

Reservation services do not usually charge a fee, as they receive a commission from the individual hotels, and some will offer discounted rates. A good travel agent can save its clients 10 to 20 percent of the standard nightly charge of many hotels. It is worth checking some package tours, such as those advertised in the Sunday paper, as they can offer significant savings for travelers. Many airlines also offer discounts as an incentive to those who reserve a room through them. If you are a member of a frequent-flyer program, you may be able to save as much as 50 percent off the normal rates when booking

Pet Suite at the Petite Auberge *(see p213)*

in an affiliated hotel, and also earn extra mileage for each night of your visit.

Disabled Travelers

All hotels in the United States are required by law to provide the disabled with accommodation, as is stated in the Americans with Disabilities Act of 1992. Older properties are exempt from this, but most of San Francisco's hotels comply with the act and provide at least one room suitable for guests who are wheelchair-bound. You will find that staff in most establishments will do all they can to assist anyone disabled, but if you do have special needs, it is advisable to inform the manager of the hotel when you reserve your room. All the hotel listings on pages 212–15 allow those who are visually impaired to bring guide dogs onto the premises. More information for travelers with special needs can be found on page 280, under *Practical Information*.

Gay and Lesbian Accommodations

Though all the hotels in San Francisco welcome lesbian and gay visitors, the city also has a number of places that cater primarily, if not exclusively, to same-sex couples. Most of these are smaller properties, which are found in and around the city's predominantly gay Castro District. A few options are listed in the Directory, and gay bookstores can also provide more information.

Traveling with Children

Children are welcome at all San Francisco hotels, and few will charge extra for one or two children under 12 staying in their parents' room. It is advisable, however, to let staff at the hotel know you are traveling with children, because not all rooms are suitable. Some hotels may provide you with a sofa that can be converted into an extra bed or alternatively may be able to set up a cot or a folding bed for an additional $10 to $15 a night. Most hotels can arrange babysitters, or licensed agencies can provide childcare, see pp262–3 for more information. Many families prefer to take rooms in an all-suite hotel, or rent a furnished apartment for extra space and freedom.

Youth and Budget Accommodations

San Francisco boasts many youth hostels. These offer bunks in dormitories plus some private rooms, at affordable prices for travelers who are on a tighter budget. There are three good, cheap hostels run by a nonprofit organization called **Hosteling International**. The best-known is located at **Fisherman's Wharf**, while the other two can be found at Ellis Street, and Mason Street near Union Square. They all have kitchens, media rooms, flat-screen TVs, nightly movies, and on-site activity coordinators to help plan your itinerary. There are also several privately run hostels in the city. Budget hotels include the **Pacific Tradewinds Hostel** and **The Herbert Hotel**.

Furnished Apartments and Rooms in Private Homes

Some travelers may prefer European-style bed-and-breakfast accommodations in a private house, and Internet services have made a much broader range of accommodations available. Options include everything from lofts and sofas in shared communal spaces to luxurious private apartments. **AMSI** are furnished high-end apartments for long-term rent. While home-rental websites are increasingly popular all over the world, tech-savvy San Francisco has more users than most locations, and sites like **AirBnB** or **VRBO** have hundreds of listings available. Rooms are rented out by a resident owner in his or her own home, or sublet by apartment tenants; breakfast is often provided. Deposits may be requested and cancellation fees imposed, so inquire when you book. There may also be a minimum stay period. If you do opt to stay in a private house, keep in mind that owners will

expect guests to be quiet and considerate. Traditional sources for these types of arrangements are also still very active. For more details contact the special rental agencies, such as **Bed and Breakfast San Francisco** or the **California Association of Bed and Breakfast Inns**.

Recommended Hotels

No matter where you plan to stay in the city, the hotels featured in this guide will provide you with excellent accommodations and services based on your budget. Farther Afield locations are close enough for daily visits to the city, while Northern California options are for longer day-trips outside of San Francisco.

Our hotels are divided into five categories: Bed and Breakfast, Boutique, Budget, Green, and Luxury and Spa. San Francisco's bed and breakfasts offer a friendly, welcoming experience, with a decent breakfast. Boutique hotels are uniquely themed, from Japanese *anime* decor to fine historical buildings; some small chains are included, but many are independently

operated, as well. Budget hotels cater to the traveler looking for reasonable accommodations at inexpensive prices. Green hotels have received local certifications for environmentally sensitive practices. Luxury hotels provide high-end amenities and services; many include spa facilities.

Throughout the listings, there are hotels marked as DK Choice. These hotels have been chosen because they highlight a surprising local gem that offers a uniquely San Francisco stay, from quirky, historical details to incredible Bay Area views or unbeatable locations.

The opulent lobby of The Fairmont hotel *(see p215)*

DIRECTORY

Where to Stay

Bed and Breakfast

Fisherman's Wharf and North Beach

Washington Square Inn $$$
1660 Stockton St, 94133
Tel *(415) 981-4220* **Map** 5 B2
W wsisf.com
This inn offers small, classy rooms. Breakfast is basic. Complimentary wine and hors d'oeuvres hour.

Financial District and Union Square

Golden Gate Hotel $$
775 Bush St, 94108
Tel *(415) 392-3702* **Map** 5 B4
W goldengatehotel.com
Rooms are small yet luxurious at this family-run hotel. Tea and cookies served in the afternoon.

Civic Center

Sleep Over Sauce $$
135 Gough St, 94102
Tel *(415) 621-0896* **Map** 10 F1
W sleepsf.com
This charming place in a trendy neighborhood has comfortable rooms and homely atmosphere.

Chateau Tivoli $$$
1057 Steiner St, 94115
Tel *(415) 776-5462* **Map** 4 D4
W chateautivoli.com
History buffs love this Victorian mansion with spacious, elegantly appointed rooms and suites.

Haight Ashbury and the Mission

Edwardian Hotel $$
1688 Market St, 94102
Tel *(415) 864-1271* **Map** 10 F1
W edwardiansf.com
Located in a classic 1913 building, this renovated hotel has modern decor and amenities.

Parker Guest House $$
520 Church St, 94114
Tel *(415) 621-3222* **Map** 10 E2
W parkerguesthouse.com
Enjoy well-appointed rooms, lush gardens, and nightly cocktails at this gay-friendly place.

Willows Inn Bed & Breakfast $$
710 14th St, 94114
Tel *(800) 431-0277* **Map** 10 E2
W willowssf.com
Well-furnished, European-style rooms and a substantial breakfast spread make this hotel excellent value for money. Bathrooms are shared, but all rooms have sinks.

Stanyan Park Hotel $$$
750 Stanyan St, 94117
Tel *(415) 751-1000* **Map** 9 B2
W stanyanpark.com
Listed on the National Historic Register, this place has spacious Victorian-styled rooms.

Farther Afield

Point Reyes Station Inn $$
11591 California 1,
Point Reyes, 94956
Tel *(415) 663-9372*
W pointreyesstationinn.com
This national seashore retreat is complete with all modern amenities. Great for nature lovers.

Rose Garden Inn $$
2740 Telegraph Ave,
Berkeley, 94705
Tel *(510) 549-2145*
W rosegardeninn.com
Small, clean rooms come with a pretty, Victorian style decor. This place attracts younger guests.

Northern California

MENDOCINO: Headlands Inn Bed & Breakfast $$
10453 Howard St, 95460
Tel *(707) 937-4431*
W headlandsinn.com
Fireplaces, feather beds, and an in-room gourmet breakfast service make this B&B the perfect romantic getaway.

NAPA: Blackbird Inn $$$
1755 First St, 94559
Tel *(707) 226-2450*
W blackbirdinnnapa.com
Large rooms with handmade furnishings and stone fireplaces are offered at this inviting B&B.

Boutique

Presidio

Inn at the Presidio $$$
42 Moraga Ave, 94129
Tel *(415) 800-7356* **Map** 3 B3
W innatthepresidio.com
All suites have fireplaces at this excellent hotel. Relax on the charming front porch, or on the outdoor patio, which has a fire pit.

Pacific Heights and the Marina

Motel Capri $$
2015 Greenwich St, 94123
Tel *(415) 346-4667* **Map** 4 D2
W sfmotelcapri.com
This family-run motel has pleasant rooms with pillowtop mattresses. There's also free parking.

Fisherman's Wharf and North Beach

Da Vinci Villa $$
2550 Van Ness Ave, 94109
Tel *(415) 529-2500* **Map** 4 F2
W davincivilla.com
Some of the comfortable rooms here have views of the Golden Gate Bridge. Outdoor pool.

Hotel Bohème $$
444 Columbus Ave, 94133
Tel *(415) 433-9111* **Map** 5 B3
W hotelboheme.com
Great for city explorers, this hotel is located amid restaurants, bars, and shops. Small, eclectic rooms.

Stone steps leading to quaint, classy Blackbird Inn, Napa

Best Western Plus
The Tuscan $$$
425 North Point St, 94133
Tel *(800) 648-4626* **Map** 5 B1
W tuscanhotel.com
The popular wine hour at this
Italianate inn offers a calm escape
from the jammed streets outside.

Financial District and Union Square

Cornell Hotel de France $$
715 Bush St, 94108
Tel *(415) 421-3154* **Map** 5 B4
W cornellhotel.com
This hotel has petite rooms,
a comfortable lounge, and a
complimentary breakfast spread.

Hotel des Arts $$
447 Bush St, 94108
Tel *(415) 956-3232* **Map** 5 C4
W sfhoteldesarts.com
True to its name, this place
features a gallery and guest
rooms designed by local artists.

DK Choice

Petite Auberge $$
863 Bush St, 94108
Tel *(415) 928-6000* **Map** 5 B4
W petiteaubergesf.com
This French Provincial-styled
hotel from hotelier Joie de Vive
offers a mix of luxurious and
rustic ambience, with brass pans
on the walls and pillowtop
mattresses on the beds. Enjoy
the complimentary breakfast
buffet, wine hour, and freshly
baked cookies.

Chancellor Hotel $$$
433 Powell St, 94102
Tel *(800) 428-4748* **Map** 5 B4
W chancellorhotel.com
Experience old-world charm at
this hotel. The rooms are small,
quiet, and well-organized.

Clift Hotel $$$
495 Geary St, 94102
Tel *(415) 775-4700* **Map** 5 B5
W clifthotel.com
A great mix of vintage and
modern, Clift Hotel is one of
the city's best celebrity-spotting
venues. The lobby has a unique
furniture collection.

Hotel Rex $$$
562 Sutter St, 94102
Tel *(415) 433-4434* **Map** 5 B4
W jdvhotels.com
Custom wall coverings and hand-
painted lamps adorn the rooms
at this welcoming place with a
literary theme. Enjoy live jazz on
Friday evenings in the Library Bar.

Plush interiors of the Library Bar at Hotel Rex

Civic Center
The Buchanan $$
1800 Sutter St, 94115
Tel *(415) 921-4000* **Map** 4 E4
W thebuchananhotel.com
This stylish Asian-inspired hotel
features quirky decor and modern
amenities. Great service.

Inn at the Opera $$
333 Fulton St, 94102
Tel *(866) 729-7182* **Map** 4 F5
W shellhospitality.com/inn-at-
the-opera
The classy, old-fashioned rooms
here all have kitchenettes. Conve-
niently located for numerous
cultural sights. Good for groups.

Phoenix Hotel $$
601 Eddy St, 94109
Tel *(415) 776-1380* **Map** 5 A5
W jdvhotels.com/phoenix
A pool lounge for guests is at
the center of this motor lodge.
Spacious rooms and free parking.

Hotel Vertigo $$$
940 Sutter St, 94109
Tel *(415) 885-6800* **Map** 5 A4
W haiyi-hotels.com/hotelvertigosf
Hitchcock fans rejoice – this
place is a fun take on the classic
film. Excellent amenities.

Queen Anne Hotel $$$
1590 Sutter St, 94109
Tel *(415) 441-2828* **Map** 4 E4
W queenanne.com
Authentic period character
and elegant decor attract guests
to this stately Victorian hotel.
Free Wi-Fi and great service.

Haight Asbury and the Mission

Best Western Carriage Inn $$$
140 7th St, 94103
Tel *(415) 552-8600* **Map** 11 A1
W carriageinnsf.com
Each guest room has a themed
decor inspired by famous San

Franciscans. The sizeable rooms
have a mix of Victorian, Asian Zen,
and modern minimalistic decor.

Farther Afield
Hotel Sausalito $$
16 El Portal St, Sausalito, 94965
Tel *(415) 332-0700*
W hotelsausalito.com
Seaside-town charm and comfy
beds await at this subtly elegant
hotel. Warm and welcoming.

Northern California
**PETALUMA: Metro Hotel &
Café** $$
508 Petaluma Blvd South, 94952
Tel *(707) 773-4900*
W metrolodging.com
This truly unique French-themed
hotel offers cheerful and cozy
rooms. Friendly owners.

**LAKE TAHOE: Fireside
Lodge** $$
*515 Emerald Bay Rd, South Lake
Tahoe, 96150*
Tel *(530) 544-5515*
W tahoefiresidelodge.com
Expect retro-kitsch charm
and great hospitality at this
1950s-style motor lodge. Pets
are welcome.

**OAKHURST: Queen's Inn
by the River** $$
41139 Hwy 41, 93644
Tel *(559) 683-4354*
W queensinn.com
Excellent, modern rooms are on
offer in ranch-style buildings. Great
on-site wine and beer garden.

**YOSEMITE: Homestead
Cottages** $$
41110 Rd 600, 93610
Tel *(559) 683-0495*
W homesteadcottages.com
These quirky, peaceful, and
well-provisioned cottages
are located near to Yosemite
National Park. Great value.

For more information on types of hotels *see pp210–11*

Budget

Pacific Heights and the Marina

Redwood Inn $
1530 Lombard St, 94123
Tel *(415) 776-3800*   **Map** 4 E2
W redwood-inn-san-francisco.
san-francisco-hotels-ca.com
This motor-lodge style inn has
spacious, inexpensive rooms. Free
parking and Wi-Fi. Non-smoking.

Inn on Broadway $$
2201 Van Ness Ave, 94109
Tel *(415) 776-7900*   **Map** 4 E3
W broadwaymanor.com
All rooms at this non-smoking
inn feature flat-screen TVs, and
coffee- and tea-making facilities.

The Greenwich Inn $$$
3201 Steiner St, 94213
Tel *(415) 921-5162*   **Map** 4 D2
W greenwichinn.com
Rooms are cozy and well furnished
at this family-friendly hotel. Free
parking and Wi-Fi available.

Fisherman's Wharf and North Beach

San Remo Hotel $$
2237 Mason St, 94133
Tel *(415) 776-8688*   **Map** 5 B2
W sanremohotel.com
Small, cozy, and neatly kept rooms
come with shared bathrooms.
Excellent rooftop penthouse.

Financial District and Union Square

Hotel 32ONE $$
321 Grant Ave, 94108
Tel *(415) 504-3950*   **Map** 5 C4
W hotel32one.com
Centrally located, this vintage
European-style hotel features
small rooms and antique tubs.

The Cartwright Hotel $$$
524 Sutter St, 94102
Tel *(415) 421-2865*   **Map** 5 B4
W cartwrightunionsquare.com
This pet-friendly hotel has a great
location near the Theater District.
Simple rooms and free Wi-Fi.

Civic Center

Hayes Valley Inn $
417 Gough St, 94102
Tel *(415) 431-9131*   **Map** 4 E5
W hayesvalleyinn.com
This charming bed-and-breakfast
has basic rooms with shared
baths and a laid-back vibe.

Key to Prices *see p212*

Haight Ashbury and the Mission

Metro Hotel $$
319 Divisadero St, 94117
Tel *(415) 861-5364*   **Map** 10 D1
W metrohotelsf.com
Comfortable, clean, and hip
rooms, some are renovated more
recently than others. Free Wi-Fi
and impeccable service.

DK Choice

**Red Victorian
Bed & Breakfast** $$
1665 Haight St, 94117
Tel *(415) 864-1978*   **Map** 9 B1
W embassynetwork.com
Locals call it the Red Vic, and
this grand building, more than
a century old, has cheerful
rooms that are a tribute to
San Francisco's Summer of Love.
There are 18 uniquely designed
guest rooms plus a café offering
great breakfasts.

Beck's Motor Lodge $$$
2222 Market St, 94114
Tel *(415) 621-8212*   **Map** 10 E1
W becksmotorlodge.com
Basic but clean rooms, a private
sundeck, free parking, and Wi-Fi
are offered in a lively area. Non-
smoking. Popular with gay men.

Farther Afield

DK Choice

Marin Headlands Hostel $
*941 Rosenstock Rd,
Sausalito, 94965*
Tel *(415) 331-2777*
W norcalhostels.org/marin
Find clean, comfortable rooms
(private or dorms) in historic
buildings for $30–130 a night.
Take a hike on the Headlands'
historic hiking trails, or spend
some time with the on-site
gallery's Artists in Residence.

The snug Roots bar at the Orchard
Garden Hotel

Point Reyes Hostel $
*1390 Limantour Spit Rd,
Point Reyes, 94956*
Tel *(415) 663-8811*
W norcalhostels.org/reyes
This secluded, historic ranch in
the Point Reyes National Seashore
park has dorms and private rooms.

Northern California

TAHOE CITY: Pepper Tree Inn $$
645 N Lake Blvd, 96145
Tel *(530) 583-3711*
W peppertreetahoe.com
Located close to the ski slopes
at Tahoe, this place offers retro
rooms with lake views.

Green

Pacific Heights and the Marina

Hotel Drisco $$$
2901 Pacific Ave, 94115
Tel *(415) 346-2880*   **Map** 3 C3
W hoteldrisco.com
Spacious and elegant, Hotel Drisco
offers 1940s glamor without being
too far from modern amenities.

DK Choice

Hotel del Sol $$$
3100 Webster St, 94123
Tel *(415) 921-5520*   **Map** 4 D2
W jdvhotels.com
Enjoy a pleasant stay in bright,
cheery, and comfortable rooms
at this beachfront-style hotel
in the city center. It caters to
families, with afternoon cookies
and milk instead of wine and
cheese. Complimentary
continental breakfast. There
are enforced quiet hours, and
a heated ground-level pool.

Fisherman's Wharf and North Beach

Argonaut Hotel $$$
495 Jefferson St, 94109
Tel *(800) 790-1415*   **Map** 5 A1
W argonauthotel.com
This place has authentic seaside
character, from the decor to the
on-site restaurant. Pet-friendly.

Chinatown and Nob Hill

Orchard Garden Hotel $$$
466 Bush St, 94108
Tel *(844) 332-5240*   **Map** 5 C4
W theorchardgardenhotel.com
Simple, eco-friendly rooms are
stocked with organic toiletries.
Personable staff.

Financial District and Union Square

Serrano Hotel $$$
405 Taylor St, 94102
Tel *(415) 885-2500*   **Map** 5 B5
W serranohotel.com
Rooms here feature cherrywood decor and white linen. Free bikes for sightseeing.

Sir Francis Drake Hotel $$$
450 Powell St, 94108
Tel *(415) 392-7755*   **Map** 5 B4
W sirfrancisdrake.com
This splendid hotel has small rooms but offers gorgeous 1930s flair. Get pampered with some in-room spa treatments. The doormen wear Beefeater costumes.

Civic Center

Hotel Whitcomb $$$
1231 Market St, 94103
Tel *(415) 626-8000*   **Map** 11 A1
W hotelwhitcomb.com
A vintage hotel with rooms that are small in size but big on style and character.

Farther Afield

Pigeon Point Lighthouse Hostel $
210 Pigeon Point Rd,
Pescadero, 94060
Tel *(650) 879-0633*
W norcalhostels.org/pigeon
Whale-watch from a hot tub on a cliff. Clean, private rooms and dorms, and lighthouse views.

Bancroft Hotel $$
2680 Bancroft Way,
Berkeley, 94704
Tel *(510) 549-1000*
W bancrofthotel.com
A former College Women's Club is restored to its Arts & Crafts glory. Organic bedding and toiletries.

Waters Edge Hotel $$$
25 Main St,
Tiburon, 94920
Tel *(415) 789-5999*
W marinhotels.com
Enjoy plush beds and in-room breakfasts at this hotel in a quaint setting. Sweeping views of the bay and city.

Northern California

BIG SUR: Treebones Resort $$$
71895 Hwy 1, 93920
Tel *(877) 424-4787*
W treebonesresort.com
Enjoy living in the yurts or the "human nest" at this unique coastal resort. Take in the gorgeous sunset views from the outdoor sushi bar.

A spacious balcony looking out over the city at The Fairmont

Luxury and Spa
Chinatown and Nob Hill

The Fairmont $$$
950 Mason St, 94108
Tel *(415) 772-5000*   **Map** 5 B4
W fairmont.com/san-francisco
Perched atop Nob Hill, The Fairmont is opulent, service-focused, and luxurious.

DK Choice

Mark Hopkins Inter-Continental Hotel $$$
1 Nob Hill, 94108
Tel *(415) 392-3434*   **Map** 5 B4
W intercontinentalmark hopkins.com
Its stately exterior and elaborate decor make this place instantly recognizable. All the rooms are excellent, but the suites are truly extravagant. The top-floor bar – Top of the Mark – attracts guests with its expansive, breathtaking, 360-degree views of San Francisco.

Ritz-Carlton San Francisco $$$
600 Stockton St, 94108
Tel *(415) 296-7465*   **Map** 5 C4
W ritzcarlton.com/sanfrancisco
Refined and ultra elegant, this place offers opulence in every aspect. Guest rooms feature original artwork by local artists.

Financial District and Union Square

Hotel Vitale $$$
8 Mission St, 94105
Tel *(415) 278-3700*   **Map** 6 E4
W hotelvitale.com
Large, de-luxe rooms are the norm at this waterfront hotel. Get pampered in the spa.

InterContinental San Francisco Hotel $$$
888 Howard St, 94103
Tel *(415) 616-6500*   **Map** 5 C5
W intercontinentalsanfrancisco.com
Sleek aesthetics, good rooms, a Michelin-starred restaurant and a spa service are on offer here.

Palace Hotel $$$
2 New Montgomery St, 94105
Tel *(415) 512-1111*   **Map** 5 C4
W sfpalace.com
This grand hotel offers refined guest rooms, spacious suites, and an excellent restaurant.

The St. Regis San Francisco $$$
125 3rd St, 94103
Tel *(415) 284-4000*   **Map** 5 C5
W stregissanfrancisco.com
Luxury at its finest, St. Regis has genteelly beautiful, welcoming spaces throughout.

W San Francisco Hotel $$$
181 3rd St, 94103
Tel *(415) 777-5300*   **Map** 5 C5
W wsanfrancisco.com
Plush beds and nicely styled, chic decor feature at this hotel. Spa services on site.

Civic Center

Hotel Kabuki $$$
1625 Post St, 94115
Tel *(415) 922-3200*   **Map** 4 E4
W jdvhotels.com
Taste a bit of Japanese-style hospitality here. Deep soaking tubs and Zen-like ambience.

Farther Afield

Cavallo Point $$$
601 Murray Circle,
Sausalito, 94965
Tel *(415) 339-4700*
W cavallopoint.com
Well-appointed, luxurious rooms are on offer at this spa resort at the base of the Golden Gate Bridge.

The Inn Above Tide $$$
30 El Portal St,
Sausalito, 94965
Tel *(415) 332-9535*
W innabovetide.com
This romantic destination has rooms perched over the bay. Cool views, hot tubs, and ferry access.

Northern California

RUTHERFORD: Auberge du Soleil $$$
180 Rutherford Hill Rd, 94573
Tel *(800) 348-5406*
W aubergedusoleil.com
Overlooking the Napa Valley, this Mediterranean-style hotel features luxury rooms and an excellent spa.

For more information on types of hotels *see pp210–11*

WHERE TO EAT AND DRINK

There are more than 10,000 places to eat and drink in San Francisco, and because competition between restaurants is fierce, visitors can find some of the world's most innovative cuisine. Surrounded by organic farms, free-range ranches, and fisheries, the Bay Area is home to gourmet eateries at all price ranges.

San Francisco's role as an international port of entry *(see pp42–3)* has brought a variety of ethnic cuisines to the city. The restaurant listings on pages 222–9 provide a selection of representative restaurants; lighter fare and quick snacks are listed on page 231. San Francisco's cafés are listed on page 230.

San Francisco's Restaurants

A wide range of food from around the world can be found in San Francisco. The most fashionable restaurants are in the center of the city, in the Mission District and South of Market areas. Chestnut Street, in the Marina District and the stretch of Divisidero between Page Street and Golden Gate Avenue, are also worth investigating. Italian food is available in the North Beach area, while Latin American fare can be found in the Mission District. Chinatown has Cambodian, Vietnamese, and Thai, as well as Chinese, restaurants. On Geary Boulevard and Clement Street, in the Richmond District, are more Chinese and Southeast Asian eateries.

Other Places to Eat

San Francisco offers a broad range of venues other than restaurants in which to consume food. Many hotels have excellent dining rooms or informal buffets open to the public at lunchtime and in the evening. Most also have coffee shops for breakfast or for late-night eating. Some delicatessens are found in the Financial District. There are fast-food outlets all over the city as well as many street vendors.

Food Trucks

An upscale version of street food, known as the food truck, offers delicious take-away meals. It can be a cheap and easy way to grab a quick meal. It can also be a foray into some of the city's most popular eats. Food trucks have become an important stepping stone for many aspiring restaurateurs; you'll find everything from Belgian waffles and crepes, to fusion "sushi burritos" and Korean BBQ tacos at the city's food trucks. Websites and phone apps can give you the exact locations of your favorite trucks, and there are a number of "pods" where trucks convene daily. The Ferry Building Farmer's Market on Tuesday, Thursday, and Friday offers a good sampling of favorites.

Hours and Prices

Prices are higher than most cities, but deals can still be found. Breakfast is available between 7am and 11am, and is the least inexpensive, costing between $10 and $25. Brunch, usually served between 10am and 2pm on Saturdays and Sundays, costs about $12 to $25. At lunchtime you can buy a light meal for about $10 between 11am and 2:30pm. In the best restaurants, lunchtime

Guests enjoying meals and drinks at NOPA, a restaurant in San Francisco *(see p225)*

prices are lower than they are at dinner, but they are still by no means cheap. In the evenings, meals are generally served from 6pm, and many kitchens begin to close around 10pm. Salads and appetizers cost between $8 and $15 each and main dishes are between $15 and $35. In the very best restaurants, however, a meal can cost upward of $100, plus $40 to $80 for a bottle of wine. A few places are open all night.

Dining on a Budget

One way of stretching your budget is to eat a large, late breakfast. Eating outside can be a real treat: at midday, buy some of the fresh fruit so abundant here, and have a picnic lunch. The Mission district's *taquerías* and falafel joints are another good option. In a restaurant, you can cut expenses by sharing, but you may be charged a small fee. Or, take advantage of the free food offered by many city-center bars between 4pm and 6pm:

Interior of the Italian restaurant, Acquerello *(see p224)*

delicacies such as fried *won ton* are often included in the price of a drink. *San Francisco's Bars* on page 258 has good recommendations. Many places serve small plates, which makes it easy to share the dishes and save money.

Tax and Tipping

A sales tax of 8.5 percent is added to all meal checks in San Francisco, although a service charge is rarely included unless there are six or more in your party. You are expected to leave a tip, however. About 20 percent of the total bill is average. The tip can be left in cash at the table, or added to the total if you are using a credit card. Restaurants in San Francisco are also subject to regulations requiring them to provide healthcare to their staff. A Healthy San Francisco surcharge may be added to your bill, ranging from $1 to $5 per table, or 1–5 percent per bill. Check menus for details.

Dress Codes

As in most of California, restaurant owners in San Francisco take a fairly relaxed approach toward dress, and most places will allow you in wearing a T-shirt and a pair of jeans. In the trendier establishments, a minimum of dark denim and casual dresses are the unofficial dress code. Formal attire requirements are quite rare.

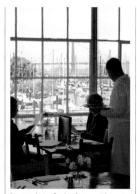

Diners ordering food at Greens, with great views of the Marina Bay *(see p222)*

Reservations

It is always best to make a reservation in advance. Popular restaurants tend to be booked a week or more ahead for Friday and Saturday nights. Weekdays, however, you should be able to book a table if you phone only a day in advance. If you don't have a reservation, and sometimes even if you do, you may have to wait for a table. Pass the time nursing a cocktail or sampling one of the city's interesting beers.

Smoking

Smoking indoors is prohibited throughout California, unless there is a separately ventilated area reserved for smoking that minimizes the risk of anyone breathing in unwanted second-hand smoke. These are often located in bar areas or within outdoor patios.

Children

All restaurants in the city are happy to serve well-behaved children, although you and your youngsters may feel less comfortable at trendier spots. At the more family-oriented establish-ments, such as North Beach Italian restaurants or a Chinatown *dim sum* house on a Sunday morning, children are welcomed. Most places supply high chairs or booster seats and offer children's portions or alternative menus. The minimum legal age of 21 for drinking beer and alcohol is strictly enforced throughout the city. Children are not allowed in any bar. However, if food is served on the premises, children can accompany adults to eat.

Wheelchair Access

Since 1992, all restaurants in San Francisco have been required by law to be accessible to those patrons who are wheel-chair-bound. As a result, wide bathroom doors and ramped entrances to restaurants and seating areas abound. It's always best to call ahead to be sure, however, as not all buildings have been brought into compliance.

Recommended Restaurants

The restaurants on the following pages have been chosen to represent a cross-section of the city's diverse and excellent dining options. From local hole-in-the-wall places to fine-dining musts, these choices offer something for everyone, in every neighbor-hood. In all areas, you'll find a combination of good food and great value.

Throughout the listings there are restaurants labeled as DK Choice. These establishments have been highlighted in recognition of an exceptional feature – either for the superb cuisine, for enjoying a uniquely San Francisco night out, for the excellent value, or a combination of these. The majority of these are very popular, so be sure to book in advance.

Dining tables surrounded by plants at Le Colonial, a fine dining restaurant *(see p224)*

The Flavors of San Francisco

If variety is the spice of life, then San Francisco's culinary scene is as red-hot as the tear-inducing salsa liberally dished out by the city's top-notch Mexican *taquerias*. You could find your way around San Francisco by scent alone: the sharp tang of espresso mingles with robust wafts of marinara sauce in the North Beach Italian sector, the sizzling *sabor de México* heats up the Mission District, and cacophonous Chinatown exudes the steamy fragrance of dim sum and crispy duck. For a sweet finale, indulge in San Francisco's very own Ghirardelli Chocolate, produced in the Bay Area for over 150 years.

Celebrated chef Yoshi Kojima prepares a carp for cooking

pulled from the earth only hours before, such as freshly plucked arugula (rocket) leaves, just washed of their dirt clumps, and heirloom tomatoes so juicy you may have to ask for an extra napkin. With such agricultural riches, San Francisco's renowned chefs are inspired to work culinary magic, creating minimalist works of art that beg to be eaten,

from baby artichokes ringed by vibrant lemon slices to wafer-thin slices of raw ahi tuna fanned atop a rainbow of grilled vegetables.

Asian Food

Explore Chinatown's web of bustling, pungent streets and you'll soon discover how the restaurants here turn out

California Cuisine

The Bay Area is the birthplace of California cuisine. The sheer variety of fresh produce in Northern California results in a culinary style that's all about the "cult of the ingredient," rather than specific dishes, leaving ample room for creativity. Many of San Francisco's best chefs cultivate a close relationship with regional growers, so what arrives at the table may have been

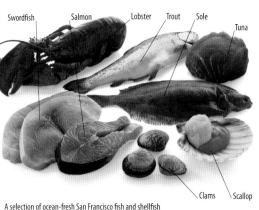

Swordfish Salmon Lobster Trout Sole Tuna

Clams Scallop

A selection of ocean-fresh San Francisco fish and shellfish

San Francisco Dishes and Specialties

A true melting pot, San Francisco not only features authentic Mexican, Italian, and Asian fare, but a creative commingling of them all. Each cuisine inspires the other, resulting in marvelous fusion dishes that have earned the city its gushing accolades as a foodie paradise. Feast on anything from wok-fried spicy greens to sautéed seafood with ginger salsa or baby vegetables with Vietnamese mint. Round out your meal with a warm hunk of the city's deservedly famous sourdough bread, widely considered among the best in the world. The bread's unique taste and texture stems from a yeast of wild micro-organisms, stumbled upon by gold miners over a century ago, that thrive only in the Bay Area's unique climate.

Dim sum

Clam chowder Restaurants on Fisherman's Wharf serve this dish of creamy soup in a hollowed-out sourdough roll.

Colorful interior of a bustling Mexican *taqueria*

exquisite Asian fare fit for an emperor. Massive aquariums are home (temporarily, that is) to giant carp swimming in languid circles, and sinewy eels unfurling amid swaying seaweed. Bulging sacks overflow with aromatic spices, and wooden crates bloom with dew-sprinkled bok choy and scallions (spring onions). Peer into an open kitchen for a glimpse of skilled chefs, knives a-blur, transforming whole ducks into paper-thin slivers that will melt in your mouth. The secret to Chinatown's culinary prowess is that the neighborhood's chefs are cooking for the most discerning of diners – their own people. San Francisco's Chinatown boasts the second-largest Asian population outside of China.

Mexican Fare

The urban fuel of San Francisco – and one of the best bargains around – is the city's fast, filling, and delicious Mexican fare. Dig into an epic burrito, filled to bursting with beans, rice and

Crab and clams on a harborside seafood stall

smoky chunks of beef, and you'll be satiated for the day. From saffron-scented rice and jumbo pinto beans to hand-rolled steamed tortillas infused with spinach and sun-dried tomato, the city's ubiquitous *taquerias* offer south-of-the-border pizzazz.

Dungeness Crab

The Dungeness crab is famed for its delicate meat. When its season arrives, from mid-November to June, locals celebrate by eating it in as many ways as possible, or simply cracked with butter and crusty sourdough bread.

On the Menu

Cioppino A tomato-based stew made with chunks of fish and shellfish.

Dim sum A Chinese lunchtime specialty, these little dumplings, steamed or fried, are stuffed with fish, meat or vegetables.

Hangtown fry A hearty omelette filled with breaded oysters and bacon.

Petrale sole This delicate local fish is usually served lightly sautéed.

Tortilla A Mexican staple, this round, flat unleavened corn- or wheat-flour bread forms the basis of many other dishes, such as burritos, quesadillas, and tacos.

Spicy marinated steak North Beach Italian restaurants often serve steak with garlic, anchovy and lemon butter.

Seared ahi tuna with Asian salsa The fusion salsa is made with shiitake mushrooms and Szechuan peppercorns.

Ghirardelli tiramisu A North Beach favorite of mascarpone cheese, Ghirardelli chocolate, cream, and coffee liqueur.

What to Drink in San Francisco

As one of the world's largest and most exciting wine-producing areas, California bottles the best-in-class vintages, particularly in Napa and Sonoma valleys. Most California wines are made from the classic European grape varieties but, unlike European wines, are identified by grape rather than by wine-growing district. Locally brewed beers, distilled spirits, and mineral waters are also popular, and the usual range of beverages are available.

Northern Sonoma vineyards, the ideal local climate for growing the fussy Pinot Noir grape

Red Wine

Vines thrive in the mild climate of Northern California where cooling fogs help the grapes reach perfection. The main red wine varieties grown in the region are Cabernet Sauvignon, Pinot Noir, Merlot, and Zinfandel. Cabernet Sauvignon is still the prime grape type, with excellent vintages produced in all major growing regions. Pinot Noir, used in the legendary French Burgundy wines, has become increasingly popular as wineries have mastered its temperamental nature, and the moist Anderson Valley in Sonoma and the Carneros in Napa Valley have emerged as prime growing regions. Merlot, used in many Bordeaux clarets, and Zinfandel, a bold and full-bodied grape popular in California, are grown all over the state.

Merlot, often used to provide more fruit in a blend, produces rich, soft wines on its own.

Pinot Noir   Cabernet Sauvignon

Red Zinfandel wines can be light and fruity, but at their best are rich, dark, and hearty.

Cabernet Sauvignon wines taste of blackcurrants with an acidic edge softened by oak.

Pinot Noir, at its best, has a floral elegance and a delicate strawberry flavor.

Wine Type	Good Vintages	Good Producers
Red Wine		
Cabernet Sauvignon	2013, 2012, 2010, 2009, 2007, 2004, 2003, 2002, 1997	Caymus Vineyards, Chateau Montelana, Jordan, Kistler Vineyards, Ridge, Robert Mondavi, Stag's Leap, Swanson
Pinot Noir	2014, 2013, 2009, 2006, 2004, 2003, 2002, 2001	De Loach, Etude, Sanford, Saintsbury
Merlot	2012, 2009, 2005, 2004, 2002, 2001	Chateau St Jean, Duckhorn Vineyards, Newton, Pine Ridge, Robert Sinskey, Whitehall Lane Reserve
Zinfandel	2014, 2013, 2011, 2010, 2008, 2003, 2001	Clos du Val, Farrell, Fetzer, Frog's Leap, Kunde, Rabbit Ridge, Ravenswood, Ridge, Turley
White Wine		
Chardonnay	2013, 2012, 2011, 2010, 2009, 2007	Loach, Far Niente Kent Rasmussen, Kitzler, Peter Michael, Robert Sinskey, Sterling Vineyards
Semillon	2006	Alban, Calera, Cline Cellars, Joseph Phelps, Niebaum-Coppola, Wild Horse
Sauvignon Blanc	2013, 2012, 2006	Phelps, Robert Mondavi Winery, Spottswoode

White Wine

As with red, California's white wines are classified by grape variety, with Chardonnay by far the most popular of recent years. Grown throughout the West Coast region, this prestige grape produces wines varying in character from dry, light, lemon, and vanilla-scented to the more headstrong and oaky. You can also find over 13 other white wine varieties and blends to try, as well as organically grown wines.

Chardonnay   Organic Chardonnay

Sauvignon Blanc wines range from clean and zingy to soft and buttery.

Chardonnay is often fermented or aged in French oak barrels, lending it smooth vanilla tones.

White Zinfandel wines, often blushed pink, are light, sweetish, and easy to drink.

Chenin Blanc, also used in blends, makes typically dry, quiet wines on its own.

The 1976 Blind Tasting

On May 24, 1976, at a blind tasting organized by the English wine consultant Steven Spurrier, French judges awarded California red (Stag's Leap Cabernet Sauvignon 1973, Napa Valley) and white (Chateau Montelana Chardonnay 1973, Napa Valley) wines the top prizes in their respective categories. Six of the top ten in each category were also California wines, a result that sent shock waves through the wine world. Within a decade, a number of illustrious French producers such as Baron de Rothschild had invested in California wineries of their own.

Sparkling Wine

If proof were needed that California is a prime spot for making sparkling wine, then look no farther than the fact that the finest French wine producers have huge investments in California. Moët & Chandon and Mumm, among others, have set up wineries in the Napa Valley and elsewhere. These companies, along with local producers Schramsberg and Korbel, have helped the West Coast establish an international reputation for excellent "Champagne" at the right price.

Sparkling wine

Beer

The resurgence in small breweries across the US can fairly be credited to the success of San Francisco's Anchor brewery, whose Steam Beer, Liberty Ale, and other products show that American beer need not be bland and tasteless. Other tasty local brews include Mendocino County's rich Boont Amber and Red Tail Ale.

Other Drinks

Coffee drinks of all kinds are available from kiosks, cafés, and restaurants across the city; you can also find a great variety of herbal teas.

Espresso   Cappuccino   Latte

Red Tail Ale   Liberty Ale   Anchor Steam Beer

Water

Health-conscious San Franciscans avail themselves of locally produced mineral water, the best of which comes from Calistoga in Napa Valley. Many mineral waters come flavored with fresh fruit, and most are carbonated. The tap water is fresh and clean.

Calistoga bottled water

Where to Eat and Drink

Presidio

Gaspare's Pizza House and Italian Restaurant $
Italian   Map 8 E2
5546 Geary Blvd, 94121
Tel (415) 387-5025
Lasagna and the anchovy pizza are popular draws at this classic Italian spot. Good art on the walls, but a weak wine list.

King's Thai Cuisine $
Thai   Map 3 A5
639 Clement St, 94118
Tel (415) 752-5198
Huge portions of Thai food – especially noodles – that is both budget-priced and crowd-pleasing. Open till late.

Pizzetta 211 $
Pizzeria   Map 2 E5
211 23rd Ave, 94121
Tel (415) 379-9880
This small spot offers an ever-changing menu of pizzas made with market-fresh ingredients.

The Warming Hut $
American   Map 2 F2
Marine Dr and Long Ave, 94129
Tel (415) 561-3042
Sip on a refreshing cup of coffee or a tasty hot chocolate and enjoy the scenic views at this café near the Golden Gate Bridge.

Burma Superstar $$
Burmese   Map 3 A5
309 Clement St, 94118
Tel (415) 387-2147
Enjoy spicy flavors here. The famous Rainbow Salad – mixed with 22 different ingredients – alone is worth the long wait.

The Presidio Social Club $$
American   Map 3 C3
563 Ruger St, 94129
Tel (415) 885-1888
Located in former military barracks, this restaurant's chic

Fresh sourdough bread on display at Boudin

decor, vibrant drinks, and excellent comfort food make for a great dining experience.

The Tipsy Pig $$
American   Map 3 C3
2231 Chestnut St, 94123
Tel (415) 292-2300
This American gastro pub serves comfort food along with a beer menu. The bar stays open beyond dinner hours. Brunch is served on weekends.

Aziza $$$
Moroccan   Map 8 E1
5800 Geary Blvd, 94121
Tel (415) 752-2222   Closed Tue
Enjoy artfully crafted cocktails and Moroccan-inspired dishes that borrow from global flavors for extra depth. Michelin starred.

Pacific Heights and the Marina

La Mediterranee $
Middle Eastern   Map 4 D5
2210 Fillmore St, 94115
Tel (415) 921-2956
Savor simple but really tasty Middle Eastern dishes in a subtly ornate setting. The menu includes mouthwatering grilled meats, vegetarian-friendly salads, dips, and soups.

Squat and Gobble $
American   Map 4 D2
2263 Chestnut St, 94123
Tel (415) 441-2200
An awkward name doesn't keep the crowds away from the hearty breakfasts and mile-high sand-wiches at this popular brunch spot. Outdoor patio with convert-ible canopy and heating lamps.

Balboa Café $$
American   Map 4 D2
3199 Fillmore St, 94123
Tel (415) 921-3944
Mix with the San Francisco elite at this wine-centric bistro. Juicy, well-seasoned burgers and creative seasonal specials are worth trying.

Belga $$
Belgian   Map 4 E2
2000 Union St, 94123
Tel (415) 872-7350
This stylish brasserie promises the sophistication of French cuisine with the heft of German food. The appealing menu features superb European bistro fare with a Californian accent.

Brazen Head $$
American   Map 4 D2
3166 Buchanan St, 94123
Tel (415) 921-7600
Reliable, pub-style food is dished up at Brazen Head, where the intimate ambience exudes an old-school vibe. The escargot is a popular draw. Open till late.

Greens $$
Vegetarian   Map 4 E1
Building A, Fort Mason Center, 94123
Tel (415) 771-6222   Closed Mon
This vegetarian restaurant wins hearts and minds with its flavorful, elegant dishes. For great views of the Marina Bay, lunch and brunch are best.

Mel's Drive-In $$
American   Map 3 C3
2165 Lombard St, 94123
Tel (415) 921-2867
The food at this kitsch,1950s-style place is a crowd-pleasing slice of Americana. Best bets include burgers, breakfasts, and the kids' menu.

Fisherman's Wharf and North Beach

Boudin $
American   Map 4 F1
160 Jefferson St, 94133
Tel (415) 351-5561
The famous sourdough breads are served up as sandwiches. There's an on-site bakery, with tours for guests. Extensive children's menu also available.

Caffè Greco $
Italian   Map 5 B3
423 Columbus Ave, 94133
Tel (415) 397-6261
North Beach is packed with Italian cafés, but this is one of the best for people-watching, tiramisu, and espresso.

Buena Vista Café $$
American   Map 5 A1
2765 Hyde St, 94109
Tel (415) 474-5044
The birthplace of the rich, creamy Irish coffee, this place dishes out hearty bar food and personable service.

Caffé Sport $$
Italian   Map 5 C3
574 Green St, 94133
Tel *(415) 981-1251*
The seafood at this Sicilian restaurant will win your heart. Sink into the buttery perfection that is the garlic shrimp.

Fog City $$
American   Map 5 C2
1300 Battery St, 94111
Tel *(415) 982-2000*
This renovated diner offers an upscale atmosphere and good food at reasonable prices. Gourmet sandwiches make for a delicious lunch.

Franchino $$
Italian   Map 5 C3
347 Columbus Ave, 94133
Tel *(415) 982-2157*   **Closed** *Mon*
A family-run gem serving up rich sauces, tender gnocchi, and freshly made pasta in an intimate setting. Service may be on the slower side.

The House $$
American-Asian   Map 5 C3
1230 Grant Ave, 94133
Tel *(415) 986-8612*
Small, congenial restaurant dishing up remarkable Asian fusion amid a sea of Italian fare nearby. Scallops and other seafood are standout picks. Service is accommodating and responsive.

DK Choice

The Stinking Rose $$
Garlic   Map 5 C3
325 Columbus Ave, 94133
Tel *(415) 781-7673*
Right in the thick of North Beach, the Stinking Rose has a gimmick that's worth a try – garlic for all. Curtained private booths, vintage decor, whimsical memorabilia, and murals that celebrate the bulb in culture and cuisine make the dining experience fun. Garlic-flavored food is buttery, pungent, and delicious. Garlic-free dishes are also available.

Gary Danko $$$
American   Map 5 A1
800 North Point St, 94109
Tel *(415) 749-2060*
The French-American menu allows you to create your own fixed-price selection. Creative meals with carefully selected ingredients. Wine and cheese lists are curated with great diligence. Impeccable service. Reservations taken two months in advance.

Entrance to the Stinking Rose, a unique garlic-themed restaurant

Scoma's $$$
Seafood   Map 5 A1
Pier 47 on Al Scoma Way, 94133
Tel *(415) 771-4383*
A Fisherman's Wharf seafood tradition since 1965, this historic spot doesn't disappoint. Fresh fish, friendly service, and a classic white-tablecloth experience – without a whiff of stodginess.

Chinatown and Nob Hill

Golden Star Vietnamese Restaurant $
Vietnamese   Map 5 C3
11 Walter U Lum Pl, 94108
Tel *(415) 398-1215*
Big bowls of *pho* (noodle soup) in many varieties and flavorful marinated, grilled pork are standout dishes. Inexpensive, family-friendly, and locally popular.

Henry's Hunan $
Chinese   Map 5 C4
674 Sacramento St, 94111
Tel *(415) 546-4999* **Closed** *Sat & Sun*
The kitschy red, black, and bamboo Chinese decor belies

Vibrant neon of the popular House of Nanking, Chinatown

authentic, blazing-hot Hunan-style dishes. The Harvest Pork is very popular.

House of Nanking $
Chinese   Map 5 C3
919 Kearny St, 94133
Tel *(415) 421-1429*
This no-frills restaurant piles plates high with delicious, authentic dishes. Lines can be long, especially during dinner. Open till late.

Great Eastern $$
Chinese   Map 5 C3
649 Jackson St, 94133
Tel *(415) 986-2500*
Great Eastern isn't a typical cart-pushing dim sum joint. Soup dumplings are popular, but also try taro cakes and other unusual fare.

Nob Hill Café $$
Italian   Map 5 B4
1152 Taylor St, 94108
Tel *(415) 776-6500*
Authentic Tuscan cuisine and a cozy feel are guaranteed at this little Italian spot. Unpretentious wine list, flavorful pasta dishes, and friendly owners.

R&G Lounge $$
Chinese   Map 5 C4
631 Kearny St, 94108
Tel *(415) 982-7877*
This upscale restaurant that dishes out traditional Cantonese fare. Salt and pepper crab is a crunchy fried treat. Also try the seafood or the special beef.

Swan Oyster Depot $$
Seafood   Map 5 A4
1517 Polk St, 94109
Tel *(415) 673-1101*   **Closed** *Sun*
Clam chowder and oysters on the half shell draw huge lunch crowds to this small café serving good, fresh seafood.

Acquerello $$$
Italian **Map** 5 A4
1722 Sacramento St, 94109
Tel *(415) 567-5432* **Closed** *Sun & Mon*
Dress up and enjoy Acquerello's elaborate set menus, which play with classic and modern interpretations of Italian cuisine.

Financial District and Union Square

21st Amendment Brewery $
American **Map** 6 D5
563 2nd St, 94107
Tel *(415) 369-0900*
Go for the Watermelon Wheat beer and a toasted sandwich in this homegrown brewpub. Huge portions of food, thick burgers, and cold, frothy pints.

Chutney $
Indian and Pakistani **Map** 5 B5
511 Jones St, 94102
Tel *(415) 931-5541*
Fragrant meat and vegetarian curries, fresh doughy naans (flatbread), and bottomless *chai* (tea) are served at low prices in a clean, simple dining room.

The Grove $
American **Map** 5 C5
690 Mission St, 94105
Tel *(415) 957-0558*
A popular lunchtime spot with downtown office workers, The Grove offers all-day breakfast, fresh salads, three-cheese macaroni, and hearty chicken pot pie. Generous portions. Sunny patio.

Hidive $
American **Map** 6 F4
Pier 28 1/2, 94105
Tel *(415) 977-0170*
Sports bar meets working waterfront charm here. The upscale versions of classic bar food aren't fancy, but they are delicious.

Anchor & Hope $$
Seafood **Map** 5 C5
83 Minna St, 94105
Tel *(415) 501-9100*
An East Coast seafood joint with a West Coast spin, this place serves great sandwiches and fries at lunch, and beer and mussels at dinner. Ambience is warm, casual.

Bouche $$
American-French **Map** 5 C4
603 Bush St, 94108
Tel *(415) 956-0396* **Closed** *Mon*
Away from the hustle and bustle of Union Square, this cozy venue has a distinctive Parisian vibe, with a great ambience and elegantly prepared dishes.

Casual ambience and wood-finish flooring of 21st Amendment Brewery

Delancey Street Restaurant $$
American **Map** 6 E5
600 Embarcadero St, 94107
Tel *(415) 512-5179* **Closed** *Mon*
Part of the Delancey Street Foundation, which provides job skills to disadvantaged individuals, this place serves excellent cuisine at inexpensive prices.

Lao Table $$
Thai **Map** 6 D5
149 2nd St, 94105
Tel *(415) 278-9991*
Classic and inventive Thai dishes are offered at this upscale spot. Generous entrée portions, small appetizers. Try the Tamarind Beef – a favorite here. Or go for the calamari, another innovative preparation. Service is lightning fast, and prices are reasonable.

Old Ship Saloon $$
American **Map** 5 C3
298 Pacific Ave, 94111
Tel *(415) 788-2222*
Named after a shipwreck site, this Jackson Square pub with an exposed brick walled interior serves draft beer and bar fare in an historic setting.

DK Choice

Sam's Grill and Seafood Restaurant $$
Seafood **Map** 5 C4
374 Bush St, 94104
Tel *(415) 421-0594* **Closed** *Sat & Sun*
Tucked underneath the Financial District's anonymous towers, this restaurant serves up classic seafood and steak lunches to local business crowds and travelers alike. Tall wooden booths, brass accents, and bright afternoon light conjure images of gentlemen in hats and dames in gloves. A great place for a hearty meal.

South Park Café $$
French **Map** 11 C1
108 South Park St, 94107
Tel *(415) 495-7275* **Closed** *Sun*
Trendy ingredients – pork belly, sweetbreads, confits – and traditional dishes blend nicely at this laid-back neighborhood bistro.

Yank Sing $$
Chinese **Map** 6 E4
101 Spear St, 94105
Tel *(415) 781-1111* **Closed** *Dinner*
A typical dim sum experience – dumplings and other traditional dishes are wheeled from table to table. Don't miss the signature Shanghai dumplings, with over 60 varieties on offer. High-end atmosphere. Weekday lunchtimes can be crowded.

54 Mint $$$
Italian **Map** 5 B3
16 Mint Plaza, 94103
Tel *(415) 543-5100*
Just steps away from Union Square shops, this hidden gem inside the historic Mint Plaza is the perfect place to savor modern Italian food and wine. Al fresco seating available.

5A5 Steak Lounge $$$
Steakhouse **Map** 6 D3
244 Jackson St, 94111
Tel *(415) 989-2539*
Melt-in-your-mouth Japanese Wagyu beef, among the best graded beef globally, sets this steakhouse apart. Smart dress code on weekends.

Le Colonial $$$
French/Vietnamese **Map** 5 B4
20 Cosmo Pl, 94109
Tel *(415) 931-3600*
This plush restaurant is a romantic hideaway away from the hustle and bustle of Union Square. It features an inner courtyard that was once home to the famous Trader Vic's, and offers a great dining experience.

DK Choice

Farallon $$$
Seafood **Map** 5 B4
450 Post St, 94102
Tel *(415) 956-6969*
Decor fit for a mermaid! Vaulted ceilings, undersea murals, and gold accents create a sunken-treasure feel. But the beautifully presented, fresh seafood is the real treasure here. At the equally elaborate Jelly Bar, caviar, oysters, and cocktails can be enjoyed at very reasonable prices. Experienced, personable staff.

Kokkari Estiatorio $$$
Greek Map 6 D3
200 Jackson St, 94111
Tel *(415) 981-0983*
Enjoy Greek fine dining in a
room with Mediterranean decor,
high ceilings and dark wood.
Succulent grilled meats pair with
flavorful vegetable dishes and
excellent Greek wines.

Michael Mina $$$
American Map 6 D4
252 California St, 94111
Tel *(415) 397-9222*
Sophisticated, modern American
cuisine with Japanese influences
is served at this restaurant.
Tasting menus, unfussy styling,
and an intimate dining room.

One Market $$$
American Map 6 D3
1 Market St, 94105
Tel *(415) 777-5577* **Closed** *Sun*
An award-winning, meat-focused
menu is on offer here. Excellent
staff, extensive wine list. Friday
and Saturday *prix fixe* "whole
animal" dinners are a bargain.

PABU $$$
Japanese Map 6 D4
101 California St, 94111
Tel *(415) 668-7228*
A sister restaurant to the classic
Michael Mina around the corner,
PABU features Izakaya-style
dining in a trendy setting. Try
the grilled squid and the miso
black cod. The tasting menu is
another highlight.

Press Club $$$
Wine bar Map 5 C5
20 Yerba Buena Ln, 94103
Tel *(415) 744-5000*
Share delectable small plates that
pair well with great wines at this
subterranean wine bar. Expansive
glass menu and plenty of bottles
to choose from, too.

Salt House $$$
American Map 6 D4
545 Mission St, 94105
Tel *(415) 543-8900*
Offering straightforward New
American food, the menu is heavy
on seafood dishes. Try the oysters
or the day boat scallops. Well-
tailored cocktails and an interesting
wine list. Exposed brick, big
windows, and an open kitchen.

Tadich Grill $$$
Seafood Map 6 D4
240 California St, 94111
Tel *(415) 391-1849*
This historic Gold Rush-era café is
still in service. Dark wood, marble
counters, strong drinks, and
seafood piled high. Excellent
cioppino (fish stew). Great service.

Civic Center

Ananda Fuara $
Vegetarian Map 11 A1
1298 Market St, 94103
Tel *(415) 621-1994*
Ananda Fuara is a calm and
clean, Indian-inspired haven for
vegetarians. Good soups and
salads, and the curries are mild.

Hinodeya Ramen Bar $
Japanese Map 4 E4
1737 Buchanan St, 94115
Tel *(415) 757-0552*
Udon, soba, and great vegetarian
options cut through the chill
of San Francisco's fog at this
Japanese gem.

Lers Ros Thai $
Thai Map 4 F3
730 Larkin St, 94109
Tel *(415) 931-6917*
The extensive, unusual menu
at this casual place features
authentic Thai food, packed with
spices and flavors. Arrive early

or you'll be standing in line down
the street. Hip Hayes Valley has
an upscale sister spot.

Saigon Sandwich $
Vietnamese Map 5 A5
560 Larkin St, 94102
Tel *(415) 474-5698*
Enjoy ridiculously cheap, delicious
Vietnamese sandwiches here.
Rich flavors more than make up
for the crude neighborhood.

Stacks $
American Map 4 E5
501 Hayes St, 94102
Tel *(415) 241-9011*
This place serves huge stacks of
thick, fruit-filled pancakes, plus
breakfast skillets, omelets, crepes,
waffles, and fruit smoothies. Worth
the money for the extensive
breakfast fare and good service.
Open breakfast and lunch only.

Tommy's Joynt $
American Map 4 F4
1101 Geary Blvd, 94109
Tel *(415) 775-4216*
A San Francisco institution, this is
the perfect place to enjoy hearty
comfort food in a wacky, and
slightly grubby, setting.

AsiaSF $$
Asian Map 11 A2
201 9th St, 94103
Tel *(415) 255-2742* **Closed** *Mon & Tue*
A raucous crowd gathers for
the nightly drag show. Male
servers in high heels dispatch
acceptable Asian dishes and
take turns on stage. Hip decor.

Dosa $$
Indian Map 4 D4
1700 Fillmore, 94110
Tel *(415) 441-3672*
Indian crepes – *dosas* – are the
star attraction at this eco-friendly
restaurant. Excellent, spiced
dishes and impressive cocktails.

1300 on Filimore $$$
Southern Map 4 D5
1300 Filimore, 94115
Tel *(415) 771-7100*
This restaurant serves traditional
southern food that is upgraded
with inventive interpretations of
low-country standards. Live music
on weekends makes this swanky
spot a fun date destination.

Absinthe Brasserie and Bar $$$
American Map 3 B5
398 Hayes St, 94102
Tel *(415) 551-1590*
Part Paris, part highbrow New
Orleans – come here for classic
cocktails and traditional French
dishes with a decidedly modern
twist. Excellent bar menu.

Gently lit interiors and cozy seating at Michael Mina

For more information on types of restaurants *see pp216–17*

Boxing Room $$$
Cajun-Creole   **Map** 10 F3
399 Grove St, 94102
Tel *(415) 430-6590*
Tuck into huge, flavorful entrées inspired by the cuisine of New Orleans. Situated between Hayes Valley and Civic Center, this is a great spot for post-shopping and pre-symphony dining.

Jardinière $$$
American   **Map** 4 F5
300 Grove St, 94102
Tel *(415) 861-5555*
Both the ultra-romantic dining room and the casual lounge bar area offer a mouthwatering, produce-filled menu of seasonal Californian ingredients.

Chefs rustling up delicious fare in the kitchen at NOPA

NOPA $$$
American   **Map** 10 D1
560 Divisadero St, 94117
Tel *(415) 864-8643*
Enjoy internationally inspired dishes, innovative cocktails, and well-priced wines in a warm, friendly atmosphere. The house burger is a budget-pleaser.

Haight Ashbury and the Mission

Axum Café $
Ethiopian   **Map** 10 D1
698 Haight St, 94117
Tel *(415) 252-7912*
Fresh, spongy *injera* (flatbread) comes piled high with generous portions of pungent Ethiopian food. Honey wine and Ethiopian beer complete the experience. Eclectic menu, great value.

El Castillito $
Mexican   **Map** 10 E1
136 Church St, 94114
Tel *(415) 621-3428*
Feast on enormous burritos, great tortillas, and delicious tacos. With generous portions, lots of choice, and speedy grillmen, this is one of the top *taquerias* in the city.

Cha Cha Cha $
Tapas   **Map** 9 B1
1801 Haight St, 94117
Tel *(415) 386-7670*
Diners are sure to find a lively atmosphere in this tapas- and sangria-serving Latin American restaurant. Most like the festive vibe of the small venue.

La Corneta Taqueria $
Mexican   **Map** 10 F4
2731 Mission St, 94110
Tel *(415) 643-7001*
Vivid colors, hand-painted murals and bright lights make this a

great dine-in option for juicy, flavorful burritos. The shrimp in particular is spectacular.

Mission Chinese Food $
Chinese   **Map** 10 F3
2234 Mission St, 94110
Tel *(415) 863-2800*   **Closed** *Tue & Wed lunch*
This gourmet sensation has diner prices and ambience. Go there for blisteringly hot dishes such as chili pickled long beans. Try the beer-brined Sichuan pickle.

Pancho Villa Taqueria $
Mexican   **Map** 10 F2
3071 16th St, 94103
Tel *(415) 864-8840*
Famous for its salsas, Pancho Villa serves up heaped plates of freshly made Mexican fare including enormous burritos and tacos.

Pork Store Café $
American   **Map** 9 C1
1451 Haight St, 94103
Tel *(415) 864-6981*
This is a great place for a hearty breakfast. Sample the Pork Store special, served with eggs, hashed brown potatoes, and toast. Huge portions and bottomless coffee.

The grand, exquisite interiors of the dining room at Jardinière

DK Choice

Rhea's Deli and Market $
Deli   **Map** 10 F3
800 Valencia St, 94110
Tel *(415) 282-5255*
This unpretentious, hidden neighborhood gem uses fresh bakery breads for unusual sandwiches such as the fiery-hot Korean BBQ and the salami-filled Cunningham. Traditional deli options are on offer too. On sunny days, take your food to Dolores Park for a picnic and people-watching. No seating.

Rosamunde Sausage Grill $
American   **Map** 10 F4
2832 Mission St, 94110
Tel *(415) 970-9015*
A wide selection of craft beers is on tap, plus freshly made sausages – from traditional to duck and wild boar – with dips.

DK Choice

SoMa StrEat Food Park $
International   **Map** 11 A2
428 11th St, 94103
Tel *(925) 408-1655*
A veritable carnival of food trucks, of every culinary stripe, roam San Francisco's streets. Don't chase them around – a rotating selection of trucks converge at this converted parking lot for convenience. There's covered seating, a beer garden, free Wi-Fi, and TVs; sit and sample away at leisure. Open late on weekends.

Sunflower $
Vietnamese   **Map** 10 F2
3111 16th St, 94103
Tel *(415) 626-5022*
Hearty bowls of Vietnamese soup appeal to vegetarians, but there is plenty for meat lovers to look forward to. There are two dining areas. Enter on Valencia Street.

Key to Prices *see p222*

La Taqueria $
Mexican   **Map** 10 F4
2889 Mission St, 94110
Tel *(415) 285-7117*
This family-run *taqueria* came to national attention in 2014 when its *carnitas* burrito won an America's Best Burrito competition. Serves superb tacos too.

Tartine Bakery $
Bakery   **Map** 10 E3
600 Guerrero St, 94110
Tel *(415) 487-2600*
Croissants, bread pudding, and crusty loaves of bread draw fast-moving lines to this corner café. Good coffee and sandwiches too.

Thep Phanom Thai Cuisine $
Thai   **Map** 10 E1
400 Waller St, 94117
Tel *(415) 431-2526*
This lovely place just off Haight Street has staff in traditional Thai dress. The dishes are good and there's an interesting drinks menu to go with the food.

Truly Mediterranean $
Middle Eastern   **Map** 10 F2
3109 16th St, 94110
Tel *(415) 252-7482*
Excellent falafel and *shawarma* (kebab) wraps are served with fiery hot sauce. Eggplant and potatoes are done to perfection.

DK Choice

Amasia Hide's Sushi Bar $$
Japanese   **Map** 10 D2
149 Noe St, 94144
Tel *(415) 861-7000*
A chorus of *"Irasshaimase!"* ("Come on in!" in Japanese) greets patrons at this neighborhood sushi bar. Fresh fish and a small selection of other Japanese dishes are available here. When it rains, all sake is discounted. Origami paper and cat's cradle entertain guests while they wait.

Chow Church $$
American   **Map** 10 E2
215 Church St, 94114
Tel *(415) 552-2469*
This cozy, organic produce-based neighborhood restaurant offers an eclectic menu – comfort food, crisp wood-fired pizzas, Asian-inspired salads, and daily specials. Guests can choose from small or large portions.

Delfina $$
Italian   **Map** 10 E3
3621 18th St, 94110
Tel *(415) 552-4055*   **Closed** *Lunch*
Perfect Italian fare, made with the freshest local ingredients, is served here. In addition to the legendary chicken and delicate pasta dishes at Delfina, you can also indulge in Neapolitan pizza at its pizzeria next door.

DK Choice

Gracias Madre $$
Mexican   **Map** 10 F2
2211 Mission St, 94110
Tel *(415) 683-1346*
A sit-down Mexican joint in the Mission comes with a California twist. Organic vegan ingredients go into the making of remarkable, original dishes. Sample spicy guacamole; thick corn tortillas; rich mole, heavy with chocolate and spice; and cashew-based sour cream that's better than the real thing. Organic house wines also served.

Indian Oven $$
Indian   **Map** 10 E1
233 Fillmore St, 94117
Tel *(415) 626-1628*
A well-decorated dining room, white tablecloths and attentive service elevate classic, flavorful curries and fresh breads from a good to a great culinary experience. Don't miss the samosas.

Limon Rotisserie $$
Peruvian   **Map** 10 F3
1001 South Van Ness Ave, 94110
Tel *(415) 821-2134*
Mouthwatering, well-seasoned rotisserie chicken is served with crispy yucca fries, unique salads, and tasty sauces at bargain prices.

Lovejoy's Tea Room $$
Tearoom   **Map** 10 E4
1351 Church St, 94114
Tel *(415) 648-5895*   **Closed** *Mon & Tue*
Expect elegant high-tea service with perfect cream scones and English teas. Homey atmosphere, mismatched silverware and chairs, and doily-heavy decor – make for an eclectic and enjoyable experience.

Magnolia Gastropub & Brewery $$
American   **Map** 9 C1
1398 Haight St, 94117
Tel *(415) 864-7468*
This boisterous brewery serves up excellently executed Southern comfort food that complements its award-winning craft beers. Small, well-curated wine list.

Memphis Minnie's BBQ Joint $$
BBQ   **Map** 10 E1
576 Haight St, 94117
Tel *(415) 864-7675*   **Closed** *Mon*
A long-standing neighborhood barbecue joint, this place has a big selection of slow-cooked, wood-smoked meats and a well-matched sake menu. A great choice for meat lovers.

Mission Cheese $$
Cheese   **Map** 10 F3
736 Valencia St, 94117
Tel *(415) 553-8667*   **Closed** *Mon*
This cheese shop and restaurant specializes in artisan cheeses from the US. Home-made pâté and local jams, alongside beer and wines, round out the offerings.

The Monk's Kettle $$
American   **Map** 10 E2
3141 16th St, 94103
Tel *(415) 865-9523*
Glamorous pub food and an extensive beer list are offered here. Long lines on most nights, so reach early. Reservations are not accepted.

Nopalito $$
Mexican   **Map** 3 C2
306 Broderick St, 94117
Tel *(415) 233-9966*
Cozy and cheerful, Nopalito serves authentic Mexican food and beverages. The *carnitas* (roasted or braised pork) are a local favorite.

Diners enjoying global delicacies at SoMa StrEat Food Park

For more information on types of restaurants *see pp216–17*

Glassware on display in the bar area at The Monk's Kettle *(see p227)*

Ragazza $$
Italian **Map** 10 D1
311 Divisadero St, 94117
Tel *(415) 255-1133*
Gourmet pizza, fresh salads, and a good wine list make this a popular neighborhood spot.

Schmidt's $$
German **Map** 11 A4
2400 Folsom St, 94110
Tel *(415) 401-0200*
Seasonal salads, dozens of sausage options, fresh pretzels, and delicious *spaetzle* (egg noodle) with bacon are dished up here. Good selection of German beers.

Zazie $$
French **Map** 9 B2
941 Cole St, 94117
Tel *(415) 564-5332*
Great food and a pleasant outdoor patio add to the charming French countryside ambience at this popular brunch spot. Less crowded at lunch and dinner.

Alembic $$$
American **Map** 9 B1
1725 Haight St, 94117
Tel *(415) 666-0822*
Stop by for a drink – craft beers and house cocktails – and stay for dinner; the food is prepared with inspiration and creative flair.

Farina $$$
Italian **Map** 10 E2
3560 18th St, 94110
Tel *(415) 565-1900*
Chic, elegant Italian cooking is complemented by an outstanding wine selection. Good service and a gorgeous, well-lit dining room.

Foreign Cinema $$$
American **Map** 10 F3
2534 Mission St, 94110
Tel *(415) 648-7600*
Watch a classic film while enjoying gourmet dinner on the patio of

this longstanding gem. Good selection of oysters and shellfish. Great spot for a leisurely brunch.

Zuni Café $$$
Mediterranean **Map** 10 F1
1658 Market St, 94102
Tel *(415) 552-2522* **Closed** *Mon*
This place is set in an unusual wedge-shaped building. Go for the restaurant's chicken and other brick-oven specialties.

Golden Gate Park and Land's End

Crepevine $
American-French **Map** 9 A2
624 Irving St, 94121
Tel *(415) 681-5858*
An expansive menu comprising excellent breakfast and lunch items is on offer here. Fresh, filling sandwiches, salads, and crepes.

San Tung Chinese Restaurant $
Chinese **Map** 8 F3
1031 Irving St, 94122
Tel *(415) 242-0828* **Closed** *Wed*
Dry-fried chicken wings are the popular draw at this spot, but the whole menu merits exploration. Long waiting time for dinner.

Ton Kiang $
Chinese **Map** 8 E1
5821 Geary Blvd, 94121
Tel *(415) 752-4440*
Home-made sauces and pickles boost the flavor of classic dim sum dishes at this place, which specializes in Hakka cuisine. Long lines on weekend lunchtimes.

DK Choice

Beach Chalet Brewery & Restaurant $$
American **Map** 7 A2
1000 Great Hwy, 94122
Tel *(415) 386-8439*
Stumble across this ocean-view restaurant on a ramble through Golden Gate Park. Cheerful crowds down pints of inventive, house-brewed beers alongside standard American dishes. Sample the elaborate weekend brunch menu. The lobby is home to gorgeous original murals from the 1930s.

Cliff House $$
Seafood **Map** 7 A1
1090 Point Lobos Ave, 94121
Tel *(415) 386-3330*
Choose between two restaurants and two bars at this historic, water's-edge spot with views of the Pacific. A classic bistro that earns top praise.

Ebisu $$
Japanese **Map** 8 F3
1283 9th Ave, 94122
Tel *(415) 566-1770* **Closed** *Sun*
Patrons eager for fresh fish sliced up by expert, entertaining sushi chefs wait in long lines. Try the quail egg-oyster shooter.

de Young Café $$
American **Map** 8 F2
50 Hagiwara Tea Garden Dr, 94118
Tel *(415) 750-2613*
Relish American and European fare while enjoying the view of the de Young Museum's Barbro Osher sculpture garden.

Grand exterior of Beach Chalet Brewery & Restaurant, a haven for beer lovers

Intimate bar area and softly lit interiors of the ultra-elegant Gather

Farther Afield

Bette's Oceanview Diner $
American
1807 4th St, Berkeley, 94710
Tel *(510) 644-3230*
A diner-style breakfast joint, Bette's draws city crowd across the bay. Hearty portions , famous scones, and Pennsylvania-style scrapple.

Sunny Side Café $
American
2136 Oxford St, Berkeley, 94704
Tel *(510) 845-9900*
This pleasing sidewalk café, known for using sustainable ingredients, has an expansive breakfast menu, and great diner coffee.

Tamarindo Antojeria $$
Mexican
468 8th St, Oakland, 94607
Tel *(510) 444-1944* **Closed** *Sun*
Rich, savory flavors highlight regional, seasonal Mexican dishes. The small plates can be shared between large groups.

DK Choice
Gather $$$
American
2200 Oxford St, Berkeley, 94704
Tel *(510) 809-0400*
The spacious dining room here feels as intimate and cozy as a café. The menu changes often and features seasonal ingredients. Creative vegetable dishes appeal to both vegetarians and carnivores alike but there's plenty of meat on the menu too. Also on offer are brick-oven pizzas.

Millennium $$$
Vegan
5912 College Ave, Oakland
Tel *(510) 735-9459*
Millennium's Vietnamese-inspired cuisine is vegan and the menu doesn't include any genetically modified food. Try the chef's five-course tasting menu.

Northern California

BOONVILLE: Table 128 $$
American
14050 Hwy 128, 95415
Tel *(707) 895-2210* **Closed** *Tue & Wed*
This romantic setting has a casual, California-rustic atmosphere. Great fixed-price menus. Seasonal ingredients, unpretentious dishes, and a well-selected wine list. Reservations required.

HEARLDSBURG: Barndiva $$$
American
231 Center St, 95448
Tel *(707) 431-0100* **Closed** *Mon & Tue*
The spacious, modern dining room at Barndiva offers a menu of delicious, locally sourced dishes. Service is warm and friendly.

LAKE TAHOE: Artemis Mediterranean Grill $
Mediterranean
2229 Lake Tahoe Blvd, South Lake Tahoe, 96150
Tel *(530) 542-2500*
Menu is mostly Greek, but not exclusively; Mediterranean extends to whatever is in season. Try the home-made pastas and morel mushrooms.

LAKE TAHOE: Bite $$
American
907 Lake Tahoe Blvd, Incline Village, 89451
Tel *(775) 831-1000* **Closed** *Sun & Mon*
The small plates of American classics are meant for sharing. Check out the long, double-sided bar, which serves great cocktails.

SEBASTOPOL: Peter Lowell's $$
American
7385 Healdsburg Ave, 95472
Tel *(707) 829-1077*
An Italian-inspired menu suits the fresh produce from California's Mediterranean climate. Fresh, flavorful foods with a focus on sustainable and organic ingredients. Patio-style seating; warm and friendly service.

SONOMA: The Girl & the Fig $$
American-French
110 West Spain St, 95476
Tel *(707) 938-3634*
A rotating menu showcases Sonoma ingredients in simple, beautiful dishes, alongside a well-chosen wine list. Extensive Sunday brunch. Don't miss the "cheese station," and do try the platters.

Modest exteriors of The Girl & the Fig, Sonoma

For more information on types of restaurants *see pp216–17*

San Francisco's Cafés

You need never search long for a place in which to taste the morning flavors of San Francisco. The city is known to be a paradise for coffee-lovers, as it teems with excellent cafés. Connoisseurs should head for those clustered in North Beach and the Mission District, to sample and enjoy local delights.

Cafès

With so many cafés from which to choose, you could spend days sampling and never visit the same place twice. With locations throughout the city, **Peet's Coffee & Tea** has offered dark, strong coffee for four decades. **Emporio Rulli Il Caffè** is ensconced on Union Square. The **Caffè Trieste**, in North Beach, is an old bohemian haunt that serves excellent coffee. It also has a jukebox that plays songs from Italian opera, and family members who sing and play instruments on occasional weekend afternoons. Columbus Avenue's **Caffè Greco**, **Caffè Puccini**, and **Caffè Roma** are also well worth a visit. This neighborhood, as well as SoMa, is a draw for many visitors because it is dotted with roasteries.

Beatniks frequented tiny **Mario's Bohemian Cigar Store Café** with Washington Square views; try a double latte with focaccia. **Vesuvio** (see p258) serves superb espresso. At **Stella Pastry**, order cappuccino with the specialty rum, marsala, and sherry zabaglione sponge cake, *Sacripantina*.

In the Mission District try **Café La Bohème**, frequented by the San Franciscan literary set. The stylish **Café Flore** on Market Street has charming outdoor seating and serves great lunch options, while **Café Mocha**, near the Civic Center, has terrific coffee and pastries. An airy and well-lit neighborhood spot, coffee lovers will appreciate **Matching Half Café**, which also serves sandwiches, salads, beer, and wine. **Café de la Presse**, across from the Chinatown Gateway, is the place to catch up with international periodicals. SoMa coffee and food choices range from **Café du Soleil** and **Grove Café** in Yerba Buena to the combination café, entertainment venue, and laundromat **Brainwash**. **Schubert's Bakery** and **Toy Boat Dessert Café** are situated on Clement Street. **Momi Toby's Revolution Café & Art Bar** combines Hayes Valley java and artwork and live music. Also in Hayes Valley is the charming **Arlequin Café**, with its community-garden seating area. Check out the Inner Sunset District art and entertainment with a coffee at the **Beanery**.

DIRECTORY

Cafès

Arlequin Café
384 Hayes St.
Map 4 E5.
Tel 626-1211.

Beanery
1307 9th Ave.
Map 8 F3.
Tel 661-1255.

Brainwash
1122 Folsom St.
Map 11 A1.
Tel 861-3663.

Café La Bohème
3318 24th St.
Map 10 F4.
Tel 643-0481.

Café Flore
2298 Market St.
Map 10 D2.
Tel 621-8579.

Café Mocha
505 Van Ness Ave.
Map 4 F5.
Tel 437-2233.

Café de la Presse
352 Grant Ave.
Map 5 C4.
Tel 398-2680.

Café du Soleil
345 3rd St.
Map 6 D5.
Tel 699-6154.

Caffè Greco
423 Columbus Ave.
Map 5 B3.
Tel 397-6261.

Caffè Puccini
411 Columbus Ave.
Map 5 B3.
Tel 989-7033.

Caffè Roma
526 Columbus Ave.
Map 5 B3.
Tel 296-7942.

885 Bryant St.
Map 11 B2.
Tel 296-7662.

Caffè Trieste
601 Vallejo St.
Map 5 C3.
Tel 982-2605.

Emporio Rulli Il Caffè
333 Stockton St,
Union Square.
Map 5 C5.
Tel 433-1122.

Grove Café
690 Mission St.
Map 6 D5. **Tel** 957-0558.

Mario's Bohemian Cigar Store Café
566 Columbus Ave.
Map 5 B2.
Tel 362-0536.

Matching Half Café
1799 McAllister St.
Map 3 C5.
Tel 674-8699.

Momi Toby's Revolution Café & Art Bar
528 Laguna St.
Map 10 E1.
Tel 400-5689.

Peet's Coffee & Tea
22 Battery St.
Map 6 D4.
Tel 981-4550.

Schubert's Bakery
521 Clement St.
Map 3 A5.
Tel 752-1580.

Stella Pastry
446 Columbus Ave.
Map 5 B3.
Tel 986-2914.

Toy Boat Dessert Café
401 Clement St.
Map 3 A5.
Tel 751-7505.

Vesuvio
255 Columbus Ave.
Map 5 C3.
Tel 362-3370.

Light Meals and Snacks

If you do not have the time to sit down for a full meal, you can get a quick bite to eat almost anywhere in San Francisco. Many establishments serve good fast food at low prices, but if you look for them, you can find places that offer something a little special.

Breakfast

Coffee and pastries, or bacon and eggs, are easy to find in San Francisco, or you can have a full American breakfast that will sustain you all day. **Sears Fine Foods** in Union Square is an institution, popular for its wonderful early morning meals. **Le Petit Café** serves great brunches on weekends. Hotel dining rooms offer good breakfasts, as do a few restaurants (see pp222–9).

Delis

If you want a perfect corned beef on rye sandwich try **David's**, the largest and most central delicatessen in San Francisco. **Tommy's Joynt** in the Civic Center, **Miller's East Coast Deli** in Russian Hill, and **Molinari's** in North Beach are also worth a visit. The **Real Food Company**, also in Russian Hill, specializes in organic food.

Hamburger Places

While you can get a quick hamburger and fries at all of the usual franchises, you would do better to try one of San Francisco's more unique places. The **Grubstake**, housed in a converted streetcar, is open late, **Mel's Drive-In** is a 1950s-style café, and **Louis'** has unbeatable views over the remains of the Sutro Baths (see p159). **Bill's Place** in the Richmond District offers two dozen different burgers, all of which are named after local celebrities, while hole-in-the-wall **Sam's Pizza & Burgers** in North Beach serves the famous double cheese-burger until after midnight.

Pizzerias

San Francisco has many good pizzerias throughout the city. Choose between the traditional **Tommaso's**, the popular **North Beach Pizza**, and the hectic, but excellent, **Golden Boy**. For a really exotic pizza, try **Pauline's** in the Mission District or the chain pizzeria **Extreme Pizza** in Pacific Heights.

Mexican Food

Mexican food, which is tasty and often extremely inexpensive, is sold by vendors all over the city. For a delicious snack, try **El Farolito**, **Pancho Villa Taqueria**, or **El Metate**. For a treat before or after a movie, try **El Super Burrito** – great prices and large portions.

DIRECTORY

Breakfast

Le Petit Café
1 Maritime Pl.
Map 6 D3.
Tel 951-8514.

Sears Fine Foods
439 Powell St.
Map 5 B4.
Tel 986-0700.

Delis

David's
474 Geary St.
Map 5 B5.
Tel 276-5950.

Miller's East Coast Deli
1725 Polk St.
Map 4 F3.
Tel 563-3542.

Molinari's
373 Columbus Ave.
Map 5 C3.
Tel 421-2337.

Real Food Company
2140 Polk St.
Map 5 A3.
Tel 673-7420.

Tommy's Joynt
1101 Geary Blvd.
Map 5 A5.
Tel 775-4216.

Hamburger Places

Bill's Place
2315 Clement St.
Map 2 D5.
Tel 221-5262.

Grubstake
1525 Pine St.
Map 4 F4.
Tel 673-8268.

Louis'
902 Point Lobos Ave.
Map 7 A1.
Tel 387-6330.

Mel's Drive-In
3355 Geary Blvd.
Map 3 B5.
Tel 387-2244.

Sam's Pizza & Burgers
618 Broadway St.
Map 5 C3.
Tel 391-1539.

Pizzerias

Extreme Pizza
1980 Union St.
Map 4 D3.
Tel 929-8234.

Golden Boy
542 Green St.
Map 5 B3.
Tel 982-9738.

North Beach Pizza
800 Stanyan St.
Map 9 B2.
Tel 751-2300.

1462 Grant Ave.
Map 5 C2.
Tel 433-2444.

Pauline's
260 Valencia St.
Map 10 F2.
Tel 552-2050.

Tommaso's
1042 Kearny St
at Pacific Ave.
Map 5 C3.
Tel 398-9696.

Mexican Food

El Farolito
2779 Mission St.
Map 10 F4.
Tel 824-7877.

El Metate
2406 Bryant St.
Map 11 A4.
Tel 641-7209.

Pancho Villa Taqueria
3071 16th St.
Map 10 F2.
Tel 864-8840.

El Super Burrito
1200 Polk St.
Map 5 A5.
Tel 771-9700.

SHOPPING IN SAN FRANCISCO

Shopping in San Francisco is much more than simply making a purchase, it's an experience that allows a glimpse into the city's culture. An enormous range of goods is available here, from the practical to the eccentric, and you can take your time in choosing because browsers are generally welcome, particularly in the city's many small specialty shops and boutiques. If you want convenience, the shopping centers, malls, and department stores are excellent. For those in search of local color, each neighborhood shopping district has a charm and personality of its own.

Emporio Armani *(see p239)*

When to Shop

Most shops in San Francisco open at 10am and stay open until 8pm, Monday to Saturday. Many malls and department stores also remain open until later in the evening and on Sundays. Stores are quietest in the mornings, but can be hectic at lunchtime (noon–2pm), on Saturdays, and during sales and holidays.

How to Pay

Major credit cards are accepted at most shops, although there will often be a minimum purchase price. Foreign checks or foreign currency are rarely taken. Some smaller shops will allow only cash purchases.

Consumer Rights and Services

Keep your receipts as proof of purchase. Each shop sets and displays its own return and exchange policies. Shops cannot charge a fee to those using credit cards, but you may get a discount for cash. If you have a problem that shop management cannot solve, the **Consumer Protection Unit** or the **California Department of Consumer Affairs** may help.

Sales

End-of-the-month, holiday, and pre-season sales are common in many stores. Keep an eye out for advertisements in local newspapers where these are announced, especially mid-week and Sundays. Shop early for the best bargains, and beware of "Going out of business" signs – these can be left up for years. Some are legitimate sales; just ask at nearby shops.

Taxes

A sales tax of 8.5 percent is added to all purchases made in San Francisco. Note that this is not refundable to overseas visitors, unlike the European Value Added Tax (VAT), but you are exempt if your purchases are forwarded to any destination outside California.

Foreign visitors may have to pay duty at customs on arrival home.

Shopping Tours

If you want to be guided to the best shops, you may want to go on a special tour. These are organized by companies such as **Glamour Girl Shopping Tours** or **Shopper Stopper Shopping Tours**. A guide takes you from shop to shop and usually knows where to find just the right things.

Malls and Shopping Centers

In contrast with a great many suburban shopping malls, those of San Francisco have character, and one or two are of architectural interest. The Embarcadero Center *(see p112)* has more than 125 shops, in an area covering eight blocks. Ghirardelli Square *(see p87)* was a chocolate factory from 1893 until the early 1960s. It is now a mall that is popular with visitors, and houses over 70 restaurants and shops, overlooking San Francisco Bay.

Lively crowd at the farmer's market, Pier 39

Ghirardelli chocolate, Fisherman's Wharf

The Westfield San Francisco Centre *(see p119)* has nine levels and contains more than 65 shops. PIER 39 *(see p82)* is a marketplace on the waterfront, with restaurants, a double-decker Venetian merry-go-round, a marina, and many specialty shops. In the Cannery *(see p87)*, located at Fisherman's Wharf, you will find a variety of charming small shops, while the Crocker Galleria *(see p118)* is one of the city's most spectacular malls, with three floors under a high glass dome built around a central plaza.

The Japan Center *(see p130)*, complete with pagoda, offers exotic foods, goods, and art from the East, as well as a Japanese-style hotel and traditional baths. The Rincon Center *(see p115)*, with a 90-ft (27-m) water column at its center, is an Art Deco haven for shopping and eating.

Department Stores

Most of San Francisco's major department stores are in or near Union Square. They are huge emporia that offer their customers an outstanding selection of goods and services. The frequent sales can get quite frantic as locals and visitors jostle for bargains. All sorts of extra services are available to make shoppers feel pampered, including cloakrooms where you can leave your belongings, assistants to guide you around the store, free gift wrapping, and beauty salons offering treatments.

Macy's department store spans two city blocks. It stocks an enormous range of goods, all beautifully presented and sold by an enthusiastic sales force. It offers all sorts of extra facilities, including a currency exchange and an interpreting service. The men's department is particularly extensive.

Neiman Marcus is another stylish emporium, housed in a modern building that caused a furor when it was opened in 1982, replacing a popular store built in the 1890s. The huge stained-glass dome in its Rotunda Restaurant was part of the original building, and is well worth coming to see. **Nordstrom**, good for fashion and shoes, is known in the city as the "store-in-the-sky," as it is located on the top five floors of the innovative Westfield San Francisco Centre.

Bloomingdale's offers a huge range of designer labels, luxury handbags, accessories, cosmetics, and shoes.

Another famous department store in the Bay Area is **Kohl's**, which carries quality clothing, shoes, accessories, and jewelry at discounted prices.

Best Buys

Gourmet shoppers should look for seafood, one of the city's specialties. Wine from California is another good buy, particularly in the Napa Valley *(see pp192–5)*. You will find blue jeans at competitive prices, also vintage clothing, ethnic art, books, and records.

DIRECTORY

Consumer Rights and Services

Consumer Protection Unit
Tel 551-9575. California Department of Consumer Affairs
Tel (1) (800) 952-5210

Shopping Tours

Glamour Girl Shopping Tours
Tel (650) 218-1734.
🆆 glamourgirlshopping tours.com

Shopper Stopper Shopping Tours
Tel (707) 829-1597

Department Stores

Bloomingdale's
845 Market St.
Map 5 C5.
Tel 856-5300.

Kohl's
1200 El Camino Real, Colma, CA 94014.
Tel (650) 992-0155.

Macy's
Stockton and O'Farrell Sts.
Map 5 C5.
Tel 397-3333.

Neiman Marcus
150 Stockton St.
Map 5 C5.
Tel 362-3900.

Nordstrom
Westfield San Francisco Centre, 865 Market St. **Map** 5 C5.
Tel 243-8500.

The interior of the upscale shopping mall, Westfield San Francisco Center

San Francisco's Best: Shopping

It is the diversity of San Francisco's stores
that makes buying anything here such
an adventure. Some of the best shopping
areas are described below, each reflecting
a different aspect of the city. Window
shoppers will find glittering displays
in Union Square, while bargain hunters
should visit the South of Market outlets.

Street Fairs
Arts, crafts, and specialty foods are sold from
booths at neighborhood fairs like this one
on Union Street, held in June.

Union Street
Clusters of boutiques in converted Victorian
houses sell antiques, books, and clothes
on this busy street (see p239).

**Pacific
Heights
and the
Marina**

Presidio

Civic Center

**Golden Gate Park
and Land's End**

**Haight Ashbury
and the Mission**

Haight Street
This is the best place in San Francisco for vintage
clothes, record shops, and books (see pp242–3).

Japan Center
You can buy authentic food and goods
from Japan here, and visit Japanese
bars and galleries (see p130).

UN Plaza
Named after the signing of the United Nations Charter, this is the site of the twice-weekly Farmers' Market (see pp244–5).

Grant Avenue
With its painted balconies, souvenir shops, and bars, this is Chinatown's main tourist street (see p244).

Crocker Galleria
Elegant shops fill the three floors of this impressive modern mall, with daylight flooding in through the glass roof. You can picnic in the rooftop gardens on sunny days (see p242).

Fisherman's Wharf and North Beach

Financial District and Union Square

Chinatown and Nob Hill

Saks Fifth Avenue
A department store synonymous with exclusive style and elegance (see p118).

Jackson Square Antique Shops
Lovers of antiques will enjoy browsing in the shops in Jackson Square (see p112).

Shopping Around Union Square

Serious shoppers should concentrate on the blocks bordered by Geary, Powell and Post streets, and on the surrounding blocks between Market and Sutter streets. Here, luxurious shops and inexpensive boutiques sell everything from designer sheets to pedigree dogs to souvenirs. Big hotels, splendid restaurants, and colorful flower stalls all add to the atmosphere.

Nordstrom
This fashion store is located in the gleaming Westfield Centre, which has 400 shops filling nine floors (see p233).

San Francisco Specials

Entrepreneurial spirit in San Francisco is strong and innovative. Owners of small shops, designers, and buyers take much pride in bringing unusual and hand-crafted wares to their customers, and will often tell you the histories of these original items. From comic postcards to fine hand-crafted Florentine paper, and from Chinese herbal teas to high-tech electronic gadgets, all kinds of goods are available. Nestling in hidden corners or clustered with other tiny shops, these specialty outlets create an environment that makes shopping in San Francisco an exciting experience.

Specialty Shops

Luxurious handbags, luggage, accessories, and scarves are the hallmark of **Coach**, one of America's preeminent designers. This city outlet also has friendly and attentive staff. At **Comix Experience** you can find a wide range of comic books and memorabilia from the newest offerings to antique, expensive oldies.

Exquisite Italian ceramics (majolica) are on display at **Biordi Art Imports** in North Beach, where hand-painted dishware, vases, and platters of all sizes are for sale. Those who would like to experience the authentic atmosphere of Chinatown will find it at **Ten Ren Tea Company of San Francisco**. At **Golden Gate Fortune Cookie Factory** (see p101), descendants of Chinese immigrants allow customers to taste samples before buying the San Francisco fortune cookies, which were a Chinatown invention. Sixty-year-old **FLAX Art and Design** features a huge selection of hand- made papers, customized stationery, and artist's tools.

Precious gems, glittering gold, and watches by some of the world's finest jewelers can be found at **Tiffany & Co.** and **Bulgari**. **Rare Device** is a unique store that offers handmade jewelery, accessories and other products from local designers.

Shops for a Good Cause

San Franciscans take great pleasure in shopping for a good cause: it assuages the conscience, and provides a temporary fix for the acquisitive urge. Here are a few establishments that cater to those shoppers who are keen to make a contribution. Proceeds from **Out of the Closet**, a treasure trove of a thrift store, directly benefit the AIDS Healthcare Foundation. The **Golden Gate National Park Store** is a not-for-profit shop offering park memorabilia, postcards, maps, and books. Co-founded by the author David Eggers, **826 Valencia Pirate Supply Store** is a quirky shop that supports their non-profit work on children's literacy.

Souvenirs

All sorts of souvenirs, such as T-shirts, keyrings, mugs, and Christmas ornaments, are decorated with motifs symbolizing San Francisco at **Only in San Francisco** and the **Cable Car Store**. Souvenir and novelty caps of every color, shape, and size are available at **Krazy Kaps**, while shop entrances in Grant Avenue and Fisherman's Wharf are lined with baskets filled with inexpensive gifts.

Antiques

Set in San Francisco's most sophisticated shopping area is the **Sacramento Street Antique Dealer's Association**. This collection of stores offers an array of antiques from furniture to small household items. It is a shoppers' paradise that is great for browsing.

Located in the North Beach District of the city, **Schein and Schein** offers an impressive collection of antique maps, books, and engraved prints, including many from the 14th to the 19th centuries.

Toys, Games, and Gadgets

The **Academy Store** and the **Exploratorium Store** sell books, kits, and games that make learning fun. At **Puppets on the Pier**, on PIER 39, new owners get puppetry lessons in the shop. There are over 500 different puppets to choose from, including marionettes and finger puppets. The comprehensively stocked **Gamescape** sells any type of game that doesn't require electricity, such as traditional gameboards, collectible cards, and role-playing books.

The **Chinatown Kite Shop** takes shopping to new heights, displaying an extra-ordinary assortment of flying objects. These range from traditional to World Champion stunt kites, all making attractive souvenirs. In the heart of the Inner Sunset District, anything and everything related to magic can be found at **Misdirections Magic Shop**, a paradise for serious magicians or those who simply want to buy a few tricks.

Museum Shops

Museum shopping is another option for visitors to San Francisco, and shops offer delightful and exquisite gifts to suit all budgets, ranging from science kits to reproduction jewelry and sculpture. In San Francisco's Golden Gate Park, visit the **Academy Store** in the California Academy of Sciences (see pp152–3), one of the leading science and natural history museums in America. Here aspiring naturalists can purchase dinosaur models, realistic rubber animals, and gifts that are environmentally friendly. Merchandise based on the Academy's Far Side Gallery, which displays the work of cartoonist Gary Larsen, is also for sale. Nearby, there is also a fine assortment of items at the **de Young Museum** shop. At Lincoln Park the **Legion of Honor Museum Store** *(see pp158–9)* offers many beautiful selections based on current exhibitions.

The **Asian Art Museum** shop in the Civic Center is well stocked with books and objects that reflect the museum's area of interest, including ceramics, basketry, textiles, jewelry, sculpture, paintings and prints, and furniture.

There is a great deal to intrigue young scientists at the unique **Exploratorium Store** *(see p94)*. Here they will find all the equipment they need for scientific experiments, games based on topics ranging from astronomy to zoology, and how-to-do-it books and toys.

In the San Francisco Museum of Modern Art *(see pp120–23)*, the **San Francisco MOMA Museum Store** sells a wide range of beautifully printed art books, posters, greetings cards, and colorful T-shirts, as well as artistically designed bags, jewelry, watches and

accessories for home and office. In fact, the shop is worth a visit just to see the stunning new building designed by Norwegian based architecture firm, Snøhetta.

Gump's *(see p118)* is so splendid it could almost be mistaken for a museum. Many of the items are American or European antiques, limited editions, or one of a kind. Well-heeled residents and visitors come here for furniture, fine art, china, crystal, jewelry, and gifts. The shop itself has had a long and storied history, having been established in 1861.

DIRECTORY

Specialty Shops

Biordi Art Imports
412 Columbus Ave.
Map 5 C3.
Tel 392-8096.

Bulgari
200 Stockton St.
Map 5 C5.
Tel 399-9141.

Coach
190 Post St.
Map 5 C4.
Tel 392-1772.

Comix Experience
305 Divisadero St.
Map 10 D1.
Tel 863-9258.

Rare Device
600 Divisadero St.
Map 1- D1.
Tel 863-3969.

FLAX Art and Design
Fort Mason Center, 2 Marina Blvd, Bldg D.
Map 10 F1.
Tel 530-3510.

Golden Gate Fortune Cookie Factory
56 Ross Alley.
Map 5 C3.
Tel 781-3956.

Ten Ren Tea Company of San Francisco
949 Grant Ave.
Map 5 C3.
Tel 362-0656.

Tiffany & Co.
350 Post St.
Map 5 C4.
Tel 781-7000.

Shops for a Good Cause

826 Valencia Pirate Supply Store
826 Valencia St.
Map 10 F3. **Tel** 642-5905.

Golden Gate National Park Store
Presidio Bldg 983.
Map 2 F2.
Tel 561-3040.

Out of the Closet
1295 Folsom St.
Map 4 F4.
Tel 558-7176.

Souvenirs

Cable Car Store
PIER 39.
Map 5 B1.
Tel 989-2040.

Krazy Kaps
PIER 39.
Map 5 B1.
Tel 296-8930.

Only in San Francisco
PIER 39. **Map** 5 B1.
Tel 705-5500.

Antiques

Sacramento Street Antique Dealers Association
3599 Sacramento St.
Map 3 B4.
Tel 637-5837.

Schein and Schein
1435 Grant Ave.
Map 5 C2.
Tel 399-8882.

Toys, Games, and Gadgets

Academy Store
See Museum Shops.

Chinatown Kite Shop
717 Grant Ave.
Map 5 C3.
Tel 989-5182.

Exploratorium Store
See Museum Shops.

Gamescape
333 Divisadero St.
Map 10 D1.
Tel 621-4263.

Misdirections Magic Shop
1236 9th Ave.
Map 9 A2.
Tel 566-2180.

Puppets on the Pier
PIER 39.
Map 5 B1.
Tel 781-4435.

Museum Shops

Academy Store
California Academy of Sciences,
55 Music Concourse Dr.
Map 8 F2.
Tel 933-6159.

Asian Art Museum
200 Larkin St.
Map 4 F5. **Tel** 581-3500.
w asianart.org

de Young Museum
50 Tea Garden Dr,
Golden Gate Park.
Map 8 F2.
Tel 750-3642.

Exploratorium Store
Pier 9.
Map 6 D2.
Tel 528-4857.

Gump's
135 Post St.
Map 5 C4.
Tel 982-1616.

Legion of Honor Museum Store
Legion of Honor, Lincoln Park.
Map 1 B5.
Tel 750-3677.

San Francisco MOMA Museum Store
Museum of Modern Art.
Map 6 D5.
Tel 357-0037.
w museumstore.sfmoma.org

Clothes and Accessories

San Francisco has a reputation for sophistication, which, judging from its clothing shops, is richly deserved. No matter what the occasion requires, from a designer outfit for a formal event to the comfort of a pair of jeans, you will find it in San Francisco.

August Fashion Week runway shows boost reputations of emerging designers from the San Francisco Bay Area, the West Coast, and New York. Unlike the department stores *(see p233)*, which offer a wide selection, most of the shops listed below are small or medium-sized, and often focus on just one or two lines. Take time to see these true gems of the retail world.

San Francisco and Other US Designers

Lines by American designers are sold in boutiques within a department store or in exclusive shops under the designer's name. Retailers such as **Wilkes Bashford** feature up-and-coming designers with a bent for conservative clothing that would be a perfect option for current denizens of the Financial District.

San Francisco designer shops to discover include **Diana Slavin** for classic Italian styles, **Joanie Char** for chic sportswear separates, and **Upper Playground** for SF-inspired T-shirts with original designs. **Emporio Armani Boutique** has an impressive selection of clothing and accessories. Fashionable knits for women can be purchased at **Weston Wear** at rock-bottom prices. Designer **Sunhee Moon** names each of her 1950s-influenced clothing items after friends. **MAC**, or Modern Appealing Clothing, sources one-third of its menswear, as well as womenswear, from San Francisco designers.

Discount Designer Clothes and Outlets

For designer clothes at concessional rates, head to the SoMa (South of Market) area. Yerba Buena Square contains several kinds of outlets, including **Burlington Coat Factory**, which stocks more than 12,000 coats. Here you can find discounted lines from many local designers. **Skechers USA** offers a wide variety of shoes at below retail prices. **Jeremy's**, in Berkeley, discounts formal clothing and designer-wear for both men and women. **Sports Basement** is a mecca of sportswear at discount prices.

Bay Area Mall Outlets

Plan a drive to the Bay Area mall outlets, for a good bargain or take home major designer brands at discounted prices. Though about an hour away from San Francisco, given the array of clothes on offer the visit would certainly be a shoppers' delight.

Find fashion outlets for Liz Claiborne, Off 5th Saks Fifth Avenue, Brooks Brothers, as well as OshKosh and Gap for children's garments, and Bass and Nine West for shoes, at the large **Petaluma Village Premium Outlets**, 46 miles (74 km) north of the city.

Fifty miles (80 km) southeast of San Francisco in Milpitas, **Great Mall** outlets stock some of the best brands. The more popular names include Tommy Hilfiger, Eddie Bauer, Polo Jeans Factory Store, St. John Knits, and Chico's casual women's styles.

Castro District

Clothing and accessories accent the dominant gay, lesbian, and transgendered

Size Chart

For Australian sizes, follow the British conversion.

Children's clothing

American	2–3	4–5	6–6x	7–8	10		12	14	16 (size)
British	2–3	4–5	6–7	8–9	10–11	12	14	14+ (years)
Continental	2–3	4–5	6–7	8–9	10–11	12	14	14+ (years)

Children's shoes

American	8½	9½	10½	11½	12½	13	1½	2½	2½
British	7	8	9	10	11	12	13	1	2
Continental	24	25½	27	28	29	30	32	33	34

Women's dresses, coats, and skirts

American	4	6	8	10	12	14	16	18
British	6	8	10	12	14	16	18	20
Continental	34	36	38	40	42	44	46	48

Women's blouses and sweaters

American	6	8	10	12	14	16	18
British	30	32	34	36	38	40	42
Continental	36	38	40	42	44	46	48

Women's shoes

American	5	6	7	8	9	10	11
British	3	4	5	6	7	8	9
Continental	36	37	38	39	40	41	44

Men's suits

American	34	36	38	40	42	44	46	48
British	34	36	38	40	42	44	46	48
Continental	44	46	48	50	52	54	56	58

Men's shirts

American	14	15	15½	16	16½	17	17½	18
British	14	15	15½	16	16½	17	17½	18
Continental	36	38	39	41	42	43	44	45

Men's shoes

American	7	7½	8	8½	9½	10½	11	11½
British	6	7	7½	8	9	10	11	12
Continental	39	40	41	42	43	44	45	46

lifestyles in this neighborhood; shopping is amusing as well as intriguing. If a garment's function or how to wear it is unclear, don't hesitate to ask. **Body SF** is a particularly well-stocked store.

Fillmore

Fillmore Street's Victorian buildings and the creation of the Jazz Preservation District lend hip history and ambience to this strolling strip, known for adorable boutique shops such as **Joie**.

Haight Ashbury

Wandering along Haight Street, it is easy to spot tie-dye T-shirts and vintage clothing stores. **Piedmont Boutique**'s landmark giantess legs adorned with fishnet stockings mark one store where clothing patterns are still cut by hand.

Hayes Valley

Proclaiming their taste for progressive style, the people at **Acrimony** pride themselves on delivering an assortment of contemporary designers. It is all about independence and an evolving style at this über-hip, street-smart shop.

Noe Valley

Beautiful clothing carefully tweaked to suit a woman's lifestyle can be found at boutique **Rabat**, in this hip part of town. Their shoes are stylish and comfortable and their handbags well designed and fashionable.

South of Market

The SoMa area, once full of warehouses and flophouses, now has swanky studios and lofts aplenty. It still possesses a gritty, no-nonsense quality

that appeals to the younger set, who patronize clubs that seem to blossom from nowhere at night.

Union Square

You won't find stiff-collared work shirts or ties at this outpost of **John Varvatos**. A truly American sensibility defines this designer's lifestyle brand, which is a favorite of many LA celebrities. The clothes have attitude, whether it be athletic punk or vintage-inspired sportswear.

Union Street

It is a short walk from the nearby apartments and mansions to this cheerful street of small boutiques. Quintessential Union Street shops such as **Marmalade** offer on-trend styles with affordable price tags.

DIRECTORY

San Francisco and Other US Designers

Diana Slavin
3 Claude Lane.
Map 5 C4.
Tel 677-9939.

Emporio Armani Boutique
1 Grant Ave.
Map 5 C5.
Tel 677-9400.

Joanie Char
537 Sutter St.
Map 5 B4.
Tel 399-9867.

MAC
387 Grove St.
Map 4 F5.
Tel 863-3011.

Sunhee Moon
3167 16th St.
Map 10 E2.
Tel 355-1800.

Upper Playground
220 Fillmore St.
Map 10 E1.
Tel 861-1960.

Weston Wear
569 Valencia St.
Map 10 F2.
Tel 621-1480.

Wilkes Bashford
375 Sutter St.
Map 5 C4.
Tel 986-4380.

Discount Designer Clothes and Outlets

Burlington Coat Factory
899 Howard St.
Map 11 B2.
Tel 495-7234.

Jeremy's
2961 College Ave, Berkeley.
Tel (510) 849-0701.

Skechers USA
2600 Mission St.
Map 10 F3.
Tel 401-6211.

Sports Basement
1590 Bryant St.
Map 11 A3.
Tel 575-3000.

Bay Area Mall Outlets

Great Mall
447 Great Mall Dr, Milpitas.
Tel 408-945-4022.

Petaluma Village Premium Outlets
2220 Petaluma Blvd, North Petaluma.
Tel 707-778-9300.

Castro District

Body SF
450 Castro St.
Map 10 D3.
Tel 575-3562.

Fillmore

Joie
2116 Fillmore St.
Map 4 D4.
Tel 400-0367.

Haight Ashbury

Piedmont Boutique
1452 Haight St.
Map 9 C1.
Tel 864-8075.

Hayes Valley

Acrimony
333 Hayes St.
Map 4 F5.
Tel 861-1025.

Noe Valley

Rabat
4001 24th St.
Map 10 D4.
Tel 415-282-7861.

Union Square

John Varvatos
152 Geary St.
Map 5 C5.
Tel 986-0138.

Union Street

Marmalade
1843 Union St.
Map 4 D3.
Tel 757-8614.

Men's Clothes

For men's designer brands, sportswear, shoes, and accessories with a European influence try **Rolo**. **Brooks Brothers** was the first retailer of ready-made clothes for men in the United States. The company is now known for its smart suits and button-down shirts.

Rugged and fashionable outdoor clothing is available from **Eddie Bauer**. **Gap** and **Old Navy** combine casual hipness with affordable prices. Men requiring larger sizes can buy travelwear and sweaters, and be fitted for both formal and business suits, at **Rochester Big and Tall**. **Body** is a mecca for form-fitting T-shirts, tops, underwear, shoes, and more.

Women's Clothes

Many of the world's famous names in fashion are in San Francisco, including **Chanel**, **Gucci**, and **Louis Vuitton**. **Banana Republic** and **Guess** provide stylish, wearable clothes.

Hip, cute, and comfortable workout attire can be found at trendy **Lululemon**. **Ann Taylor** has well-made suits, blouses, evening dresses, and sweaters. **Bebe** stocks contemporary clothing for the chic and slim. **Lane Bryant** offers stylish and flattering designs in sizes 12–26. **Urban Outfitters** has chic secondhand and new clothes, and **Anthropologie** has stylish vintage-inspired looks that include denim and dresses.

Children's Clothes

Colorful collections of cotton attire, as well as accessories for kids can be found at the local favourite, **Small Frys**. **Gap Kids** and **Baby Gap** are good on selection, size, and color. **Dottie Doolittle** in Presidio Heights stocks the best in American and European clothes for children of all ages, from newborn to pre-teen. **Sprout**, which has a handful of locations, offers natural and organic children's clothing and gifts.

Shoes

Top-quality footwear is available at **Kate Spade**, which delivers classic yet inspired shoes, bags, and accessories. Best names in comfort are at **Ria's**, including Clarks, Birkenstock, Timberland, Sebago, and Rockport. **Nike Town** is a megastore for sneakers, and **DSW Shoe Warehouse** offers an enormous range of discounted shoes.

Shoe Biz II, one of two Shoe Biz stores on Haight Street, is easy to spot, with its dinosaur mascot figure outside. The music and relaxing chairs in the store are an easy way to slide in and out of a large sneaker selection. **Shoe Biz I** has fashion-aware, value-priced everyday shoes. **Merrell** shoes are reliably stylish and comfortable.

Foot Worship stocks women's sizes from 5–14, personally assisting a clientele that enjoys a precarious stiletto heel.

Lingerie

San Francisco's playful side gets indulged, too. **Alla Prima Fine Lingerie** fits the finest European brand-name underwear, silky gowns, and camisoles. **Victoria's Secret** has San Francisco outposts, including Union Square. The international boutique, **Agent Provocateur**, offers lingerie as well as sleepwear and swimwear.

Leather Clothing

In San Francisco, leatherwear is an antidote to fog effects as well as a lifestyle declaration. **Fog City Leather** custom-makes alligator jackets and purveys head-to-pants leather clothing. A local institution for more than 80 years, **Golden Bear Sportswear** uses the highest-quality leather for its handmade jackets in a variety of modern and classic styles.

Outdoor Outfitters

There is a lot of accessible outdoor space around the city and Northern California, with active adult clothing, gear, and equipment stores to provide for adventuring whims. **REI** bargain prices on the first Saturday of the month and seasonal sales are a good bet for skiing, snowboarding, cycling, paddling, and comfortable travelwear.

The **North Face** started in North Beach in 1966 and provides outerwear designed for sub-freezing temperatures. **Patagonia**'s mountain-climbing roots developed organic cotton, and moisture- and heat-resistant clothing for activities ranging from climbing, surfing, running, and mountain biking to yoga.

Sportswear

Devoted baseball fans shop for logo caps to pants at **SF Giants Dugout** stores. A wide display of authorized NFL and NBA team sweatshirts and sweatpants are available at the **NFL College Shop** at PIER 39. San Francisco 49er jerseys and varsity jackets are popular buys at **Champs Sports**. A more complete range of team merchandise is available at the **49ers Team Store**, which has T-shirts, hats, tailgating gear, and much more.

The **Adidas Store** has a great variety of classic shoes, sporty apparel, and genuine athletic wear for men and women. Specialty sportswear and gear shops include **Golfsmith**, for both golf and tennis, and **Athleta**, which offers all types of exercise clothes for women.

For name-embossed San Francisco T-shirts, hoodies, or sleepwear, **Only in San Francisco** at Fisherman's Wharf has one of the widest selections available.

Vintage Clothing

Buffalo Exchange and **Crossroads Trading** offer secondhand clothing with something of a history. **Wasteland** in the Haight Ashbury District is known for its vintage clothes and, in the same district, **Static** offers a wide range of carefully selected high-end vintage items.

DIRECTORY

Men's Clothes

Body
450 Castro St. **Map** 10 D3.
Tel 575-3562.

Brooks Brothers
240 Post St. **Map** 5 C4.
Tel 402-0476.

Eddie Bauer
Westfield Centre, Level 3.
Map 5 C5.
Tel 343-0146.

Gap
2169 Chestnut St.
Map 4 D2.
Tel 929-1744.

890 Market St.
Map 5 C5.
Tel 788-5909.

Old Navy
801 Market St. **Map** 5 C5.
Tel 344-0375.

**Rochester Big
and Tall**
1202 El Camino Real, San
Bruno **Tel** (650) 757-1366.

Rolo
2351 Market St.
Map 10 D2.
Tel 431-4545.

Women's Clothes

Ann Taylor
3 Embarcadero Center.
Map 6 D3.
Tel 989-5355.

Anthropologie
880 Market St. **Map** 5 C5.
Tel 434-2210.

Banana Republic
256 Grant Ave. **Map** 5 C4.
Tel 788-3087.

Bebe
Westfield Centre, Level 2.
Map 5 C5. **Tel** 543-2323.

Chanel
156 Geary St. **Map** 5 C4.
Tel 981-1550.

Gucci
240 Stockton St.
Map 5 C5. **Tel** 392-2808.

Guess
Westfield Centre, Level 3.
Map 5 C5.
Tel 543-4636.

Lane Bryant
1150 El Camino Real #297
Tel (650) 238 5442.

Louis Vuitton
233 Geary St.
Map 5 C5.
Tel 391-6200.

Lululemon
327 Grant Ave.
Map 5 C4.
Tel 402-0914.

Urban Outfitters
80 Powell St.
Map 5 B5.
Tel 989-1515.

Children's Clothes

Dottie Doolittle
3680 Sacramento St.
Map 3 B4.
Tel 673-1334.

Gap Kids/Baby Gap
3491 California St.
Map 3 B4.
Tel 386-7517.

Small Frys
4066 24th St.
Map 10 D4.
Tel 648-3954.

Sprout
1828 Union St.
Map 4 E2.
Tel 359-9205.
(one of several locations)

Shoes

**DSW Shoe
Warehouse**
400 Post St. **Map** 5 B5.
Tel 956-3453.

Foot Worship
1214 Sutter St.
Map 5 A5.
Tel 921-3668.

Kate Spade
865 Market St.
Map 5 C5.
Tel 222-9638.

Merrell
285 Geary St.
Map 5 B5.
Tel 834-9605.

Nike Town
278 Post St.
Map 5 C4.
Tel 392-6453.

Ria's
301 Grant Ave.
Map 5 C4.
Tel 834-1420.

Shoe Biz I
1420 Haight St.
Map 9 C1.
Tel 861-0313.

Shoe Biz II
1553 Haight St.
Map 9 C1.
Tel 861-3933.

Lingerie

Agent Provocateur
54 Geary St..
Map 4 E2.
Tel 421-0229.

**Alla Prima Fine
Lingerie**
539 Hayes St.
Map 5 C2.
Tel 864-8180.

Victoria's Secret
865 Market St.
Map 5 B5.
Tel 974-1760.

Leather Clothing

Fog City Leather
2060 Union St.
Map 4 D2.
Tel 567-1996.

**Golden Bear
Sportswear**
200 Potrero Ave.
Map 11 A3.
Tel 863-6171.

Outdoor Outfitters

North Face
180 Post St.
Map 5 C4.
Tel 433-3223.

Patagonia
770 North Point St.
Map 5 A2.
Tel 771-2050.

REI
840 Brannan St.
Map 11 B2.
Tel 934-1938.

Sportswear

49ers Team Store
865 Market St
Tel 666-2296

Adidas Store
Westfield Centre,
Level 1. **Map** 5 C5.
Tel 975-0934.

Athleta
2226 Fillmore St.
Map 4 D4. **Tel** 345-8501.

Champs Sports
Westfield Centre, Level LC.
Map 5 C5.
Tel 975-0883.

Golfsmith
735 Market St.
Map 5 C5.
Tel 974-6979.

NFL College Shop
PIER 39. **Map** 5 B1.
Tel 397-2027.

Only in San Francisco
PIER 39 at Jefferson St.
Map 5 B1.
Tel 397-0143.

SF Giants Dugout
AT&T Park.
Map 11 C1.
Tel 947-3419.

Vintage Clothing

Buffalo Exchange
1555 Haight St.
Map 9 C1.
Tel 431-7733.

1210 Valencia St.
Map 10 F4.
Tel 647-8332.

Crossroads Trading
1901 Fillmore.
Map 4 D4.
Tel 775-8885.

2123 Market St.
Map 10 E2.
Tel 552-8740.

Static
1764 Haight St.
Map 9 B1.
Tel 422-0046.

Wasteland
1660 Haight St.
Map 9 B1.
Tel 863-3150.

Books, Music, Art, and Antiques

Hundreds of shops cater to the many writers, artists, and collectors living in and visiting San Francisco. Residents decorate their houses with items from local art and antiques galleries. Visitors who love shopping for fine and unusual objects – from that rare one-of-a-kind piece to distinctive contemporary ethnic arts – are sure to find a treasure in one of San Francisco's shops.

General Interest Bookstores

The artists of the Beat Generation once gathered to talk about America's emerging 1960s social revolution at the **City Lights Bookstore** *(see p88)*, a famous San Francisco institution. It stays open till late, making it a favorite hangout for students. **Reader's Bookstore** at the Fort Mason Center is a great place to relax and peruse the books. **Green Apple Books** has both new and used books, and is open until 10:30pm, or 11:30pm on Fridays and Saturdays. **Folio Books** is a neighborhood bookstore situated in the heart of Noe Valley that also sells new and used books, while **The Booksmith**, located in Haight Ashbury, is notable for its stock of foreign and political periodicals. The **Alexander Book Company** located in the downtown SoMa district has good selections of children's and general interest books.

Specialty Bookstores

If science fiction, mystery, and horror are what excites you, head over to **Borderland Books** for the most extensive selection of titles in these genres. If your interests include the environment, politics, and sustainability, **The Green Arcade** is the place to visit. **Omnivore Books** is a food lover's dream, filled with a wide range of cookbooks and other types of food-inspired books. **Kinokuniya** is a popular Japanese retailer that stocks a massive selection of periodicals, DVDs and stationery.

New and Used Music

Streetlight Records offers a varied selection of new and used music as well as bargain DVDs, CDs, and video games. Obscure sounds are available at **Recycled Records** on Haight Street, where new and used recordings are bought, sold, and traded as eagerly as stocks in the Financial District. Tiny **Groove Merchant Records** in the Lower Haight specializes in soul, funk, and hip-hop vinyl, and is colorfully decorated with vintage gig posters. Most of its staff DJ regular gigs around the city. **Amoeba Music** has the largest selection of CDs and tapes in the country. It has 500,000 titles, both new and secondhand, including jazz, international blues, and rock music. A music collector's paradise, this is *the* place to go if you are looking for hard-to-find music at low prices.

Sheet Music

For all your musical needs, pay a visit to **Sunset Music Company**, a one-stop shop selling sheet music, music books, instruments, and music accessories. They also offer services such as lessons, rehearsal room rental, and instrument hire. All types of music and books of collections can be found at the **Union Music Company**.

Art Galleries

New enthusiasts as well as serious art lovers will find something to their liking in the hundreds of galleries. The **John Berggruen Gallery** *(see p40)* has the biggest collection in San Francisco of works by both emerging and well-established artists. The **Fraenkel Gallery** is known for its collection of 19th- and 20th-century photography. The **Haines Gallery**, in the same building, stocks paintings, drawings, sculpture, and photography. **SF Camerawork** sells limited-edition prints by renowned photographic artists, while **The Shooting Gallery** located in the Tenderloin shows edgy, interesting art pieces. **Art Haus Gallery** is a top boutique gallery with museum-quality contemporary fine art. New works by American artists are hung at **Gallery Paule Anglim**, while realism is the theme at the **John Pence Gallery**.

For affordable art by local Bay Area artists, visit **Hang Art** gallery. **Vista Point Studios Gallery** shows amazing photos of the Bay Area and beyond.

Ethnic and American Folk Art

Good collections of ethnic art are at several galleries. Find beautiful handmade African masks, jewelry, and textiles at **African Outlet**. Pottery and masks from Japan are hard to resist at **Ma-Shi'-Ko Folk Craft**. Traditional and contemporary works by local artists can be found at **Galeria de la Raza**.

International Antiques

San Francisco's Barbary Coast area *(see pp28–9)* has been transformed into a shopping district for antiques, and is now called **Jackson Square** *(see p112)*. More antiques can be found at the vast **San Francisco Antique and Design Mall**.

Aria Antiques offers true finds in its eclectic shop and **Lang Antiques** has all kinds of items from the Victorian, Art Nouveau, Art Deco, and Edwardian periods. **JRM International** sells a unique assortment of fine art and antiques from world cultures. All sorts of antique books, prints, and maps can be seen at **Prints Old & Rare** – although you will need to make an appointment.

DIRECTORY

General Interest Bookstores

Alexander Book Company
50 Second St.
Map 6 D4.
Tel 495-2992.
w alexanderbook.com

The Booksmith
1644 Haight St.
Map 9 B1.
Tel 863-8688.
w booksmith.com

City Lights Bookstore
261 Columbus Ave.
Map 5 C3.
Tel 362-8193.
w citylights.com

Folio Books
3957 24th St.
Map 10 E4.
Tel 821-3477.
w foliosf.com

Green Apple Books
506 Clement St.
Map 3 A5.
Tel 387-2272.
w greenapplebooks.com

Reader's Bookstore
Room 165, Building C,
Fort Mason Center.
Map 4 D1.
Tel 771-1011.
w friendssfpl.org

Specialty Bookstores

Borderland Books
866 Valencia St.
Map 10 F3.
Tel 824-8203.

The Green Arcade
1680 Market St.
Map 10 F1.
Tel 431-6800.

Kinokuniya
1581 Webster St.
Map 4 E4.
Tel 567-7625.

Omnivore Books
3885A Cesar Chavez St.
Map 10 E4.
Tel 282-4712.

New and Used Music

Amoeba Music
1855 Haight St.
Map 9 B1.
Tel 831-1200.

Groove Merchant Records
687 Haight St.
Map 10 D1.
Tel 252-5766.

Recycled Records
1377 Haight St.
Map 9 C1.
Tel 626-4075.

Streetlight Records
980 South Bascom Ave,
San Jose.
Tel (408) 292-1404.

Sheet Music

Sunset Music Company
2311 Irving St.
Map 8 E3.
Tel 731-1725.

Union Music Company
1710B Market St.
Map 10 E1.
Tel 775-6043.

Art Galleries

Art Haus Gallery
411 Brannan St.
Map 11 C1.
Tel 977-0223.

Fraenkel Gallery
49 Geary St.
Map 5 C5.
Tel 981-2661.

Gallery Paule Anglim
14 Geary St.
Map 5 C5.
Tel 433-2710.

Haines Gallery
49 Geary St,
5th Floor.
Map 5 C5.
Tel 397-8114.

Hang Art
567 Sutter St,
2nd Floor.
Map 3 C4.
Tel 434-4264.

John Berggruen Gallery
228 Grant Ave.
Map 5 C4.
Tel 781-4629.

John Pence Gallery
750 Post St.
Map 5 B5.
Tel 441-1138.

SF Camerawork
1011 Market St.
Map 11 A1.
Tel 487-1011.

The Shooting Gallery
886 Geary St.
Map 5 A5.
Tel 931-8035.

Vista Point Studios Gallery
405 Florida St.
Map 11 A3.
Tel 215-9073.

Ethnic and American Folk Art

African Outlet
4942 3rd St.
Tel (415) 864-3576.

Galeria de la Raza
Studio 24,
2857 24th St.
Map 10 F4.
Tel 826-8009.

Ma-Shi'-Ko Folk Craft
1581 Webster St,
Japan Center.
Map 4 E4.
Tel 346-0748.

International Antiques

Aria Antiques
1522 Grant Ave.
Map 5 C2.
Tel 433-0219.

Jackson Square Art & Antique Dealers Association
445 Jackson St
(at Jackson Square).
Map 5 C3.
Tel 398-8115.

JRM International
2015 17th St.
Map 11 B3.
Tel 864-8118.

Lang Antiques
309 Sutter St.
Map 5 C4.
Tel 982-2213.

Prints Old & Rare
580 Mount Crespi
Drive, Pacifica,
CA 94044.
Tel (650) 355-6325.

San Francisco Antique and Design Mall
538 Castro St.
Map 10 D3.
Tel 626-1283.

Food and Household Goods

San Francisco's "foodies" are a sophisticated breed, and they thrive on the city's reputation for fine food. When not dining out, they cook at home from well-stocked pantries in their ultra-equipped kitchens. Cravings for good wine, gourmet groceries, and for the items that make cooking into an art form can easily be satisfied here. For the home, there are dozens of stores carrying the latest household goods, computers, and photographic and electronic equipment.

Gourmet Groceries

From abalone to zucchini (courgettes), and from fresh Californian produce to imported specialty foods, gourmet grocers such as **Whole Foods** carry a variety of items. **Williams-Sonoma** has jams, mustards, and much more for gifts or as a special treat. **David's** is known for its lox (smoked salmon), bagels, and New York cheesecake. For a quick takeout lunch or a choice of beautifully packaged foods, try one of the department store food sections such as **Macy's Cellar**. Most large-chain grocery stores have good international sections.

In addition to fresh takeout items, Italian delicatessens stock olive oil, polenta, and pasta from Italy. **Molinari Delicatessen** is famous for its ravioli and tortellini, ready to throw in the saucepan. **Lucca Ravioli** has a friendly staff, who makes their pasta on the premises. **Pasta Gina**, located in lovely Noe Valley, sells pasta, prepared pesto, and other sauces with ample meatballs.

It is worth going to the two Chinese quarters – Chinatown (see pp96–102) in the city center and Clement Street (see p63) – for Asian food products and produce. At **Casa Lucas Market** you will find Spanish and Latin American specialties.

Specialty Food and Wine Shops

A baguette of fresh sourdough bread from **Boudin Bakery** is an addiction with locals and a tradition with visitors. **La Boulangerie San Francisco** brings Paris to San Francisco, with some of the best bread in the city. More Italian specialties come from **Il Fornaio Bakery**, a popular offshoot from their restaurant on Battery Street. Head to **Fillmore Bake Shop** for heavenly pastries, while the gourmet cupcakes made fresh throughout the day from **Kara's** are also delicious.

San Franciscans are coffee connoisseurs and there are many specialty shops. **Caffè Trieste** sells custom-roasted and blended coffees and a variety of brewing equipment. **Caffè Roma Coffee Roasting Company** and the **Graffeo Coffee Roasting Company** both sell excellent beans. The locals are also loyal to **Peet's Coffee & Tea** and **Blue Bottle Coffee**.

Chocoholics usually frequent **See's Candies** and San Francisco's own **Ghirardelli's**. Ice cream is good from **Ben & Jerry's** and **Hot Cookie**. If you have a sweet tooth, be sure to stop by **Miette**, which specializes in home-made caramels and other delectables. Head for **Bi-Rite Market** for locally grown products and to **Cheese Plus** for a huge selection of cheeses.

The staff at the **California Wine Merchant** makes good recommendations and are very knowledgeable about their affordable wines.

Farmers' Markets and Flea Markets

Locally grown produce arrives by the truckload at farmers' markets in the center of the city. Stalls are erected for the day, and farmers sell directly to the public. The **Heart of the City** is open from 7am to 5:30pm on Wednesdays and until 5pm on Sundays. The **Ferry Plaza** on Saturdays is from 9am to 2pm. Chinatown's produce stores have the feel of an exotic farmers' market and are open every day. All kinds of things are sold at the flea markets. The one in **Berkeley** is within easy reach. Be prepared to barter and to pay in cash. There may also be a nominal entrance fee.

Household Goods

Gourmet cooks dream of **Williams-Sonoma**'s many kitchen gadgets and quality cookware. From practical pots and pans to beautiful serving plates, **Crate & Barrel** sells moderately priced items for your kitchen and patio. Chinese cooking gear is the specialty of the house at **The Wok Shop**. For bed, bath, and table linens and general household goods, visit **Bed, Bath & Beyond**. **Sue Fisher King** sells elegant, fashionable items for the home and bath. For a kaleidoscopic range of fabrics and accessories, from silks, woolens, and cottons, to buttons, ribbons and laces, and even upholstery materials, look no farther than **Britex Fabrics**.

Computers, Electronics, and Photographic Equipment

One of the best places to head to for computers is **Central Computers**. For software and for anything else electronic, pay a visit to **Best Buy**. It's "one-stop shopping for the nerd population."

For new and secondhand camera gear, repairs, and film, go to **Adolph Gasser**. Some of the discount camera shops along Market Street have shady reputations, so it is advisable to check with the Visitor Information Center (see p119) for the best and most reputable places to shop. If you just need film or other photographic supplies, **Camera Zone and Art Gallery**, in Fisherman's Wharf, offers very low prices along with good advice.

DIRECTORY

Gourmet Groceries

Casa Lucas Market
2934 24th St.
Map 9 C3.
Tel 826-4334.

David's
474 Geary St.
Map 5 A5. **Tel** 276-5950.

Lucca Ravioli
1100 Valencia St.
Map 10 F3.
Tel 647-5581.

Macy's Cellar
170 O'Farrell St.
Map 5 C1.
Tel 397-3333.

Molinari Delicatessen
373 Columbus Ave.
Map 5 C3.
Tel 421-2337.

Pasta Gina
741 Diamond St.
Map 10 D4.
Tel 282-0738.

Whole Foods
1765 California St.
Map 4 F4.
Tel 674-0500.

Williams-Sonoma
340 Post St.
Map 5 C4.
Tel 362-9450.
W williams-sonoma.com
One of several branches.

Specialty Food and Wine Shops

Ben & Jerry's Ice Cream
1480 Haight St.
Map 9 C1.
Tel 626-4143.
W ben&jerrys.com

Bi-Rite Market
3639 18th St.
Map 10 E3.
Tel 241-9760.
550 Divisadero St.
Map 10 D1.
Tel (415) 551-7900.

Blue Bottle Coffee
1 Ferry Building.
Map 6 D3.
Tel (510) 653-3394.
One of several branches.

Boudin Bakery
4 Embarcadero Center.
Map 6 D3.
Tel 362-3330.
One of many branches.

La Boulangerie San Francisco
2325 Pine St.
Map 4 D4.
Tel 440-0356.

Caffè Roma Coffee Roasting Company
526 Columbus Ave.
Map 5 B2.
Tel 296-7942.

Caffè Trieste
601 Vallejo St.
Map 5 C3. **Tel** 982-2605.

California Wine Merchant
2113 Chestnut St.
Map 4 D2.
Tel 567-0646.

Cheese Plus
2001 Polk St.
Map 5 A3.
Tel 921-2001.

Fillmore Bake Shop
1890 Fillmore St.
Map 4 D4.
Tel 923-0711.

Il Fornaio Bakery
1265 Battery St.
Map 5 C2.
Tel 986-0100.

Ghirardelli's
Ghirardelli Square.
Map 4 F1.
Tel 474-2846.
42 Stockton St.
Map 5 C1.
Tel 397-3030.

Graffeo Coffee Roasting Company
735 Columbus Ave.
Map 5 B2.
Tel 986-2420.

Hot Cookie
407 Castro St.
Map 10 D2.
Tel 621-2350.
One of several branches.

Kara's Cupcakes
3249 Scott St.
Map 3 C2.
Tel 563-2253.

Miette
449 Octavia St.
Map 4 E5.
Tel 626-6221.
One of several branches.

Peet's Coffee & Tea
2257 Market St.
Map 10 D2.
Tel 626-6416.
One of several branches.

See's Candies
3 Embarcadero Center.
Map 6 D3.
Tel 391-1622.
One of several branches.

Farmers' Markets and Flea Markets

Berkeley Flea Market
1937 Ashby Ave, Berkeley,
CA 94703.
Tel (510) 644-0744.

Ferry Plaza Farmers' Market
Base of Market at
the Embarcadero.
Map 6 D3.
Tel 291-3276
W ferrybuildingmarket
place.com

Heart of the City Farmers' Market
United Nations Plaza.
Map 11 A1.
Tel 558-9455.

Household Goods

Bed, Bath & Beyond
555 9th St.
Map 11 A4.
Tel 252-0490.

Britex Fabrics
146 Geary St.
Map 5 C5.
Tel 392-2910.

Crate & Barrel
55 Stockton St.
Map 5 C5.
Tel 982-5200.
W crateandbarrel.com

Sue Fisher King
3067 Sacramento St.
Map 3 C4.
Tel 922-7276.

Williams-Sonoma
See Gourmet Groceries.

The Wok Shop
718 Grant Ave.
Map 5 C4.
Tel 989-3797.

Computers, Electronics, and Photographic Equipment

Adolph Gasser, Inc
181 Second St.
Map 6 D5.
Tel 495-3852.

Best Buy
1717 Harrison St.
Map 11 A3.
Tel 626-9682.

Camera Zone and Art Gallery
1365 Columbus St.
Map 5 A1.
Tel 359-0947.

Central Computers
837 Howard St.
Map 5 C5.
Tel 495-5888.

ENTERTAINMENT IN SAN FRANCISCO

San Francisco has prided itself on being the cultural capital of the West Coast since the city first began to prosper in the 1850s, and here entertainment is generally of high quality. The performing arts complex of the Civic Center is the major location for the best classical music, opera, and ballet. The latest addition to the cultural life here is the excellent Center for the Arts Theater at Yerba Buena Gardens. International touring shows can be seen here. Numerous repertory movie theaters *(see pp250–51)* offer filmgoers a wide range of choices, but theater, except for some independent productions is not the city's strongest suit. Popular music, especially jazz and blues, is where San Francisco excels, and you can hear good bands in intimate locales for the price of a drink, or at the street fairs and music festivals held during the summer months *(see pp50–53)*. Facilities are also available around the city for all kinds of sports, from bicycling to golf or sailing.

Information

Complete listings of what's on and where are given in the *San Francisco Chronicle* and *Examiner* newspapers *(see p275)*. The Chronicle's Sunday edition is most useful, with a "Datebook" section (also called the "Pink Pages") that gives details of hundreds of events taking place each week. Other good sources include the free *San Francisco Weekly* (available at newsstands, kiosks, cafés, and bars). These give both listings and reviews, especially of live music, films, and nightclubs.

Visitors planning further in advance will find the *San Francisco Book* very helpful. This is published twice yearly by the San Francisco Visitor Information Center, and contains listings of both short- and long-running cultural events. The book is available free if you go to the Visitor Information Center at Hallidie Plaza. You can also phone the bureau's events line for recorded information. Numerous free magazines for visitors are available, as well as calendars of events.

Among these are *Key This Week San Francisco* and *Where San Francisco*.

Buying Tickets

The main source for tickets to concerts, theater, and sports events is **Ticketmaster.** This company has a virtual monopoly on ticket sales, running an extensive charge-by-phone operation in Tower Record shops all over Northern California. They ask for a "convenience charge" of around $7 per ticket. The only alternative to Ticketmaster is to buy directly from the box offices, though many of these are open only just before the start of evening performances.

Many productions by the San Francisco Symphony and ballet and opera companies are sold out in advance. So if you want to see one of these performan-ces, advance planning is essential. All have subscription programs through which you can buy tickets for the season, useful if you are planning to stay in the city for a lengthy period of time.

There are only a few ticket agencies in San Francisco, mostly

People enjoying the outdoors in Portsmouth Square, Chinatown

specializing in selling hard-to-get seats at marked-up prices. All are listed in the Yellow Pages of the telephone directory. "Scalpers," or ticket hawkers, can be found lurking outside most sold-out events, offering seats at extortionate prices. If you are willing to bargain (and miss the opening), you can sometimes get a good deal.

Discount Tickets

Discount tickets for selected theater, dance, and music events are available from **TIX Bay Area**, which offers half-price seats from a booth on the east side of Union Square. Tickets are sold from 11am on the day of the performance, and can be purchased with cash or

Banner for the Jazz Festival *(see p254)*

Johnny Winter, Blues guitar legend, performing at the Blues Festival *(see p255)*

traveler's checks. There are also some half-price tickets available on weekends for events taking place on the following Sunday and Monday.

TIX Bay Area is also a full-service ticket outlet, and will accept credit cards for advance sales. It is open Tuesday to Friday 11am to 6pm, Saturday 10am to 6pm, and Sunday 10am to 3pm.

Free Events

In addition to San Francisco's many ticket-only events, a number of free concerts and performances are staged all over the city. Most of these take place during the day. The San Francisco Symphony gives a late summer series of Sunday concerts at Stern Grove, south of the Sunset District, and is occasionally used for ballets.

Cobbs Comedy Club, Fisherman's Wharf, hosts the San Francisco International Comedy Competition for four weeks in August/September. Over 300 entertainers join in.

Performers from the San Francisco Opera sing outdoors in the Financial District, as part of the "Brown Bag Operas" series. In the summer the park is host to the Shakespeare Festival, Comedy Celebration Day, and the San Francisco Mime Troupe. A series of concerts called "Jewels in the Square" brings live music to Union Square on Wednesdays at 12:30pm and 6pm, and Sundays at 2pm, and at Old St. Mary's Cathedral *(see p100)* there are sometimes lunchtime recitals at 12:30pm during the week.

Facilities for the Disabled

California is a national leader in providing the handicapped with access to facilities. Most theaters and concert halls in San Francisco are therefore fully accessible, and have special open areas set aside for wheelchair-bound patrons. A few of the smaller houses may require you to use special entrances, or elevators to reach the upper tiers, but in general access is free of obstacles. Many movie theaters also offer amplifying headphones for the hearing impaired. Contact the theaters to be sure of their facilities, and see *Practical Information* on page 268.

The façade of Castro Theater, a landmark theater in San Francisco *(see p138)*

DIRECTORY

Useful Numbers

San Francisco Visitor Information Center
Powell St at Market St,
lower level Hallidie Plaza.
Tel 391-2000.
W sftravel.com

California Welcome Center
PIER 39,
Building B, 2nd Level.
Tel (415) 981-1280.
W visitcalifornia.com

Ticket Agencies

Ticketmaster
Charge-by-phone.
Tel (1-800) 745-3000.
W ticketmaster.com or
W tickets.com

TIX Bay Area
East Side of Union Sq, Powell St between Geary and Post streets.
Tel 430-1140.
W theatrebayarea.org or
W tixbayarea.com

AT&T Park, home of the San Francisco Giants *(see p260)*

San Francisco's Best: Entertainment

With a huge variety of entertainment
options, San Francisco is one of the most
enjoyable cities in the world. Big names
in every branch of the arts perform here,
and many also make the city their home,
attracted by the creative local community.
In addition to the West Coast's best opera,
ballet, and symphony orchestra, the city
supports a wide range of jazz and rock music
plus diverse theater and dance companies.
For the sports-minded, there are numerous
events to watch or take part in. And finally,
the spectacular parks and recreation areas
allow visitors to design their own outdoor
activities, many of them costing nothing.

Clay Theatre
For foreign films try the Clay Theatre
on Fillmore Street, which was built
in 1910 and is one of the city's
oldest theaters (see p250).

**San Francisco Comedy
Celebration Day**
This annual festival in Golden Gate
Park offers spectators a chance to see
new talent that could, like Whoopi
Goldberg, make it big (see p247).

Pacific
Heights a
the Marir

Presidio

Civic Center

Golden Gate Park
and Land's End

Haight Ashbury
and the Mission

0 kilometers   2
0 miles   1

Fillmore Auditorium
Famous for acts such as
Jefferson Airplane in the
1960s, the Auditorium
remains a premier music
venue (see p254).

Outdoor Ballet at Stern Grove
The natural outdoor amphitheater is
a tranquil setting for ballet (see p247).

Street Entertainers on Fisherman's Wharf
A lively mix of street musicians, jugglers, and various other impromptu performers entertain the crowds at Fisherman's Wharf *(see p247).*

The Saloon
Local blues bands perform nightly at this popular North Beach bar. Dating from 1861, the Saloon is an authentic Gold Rush survivor *(see p254).*

The Fairmont Hotel
Some of the best live music can be heard in piano bars at big hotels. The Tonga Room at the Fairmont is where Tony Bennett made "I Left My Heart in San Francisco" famous *(see p257).*

Fisherman's Wharf and North Beach

Chinatown and Nob Hill

Financial District and Union Square

The Geary Theater
This landmark building, home of the renowned American Conservatory Theater, has been extensively renovated since the 1989 earthquake *(see p251).*

War Memorial Opera House
Book tickets in advance for the acclaimed San Francisco Opera Association *(see p252).*

Slim's
One of the classiest of the SoMa nightclubs, Slim's offers a mixture of jazz, rock and blues *(see p255).*

Film and Theater

San Francisco has an avid filmgoing community, and newly released blockbusters often get shown at neighborhood theaters. In keeping with its reputation as a center of the arts, San Francisco really excels at film festivals. In addition to the well-known International and Mill Valley festivals, there are annual celebrations of the best of Native American, Asian-American, Women's, and Gay and Lesbian film and video productions.

Theater offerings are much less varied and more expensive than films, and at any one time there may be only a handful of productions from which to choose. Mainstream theaters, which host a range of touring Broadway productions as well as those by local companies, are concentrated in the Theater District *(see p118)*, along Geary Street just west of Union Square. The Fort Mason Center *(see pp74–5)* is another theatrical nexus, with a more avant-garde reputation.

First-Run Films

For an enjoyable multimedia experience, head to the **Metreon 16**, a 15-screen complex plus IMAX. There are shops, restaurants, special programs, and other attractions. The **Sundance Kabuki** Japan Center *(see p130)* and the modern **Embarcadero Center Cinema**, and **Presidio Theatre** are other excellent movie houses for first-run films; the Embarcadero also excels at foreign and indie films. Prices for all first-run venues are roughly the same.

Other popular venues include the **AMC Van Ness 14** and the **Century San Francisco Centre. The latter** is located in the West-field San Francisco Centre and has luxurious seats and a gourmet snack bar.

Programs usually start around noon, with shows every 2 hours until around 10pm. On occasion, there are midnight shows on weekends. Half-price tickets may be available for at least the first showing, although this varies greatly from theater to theater. The Kabuki offers its best discounts every day from 4pm to 6pm.

Foreign Films and Art Houses

Main venues for first-run foreign films are the **Clay Theatre** in Pacific Heights and **Opera Plaza**, a four-screen complex. Both of these are owned and operated by the Landmark chain, which sells a discount card that gives five admissions for a saving of 30 percent.

The **Castro Theatre** *(see p138)*, San Francisco's finest older theater, shows Hollywood classics as well as unusual newer films, with programs changing daily. The chic **Roxie**, an independent rep house in the Mission District, and the historic **Victoria Theater**, also screen forgotten classics and unusual new releases.

More obscure but intriguing fare is at **Cinematheque**, which has programs on Sunday nights at the San Francisco Art Institute, and on Thursday nights at the **Yerba Buena Center for the Arts**.

Film Festivals

Held at the Kabuki complex for two weeks in May, the **San Francisco International Film Festival** usually has some commercial hits. Generally, however, it shows independent and foreign releases that might not otherwise get shown. The tickets sell extremely fast, and you will need to book three or four days in advance. The **Mill Valley Film Festival**, held early in October, is also a mainstay of the circuit, as is the increasingly high-profile **San Francisco International LGBT Film Festival** held each June at the Castro, Roxie, and the Yerba Buena Center for the Arts.

Mainstream Theaters

Many residents of San Francisco show apparent disdain for the international commercial successes, which

Film Ratings

Films in the US are graded as follows:
G General audiences, all ages admitted.
PG Parental guidance suggested. Some material unsuitable for children.
PG-13 Parents strongly cautioned. Some material inappropriate for children under age 13.
R Restricted. Children under 17 need to be accompanied by a parent or adult guardian.
NC-17 No children under 17 admitted.

On Location

Many places in and around San Francisco have played starring roles in films:

Alcatraz is the famous high-security prison in *Bird Man of Alcatraz* and *Escape from Alcatraz*.
Alta Plaza Park is where Barbra Streisand drove a car down the steps in *What's Up, Doc?*
Bodega Bay, on the coast just north of San Francisco, is the small town in Hitchcock's *The Birds*.
Chinatown as tourists don't usually see it is the setting for *Chan is Missing*, *The Dead Pool*, *Dim Sum*, and *Hammett*.
Fillmore Auditorium's final week, with footage of the Grateful Dead, is the theme of *Fillmore*.
Mission District featured in the violent cop thriller *The Laughing Policeman*.
Presidio is where a brutal murder takes place in the crime thriller *The Presidio*.
Union Square is the scene for the key sequence of *The Conversation*.

explains why theater has a lower profile here than in other large cities. There are likely to be at least a couple of major shows, however, playing at the main Theater District spots; three of the largest theaters are the **Golden Gate Theater**, the **Curran Theater**, and the **Orpheum Theater**, all part of the Best of Broadway performance series. Others include the **New Conservatory Theatre Center** and the **Marines Memorial Theatre**. At the center of the San Francisco's Mission District, **The Marsh Theater** is dedicated to staging new and original performing arts shows.

The most respected major company in the city is the **American Conservatory Theater (ACT)**, whose longtime home, the landmark Geary Theater, is located near Union Square. A variety of plays are performed during its October to May season.

Alternative Theater

With dozens of small theaters spread around the city, and many more in the Bay Area, San Francisco's off-Broadway scene is alive and well, if hard to find. **Fort Mason** is the most obvious center, home to the nationally known **Magic Theatre** and diverse other groups, as well as the Playwrights Festival each August (see p51).

The historic **San Francisco Playhouse** is known for hosting premiers from celebrities such as Lily Tomlin and Steve Martin. The Mission District boasts the satirical **Theater Rhinoceros** and risk-taking **Project Artaud** (see p253). The city's best-loved production, the uniquely San Franciscan revue *Beach Blanket Babylon*, still plays at North Beach's **Club Fugazi** (see p89).

Other companies to look out for are **Intersection for the Arts**, the multimedia-oriented **Exit Theater**, and the highly regarded **Berkeley Repertory Theater** in the East Bay.

DIRECTORY

First-Run Films, Foreign Films, and Art Houses

AMC Van Ness 14
Map 4 F4.
Tel 674-4630.

Castro Theatre
Map 10 D2.
Tel 621-6120.

Century San Francisco Centre
Map 5 C5.
Tel 538-8422.

Cinematheque
Map 11 B3.
Tel 552-1990.

Clay Theatre
Map 4 D3.
Tel 561-9921.

Embarcadero Center Cinema
Map 6 C3.
Tel 352-0835.

Metreon 16
Map 5 C5.
Tel (1-888) 262-4386
or 369-6207.

Opera Plaza
Map 4 F5.
Tel 771-0183.

Presidio Theatre
Map 3 C2.
Tel 776-2388.

Roxie
Map 10 F2.
Tel 863-1087.

Sundance Kabuki
Map 4 E4.
Tel 346-3243.

Victoria Theater
Map 10 F2.
Tel 863-7576.

Yerba Buena Center for the Arts
Map 5 C5.
Tel 978-2787.

Film Festivals

San Francisco International LGBT Film Festival
Map 11 A2.
Tel 703-8655.
W frameline.org

Mill Valley Film Festival
38 Miller Ave, Mill Valley.
Tel 383-5256.

San Francisco International Film Festival
Map 4 D5.
Tel 561-5000.
W sffs.org

Mainstream Theaters

American Conservatory Theater (ACT)
Map 5 B5.
Tel 749-2228.
W act-sf.org

Curran Theater
Map 5 B5.
Tel (415) 358-1220.

Golden Gate Theater
Map 5 B5. Tel 673-6757.

Marines Memorial Theatre
Map 5 B4. Tel 771-6900.
W marinesmemorial theatre.com

The Marsh Theater
Map 10 F3. Tel 282-3055.
W themarsh.org

New Conservatory Theatre Center
Map 10 F1.
Tel 861-8972.
W nctcsf.org

Orpheum Theater
Map 11 A1.
Tel 551-2000.
W orpheum-theater. com

Alternative Theater

Berkeley Repertory Theater
2025 Addison St, Berkeley.
Tel (510) 647-2900 or
(510) 647-2949.

Club Fugazi
Map 5 B3.
Tel 421-4222.
W beachblanket babylon.com

Exit Theater
156 Eddy St.
Map 5 B5.
Tel 673-3847.
W theexit.org

Fort Mason Center
Map 4 E1.
Tel 345-7500.

Intersection for the Arts
Map 10 F2.
Tel 626-2787.

Magic Theatre
Map 4 E1.
Tel 441-8822.

Project Artaud
Map 11 A3.
Tel 621-4240.

San Francisco Playhouse
Map 5 B4.
Tel 771-6900.
W sfplayhouse.org

Theater Rhinoceros
Map 10 F2.
Tel (800) 838-3006.

Opera, Classical Music, and Dance

Since the Gold Rush days of 1849, San Francisco has prided itself on the variety of its cultural institutions, and its ability to attract world-class performers. Black-tie fundraisers and the Hotel Tax Fund help support the performing arts, and there is great popular support as well, evidenced by the full houses. The main halls, including the War Memorial Opera House and the Louise M. Davies Symphony Hall, are in the Civic Center performing arts complex (see pp128–9). The best times to see a performance are winter and spring, when the opera, symphony, and ballet seasons are all in full swing. However, tickets can be hard to obtain, so it is sensible to book well in advance.

Opera

Beginning well before 1932, when San Francisco built the first municipally owned opera house in the US, opera has been popular in the city. In recent years the San Francisco Opera has achieved international fame as one of the world's finest attracting such stars as Placido Domingo and Dame Kiri Te Kanawa, and artist David Hockney to design the sets. All performances feature English translations of the lyrics, which are projected as "supertitles" above the stage.

The main season runs from September to December, and the opening night is one of the principal social events on the West Coast. Summer special events are held in June and July, when tickets may be easier to obtain.

Ticket prices range from about $10 to $15 (for standing room, sold on day of performance) to more than $100. For advance information, contact the **San Francisco Opera Association**. To find out about ticket availability, contact **War Memorial Opera House** box office.

Across the bay, the high-caliber **West Edge Opera** performs in April and May at the El Cerrito Performing Arts Center.

Classical Music

The **Louise M. Davies Symphony Hall**, part of the Civic Center performing arts complex, was inaugurated on September 16, 1980. Following a great deal of criticism about the acoustics, a decision was made to make alterations, and building work began in 1991. The hall reopened in 1992. It is now San Francisco's principal location for fine classical music performances, and home to the highly regarded **San Francisco Symphony**.

The orchestra performs up to five concerts a week during its September to June season. Guest conductors, performers, and various touring orchestras perform additional special concerts, and in July a "Symphony Pops" program is held at the Louise M. Davies Symphony Hall. Next door to the Opera House, the **Herbst Theatre** (closed for renovation until 2015) hosts recitals by prominent performers.

In addition to these big events, there are numerous less formal recitals and concerts in the Bay Area. The **Philharmonia Baroque Orchestra**, a period instrument ensemble, plays at various sites around the city, while the historic **Old First Presbyterian Church** has a series of chamber music and individual recitals on Friday nights and Sunday afternoons throughout the year. The **Florence Gould Theater** in the Legion of Honor (see pp158–9) is often used for classical small group performances, including quartets, and there are also demonstrations of classical or pre-classical musical instruments, such as the clavichord.

Across the bay, **Hertz Hall** on the UC Berkeley campus (see pp178–9) attracts rising stars of the classical world for its winter and spring seasons, while the innovative **Oakland Symphony** performs at the Art Deco landmark Paramount Theater.

Contemporary Music

One of San Francisco's leading cultural centers, the **Yerba Buena Center for the Arts** has given a significant boost to contemporary music. Bay Area composers and performers, including John Adams and the internationally acclaimed **Kronos Quartet**, along with others from all over the world, give concerts in the Center's theater as well as in the much smaller Forum. Contemporary composers occasionally hold concerts in the Louise M. Davies Symphony Hall.

The other main spot for new music in the Bay Area is **Zellerbach Hall** on the UC Berkeley campus, while the **Cowell Theater** at Fort Mason also holds events approximately twice a month.

One of the more unusual musical adventures to be found in San Francisco is **Audium**. In this dynamic "sound sculpture," the audience sits through the performance in total darkness, surrounded by hundreds of speakers.

Ballet and Dance

Founded in 1933, the **San Francisco Ballet** is the oldest professional ballet company in the US. Under the direction of Helgi Tomasson it has proved itself to be among the best in the world. Starting off with an annual production of Tchaikovsky's Christmas classic The Nutcracker, the season runs from February to May. The schedule includes classic works choreographed by Balanchine and others, as well as premières by such leading artists as Mark Morris.

Performances by local talent take place at the intimate **Project Artaud** and the **ODC Performance Gallery**, both located in the Mission District. The **Yerba Buena Center for the Arts** is home to the **Alonzo**

King LINES Contemporary Ballet, while Zellerbach Hall across the Bay attracts the best touring productions, with annual visits by Pilobolus, the Dance Theater of Harlem, and Merce Cunningham.

Backstage Tours

Scheduled backstage tours are organized at the Louise M. Davies Symphony Hall and the War Memorial Opera House. You can tour both buildings on Mondays, every half hour from 10am to 2pm. Tours of the Davies Symphony Hall only can be arranged on Wednesdays and Saturdays, but reservations must be made a week ahead. All tours begin at the Grove Street entrance and offer an intriguing firsthand look behind the scene.

Free Events

In addition to the numerous ticketed events, free concerts and performances are staged all over the city. Most of these are outdoor daytime summer events. For example, the San Francisco Symphony Orchestra holds a late-summer series of Sunday concerts in a natural, wooded amphitheater at Stern Grove (see p247). Members of the San Francisco Opera Company sing a selection of favorite arias for lunchtime crowds in the Financial District on Bush Street as part of the "Brown Bag Operas" series, and in Sharon Meadow, Golden Gate Park (see pp145–57), during "Opera in the Park." Also free are the Tuesday lunchtime recitals at 12:30 at Old St. Mary's Cathedral (see p100).

On Fridays at noon during the summer there is "Music in the Park" in the redwood grove behind the Transamerica Pyramid (see p113).

Grace Cathedral is a particularly striking setting for choral church music, performed by the Grace Cathedral Choir of men and boys, founded in 1913. The choir sings at Evensong on Thursdays at 5:15pm, while Choral Eucharist is celebrated on Sundays at 11am.

For details of free and other events, contact the San Francisco Visitor Information Center (see p266), or call their 24-hour hotline for updates: 415-391-2001. You can also check the "Datebook" section of the Sunday San Francisco Chronicle/Examiner or one of the weekly events papers.

DIRECTORY

Opera

San Francisco Opera Association
301 Van Ness Ave.
Map 4 F5.
Tel 864-3330.

War Memorial Opera House Box Office
199 Grove St (day).
Map 4 E5.
301 Van Ness Ave (eve).
Map 4 F5.
Tel 864-3330.
🔲 sfopera.com

West Edge Opera
540 Ashbury Ave.
El Cerrito.
Tel (510) 841-1903.

Classical Music

Florence Gould Theater
Legion of Honor,
Lincoln Park.
Map 1 C5.
Tel 750-3600.

Herbst Theatre
401 Van Ness Ave.
Map 4 F5.
Tel 621-6000.

Hertz Hall
UC Berkeley.
Tel (510) 642-0212.

Louise M. Davies Symphony Hall Box Office
201 Van Ness Ave.
Map 4 F5.
Tel 864-6000.

Oakland Symphony Box Office
1440 Broadway, Suite 405,
Oakland. Tel (510) 444-0801.

Old First Presbyterian Church
1751 Sacramento St.
Map 4 F3.
Tel 776-5552.

Philharmonia Baroque Orchestra Box Office
414 Mason St. Map 4 F5.
Tel 252-1288.
🔲 philharmonia.org

San Francisco Symphony Box Office
201 Van Ness Ave.
Map 4 F5.
Tel 864-6000.

Contemporary Music

Audium
1616 Bush St.
Map 4 F4.
Tel 771-1616.

Cowell Theater
Fort Mason Center
Pier 2.
Map 4 E1.
Tel 345-7500.

Kronos Quartet
1235 9th Ave.
Map 8 F3.
Tel 731-3533.
🔲 kronosquartet.org

Yerba Buena Center for the Arts
701 Mission St.
Map 5 C5. Tel 978-2787.
🔲 ybca.org

Zellerbach Hall
UC Berkeley.
Tel (510) 642-9988.

Ballet and Dance

Alonzo King LINES Contemporary Ballet
Yerba Buena Center for the Arts, 700 Howard St.
Map 5 C5.
Tel 863-3040.

ODC Performance Gallery
3153 17th St.
Map 10 E3. Tel 863-9834.

Project Artaud
450 Florida St.
Map 11 A3.
Tel 621-4240.

San Francisco Ballet
301 Van Ness Ave.
Map 4 F4. Tel 861-5600 or 865-2000 (box office).
🔲 sfballet.org

Yerba Buena Center for the Arts
See Contemporary Music.

Zellerbach Hall
See Contemporary Music.

Backstage Tours

War Memorial Performing Arts Center
401 Van Ness Ave.
Map 4 E5.
Tel 621-6600.

Free Events

Grace Cathedral
1100 California St.
Map 5 B4.
Tel 749-6300.
🔲 gracecathedral.org

Rock, Jazz, Blues, and Country Music

You will find almost every genre of popular music played somewhere in San Francisco. It may be Dixieland jazz, country and western, Delta blues, urban rap, psychedelic rock, or the latest sounds from West Africa or Eastern Europe. Good groups can be found in ordinary neighborhood bars, and there are a number of good small places with only a minimum charge.

The city's music scene has a long and varied tradition of excellence. It changes swiftly and there is no way to predict what you may find, but whatever it is, it's bound to be good.

Major Arenas

Big-name international performers are likely to be found at the large, municipal arenas around the Bay Area. In San Francisco itself, one of the prime places is the small **Nob Hill Masonic Auditorium**. Two larger venues, the **Cow Palace** and the outdoor **Shoreline Amphitheater**, are south of the city, while the main stadium-scale shows are held across the bay.

Berkeley's outdoor **Greek Theatre** hosts a summer-long series of concerts by leading bands and artists. Concord's huge **Concord Pavilion** features such favorites as Bonnie Raitt, Dave Matthews, and Santana.

The best medium-scale spot in the city is the grand old **Warfield**, which has dancing downstairs and seating in the balcony during its year-round, mostly rock season. Smaller clubs are throughout the city, with the densest concentration in the South of Market (SoMa) area around 11th and Folsom streets, where a handful of rock and jazz clubs are within walking distance of one another. Cover charges at clubs vary from $5 to $20, with the highest prices on weekends. Some places also impose a one- or two-drink minimum. Tickets for concerts cost from $15 to $25 and are available at the box office or through BASS or Ticketmaster, for a small fee (see p247).

For listings and details of events in the city and the Bay Area as a whole, check the SF Weekly, or other local newspapers (see p275); or pick up a free copy of Bay Area Music (BAM), which is readily found in record stores and clubs.

Rock Music

From Metallica and En Vogue to the more mainstream contemporary bands such as Counting Crows and Chris Isaak, San Francisco has a strong, if offbeat, rock music scene. The local bands tend to eschew the trappings of stardom, and most clubs are small, casual places. Bands and performers come from all over the US to give showcase performances at the radio industry's Gavin Convention every February. Events are generally cool, low-key, and unpretentious, however, for the rest of the year.

Two of the best rock clubs to hear live music are **Slim's** and **Bimbo's 365 Club**. Bimbo's hosts rock, jazz, country, and R&B – and attracts a similarly diverse crowd. Slim's, which is part-owned by musician Boz Scaggs, is a bit more upscale, tending to feature established performers in its comfortable, 436-seat room. Another popular place is the **Fillmore Auditorium**, which is the legendary birthplace of psychedelic rock during the Flower Power 1960s (see p131).

Smaller places to hear good rock music include the **Bottom of the Hill** club in Potrero Hill, the **Hotel Utah Saloon** under the I-80 freeway south of Market Street, and **Great American Music Hall**. The Bay Area's punk rock world focuses on Berkeley's all-ages **924 Gilman Street** club.

Jazz

In the late 1950s, the heyday of the Beat Generation (see p34), San Francisco enjoyed one of the liveliest jazz scenes in the entire country. Nightclubs like the legendary Blackhawk vied with the nation's hottest spots for performers such as Miles Davis, John Coltrane, and Thelonious Monk. Things have quietened down considerably since then, but there is still a number of places in the Bay Area where you can hear excellent live jazz.

For traditional Dixieland in an informal (and free) setting, visit the amiable **Gold Dust Lounge**, near Fisherman's Wharf. If you prefer more modern sounds, choose a club such as **Yoshi's** in Oakland's Jack London Square. Many major jazz and blues artists, like B. B. King and Pat Metheny, perform here.

For an elegant evening of jazz, rhythm and blues, or cabaret, head to **Feinstein's** at the Hotel Nikko for outstanding acts and delicious food. For a more downtown experience, **Club Deluxe** offers a wide array of jazz bands as well as DJs and a monthly burlesque show. **Comstock Saloon** is not a traditional jazz club, but on Saturday nights, this hip cocktail bar on Columbus Avenue undergoes a transformation, thanks to its long standing resident pianist, Jay Sanders, along with his quartet of fellow musicians.

Patrons at the Italian American **Verdi Club** enjoy the live music and swing dancing. The SFJAZZ institution built the state-of-the-art **SFJAZZ Center**, which opened in Hayes Valley in January 2013.

Many jazz fans plan their trips to San Francisco to coincide with the world-famous **Monterey Jazz Festival**, which is held every September in Monterey (see pp188–9), just 2 hours by car south of San Francisco.

Blues

San Francisco probably has more blues clubs than anywhere else in the world, except Chicago. Every night of the week, live blues is played somewhere in town, from bars like **The Saloon** to **The Boom Boom Room**, which is owned by musician John Lee Hooker. **Lou's Fish Shack**, on Fisherman's Wharf, has live blues bands on the bill almost every day, with special shows on weekends. The award-winning **Biscuits and Blues** has local blues spotlights on weekdays and special shows on weekends.

Folk, Country, and World Music

Although folk music's mass appeal has faded since the fervent days of the 1960s, when singers like Joan Baez and Pete Seeger appeared regularly, fans of the genre can find live performers playing in clubs and coffee-houses all around the Bay Area. Berkeley's **Freight & Salvage Coffeehouse** hosts country and bluegrass bands as well as singer-songwriters, and it is probably the prime folk music club in San Francisco and surrounding area. **Starry Plough** in Berkeley

is also mostly folk-oriented, although many country and western music stars perform here. **Café Du Nord** has acoustic performers in its underground club.

While down-home country music fans may have to search hard to find anything that suits their tastes, the Bay Area is rich in "World Music," which covers every-thing from reggae and soca to Taiko drumming and klezmer music. The cozy **Ashkenaz Music & Dance Café** hosts a wildly diverse range of performers.

DIRECTORY

Major Arenas

Concord Pavilion
2000 Kirker Pass Rd, Concord.
Tel (925) 676-8742.

Cow Palace
Geneva Ave & Santos St.
Tel 404-4100.

Greek Theatre
UC Berkeley.
Tel (510) 642-9988.
w thegreektheatre
berkeley.com

Nob Hill Masonic Auditorium
1111 California St.
Map 4 F3.
Tel 776-7457.
w sfmasonic.com

Shoreline Amphitheater
1 Amphitheater Parkway, Mountain View.
Tel (650) 967-4040.
w mountainview
amphitheater.com

Warfield
982 Market St.
Map 5 C5. **Tel** 345-0900.
w thewarfieldtheatre.
com

Rock Music

924 Gilman Street
924 Gilman St, Berkeley.
Tel (510) 524-8180.
w 924gilman.org

Bimbo's 365 Club
1025 Columbus Ave.
Map 5 A2. **Tel** 474-0365.
w bimbo365club.com

Bottom of the Hill
1233 17th St.
Map 11 C3. **Tel** 626-4455.
w bottomofthehill.com

Fillmore Auditorium
1805 Geary Blvd.
Map 4 D4.
Tel 346-6000.
w thefillmore.com

Great American Music Hall
859 O'Farrell St.
Map 5 A5.
Tel 885-0750.

Hotel Utah Saloon
500 4th St.
Map 5 C5.
Tel 546-6300.
w hotelutah.com

Slim's
333 11th St.
Map 10 F1.
Tel 255-0333.
w slimspresents.com

Jazz

Club Deluxe
1511 Haight St.
Map 9 C1.
Tel 552-6949.

Comstock Saloon
155 Columbus Ave
Tel 617-0071

Feinstein's
222 Mason St.
Map 5 B5. **Tel** 394-1188.
w feinsteins-
atthenikko.com

Gold Dust Lounge
165 Jefferson St.
Map 4 F1. **Tel** 397-1695.
w golddustsf.com

Monterey Jazz Festival
2000 Fairgrounds Rd at Casa Verde, Monterey.
Tel (831) 373-3366.
w montereyjazz
festival.org

SFJAZZ Center
201 Franklin St.
Tel 920-5299
Map 4 F5.
w sfjazz.org

Verdi Club
2424 Mariposa St.
Map 11 A3.
Tel 861-9199.

Yoshi's
510 Embarcadero West, Jack London Sq, Oakland.
Tel (510) 238-9200.

Blues

Biscuits and Blues
401 Mason St.
Map 5 B5. **Tel** 292-2583.

The Boom Boom Room
1601 Fillmore St.
Map 10 F2.
Tel 673-8000.
w boomboom
room.com

Lou's Fish Shack
300 Jefferson St.
Map 5 B1.
Tel 771-5687.
w lousfishshacksf.com

The Saloon
1232 Grant Ave.
Map 5 C3.
Tel 989-7666.

Folk, Country, and World Music

Ashkenaz Music & Dance Café
1317 San Pablo Ave, Berkeley.
Tel (510) 525-5054.
w ashkenaz.com

Café Du Nord
2170 Market St.
Map 10 E2.
Tel 471-2969.
w cafedunord.com

Freight & Salvage Coffeehouse
2020 Addison St, Berkeley.
Tel (510) 644-2020.
w thefreight.org

Starry Plough
3101 Shattuck Ave, Berkeley.
Tel (510) 841-0188.
w thestarryplough.
com

Nightclubs

Like almost everything else in San Francisco, the city's nightlife is fairly casual, friendly, and low key. There is little of the fashion consciousness of London, New York, or Paris, and flashy discos are few and far between. Many of the trendy clubs are open only one or two nights a week, but cover charges and drink prices are generally low.

If you want to sample an aspect of nightlife that is "uniquely San Franciscan," try the stand-up comedy clubs. Although some of the once-vaunted places have closed, you can still find stand-up done with a special eccentric flair. In addition, San Francisco has many comfortable piano bars in luxurious hotels or restaurants, which are perfect for an entertaining, intimate night out. It is a good idea to rest up after the day so you can enjoy the city after hours, too.

Where and When

Names, times, and locations of nightclubs change constantly, and even the most popular-places may last no longer than a year. In many ways your best bet is to check the *SF Weekly*, *Bay Times*, and other magazines and newspapers to see what is happening. Most of the larger clubs are located in the industrial South of Market (SoMa) area, and run from around 9pm until 2am. A few stay open all night, especially on weekends, but all places stop serving alcohol at 2am. Always bring valid ID to prove you are over 21, or you will not be admitted.

Dancing

One of San Francisco's liveliest nightclubs is **Ruby Skye** on Mason Street, with its flashy decor, great sound system, and fashionably mainstream clientele. RnB, hip-hop, and jazz are played at **Nickies Bar** in Haight Ashbury; while **The Sound Factory** and **City Nights**, both on Harrison, feature alternative rock and modern dance music; take a cab home after club hours in this iffy neighborhood.

Located in the historic Mission District, **Elbo Room** has multi-level lounges and pool tables in case you want a break from the dancing. **The Mexican Bus** is a real bus that takes you to three different salsa dance clubs in one evening. **Ten 15** is another venue where the music is varied and the atmosphere electric. Also in this area is the after-hours **Cat Club**, which stays lively until dawn with acid jazz and alternative-industrial sounds, as well as a popular 1980s night. **Hemlock Tavern** is another great place for music enthusiasts, with a free juke-box and a back room featuring live music most nights.

For a truly San Franciscan club experience, head to **The Roc**, an Alcatraz-themed bar and nightclub with DJs every night.

Gay and Lesbian Clubs

Some of San Francisco's most popular clubs are primarily, though rarely exclusively, homosexual. These include the ever-popular **EndUp**, which is open around the clock from Friday night until Monday morning for nonstop dancing. Other gay and lesbian clubs include **El Rio** in the Mission District and **440 Castro**.

There are also a number of dance clubs on and around 18th Street in the Castro District, such as the **Midnight Sun**. In the East Bay, the **White Horse Inn** has been a popular bar and dance club since the early 1960s. Also in the Castro is **The Café**, which has a massive dance floor and three separate bars that draw friendly guys and girls, as well as go-go dancers and drag queens.

Gay and lesbian nightclubs tend to change even more quickly than their straight counterparts, so check listings and ads beforehand in local papers like the *Bay Times* and *Bay Area Reporter*. Gay men in particular can check *Betty and Pansy's Severe Queer Review*.

Piano Bars

The name "piano bar" does not really do justice to the variety of bars and nightclubs presented here. They all have nightly live music, usually jazz, to enjoy just for the price of a drink. Many of the most fabulous clubs in the city are in four-star hotels. A few blocks from the Theater District, **Lush Lounge** offers stiff martinis in a funky setting. The Art Deco-style **Top of the Mark** sits high above Nob Hill at the top of the Mark Hopkins Hotel. **MKT Restaurant–Bar** at the Four Seasons, an elegant hotel piano bar with cozy fireplaces and leather chairs, offers spectacular views of the Financial District.

Other piano bars are found in the better restaurants, where you can enjoy music before, during, or after dinner. Drop into **Lefty O'Doul's** for good piano bar music with an obvious Irish lilt and a fine selection of ales, or head for **The Burritt Room**, which is renowned for its American food and sleek modern decor. Right off Union Square is **Zingari**, an Italian restaurant that serves up live jazz in their Piano Lounge seven nights a week.

The Theater District west of Union Square has lively venues, such as **Johnny Foley's Irish House**. Talented pianists "duel" in this dark basement bar that encourages the crowd to sing along. Farther west still, the **Sheba Piano Lounge** is a romantic spot that serves up live music and delicious

Ethiopian fare seven nights a week. **The Starlight Room** has nightly live music in a classy setting on the 21st floor at the Sir Francis Drake Hotel. Just off Market Street, **Martuni's** offers stiff martinis and classic singalongs for a diverse crowd. Last but not least is the **Tonga Room** in the lower level of the Fairmont Hotel *(see p215)*. In this elaborate Polynesian-style cocktail bar you can dance or just listen to jazz – interrupted every half-hour by a simulated rainstorm.

Comedy Clubs

The city's once-thriving live comedy scene spawned the famous comedian and movie actor Robin Williams, among many other talents. While the comedy scene has been cut back considerably, there is usually something happening somewhere in the city every night of the week at a bar or café. Check local newspapers for listings *(see p275)*.

Some of the best shows take place at **Tommy T's Comedy House**, with such regular artists as Bobby Slayton, Will Durst,

and Richard Stockton. Other clubs with stand-up comedy acts and improvisation are **Marsh's Mock Cafe-Theater** in the Mission and **Cobb's Comedy Club** in North Beach, as well as **The Punchline**. **Down Town Comedy Theater** is an intimate space in Union Square where you can see great comedy talent.

Shows usually start at 8pm, with late-night performances at weekends beginning at around 10pm. Most venues cost around $15 and can operate a one- or two-drink minimum policy.

DIRECTORY

Dancing

Cat Club
1190 Folsom St.
Map 11 A2.
Tel 703-8965.
w sfcatclub.com

City Nights
715 Harrison St.
Map 5 D5.
Tel 546-7938.

Elbo Room
647 Valencia St.
Map 10 F2.
Tel 552-7788.

Hemlock Tavern
1131 Polk St.
Map 5 A5.
Tel 923-0923.

The Mexican Bus
Call for bus pick-up.
Tel 546-3747.
w mexicanbus.net

Nickies Bar
466 Haight St.
Map 10 E1. **Tel** 255-0300.
w nickies.com

The Roc
2801 Leavenworth St.
Map 4 E1.
Tel 650-6038.
w playasf.com

Ruby Skye
420 Mason St.
Map 5 B5. **Tel** 693-0777.

The Sound Factory
525 Harrison St.
Map 5 D5.
Tel 339-8686.

Ten 15
1015 Folsom St.
Map 11 B1.
Tel 431-1200.

Gay and Lesbian Clubs

440 Castro
440 Castro St.
Map 10 D3.
Tel 621-8732.

The Café
2369 Market St.
Map 10 D2.
Tel 523-0133.

El Rio
3158 Mission St.
Map 10 F4.
Tel 282-3325.
w elriosf.com

The EndUp
401 6th St.
Map 11 B1.
Tel 646-0999.

Midnight Sun
4067 18th St.
Map 10 D3.
Tel 861-4186.

White Horse Bar
6551 Telegraph Ave,
Oakland.
Tel (510) 652-3820.

Piano Bars

The Burritt Room
417 Stockton St.
Map 5 C4.
Tel 400-0561.
w burritttavern.com

Johnny Foley's Irish House
243 O'Farrell St.
Map 5 B5.
Tel 954-0777.

Lefty O'Doul's
333 Geary St.
Map 5 B5.
Tel 982-8900.

Lush Lounge
1221 Polk St.
Map 5 A5.
Tel 771-2022.
w lushloungesf.com

Martuni's
4 Valencia St.
Map 10 F1.
Tel 241-0205.

MKT Restaurant–Bar
Four Seasons Hotel,
757 Market St.
Map 5 C5.
Tel 633-3838.

Sheba Piano Lounge
1419 Fillmore St.
Map 4 D5.
Tel 440-7414.

The Starlight Room
450 Powell St.
Map 5 B5.
Tel 395-8595.
w starlightroomsf.com

Tonga Room
950 Mason St.
Map 5 B4. **Tel** 772-5278.
w tongaroom.com

Top of the Mark
Mark Hopkins
InterContinental Hotel,
1 Nob Hill.
Map 5 B4.
Tel 392-3434.

Zingari
501 Post St.
Map 5 B5.
Tel 885-8850.
w zingari.com

Comedy Clubs

Cobb's Comedy Club
915 Columbus Ave.
Map 5 B2.
Tel 928-4320.
w cobbscomedy.com

Down Town Comedy Theater
287 Ellis St.
Map 5 B5.
Tel 378-4413.

The Marsh
1062 Valencia St.
Map 10 F3.
Tel 641-0235.
w themarsh.org

The Punchline
444 Battery St.
Map 6 D3.
Tel 397-7573.
w punchline comedyclub.com

Tommy T's Comedy House
5104 Hopyard Rd,
Pleasanton.
Tel (925) 227-1800.
w tommyts.com

San Francisco's Bars

San Francisco has been a drinkers' town ever since the heady days of the Gold Rush *(see pp26–7)*, when there was a saloon for every 50 residents. The bawdy public houses of the mid-19th century no longer exist. Instead, today, you can drink with a view; grab a local brew; sip an elegant cocktail in a chic lounge; sample a fine local country vintage wine; mingle with cheering local fans at a sports bar; see satellite-broadcast matches from Europe; and soak up charm and an occasional concert at an Irish Bar. Alternatively, you can observe how a notable segment of San Francisco's population parties at a gay bar.

Rooftop Bars

Those with a head for heights and a craving to be above the hills can visit the bars at the top of the towers in the city center. **The View** at Marriott Marquis offers splendid views and evening jazz along with dance music. **El Techo de Lolinda** is a festive rooftop bar worth visiting in the Mission. The quaint rooftop patio at **Jones** is more low-key and relaxing.

Beer Bars

For a more down-to-earth experience, visit one of the city's many beer bars, popular gathering places for the after-work crowd and weekend revelers. The best of these specialize in beers brewed by West Coast breweries, including San Francisco's fine Anchor Steam and Liberty Ale.

One of the best, the English **Mad Dog in the Fog**, is situated on Haight Street. **Magnolia Gastropub & Brewery**, in a 1903 Haight Victorian building, retains its original wooden bar and name from ex-dancer Magnolia Thunderpussy. **ThirstyBear** is known for its tapas, while the hip **The Monk's Kettle** draws the crowds with its craft beers and excellent food pairings. In North Beach, **The Church Key** is a charming dive bar with a huge beer list. This popular hangout is easy to miss – its entrance is marked simply by a sign featuring a key. At the Pacific Ocean edge of Golden Gate Park, **Beach Chalet**'s brews combine with fine views.

Cocktail Bars

Traditional cocktail bars, with a chatty bartender holding court in front of rows of gleaming bottles, are great fun in San Francisco, and there are plenty of venues to choose from.

Singles often drink at **The Starlight Room**, and those in the need-to-be-seen crowd are in the Clift Hotel **Redwood Room**, with a back-lit bar and upper-tier cocktail prices. A lively bohemian crowd can be found along Columbus Avenue at **Specs' Twelve Adler Museum Cafe**, **Tosca**, and **Vesuvio** – a one-time beatnik hangout where a popular house drink is the Jack Kerouac (rum, tequila, orange/cranberry juice, and lime). Banquettes, potent cocktails, and Rat Pack-era decor mix with a relaxed North Beach crowd at **Tony Nik's**.

Across town in the Mission District, **Elixir** is a neighborhood bar with darts, and a wooden back-bar in a Victorian building that once had a bootblack on the premises. Also in the Mission, **Nihon Whiskey Lounge** has the largest single-malt selection on the West Coast, plus innovative whiskey and champagne cocktails, and a delectable menu of Japanese food. **Buena Vista Café** is the 1952 birthplace of Irish coffee and serves 2,000 glasses per day. The wood-paneled **Rickhouse** provides a cozy, intimate space. Other bars, such as **Café du Nord**, in a former Prohibition speakeasy, and the award-winning **Biscuits and Blues**, have live jazz.

Wine Bars

With the proximity to Northern California Wine Country, the **Ferry Plaza Wine Merchant Bar**, surrounded by artisan cheese-makers, bakers, and other gourmet outlets, is a fine spot to sample wines.

Champagne and candlelight create the atmosphere of the **Barbarossa Lounge**. Not far from Union Square is **Press Club**, a wine-tasting bar and lounge serving wines from six of Northern California's most prestigious wineries. At **The Hidden Vine**, also in Union Square, patrons can share and taste delectable California wines, as well as rare offerings from other regions. In the vibrant Marina District, **The Scotland Yard** entices with a great selection of small-production wines, while **Amelie** is a quaint place to enjoy fine wines and cheese.

Themed Bars

One of the best spots to connect with local passion is **Brick & Beam**. Bring your own food or snacks to the drinks-only **Greens Sports Bar**. **Smuggler's Cove** is a renowned tiki bar that boasts more than 200 rums in a kitschy, pirate-themed setting, with excellent cocktails. Irish cheer and Guinness are quaffed at **The Irish Bank** and **The Chieftain**.

Gay Bars

Watering holes popular with the gay, lesbian, bisexual, and transgendered range from leather-, biker-, latex-, and fetish-specialized to bars favored simply because the clientele is predominantly of one type. The Castro, SoMa, and Mission Districts are magnet areas. **The Twin Peaks Tavern** has a relaxed, warm atmosphere; **The Stud** and **The EndUp** keep drinks flowing with the dancing; the **Last Call Bar** offers a cozy, friendly, pub-like atmosphere; while **Divas** is a well-known spot serving the transgender community.

DIRECTORY

Rooftop Bars

Jones
620 Jones St.
Map 5 B5.
Tel 496-6858.
W 620-jones.com

El Techo de Lolinda
2518 Mission St.
Map 10 DF.
Tel 550-6970.

The View
39th floor,
Marriott Marquis, 780
Mission St.
Map 5 C5.
Tel 896-1600.
W sfviewlounge.com

Beer Bars

Beach Chalet
1000 Great Hwy.
Map 7 A2.
Tel 386-8439.
W beachchalet.com

The Church Key
1402 Grant Ave.
Map 5 C3.
Tel 986-3511.

**Mad Dog
in the Fog**
530 Haight St.
Map 10 E1.
Tel 626-7279.
W themaddoginthe
fog.com

**Magnolia Gastropub
& Brewery**
1398 Haight St.
Map 9 C1.
Tel 864-7468.
W magnoliapub.com

The Monk's Kettle
3141 16th St.
Map 10 F2.
Tel 865-9523.
W monkskettle.com

ThirstyBear
661 Howard St.
Map 6 D5.
Tel 974-0905.
W thirstybear.com

Cocktail Bars

Biscuits and Blues
401 Mason St.
Map 5 B5.
Tel 292-2583.
W biscuitsand
blues.com

Buena Vista Café
2765 Hyde St.
Map 4 F1.
Tel 474-5044.
W thebuenavista.com

Café du Nord
2170 Market St.
Map 10 D2.
Tel 471-2969.
W cafedunord.com

Elixir
3200 16th St
at Guerrero St.
Map 10 E2.
Tel 552-1633.
W elixirsf.com

**Nihon Whiskey
Lounge**
1779 Folsom St.
Map 10 F2.
Tel 552-4400.

Redwood Room
495 Geary St
(at Clift Hotel).
Map 5 B5.
Tel 929-2372.

Rickhouse
246 Kearny St.
Map 5 C4.
Tel 398-2827.
W rickhousebar.com

**Specs' Twelve Adler
Museum Cafe**
12 Williams Pl
(across Columbus Ave
from Vesuvio).
Map 5 C3.
Tel 421-4112.

The Starlight Room
450 Powell St.
Map 5 B4.
Tel 395-8595.
W starlightroomsf.com

Tony Nik's
1534 Stockton St.
Map 5 B2.
Tel 693-0990.
W tonyniks.com

Tosca
242 Columbus Ave.
Map 5 C3.
Tel 986-9651.
W toscacafesf.com

Vesuvio
255 Columbus Ave.
Map 5 C3.
Tel 362-3370.

Wine Bars

Amelie
1754 Polk St.
Map 4 F3.
Tel 292-6916.
W ameliewinebar.com

Barbarossa Lounge
714 Montgomery St.
Map 5 C3.
Tel 434-4204.
W barbarossa
lounge.com

**Ferry Plaza Wine
Merchant Bar**
One Ferry Building,
Shop 23.
Map 6 E3.
Tel 391-9400.
W fpwm.com

The Hidden Vine
408 Merchant St.
Map 5 B5.
Tel 674-3567.
W thehiddenvine.com

Press Club
20 Yerba Buena Lane.
Map 5 C5.
Tel 744-5000.

The Scotland Yard
3232 Scott St.
Map 3 C2.
Tel 872-6853.
W thehiddenvine.com

Themed Bars

**Brick & Beam at Hyatt
Fisherman's Wharf**
555 North Point St.
Map 5 A1.
Tel 202-3612.

The Chieftain
198 5th St.
Map 11 B1.
Tel 625-0436.

Greens Sports Bar
2239 Polk St.
Map 5 A3.
Tel 775-4287.

The Irish Bank
10 Mark Lane
(off Bush St).
Map 5 B4.
Tel 788-7152.
W theirishbank.com

Smuggler's Cove
650 Gough St.
Map 4 F5.
Tel 869-1900.
W smugglers
covesf.com

Gay Bars

Divas
1081 Post St.
Map 4 F4.
Tel 474-3482.

The EndUp
401 6th St.
Map 11 B2.
Tel 646-0999.

Last Call Bar
3988 18th St.
Map 10 D3.
Tel 861-1310.
W thelastcallbar.com

The Stud
399 9th St.
Map 11 A2.
Tel 863-6623.
W studsf.com

Twin Peaks Tavern
401 Castro.
Map 10 D2.
Tel 864-9470.
W twinpeaks
tavern.com

Sports and Outdoor Activities

San Franciscans are sports enthusiasts, and there are plenty of activities to suit every taste. You can choose from a range of public and private health clubs, swimming pools, tennis courts, and golf courses. Spectator sports are provided by two baseball teams, professional football, basketball, and hockey, plus numerous Bay Area college games. Outdoor activities include cycling, skiing, boat trips, and kayaking. Whale-watching adventures are also fun to try. Tickets are available through **Ticketmaster** *(see p247)* or other ticket agents *(see p261)*.

Football

Levi's Stadium, in Santa Clara, is the new home of the **San Francisco 49ers** and will also host the 2016 NFL Super Bowl in 2016. **Oakland Raiders** play at Coliseum. The **University of California** at Berkeley and **Stanford University** in Palo Alto, also have good football teams.

Baseball

Two professional baseball teams play in the Bay Area. The National League **San Francisco Giants** play their home games at the state-of-the art stadium at AT&T Park. The American League **Oakland Athletics** (the A's) play at the O.co Coliseum in Oakland.

Basketball

The Bay Area's only NBA basketball team is the **Golden State Warriors**, who play at the Oracle Arena. The Golden Bears of **UC Berkeley** also play some games there, but most of their home games actually take place on campus, as do all of **Stanford University's**.

Ice Hockey

Home games of the **San José Sharks**, the Bay Area's only professional ice hockey team, are played at the SAP Center in central San José, about an hour's drive south of San Francisco.

Gyms and Health Clubs

Large business hotels usually have health club facilities on the premises. Those that don't usually have an agreement with a private club that gives short-term membership to hotel guests. If neither option is available, choose from the upscale **Bay Club**, near the Financial District, the well-maintained **Crunch Fitness**, or the basic **24-Hour Nautilus Fitness Center**.

Boating

Unless you are fortunate to know someone willing to take you out on their yacht, the only way to sail around the bay is to rent a boat from **Cass' Marina** in Sausalito, where lessons and piloted charters are also available. For more limited water trips, rent a kayak from the **Sea Trek Ocean Kayak Center** or a rowboat, pedal boat, or motorboat from the **Stow Lake Boathouse** in Golden Gate Park.

Golf Courses

Golfers have a wide range of courses to choose from, including municipal links in **Lincoln Park** and **Golden Gate Park** and the beautiful **Presidio Golf Club**. Farther away, some of the world's most famous courses line the Pacific Ocean in Carmel *(see pp188–9)*, where for about $275–$300 you can test your skills and play a round or two at the renowned **Pebble Beach Golf Links**.

Skiing

For skiing, San Franciscans head east to the mountains of Lake Tahoe *(see pp198–9)*, where resorts like **Heavenly** and **Alpine Meadows** provide excellent slopes for all levels of ability, amid gorgeous alpine vistas. The biggest resort, **Squaw Valley**, is just north of the lake and was the site of the 1960 Winter Olympics. Also within reach of the Bay Area are **Yosemite Ski & Snowboard Area**, in Yosemite National Park *(see pp202–3)*, and cross-country oriented **Kirkwood Ski Resort**. Skiing equipment can be rented at all these resorts, and lessons are also available.

Swimming

Most public swimming pools are out in the suburban fringes, so for times and fees contact **City of San Francisco Recreation and Parks Department** swimming information line. To swim in the chilly ocean, head to China Beach, the only safe beach in the city. Join the "Polar Bear Club" and swim in the bay. There are also two swimming clubs at Aquatic Park *(see pp174–5)*, the **Dolphin Club** and the **South End Rowing Club**. If you are in San Francisco over the New Year, watch the New Year's Day sponsored swim organized by these two clubs for their members *(see p53)*.

Bicycling

Cycling up and down San Francisco's steep hills may not seem like a sensible idea, but if you plan your route well a bike can be the best way to appreciate the city, explore neighborhoods, and gaze at breathtaking views. There are dozens of **Bay Area Bike Share** stations near the Embarcadero and Mission, where you can rent and return bikes. The Presidio and Golden Gate Park, where you will find **Stow Lake Bike Rentals**, are also ideal for cycling. Biking over the Golden Gate is a memorable experience.

In the Wine Country *(see pp192–5)*, you can take advantage of the tours organized by **Backroads**

Bicycle Tours. Many are multi-day tours through Napa and Sonoma counties as well as through the Alexander Valley.

Tennis

There are good tennis courts in almost all of the city's public parks, with the largest group in Golden Gate Park. All city courts have been renovated, and many have lights for night games. They are all operated by the **City of San Francisco Recreation and Parks Department**. For details,

phone their information line. The **Bay Club SF Tennis** has 24 indoor and outdoor courts and offers private and group lessons. Guests staying at the famed **Claremont Resort, Spa and Tennis Club** *(see p165)* can have lessons and play tennis to their heart's content.

Whale Watching

If you visit San Francisco in winter, don't miss the chance to experience one of nature's greatest shows, the annual migration of the California gray whale. These huge mammals

are sometimes visible from headlands like Point Reyes *(see p162)*, but the best way to see them is to join an ocean-going charter trip, tickets for which are available from **Tickets.com** or Ticketmaster *(see p247)*.

The most informative trips are those offered by the **Oceanic Society Expeditions**. They sail west to the Farallon Islands, where you may also see rare birds and blue whales as well as migrating gray whales. Many whale-watching trips leave from Half Moon Bay, 20 miles (32 km) south of San Francisco.

DIRECTORY

Tickets

Golden State Warriors
Oracle Arena.
Tel (1-888) 479-4667.

Oakland Athletics
Tel (510) 638-0500.

Oakland Raiders
Tel (1-800) 724-3377.

San Francisco 49ers
Levi's Stadium.
Tel 464-9377.

San Francisco Giants
AT&T Park.
Tel 972-2000.
w sfgiants.com

San José Sharks
SAP Center.
Tel (408) 287-7070.

Stanford University Athletics
Stanford University.
Tel (1-800) STANFORD.

Tickets.com
w tickets.com

UC Berkeley Intercollegiate Athletics
UC Berkeley.
Tel (1-800) 462-3277.

Health Clubs

Bay Club
150 Greenwich St.
Map 5 C2.
Tel 433-2200.

Crunch Fitness
345 Spear St.
Map 6 E4. **Tel** 495-1939.
w crunch.com
One of several branches.

24-Hour Nautilus Fitness Center
1200 Van Ness St.
Map 4 F4.
Tel 776-2200.
w 24hourfitness.com
One of several branches.

Boating

Cass' Marina
1702 Bridgeway, Sausalito.

Sea Trek Ocean Kayak Center
Schoonmaker Point Marina, Sausalito.
Tel 332-8494.

Stow Lake Boathouse
Golden Gate Park.
Map 8 E2.
Tel 386-2531.

Golf Courses

Golden Gate Park
(Municipal 9-hole)
Map 7 B2.
Tel 751-8987.

Lincoln Park
(Municipal 18-hole).
Map 1 C5.
Tel 221-9911.

Pebble Beach Golf Links
Pebble Beach.
Tel (831) 624 3811.

Presidio Golf Clubv
300 Finley Rd. **Map** 3 A3.
Tel 561-4653.

Skiing

Alpine Meadows
Tahoe City.
Tel (530) 583-4232.

Yosemite Ski & Snowboard Area
Yosemite National Park.
Tel (209) 372-8430.

Heavenly Ski Resort
Stateline, NV.
Tel (775) 586-7000.

Kirkwood Ski Resort
Kirkwood.
Tel (209) 258-6000.

Squaw Valley USA
Squaw Valley.
Tel (530) 583-6985.

Swimming

City of San Francisco Recreation and Parks Department
Tel 831-2700.
w parks.sf.gov.org

Dolphin Club
502 Jefferson St.
Map 4 F1.
Tel 441-9329.
w dolphinclub.com

South End Rowing Club
500 Jefferson St.
Map 4 F1.
Tel 776-7372.
w southend.org

Bicycling

Backroads Bicycle Tours
1516 Fifth St,
Berkeley.
Tel (800) 462-2848.
w backroads.com

Bay Area Bike Share
The Embarcadero St.
Map 6 D3
Tel 855-480-BIKE.
w bayareabike share.com
One of many branches.

Stow Lake Bike Rentals
Golden Gate Park.
Map 8 E2.
Tel 386-2531.

Tennis

Bay Club SF Tennis
645 5th St.
Map 11 B1.
Tel 777-9000.

City of San Francisco Recreation and Parks Department
Tel 831-2700.
w parks.sf.gov.org

Claremont Resort, Spa & Tennis Club
41 Tunnel Rd,
Berkeley.
Tel (510) 843-3000.
w claremontresort.com

Whale Watching

Oceanic Society Expeditions
Fort Mason.
Map 4 E1.
Tel 256-9604.

Tickets.com
w tickets.com

CHILDREN'S SAN FRANCISCO

San Francisco is full of attractions that can satisfy children's curiosity and never-ending quest for adventure and fun. Many museums tailor their exhibits to spark a child's imagination and occupy busy little hands. Colorful street fairs run from spring to fall. And, year-round, the days of the Gold Rush, the Wild West, and gangsters imprisoned on Alcatraz come alive with a visit to historic sites. Children can see exotic animals up close at the zoo, or enjoy the varied attractions of Golden Gate Park. This is a city for families, and many places offer free or discounted admission for children.

Practical Advice

Families are well provided for in San Francisco. Family discounts at most hotels allow children to stay in their parents' room free of charge, and cots and cribs are usually available. Most hotels will arrange babysitters, or licensed agencies such as the **American Child Care Services, Inc.** will provide experienced childcare.

Parking is costly, but public transportation is excellent. Plan your trip, using the map on the inside back cover of this book, to include an exciting combination of buses, streetcars, and cable cars; each is an adventure in itself. Under-5s travel free on public transportation. There are reduced fares for children aged 5 to 17, and 1-, 3-, and 7-day Muni Passports for all age groups *(see p282)*.

Use the pay public toilets *(see p267)* or rest rooms in large hotels and stores; they are usually well kept. Medications are available 24 hours a day at Walgreens Drugstore *(see p271)*.

Current activities that are recommended for families are listed in the quarterly *San Francisco Book* and *Arts Monthly* calendar *(see p275)*.

Crazy Castle at San Francisco Zoo

Wildlife

Animal lovers will find a wealth of wildlife in the Bay Area. Drive or take the ferry to **Six Flags Discovery Kingdom** in Vallejo and spend the day riding an elephant or coming nose-to-nose with a dolphin. At the Marine Mammal Center in the Marin Headlands *(see pp176–7)* you can get close to rescued sea lions. San Francisco Zoo *(see p162)* makes a good day or half-day trip. Here you can watch the antics of a lowland gorilla family in Gorilla World and feed penguin chicks in the world's most successful breeding colony. The **Josephine D. Randall Junior Museum** has a petting zoo and nature walks. Oceanic Society Expeditions *(see p287)* sail 25 miles (40 km) into the Pacific to the Farallones National Marine Sanctuary. Trips run all through the year, but gray whales are best seen from December to April.

Museums

Many museums are action-packed for children. At the California Academy of Sciences *(see pp152–3)* you can ride out an earthquake in the Earthquake! Theater. The Academy is also home to the Morrison Planetarium and the huge Steinhart Aquarium. The **Children's Creativity Museum**, at the Rooftop in Yerba Buena Gardens, is an interactive facility where kids can explore the media arts. The Rooftop includes an ice-skating rink and a 1906 carousel.

The **Bay Area Discovery Museum** is for 2- to 12-year-olds, offering activities to encourage budding imaginations. The **Exploratorium** *(see pp94–5)* is a state-of-the-art science museum acclaimed for its numerous interactive exhibits both inside and outside. The huge site it inhabits at Pier 15 has plenty to keep the family amused for hours. Don't miss the Wells Fargo History Museum *(see p112)*, where your children can relive the Gold Rush days, hopping aboard a stagecoach, tapping out a telegraph message, and discovering

Giraffes at San Francisco Zoo

gold, as well as engaging in interactive media exhibits. Admission is free, and also at the Maritime Historical Park *(see p87)*, a nautical treasure-house of ship models and relics. Three of the museum's restored historic ships can be explored at Hyde Street Pier.

Museums at Fisherman's Wharf are designed to amuse, mystify, horrify, and fascinate youngsters. Sample the delights of Ripley's Believe It Or Not! *(see pp86–7)* and Madame Tussaud's *(see p86)*. Everyone can enjoy the restored marshland, dunes, and beach at Crissy Field in the Presidio.

Outdoor Fun

The most exciting way to take children around town is on the cable cars *(see pp284–5)*. For a thrilling descent, ride the last leg of the Powell–Hyde line to Aquatic Park *(see pp174–5)*, then take the nearby ferry to Alcatraz Island *(see pp82–5)*.

In Golden Gate Park *(see pp144–59)* there are riding stables, bike trails, boating lakes, a carousel in the Children's Playground, and even a herd of bison. In the South Bay, **Great America** is a theme park with 100 acres (40 ha) of rides and shows.

Shopping

At **Build-A-Bear** shoppers make and "adopt" their own huggable bear. For an incred-ible selection of games, head down to **Gamescape**, or watch chocolate being made at the Ghirardelli Chocolate Manufactory *(see p87)*, and then buy delicious candy to eat or to take home as presents and souvenirs.

Riding stables in Golden Gate Park

Children on the beach at Crissy Field *(see p62)*

Indoor Fun

Slightly older children can burn off their excess energy at **Mission Cliffs**, an enormous indoor rock-climbing gym. For creative fun, try the Exploratium for interesting, hands-on exhibits. The Children's Creativity Museum is a must for kids of all ages. **AcroSports** is a huge acrobatic arena that caters to both kids and adults. Check out the interactive Circus Workshop, book a private lesson in contortion or tumbling, or simply catch a show.

Eating Out

Fast food is available all over the city, from takeout dim sum in Chinatown to burgers in Union Square. For those who prefer a more relaxed meal, most restaurants welcome children and provide highchairs and special menus for them. **California Pizza Kitchen** serves tasty pizzas with unique toppings, sandwiches, and salads. Surrounded by animated wildlife and other special effects little ones will love, eating out at the **Rain-forest Café** is a wonderful experience.

DIRECTORY

Babysitters

American Child Care Services, Inc.
Tel 285-2300.

Wildlife

Josephine D. Randall Junior Museum
199 Museum Way. **Map** 10 D2.
Tel 554-9600.
W randallmuseum.org

Six Flags Discovery Kingdom
Marine World Parkway, Vallejo.
Tel (707) 644-4000.

Museums

Bay Area Discovery Museum
557 East Fort Baker, Sausalito.
Tel 339-3900.
W badm.org

Children's Creativity Museum
221 4th St. **Map** 5 C5.
Tel 820-3320.

Exploratorium
Pier 15. **Map** 5 D2.
Tel 563-7337.

Outdoor Fun

Great America
Tel (408) 988-1776.

Shopping

Build-A-Bear Workshop
Hillsdale Mall, San Mateo.
Tel (650) 577-8713.

Gamescape
333 Divisadero St. **Map** 10 D1.
Tel 621-4263.

Indoor Fun

AcroSports
639 Frederick St. **Map** 9 B2.
Tel 665-2276.

Mission Cliffs
2295 Harrison St. **Map** 11 A4.
Tel 550-0515.

Eating Out

California Pizza Kitchen
53 3rd St. **Map** 5 C5.
Tel 278-0443.

Rainforest Café
145 Jefferson St. **Map** 5 A1.
Tel 440-5610.

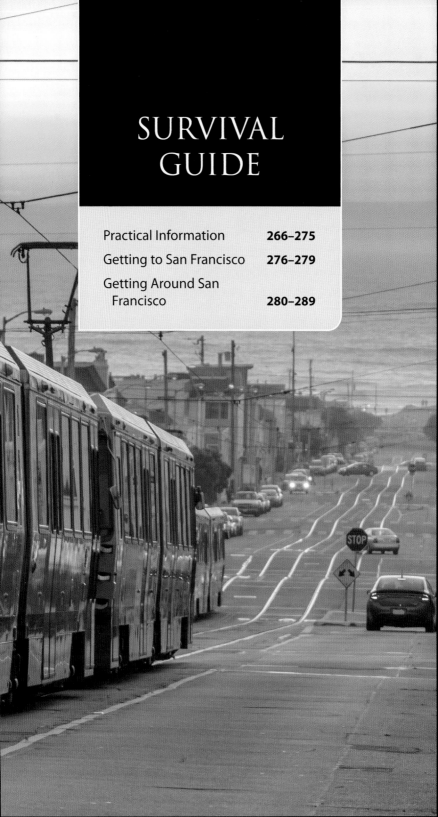

SURVIVAL
GUIDE

PRACTICAL INFORMATION

San Francisco proclaims itself as "Everybody's Favorite City," an accolade that is confirmed by the many awards heaped on its facilities. All visitors, from the economy-minded to the extravagant, will find a wide range of hotels *(see pp212–15)*, restaurants *(pp222–9)*, shops *(pp232–45)*, entertainment options *(pp246–61)*, and guided tours *(p281)* to suit

their budget. Getting around the city is easy and usually safe, provided you use common sense *(p270)*. The practical information on these pages will help you locate banks *(pp272–3)* and medical resources *(p281)*, and the tips included here address everything from making long-distance phone calls *(p274)* to riding a cable car *(pp284–5)*.

Visas and Passports

Holders of a valid European Union, Australian, or New Zealand passport who are also in possession of a return ticket are not required to have visas if staying in the US for 90 days or less. However, they must register online via the Electronic System for Travel Authorization (https://esta.cbp.dhs.gov). Applications must be made at least 72 hours before travel, and there is a charge.

Canadians and returning Americans must have a passport or other accepted form of official ID.

Entry requirements are prone to change, so contact your local US embassy for current requirements.

Customs Information

Upon arrival at San Francisco International Airport *(see pp276–7)*, travelers from outside the US should follow the signs that read "Other than American Passports" to immigration counters for passport inspection and stamping. Proceed to customs, where an officer will check your passport, take your fingerprints and a digital picture, and review the declaration you filled in on your flight. You will then be directed either to the exit or to another officer, who may search your luggage. It takes on average 30–60 minutes to complete these formalities.

Customs allowances for visitors over the age of 21 entering the US are: 200 cigarettes, 100 cigars (not from Cuba), or 3 lb (1.4 kg) of tobacco; no more than 1 liter (2 pints) of alcohol; and gifts that are worth no more than $100. Meat or meat products (even in cans), illegal drugs,

Rows of brochures at the San Francisco Visitor Information Center

cheese, seeds, live plants, and fresh fruit are not allowed. Foreign visitors to the US may bring in or take out up to $10,000 in US or foreign currency.

Travel Safety

Visitors can get up-to-date travel safety information from the **Foreign and Commonwealth Office** in the UK, the **State Department** in the US and the **Department of Foreign Affairs and Trade** in Australia.

Tourist Information

Maps, guides, listings, and passes for attractions and public transportation can be found at the **San Francisco Visitor Information Center** *(see p119)*. The office prides itself on offering personalized service: its efficient staff are available for one-on-one sit-downs to help plan itineraries, book tours, and reserve hotel rooms. *This Week in San Francisco* and the monthly

Where Magazine are available free from hotels and stores.

The "Datebook" section of Sunday's *San Francisco Chronicle* lists the major arts and entertainment events in the city. Other good sources of information are Friday's "Weekend" section of the *San Francisco Examiner* and the listings section in the *SF Weekly,* which is available free of cost.

Admission Charges

Although there are a number of free entertainment options in the city, most attractions charge an admission fee of between $5 and $10. The Conservatory of Flowers and Japanese Tea Garden, both in Golden Gate Park *(see pp145–57)*, charge $8. A trip to Alcatraz *(see pp84–7)*, including the ferry ride there and back, costs $38 ($45 for the night tour), with discounts for seniors and children under 11; kids under the age of 4 go free *(see p287)*.

San Francisco is well known for its live music scene, which features both emerging local

CityPASS ticket

bands and established international artists. Cover charges and tickets for concerts run from $5 to $30. In the summer, free weekly Sunday concerts are held amid the redwoods in Stern Grove, but be sure to arrive early to get a decent seat.

Major museums, such as the Museum of Modern Art (see pp120–23), have entry fees ranging from $5 to $10, but discounts are available for senior citizens, children, and students. Many museums offer reduced admission on Thursdays, and most large institutions offer free entrance once a month (phone for details), in addition to free guided tours, demonstrations, and lectures. Smaller museums are either free or request a donation.

In Fort Mason (see pp74–5), Yerba Buena Gardens (see pp116–17), and Golden Gate Park, several museums and venues are grouped together. A CityPASS, available from the San Francisco Visitor Information Center, offers reduced rates on several must-see sights and public transportation.

The Conservatory of Flowers in Golden Gate Park

Opening Hours

Most businesses in San Francisco are open on weekdays from 9am to 5pm. Shops (see p232) typically stay open until 8pm to allow for after-work errands. All banks operate from 10am to 3pm Monday to Friday; in addition, some banks open as early as 7:30am, some close at 6pm, and some offer Saturday-morning hours. Almost all banks have cash machines operating round the clock.

Some museums are closed on Mondays and/or Tuesdays and major public holidays. Some occasionally stay open in the evening. Closing time for bars is 2am; no liquor can be served in California between the hours of 2am and 6am.

Etiquette and Smoking

Usually too chilly for the carefree sandals-and-shorts approach of Southern California, Northern California is still fairly laid-back. Even at elegant restaurants in San Francisco, it's not uncommon to see jeans, albeit a dark wash, paired with a nice shirt.

Bring identification with you everywhere you go: bars and restaurants are required by law to ask anyone who looks under 35 for ID before serving them a drink. Moreover, the United States is not yet on the PIN system used by many European establishments, so be prepared to sign and show photo ID whenever you use a credit card.

It is illegal to smoke in all workplaces, stores, bars, and restaurants, and in the seating areas at AT&T Park (see p261). However, smoking is allowed in owner-operated bars where the owners have opted to allow it. Hotels must designate 35 percent of their rooms and 75 percent of the lobby as non-smoking zones, though many have adopted a complete non-smoking policy. Inquire about smoking policies when booking a room.

Public Restrooms

Public facilities in bus depots and underground BART stations (see p286) are often frequented by the city's homeless and drug users. The same holds true for the large, green, self-cleaning toilets that line Market Street. As an alternative, major hotels and department stores have facilities that are free and usually well maintained.

Taxes and Tipping

Sales tax in San Francisco is 8.5 percent, and it is charged on everything except takeout food. In restaurants, tip around 20 percent of the total bill. However, a few places have gone tip-free, in which case it will be noted on your bill. A useful trick to figure out the tip is to double the tax. Allow for an average tip of 20 percent for taxi drivers, bar staff, and hair stylists. Hotel and airport baggage handlers expect $1 to $1.50 per bag. Leave hotel chambermaids $1 to $2 for each day of your stay.

SS *Balclutha* at the Maritime Museum, closed on major public holidays

Muni bus, adapted for disabled travelers

Disabled Travelers

Most public transportation in the city is equipped for easy access. See the **Muni Access Guide** for details. Hotels usually have a few accessible rooms, and major entertainment venues have seats adapted for the disabled. Direction signs, toilets, and entrances are specially adapted for blind and disabled visitors, while some movie theaters offer special audio equipment for hearing-impaired patrons. Parking spaces reserved for the disabled are marked by a blue-and-white sign and a blue curb. A wheelchair outline is often painted on the sidewalk. Parking and public transportation are discounted for the disabled.

Traveling with Children

San Francisco is a family-friendly destination: many hotels offer "kids stay free" deals, and many restaurants have children's menus. Kids also enjoy discounts on tickets to sporting events, movies, and museums. Except for cable cars, which charge a flat rate ($7), children under the age of 4 ride the city's public transportation system for free, and those between the ages of 5 and 17 ride for just $1 (the adult fare is $2.25). San Francisco has many free parks and playgrounds; for a full list, visit the **City and County of San Francisco** website. More useful information and ideas are available on the **Travel for Kids** website.

Senior Travelers

Senior travelers might struggle a bit with San Francisco's ubiquitous hills, but public transportation is extensive and reliable, and there are many senior-friendly attractions. Movie tickets, museum entry fees, and some sporting events are discounted for people aged 65 or older (ID must be shown). Transportation is also cheaper ($1 instead of $2.25 for a standard return fare), and many restaurants offer senior discounts as well. For more information on senior travel, contact the **American Association of Retired People (AARP)**.

Gay and Lesbian Travelers

San Francisco is arguably the most gay-friendly city in the world, and it is completely accepted for same-sex couples to show affection in public. It was one of the first US cities to legalize gay marriage; state legislation subsequently revoked that right, but it has since been reinstated. It is a judicial battle that is likely to continue. The annual San Francisco Pride parade at the end of June is one of the city's main attractions *(see p51)*. The Castro is the center of gay life in San Francisco, marked as such by a giant rainbow flag at the intersection of Market and Castro streets. Although all of the Bay Area is gay-friendly, there are a few hotels that cater specifically for a gay clientele; visit www.sfgay.org for a detailed directory.

Traveling on a Budget

San Francisco is notoriously expensive, but that doesn't mean there aren't any deals to be found. In addition to the many inexpensive hostels, a local chain of nicely designed hotels, **Joie de Vivre**, offers several bargain-priced options. Visitors can also sign up for websites such as **Jetsetter**, **Groupon**, and **Living Social**, which send out daily emails with discounts on everything from restaurant dinners to spa services. The website **Goldstar** offers discounts on tickets to concerts, comedy shows, and other events.

Visitors with proof of student status receive discounts at many museums and theaters. The most widely accepted form of student ID is an International Student Identity Card (ISIC). Apply for one at your local student center, youth hostel organization, or student travel association prior to traveling.

Working vacations for foreign students may be arranged through **STA Travel**, which has one office in the Bay Area.

The International Student Identity Card, offering many benefits

What to Take

Despite its location in sunny California, San Francisco is not typically a warm city. Bring clothing appropriate for every season and be prepared to dress in layers, especially in the summer, when the city is at its foggiest. There are two main swimming beaches (Ocean Beach and Baker Beach), and many hotels have either indoor or heated outdoor pools, so packing a bathing suit is a good idea. Comfortable shoes are a must: not only is it often more practical to walk to a particular destination, but it is also the most enjoyable option *(see p281)*.

San Francisco Time

San Francisco is in the Pacific Time Zone. Daylight Saving Time (when clocks are set ahead 1 hour) begins on the second Sunday in March and ends on the first Sunday in November. San Francisco is 3 hours behind New York, 8 hours behind London, and 18 hours behind Sydney.

Electricity

Electric current in the US flows at a standard 110–120 volts AC (alternating current). Visitors from abroad will need a voltage converter and an adaptor plug. Some hotels hand out adaptors at the front desk, but it is also possible to purchase them at the airport. Special plugs for electric shavers carry either 110- or 220-volt current.

Responsible Tourism

San Francisco and the Bay Area are on the cutting edge of all things green in the US. The area boasts a number of eco-lodges and hotels, most of which are members of the **Green Hotels Association**. The organic food movement is huge in Northern California: a good number of restaurants will list which local farm their ingredients come from, and there are weekly farmers' markets throughout the area. One of the best is the **Ferry Building Market Place**, where local growers sell everything from fresh produce to delicious prepared foods.

Large tracts of open space in the city – including the Presidio, Golden Gate Park, Marin Headlands, and Muir Woods – have been set aside for preservation, and San Francisco also features several eco-friendly buildings, such as the California Academy of Sciences *(see pp152–3)*.

To find businesses that operate an environmentally sustainable policy, visit the website of the **Bay Area Green Business Program**.

Colorful vegetables stall at a farmers' market in San Francisco

DIRECTORY

Foreign Consulates

Australian Consulate General
575 Market St, Suite 1800.
Map 5 C4.
Tel 644-3620.

British Consulate General
1 Sansome St, Suite 850.
Map 6 D4.
Tel 617-1300.

Canadian Consulate General
580 California St, 14th Floor.
Map 5 C4.
Tel 834-3180.

Consulate General of Ireland
100 Pine St, 33rd Floor.
Map 6 D4.
Tel 392-4214.

New Zealand Consulate General
Tel (650) 342-4443.

Travel Safety

Australia Department of Foreign Affairs and Trade
ⓦ dfat.gov.au
ⓦ smartraveller.gov.au

UK Foreign and Commonwealth Office
ⓦ gov.uk/foreign-travel-advice

US Department of State
ⓦ travel.state.gov

Tourist Information

San Francisco Visitor Information Center
900 Market St at Powell St, Lower Level of Hallidie Plaza.
Map 5 B5.
Tel 391-2000.
ⓦ sftravel.com

Visit California
Tel (916) 444-4429.
ⓦ visitcalifornia.com

Disabled Travelers

Mayor's Office on Disability
Tel 554-6789
ⓦ sfgov.org/mod

Muni Access Guide
949 Presidio Ave.
Map 3 C4. **Tel** 923-6142
(weekdays) or 673-MUNI.
ⓦ sfmta.com

Traveling with Children

City and County of San Francisco
ⓦ sfrecpark.org

Travel for Kids
ⓦ travelforkids.com/Funtodo/California/San_Francisco/sanfrancisco.htm

Senior Travelers

American Association of Retired People (AARP)
Tel (1-888) 687-2277.
ⓦ aarp.org

Gay and Lesbian Travelers

Gay and Lesbian Convention Visitors Bureau
ⓦ glcvb.org

Traveling on a Budget

Goldstar
ⓦ goldstar.com

Groupon
ⓦ groupon.com

Jetsetter
ⓦ jetsetter.com

Joie de Vivre
ⓦ jdvhospitality.com

Living Social
ⓦ livingsocial.com

STA Travel
Tel (1-800) 781-4040.
ⓦ statravel.com

Responsible Tourism

Bay Area Green Business Program
ⓦ greenbiz.ca.gov

California Farmers' Market Association
Tel (1-800) 806-3276.
ⓦ cafarmersmkts.com

Ferry Building Market Place
ⓦ ferrybuildingmarketplace.com

Green Hotels Association
ⓦ greenhotels.com

Personal Security and Health

San Francisco is one of the safest large cities in the US. Police officers patrol tourist areas regularly, and very few visitors are victims of any form of street crime. Community groups in areas such as the Civic Center, Tenderloin, Western Addition, and Mission District have also taken steps to improve their locale and image. During the late afternoon and after dark, however, it is advisable to take a taxi to and from these districts, since tourist sights often border sleazy theaters and vacant buildings. If you follow the guidelines below, set by the Police Department, and use common sense, your stay should be safe and pleasant.

Police

The San Francisco Police Department provides foot, horse, motorcycle, and car patrols day and night. All major events are overseen by the police, especially at night in the Tenderloin area. Police kiosks are located in Chinatown, Japantown, Union Square, the Mission District, and at Hallidie Plaza. Traffic and parking enforcement officers make their rounds on foot, in police cars, or in small three-wheeled vehicles. Airports, stores, hotels, and the transit system have their own uniformed and plain-clothes security staff.

Police car

Fire engine

Ambulance

What to be Aware of

Mild weather, a progressive population, and extensive social welfare programs draw many homeless people to San Francisco. Street people are mostly not dangerous, but some are mentally unstable or addicted to drugs, so treat them with caution. Do not advertise the fact that you are a visitor; plan your route in your hotel room and look at maps discreetly. Walk confidently even if you do not know where you are; if you look lost, you may be an easy target for crime. Be aware of your surroundings, and if an area appears unsafe, leave. If you need directions, ask only hotel, shop, or office staff, or police officers, and avoid talking to strangers on the street.

Do not carry large amounts of cash. Never display cash; money belts concealed under clothing are better than purses and wallets. If you must carry a purse, hold it securely under your arm, and keep your wallet in the inside front pocket of your pants or jacket. Carry some cash and credit cards in a concealed secondary wallet. Be alert in crowds, especially in stores, at bus stops, and on public transportation. Make copies of all your travel documents and carry them separately.

In your hotel, keep an eye on your luggage while you check in and out, and do not broadcast your name and room number. Do not leave cash or valuables in your room, and keep your luggage locked. Most hotels offer an in-room safe for valuables, and many also have safety deposit boxes at the front desk. Keep an inventory of items that you deposit in the room safe or hotel safe. Learn how to double-lock your hotel room door, and use the door viewer before letting anyone in. Always verify the identity of room service and repair personnel with reception before you let them into your room, especially if you did not call for them. Report any suspicious activity, and keep the key with you until you check out.

If you have a car, lock it and keep the keys with you; always check the interior before you get in. Park in busy, well-lit areas, and remove all luggage and valuables, especially GPS systems.

In an Emergency

For emergencies that require medical, police, or fire services, dial 911. The Blue Pages of the telephone book list hospital emergency rooms and city hospitals. These can be crowded but are less expensive than private hospitals, which are listed in the Yellow Pages.

Hotels may be able to arrange for a doctor or dentist to visit you in your room.

Hospitals and Pharmacies

If you do not have comprehensive medical insurance, a visit to a doctor, hospital, or clinic can be very expensive. Even with medical insurance you may find that you have to pay for the services in advance, then claim reimbursement from your insurance company. Many doctors, dentists, and hospitals accept credit cards, but traveler's checks and cash are sometimes the only form of payment allowed for visitors.

For non-emergency medical care, a handful of walk-in clinics in San Francisco charge reasonable prices; these can be found in the "Personal Services" section of the San Francisco Visitor Information Center website (see p269). There's even a clinic at San Francisco International Airport.

If you get a prescription from a doctor, ask that it be called into a pharmacy near your hotel. Some **Walgreens** drugstores stay open late or round the clock. If you take medication, it is a good idea to bring a backup prescription with you.

Walgreens
pharmacy logo

Lost and Stolen Property

Although the chances of retrieving property lost on the street are remote, you can phone the **Police Non-Emergency Line**. The Muni transportation system and BART both have **Lost-and-Found** offices, as do many shops and restaurants. Note the company name, driver name, color, and number of any taxi you take. If you lose an item, you will need this information when calling the relevant cab company to report your loss.

Travel Insurance

Medical care in the US is first-class but costly, making travel insurance essential for foreign visitors. Travelers should check that their coverage includes emergency medical and dental care, lost or stolen baggage and travel documents, accidental death, and trip-cancellation fees.

Natural Disasters

The Bay Area lies on several fault lines, a fact that has led to a few devastating earthquakes in the past. According to the US Geological Service (USGS), a damaging earthquake hits the Bay Area every four years on average. Since the 7.8 magnitude earthquake of 1906, the area has seen less activity because stresses on the fault lines were relieved. However, according to the USGS, those stresses are building up again, and there is a 62 percent chance of a magnitude 6.7 or larger quake hitting the area by 2032. The good news is that the area is fairly well prepared for earthquakes – by law, buildings have to be retrofitted to function well in a tremor. Although earthquakes can be extremely frightening, they typically last less than one minute. The best course of action in the event of an earthquake is to crouch under a desk or brace yourself in a doorway.

DIRECTORY

Emergency Services

All Emergencies (Police, Fire, and Medical Services)
Tel 911.

Victims of Crime Resource Center
Tel (1-800) 842-8467.
W 1800victims.org

Hospitals

Saint Francis Memorial Hospital
900 Hyde St.
Map 5 A4.
Tel 353-6000.
Emergency Services
Tel 353-6300 (24-hour emergency care).
W saintfrancis memorial.org

San Francisco General Hospital
1001 Potrero Ave.
Map 11 A3.
Tel 206-8000.

Traveler Medical Group
490 Post St, Suite 225.
Map 5 A5.
Tel 981-1102.
W traveler medicalgroup.net

Pharmacies

450 Sutter Pharmacy
450 Sutter St, 7th Floor.
Map 5 B4.
Tel 392-4137. (Will deliver.)

Saint Francis Medical Center
901 Hyde St. Map 5 A4.
Tel 776-4650. (Will deliver.)

Walgreens
135 Powell St. Map 5 B5.
Tel 391-7222.

498 Castro St. Map 10 D3.
Tel 861-3136 (24 hours).

3201 Divisadero St.
Map 3 C2.
Tel 931-6417 (24 hours).

Walk-In Clinics

Concentra Medical Center
26 California St.
Map 6 D4. Tel 781-7077.

University of California San Francisco Clinic
400 Parnassus Ave.
Map 9 B2.
Tel 353-7500.

Wall Medical Group
2001 Union St.
Map 4 E3. Tel 447-6800.

Dental Services

Emergency Dentist 24/7
Tel 702-4543.

San Francisco Dental Society Referral Service
Tel 928-7337 (24 hours).

Lost and Stolen Property

Lost-and-Found (BART)
W bart.gov/guide/lostandfound

Lost-and-Found (Muni)
Tel 701-2311.

Police Non-Emergency Line
Tel 553-0123.

Banking and Currency

San Francisco's Financial District *(see pp108–23)* is the banking center of the West Coast. The imposing corporate headquarters of major US banks and foreign branches of some of the world's leading financial institutions can be found in this prestigious area. For the convenience of residents and visitors alike, hundreds of cash machines (ATMs) throughout the city allow automatic transactions 24 hours a day.

Wells Fargo cash-dispensing machines (ATMs)

Banks and Bureaux de Change

Banks in San Francisco are generally open from 9am to 5pm Monday to Friday. Some, however, open as early as 7:30am, close as late as 6pm, and are open on Saturday mornings. Always ask if any special fees apply before making your transaction. US-dollar traveler's checks can be cashed at most banks, provided you have a government-issued form of photographic identification.

Credit unions will serve only their members, so look for banks that offer services to the general public. **Bank of America** and **Wells Fargo** have headquarters in the city, and **Chase** has a major presence as well. You will see local branches of all three in the Financial District and in shopping areas.

Foreign currency exchange is available at the main branches of large banks, at bureaux de change throughout the Financial District, and at the area's international airports (SFO, Oakland, and San José; *see pp276–7*). Foreign currency exchange offices charge fees and commissions, and they are generally open on weekdays from 9am to 5pm. One of the best-known firms is **Travelex**.

There are several Travelex America Currency Exchange offices and ATMs located throughout the International terminal at SFO.

ATMs

Automated Teller Machines (ATMs) can be found in most bank lobbies or on an outside wall near the bank's entrance. US currency, usually in $20 bills, can be electronically withdrawn from your bank or credit card account in seconds. ATM withdrawals may provide a better foreign currency exchange rate than cash transactions. Before you travel, ask your bank which ATM systems your card can access in San Francisco and how much each transaction will cost, as a conversion charge may apply. Popular systems include Cirrus, Plus, and Star, and they accept various US bank cards, in addition to MasterCard, VISA, and others. Although they are likely to be less secure, the small ATM kiosks at grocery stores, liquor stores, and on city streets sometimes handle foreign cards better. However, you may be charged around $2.50–$3 to use them.

Be aware that robberies can occur at ATM machines, so use them only in daylight or when

there are plenty of people nearby, and make sure that nobody can see your PIN as you type it in.

Be sure to notify your bank and credit card companies that you will be traveling. In some cases, access to funds can be cut off when banks see what seem to be suspicious charges.

Credit Cards and Currency Cards

Credit cards are widely accepted in San Francisco, but be prepared to show photo ID when using them. The majority of credit cards offer merchandise guarantees or other benefits. **American Express**, **MasterCard**, and **VISA** are accepted at most establishments. In most instances you'll be asked to sign a slip; in a very few cases, retailers will print your credit card number on receipts, so be sure to check and black it out if necessary. Most hotels ask for a credit card imprint on check-in. Car rental agencies put a hold on renters' cards equal to a deposit of anywhere between $100 and $300, and they penalize patrons without credit cards by asking for large cash deposits. Most hospitals *(see p271)* will accept the credit cards listed above as payment for treatment.

Prepaid currency cards can be used to withdraw money from ATMs or to pay for services in shops and restaurants. These cards are available through several providers, including Thomas Cook, Travelex, and major credit card companies. Look for one that offers fair exchange rates, no ATM fees, and no charges for purchases.

A large branch of Chase bank in downtown San Francisco

Coins

Units of currency in the US are dollars and cents. There are 100 cents to a dollar. Coins come in $1, and 50-, 25-, 10-, 5-, and 1-cent pieces. Gold-tone $1 coins and state quarters are also in circulation. Each coin has a popular name: 1-cent pieces are called pennies; 5-cent pieces, nickels; 10-cent pieces, dimes; and 25-cent pieces, quarters.

25-cent coin (a quarter)

10-cent coin (a dime)

5-cent coin (a nickel)

1-cent coin (a penny)

1-dollar coin (a buck)

Bank Notes (Bills)

American bank notes come in $1, $5, $10, $20, $50, and $100 denominations. They are all the same color, but each features a different US President. The $20 and $50 bills in circulation have extra security features. Paper bills were first issued in 1862, when coins were in short supply and the Civil War needed financing.

1-dollar bill ($1)

5-dollar bill ($5)

10-dollar bill ($10)

20-dollar bill ($20)

50-dollar bill ($50)

100-dollar bill ($100)

Communications and Media

The Bay Area is where the American tech boom was born, so it should come as no surprise that most places in San Francisco have wireless Internet access; indeed, many hotels and cafés offer it to customers free of charge. San Francisco is also a fairly international and cultural city, so it's relatively easy to find foreign publications, films, and television broadcasts. Coin-operated public pay phones are not as common as they once were, but they are still available at the airport and on some streets in downtown neighborhoods. Note that hotels set their own telephone rates, so calls from your room may be more expensive than those made from a pay phone or cell phone.

International and Local Telephone Calls

Within the city limits of San Francisco, the standard charge of 50 cents buys 3 minutes' time. If you talk for longer than that, the operator may request additional payment. The area code for the city is 415. The prefixes 650 and 408 serve the southern suburbs; 510 is for Oakland, Berkeley, and the East Bay; and 707 is for Napa and Sonoma. These and other numbers called from San Francisco are long-distance. The prefixes 800, 866, 877, and 888 indicate toll-free numbers.

All international calls can be dialed direct, but operators can help if your call is not going through. Their advice is free, but if they connect your call you will have to pay a surcharge. Long-distance direct-dial calls within the US are cheaper at night and weekends. The White Pages of the telephone book offer current rate and long-distance calling information in the "Customer Guide" section. The times of day when discounted rates apply for calls to foreign countries vary; the international operator will be able to advise you. Prepaid international calling cards, available from most newsstands and convenience stores, as well as online, offer discounted rates on international calls.

Public Telephones

Pay phones in San Francisco are slowly disappearing, but they can still be found at the airport, on major streets, and in some shopping centers. AT&T operates most of the pay phones in the city, which have a blue-and-white sign with a receiver and the word "phone" or a bell with a circle around it. Charges must be posted by law, as well as toll-free numbers, how to make calls using other long-distance service carriers, and the phone's location. To complain about service, call the operator (0).

Chinatown phone box

Cell Phones

Triband or multiband cell phones from elsewhere in the world should work in the US, but your service provider may have to unlock international roaming. They can also advise on costs of calls.

The main US providers are **T-Mobile**, **Verizon**, **AT&T**, and **Sprint**. Except for Sprint, they all offer prepaid, pay-as-you-go phones with a "starter" SIM card (with 10–15 minutes' talk time) for $30 and up. Local and national calls are very cheap on these phones, but international calls are not, so it is wise to buy a calling card to use with your pay-as-you-go phone. Alternatively, look for a plan with international calling options. **Virgin Mobile** offers a flat-rate, $25-a-month, no-contract-service option with good international rates. You will also need a phone, but the company sells a basic one for $20. This is a good option if you are staying in the US longer than a week and plan on making frequent calls.

Reaching the Right Number

- Long-distance direct-dial calls outside your local area code, but within the US and Canada: dial 1.

- International direct-dial calls: dial 011, followed by the country code (Australia: 61; New Zealand: 64; UK: 44), then the city or area code (omitting the first 0), and then the local number.

- International calls via the operator: dial 01, followed by the country code, and the city code (without the first 0), then the local number.

- National directory inquiries: dial 411. There may be a charge.

- International directory inquiries: dial 00.

- Local operator assistance: dial 0.

- International operator assistance: dial 01.

- An 800, 866, 877, or 888 prefix indicates that the call is free. Dial 1 before the 800.

- Emergencies: dial 911.

Internet

High-speed Internet (often wireless) is available throughout the city, including on many trains and in the underwater subway tunnel linking San Francisco to Oakland. Many cafés, such as **Ritual Coffee Roasters**, offer free Wi-Fi, although you are expected to purchase something before using it. Hotels are increasingly offering free Wi-Fi as well, either in the lobby or in all rooms. Those that charge for access bill $10–$15 a day. It is rare to find an Internet café with computers, so take your laptop.

Customers at the popular Café de la Presse

Postal Services

Stamps can be purchased at post offices, hotel reception desks, and vending machines. Some ATMs also sell stamps; most banks charge a fee for this service, but so do most non-US Postal Service outlets. Check current postal rates at post offices or online, at the **US Postal Service** website.

Letters can be mailed in post offices, at your hotel, at the airport, and in mailboxes on the street. Collection times are printed on the inside of the mailbox's pull-down door.

All domestic mail is first class and will arrive within one to five days. Air mail to Australia, Canada, Ireland, New Zealand, and the UK takes five to ten business days. Packages sent overseas by surface rate may take four to six weeks. The federal post office offers a range of special services: Priority Mail promises delivery faster than first-class mail, while Global Priority arrives to most international destinations within five days. The more expensive Express Mail delivers next day within the US, and within two to three days to many international destinations. Express mail can also be arranged through private delivery companies, such as **DHL**, **FedEx**, and **UPS**.

Correspondence sent to you c/o General Delivery, Civic Center, 101 Hyde Street, San Francisco, CA 94142 will be held for 30 days. Show photographic proof of identity on collection. The main **post offices** in San Francisco are marked on the Street Finder maps *(see pp290–300)*.

Newspapers, Magazines, and Websites

Foreign newspapers and magazines are for sale at several shops and newsstands, including **Fog City News** and **Café de la Presse**. The local newspaper is the *San Francisco Chronicle*. The *SF Weekly* offers entertainment reviews and listings. *San Francisco Magazine* and *7x7* are glossy lifestyle magazines covering the cultural happenings in the city.

Useful websites for visitors include **Yelp**, which has user-generated reviews on everything from spas to restaurants and bars, and **The Bold Italic**, which lists things to do in the city, such as where to find the best coffee or the best brunch.

Television and Radio

Four TV networks operate in San Francisco: CBS is on channel 5 (KPIX), ABC on channel 7 (KGO), NBC on channel 11 (KNTV), and Fox on channel 2 (KTVU). The local PBS station, which offers cultural programs as well as some classic BBC shows, is on channel 9 (KQED). Cable offerings include CNN, ESPN, BBC America, and pay channels. Some pay channels, such as HBO and Showtime, are free in most hotels.

AM radio stations include KCBS (740 Hz; news), KOIT (1260 Hz; soft rock), and KNBR (680 Hz; sport). FM stations include KALW (91.7 FM; news), KLLC Alice (97.3 FM; pop), KBLX (102.9 FM; jazz), and KDFC (102.1 FM; classical).

GETTING TO SAN FRANCISCO

Several international airlines offer direct flights to San Francisco, and charter and domestic services are also numerous. Amtrak trains run from all parts of the US to nearby Oakland, and bus shuttles operate from this station into San Francisco. Long-distance luxury bus services offer a less frenetic and often cheaper way to travel for those arriving from other North American cities. Several cruise liners dock at Pier 35 on their way north to Alaska or south to the Mexican Riviera. Check with your travel agent or individual operators for the best deals. For visitors arriving by car or bus, there can be little to beat the views of the city and its surroundings when driving over the Golden Gate and Bay bridges.

Airport locations around the Bay Area

Arriving by Air

San Francisco International Airport (SFO) is one of the busiest airports in the world. Not only is it one of the largest in the United States, but it is also one of the most user-friendly. The major carriers operating there include **Air Canada**, **American Airlines**, **British Airways**, **Delta**, **KLM Airlines**, **Qantas**, **United Airlines**, **US Airways**, and **Virgin Atlantic**.

Other airports near the city include San José International Airport (SJC), which is about 1 hour away from San Francisco, and Oakland International Airport (OAK), which is 30 minutes away.

San Francisco International Airport (SFO)

San Francisco International Airport is located south of the city, 14 miles (23 km) from the center of town. Its main runways are right next to San Francisco Bay. SFO is convenient for access to the Greater San Francisco and metro Bay areas and Silicon Valley, with international connections to and from the Pacific Rim, Europe, and Latin America. The arrival and departure gates are arranged around each of four terminals (1, 2, 3, and International). All international airlines are located in the state-of-the-art International Terminal. Domestic flights on **Virgin America** and **JetBlue** airlines depart from the International Terminal, while flights to and from Canada are located in the domestic terminals. Always check the **Airport Information website** in advance.

Walkways link all the terminals, which surround a short-term parking area. Long-term parking garages, a global communications center, a consolidated car-rental center, and the airport's Bay Area Rapid Transit (BART) station *(see p286)* are connected to the terminals by a light-rail shuttle.

Visitors arriving at SFO will find customs, baggage claim, sightseeing information, car-rental booths, and ground transportation into the city on the lower level. The top level has services for those departing from San Francisco, including baggage handlers, ticket and insurance counters, restaurants, bars, shops, and security checkpoints. All car rental and parking shuttles, public buses, and door-to-door shuttle minibus services deliver (and pick up) their passengers at this level. The airport's 24-hour shuttle, which operates between terminals and long-term parking, picks passengers up on the center island near the ticket counters every 5 to 20 minutes.

Bank of America branches and currency exchange services are available from 7am to 11pm in all terminals, and there are Wells Fargo ATMs in all areas. Each terminal also has a range of newsstands, restaurants, and snack bars. Other services provided include baby-changing facilities, free wireless Internet, mailboxes, and postage-stamp

Escalators between levels in SFO's International Terminal

vending machines. There is also a clinic for those with medical problems *(see p271)*.

Wheelchairs, TDD terminals for the hearing-impaired, and an airport shuttle service for the disabled are readily available. You can also use the white courtesy phones that allow you to contact all airport services and facilities free of charge.

Throughout the airport, a series of galleries display changing exhibits on a wide range of subjects. There is also a museum dedicated to the history of aviation in the International Terminal.

Getting into the City from SFO

Information booths on the lower level of the airport offer advice on ground transportation, fares, and boarding locations. Follow the arrows marked "Ground Transportation." Buses operated by **SuperShuttle** depart every 20 minutes from 5am to 11pm, serving three city-center areas with dropoffs at major hotels.

The area in front of the terminal at Oakland International Airport

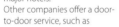

A SuperShuttle minibus service

Other companies offer a door-to-door service, such as **Bayporter Express** and **American Airporter Shuttle**. These minibus shuttles and shared limousines will take you to a specific address. You share the cost of the trip with other passengers for an average of $19 to $40.

The average fare for a metered cab ride into San Francisco is $45. This nonstop trip can take as little as 25 minutes or as long as 40 minutes or even longer during rush hour (7–9am and 4–7pm).

Travelers on a budget, with plenty of time (to allow for frequent stops), can hop on SFO's light-rail shuttle to the airport's BART station and take the subway to San Francisco, the East Bay, or the CalTrain depot. A one-way fare to downtown is $8.65.

Other International Airports

Most international flights arrive at SFO, but **Oakland International** and **San José International** airports are also viable options. Both offer good ground transportation into San Francisco by door-to-door bus shuttle and limousine. BART serves Oakland International in conjunction with a shuttle, getting people into the city within an hour.

Visitors flying into San José can take a **SamTrans** shuttle bus to the CalTrain station *(see p278)*, arriving in San Francisco in about 90 minutes. San José airport has expanded significantly, and the city's transportation authority has managed to connect it to the light-rail system by means of a looping shuttle service.

The airy interior of San José International Airport

Tickets and Fares

Flights to San Francisco (and hotel rates) are most expensive in the summer. Fortunately, though, the city's best weather is in the fall, from September to the end of October, and flight prices are often a bit cheaper then. Late June is particularly expensive and crowded in the city due to the annual San Francisco Pride parade *(see p51)*. Websites such as **Priceline**, **Expedia**, and **Travelocity** often offer deals on airfares, and **Kayak** compares prices from all of these sites, as well as the airline sites, to deliver the best possible deal.

Package Deals

By far the best value for visitors can be found by purchasing a package that includes airfare and hotel, and sometimes a rental car. Websites such as Expedia.com and Travelocity.com offer exclusive package deals that are not available through travel agents. However, be sure to check the hotel component, since it is not uncommon for sites to bundle a mediocre hotel into a package. Bear in mind that if you have booked a package through a third party, any changes or complaints will have to be handled by the booking party; you will not be able to make changes to your reservation directly. In addition to the travel sites, hotels also sometimes offer packages that include meals, a rental car, tourist activities, or spa services.

Arriving by Train

The national passenger rail network, **Amtrak**, links most major US cities. It also connects with bus, ferry, and air carriers and operates a joint service across the border with Rail Canada. All long-distance trains offer sleeping quarters and full refreshment facilities. Often there is a sightseeing lounge with large windows allowing good views of the passing landscape. Unfortunately, some of the trains are quite dated and long-distance routes are often delayed. However, if you have time, traveling by train is a great way to see parts of the country you would not otherwise experience.

Passengers are required to reserve seats in advance on many services. Advance booking is recommended for all travel during peak periods. Amtrak offers a varied program of special discounts and packages, including 15- and 30-day passes allowing unlimited travel within specified zones. Ask your travel agent for details.

Visitors traveling to San Francisco by train will arrive at Amtrak's station in Emeryville, to the north of Oakland. The station is in an industrial area, so most passengers continue their journeys as soon as possible. Amtrak runs a free shuttle to the city center. The ride takes approximately 45 minutes and terminates at the Ferry Building

(see pp114–15). From here, you can then take ferries, buses, BART trains, and streetcars *(see pp282–3)* to other parts of the city.

Amtrak passengers arriving at San José can transfer via the **CalTrain** commuter rail system to San Francisco. A separate ticket ($9 one way) is required for this trip and must be purchased at the vending machine located on the platform. Most shuttle buses from Oakland also stop at San Francisco's CalTrain station, which is located on the corner of Fourth Street and Townsend Street.

Arriving by Car

You will get a spectacular introduction to the city by driving over Golden Gate Bridge or Bay Bridge. Both are toll bridges, but the toll ($7.50 for Golden Gate Bridge and between $4 and $6 for Bay Bridge depending on the time and day) is charged only one way. If your route is from the north via US 101, the Golden Gate Bridge toll will be collected as you enter the city. To get into the city center from Golden Gate Bridge, follow the US 101 signs to Lombard Street and Van Ness Avenue.

Approaching the city from the east via I-80 through Oakland, the Bay Bridge toll is again collected only on the approach to San Francisco. This bridge has two main sections *(see pp166–7)*,

joining at Yerba Buena Island, and its highway runs alongside the skyscrapers of the Financial District. The first two exits take you to the city center. Arriving from the south via the peninsula, you can choose to follow either US 101 or 280 into the city. Both routes are well marked, and there are no tolls on the roads.

Driving in the States is on the righthand side of the road. Red stop lights and stop signs are compulsory stops. More useful tips for driving in San Francisco can be found on page 288.

One-way toll system operating on Bay Bridge

Arriving by Long-Distance Bus

Regular services operated by **Greyhound Bus Line** reach most parts of the United States. The buses are modern and clean, and include wireless Internet and electrical outlets. Ask at Greyhound ticket counters in bus stations or look online for special rates. The average 8-hour San Francisco–Los Angeles adult fare is $59 (one-way), and discounts are usually offered for online purchases, 14-day advance purchases, students, seniors, and children. International travelers can purchase tickets online and have them waiting at the Will Call counter of the appropriate bus station. If you are planning to make several stops along the way, or if you want to tour the country on an extended trip, there may be a package designed to suit your requirements.

Green Tortoise offers an inexpensive and sometimes adventurous way to travel by bus, but it is not for everyone. Facilities and stops are limited, so passengers have to prepare and share meals among the group.

Amtrak train on the tracks at Emeryville station, near Oakland

On some routes, buses stop to let riders explore a national park or freshen up in a natural hot spring. The popular Coastal Crawler tour spends a week winding down the California coast from San Francisco to Los Angeles, with stops in Monterey, Big Sur, and Hearst Castle ($320 round trip for the travel, not including the three nights' hostel accommodations in Los Angeles). Other Green Tortoise routes include Los Angeles, Yosemite National Park, the Grand Canyon, Death Valley, and Las Vegas. Journeys are slow, so if you need to reach your destination at a precise time, it may be better to take the Greyhound or a train.

The Transbay Terminal, located at Main and Howard Streets until 2017, is used by long-distance, regional, and local public transit bus lines, as well as a few sightseeing

Sailing under Golden Gate Bridge, an unforgettable experience

tour companies. It can attract petty criminals, so stay alert and watch your belongings.

Arriving by Sea

Sailing under Golden Gate Bridge into San Francisco Bay is a highlight of arriving at the **Port of San Francisco**. Luxury cruise

ships dock near Fisherman's Wharf at Pier 35. The city is the embarkation and debarkation point of many operators' Alaskan or Mexican Riviera cruises. Taxis and public transportation such as BART, buses, and Muni Metro streetcars are available at the dock; the city center is only a few minutes' ride away.

DIRECTORY

Arriving by Air

Air Canada
Tel (1-888) 247-2262.

American Airlines
Tel (1-800) 433-7300.

British Airways
Tel (1-800) 247-9297.

Delta/KLM Airlines
Tel (1-800) 618-0104.

Qantas
Tel (1-800) 227-4500.

United Airlines
Tel (1-800) 864-8331.

US Airways
Tel (1-800) 433-7300.

Virgin Atlantic
Tel (1-800) 862-8621.

San Francisco International Airport (SFO)

Airport Information
Tel (650) 821-8211 or
(1-800) 435-9736.
w flysfo.com

Airport Police
Tel (650) 821-7111.

Info Service
Tel (650) 821-HELP.

JetBlue
Tel (1-800) 538-2583.

Parking Garage
Tel (650) 821-8211.

Traveler's Aid
Tel (650) 821-2730.

Virgin America
Tel (1-877) 359-8474.

Other International Airports

Oakland Airport Information
Tel (510) 563-3300.
w oaklandairport.com

San José Airport Information
Tel (408) 392-3600.
w sjc.org

Airport Transportation

American Airporter Shuttle
Tel 202-0733.
(Reservations recommended.)

BayPorter Express
Tel 467-1800.
(Scheduled service between SFO and Oakland airports.)

SamTrans
Tel (1-800) 660-4287.
w samtrans.com

SuperShuttle
Tel (1-800) 258-3826.
w supershuttle.com

Tickets and Fares

Expedia
w expedia.com

Kayak
w kayak.com

Priceline
w priceline.com

Travelocity
w travelocity.com

Arriving by Train

Amtrak
Tel (1-800) 872-7245.
w amtrak.com

CalTrain
Tel (1-800) 660-4287.
w caltrain.com

Arriving by Long-Distance Bus

Green Tortoise
Tel 956-7500.
w greentortoise.com

Greyhound Bus Line
Tel (1-800) 231-2222.
w greyhound.com

Arriving by Sea

Port of San Francisco
Pier 1, The Embarcadero.
Tel 274-0400.
w sfgov.org

GETTING AROUND SAN FRANCISCO

San Francisco occupies a fairly compact area, and many of its most famous sights are only a short walk from one another. The public transportation system is very efficient and easy to use. Bus routes crisscross the city and pass by many attractions. Muni Metro streetcars and BART lines serve downtown neighborhoods, as well as the suburbs and outlying areas. Most visitors make time to ride on one of the city's famous cable cars. Taxis can be hard to find, particularly outside the major tourist areas, but Uber and Lyft provide services in all parts of the city. Passenger ferries and boats run regular trips east and north across San Francisco Bay.

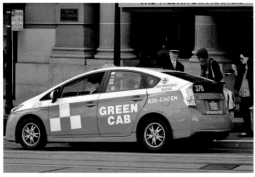

San Francisco's fleet of Green Cabs, using hybrid or electric cars

Green Travel

As well as boasting a reliable, clean, and safe public transportation system, San Francisco is easily explored on foot. There are also many cycle paths. The Bay Area has more hybrid cars than any other region in the US. Half of the city's taxi fleet, such as **Lyft** and **Uber**, consists of "green" cabs that are either hybrid or electric vehicles, or run on biofuel. Streetcars run down Market Street all the way to the waterfront.

They are all electric, as are the buses – hence the maze of power lines throughout the city.

Planning Your Journey

The public transit system is best avoided at rush hour (7–9am and 4–7pm Mon–Fri). Ask your hotel concierge for directions or use the Trip Planner on the **511** website. There are several ticket options. Single tickets can be bought for most services. A Muni Passport *(see p282)* gives unlimited rides for one, three or seven days on light-rail cars, streetcars, buses, and cable cars. The electronic pre-pay Clipper card is accepted on Muni and BART. It deducts the exact fare each time you use it. Contact the **Transport Agency** for more information.

Street Layout and Numbering

Most of San Francisco's streets are based on a grid system. Market Street crosses the city from southwest to northeast, creating the northern and southern sections. With few exceptions, each block is designated a number by hundreds, starting at zero. So, the first block from Market Street has addresses between 1 and 99; the second block has addresses between 100 and 199; and so on. House numbers on east–west streets increase as they move west from San Francisco Bay. Numbers on north–south streets increase going north of Market Street, but also as they move south of Market Street. When asking for an address, make sure you also get the name of the nearest cross street and the neighborhood of your destination.

Local residents refer to the numerically named avenues in the Richmond District as "The Avenues." Numerically named streets begin on the south side of Market Street, in the city center, and end in the Mission District. The Street Finder *(see pp290–300)* provides a comprehensive map with details of the city.

Street numbering increases north and south of Market Street and west from San Francisco Bay

Walking in San Francisco

San Francisco is easy to explore on foot. The main tourist areas are all within 15 to 20 minutes of one another, and although the hills, particularly Nob Hill *(see pp103–105)* and Telegraph Hill *(see pp90–93)*, can be a struggle, the views from the top make them well worth the strenuous climb.

At traffic lights, electronic signs for pedestrians show an illuminated white human figure when it is OK to go; a countdown in flashing red lights tells you how long you have to cross before the light changes to the red hand "Don't Walk" signal. Jaywalking (crossing in the middle of a block, or using a crosswalk when the "Don't Walk" signal is showing) can result in a minimum $50 fine.

Vehicles are driven on the righthand side of the road in the US. Always look both ways before you cross. Take care at traffic lights – vehicles are allowed to turn right on a red light if the way is clear.

Motorcycles and Mopeds

A helmet, a valid US or international motorcycle license, a deposit, and prior riding experience are required when hiring motorcycles or mopeds. Parking for these vehicles is either deeply discounted or free, but they are not allowed on the highways or bridges.

Cycling

Cycling is very popular in San Francisco. There are many bicycle lanes and all buses are equipped to carry bikes strapped to the outside. Bikes can also be taken on the light-rail Muni cars and on BART, although they are not allowed when it gets too crowded. There are two marked scenic bicycle routes. One goes from Golden Gate Park *(see pp144–59)* south to Lake Merced; the other starts at the southern end of Golden Gate Bridge *(see pp64–7)* and crosses to Marin County.

Bicycles, equipment, repairs, and tours are available from **Bay City Bike** and **Blazing Saddles**. They rent bikes for around $32 a day or $220 a week. **Bay Area Bike Share** stations that are spread across the city, also rent bikes charging $9 for a day and $22 for 3 days.

Tours and Other Ways to Get Around

GoCar Tours rents out small vehicles that come equipped with recorded GPS tours of the city. **Extranomical Tours** offers affordable small group tours, while **Cable Car Charters** runs guided tours on motorized cable cars. Visitors can go on half- or full-day **bus tours** and themed **walking tours**, or take a **Segway tour** or a **helicopter tour**. To get away from the city, try taking the **Wine Country Tour Shuttle** out to Napa Valley. Pedicabs and horse-drawn carriages can be found near Fisherman's Wharf *(see pp80–81)*.

A GoCar with GPS

DIRECTORY

Green Travel

Green Cab
Tel 626-4733.

Lyft
w lyft.com

Uber
w uber.com

Planning Your Journey

511
Tel 511. w 511.org

Transport Agency
w sfmta.com

Motorcycle and Moped Rental

EagleRider Rentals
488 8th St. **Map** 11 A2.
Tel 503-1900. w eagle
rider.com/sanfrancisco

Bicycle Rental

Bay Area Bike Share
The Embarcadero St.

Map 6 D3. **Tel** 855-480-BIKE.
w bayareabike
share.com
One of many stations

Bay City Bike
2661 Taylor St. **Map** 5 A1.
Tel 346-2453.

Blazing Saddles
1095 Columbus Ave,
2715 Hyde St,
and 550 North Point.
Map 5 A2, 5 A1, and 5 A1.
Tel 202-8888.

City Bike Hotline
Tel 311.

Tours

**Bus Tours: Gray Line
of San Francisco**
2627 Taylor St.
Map 5 A1.
Also at: Transbay Terminal.
Tel 353-5310.
w graylineof
sanfrancisco.com

**Cruisin' the
Castro Tours**
Tel 255-1821.
w cruisinthecastro.com

Extranomical Tours
501 Bay St. **Map** 5 A1.
Tel 357-0700.

GoCar Tours:
Tel 441-5695.
w gocartours.com

**Helicopter Tours:
SF Helicopter Tours**
Tel (1-800) 400-2404.
w sfhelicopters.com

Heritage Walks
2007 Franklin St.
Map 4 E3. **Tel** 441-3000.
w sfheritage.org

**Horse and Carriage
Tours: Hackney Horse
& Carriage**
Pier 41. **Tel** (408) 535-0277.

**Real SF Tour: Wine
Bars and Cable Cars**
Tel (1-888) 9-SF-TOUR.
w therealsftour.com

**San Francisco Parks
Alliance**
451 Hayes St.
Map 9 B1.**Tel** 621-3260.
w sfparksalliance.org

**Segway Tours:
City Segway Tours**
333 Jefferson St.
Map 3 C2. **Tel** 409-0672.
w citysegwaytours.com

**SF Comprehensive
Shuttle Tours**
Tel (1-866) 991-8687.

**Walking Tours: All
About Chinatown**
660 California St.
Map 5 C4. **Tel** 982-8839.
w allaboutchina
town.com

**Wine Tours:
Wine Country
Tour Shuttle**
Tel 513-5400
or (1-866) 991-8687.
w winecountrytour
shuttle.com

Traveling by Bus and Muni Metro Streetcar

San Francisco Municipal Railway, or Muni as it is commonly called, is the organization that runs the city's public transportation system. You can use one interchangeable pass – Muni Passport – to travel on Muni buses, Muni Metro streetcars (electric trams), and the cable-car lines, which are mainly used by tourists *(see pp284–5)*. Buses and streetcars serve most tourist attractions and all neighborhoods. Using the bus and streetcar map on the inside back cover, and a Muni Passport, you can ride the city's public transportation all day at a fraction of the cost of car rentals and parking fees.

Fares and Tickets

Buses and streetcars both cost $2.50 per ride. When paying your fare, you can request a free transfer, which will allow you to change to another bus or streetcar without paying an additional fare. The transfer is valid for 90 minutes.

If you are planning to make a number of trips by Muni, a **Muni Passport**, valid for 1, 3, or 7 days, allows unlimited travel on buses, streetcars, and cable cars ($21–$42). Muni Passports are available at many stores and information kiosks throughout the city, including the kiosk at SFO, and at the **Visitor Information Center**.

The Clipper card is a convenient payment option, and is accepted on all Muni services. This electronic pre-pay card can be bought on the **SFMTA** website (www.sfmta.com), as well as at Muni metro stations. Hold it against the reader at station gates or when boarding a vehicle, and the exact fare is automatically deducted.

Using Buses

Buses stop only at designated bus stops, every two or three blocks. On boarding, put the exact change in the fare box, or show your Muni Passport to the driver. Ask your driver to let you know when you are near your destination, and watch the sign above the driver's head, which will flash the name of the next stop. Senior citizens and disabled passengers have priority at the front of the

Route numbers are displayed on the front and side of the bus

bus, so be prepared to give up your seat.

Smoking, drinking, eating, and playing music are prohibited on buses. Guide dogs for the blind can ride for free at any time; other animals may be allowed at certain times of day, at the driver's discretion.

To indicate that you want to get off at the next stop, pull the cord that runs along the windows. A "Stop Requested" sign will light up. Instructions about how to open the doors are posted near the exit. Look carefully for oncoming traffic when alighting from the bus,

especially at those stops that are located at islands in the middle of the street.

The route number and name of the destination are shown on the front and side of every bus, near the front door. Route numbers that are followed by a letter (L, X, AX, BX, etc.) are either express services or make limited stops. Ask the driver if you are not sure where the bus stops. Some lines offer a Night Owl Service (midnight–6am), but taxis *(see p289)* are often the safest means of getting around after dark.

Bus Stops

Bus stops are indicated by signs displaying the Muni logo or by yellow bands on poles. Route numbers of buses that stop there are listed below the sign and on the exterior wall of the shelter. Most bus shelters now have digital signs showing which routes are running and when the next bus will arrive. Route maps and service frequency guides are posted inside most bus shelters.

Using Streetcars

Streetcars operate both above and below ground. Streetcar lines J (Church), K (Ingleside), L (Taraval), M (Ocean View), N (Judah), and T (Third) all share the same tracks, which run beneath Market Street. So if you intend to catch a streetcar at a Market Street station, it is a good idea to check the letter and name of the one you are about to board to avoid taking the wrong line.

Muni bus shelter, with glass walls and a digital timetable

A Muni Metro streetcar, with its distinctive silver-and-red cars

Along Market Street, four of the seven underground stations are shared by both Muni Metro streetcars and BART (see p286). Entrances to Muni and BART are clearly signposted throughout. In the station, look for the separate "Muni" entrance.

Pay, use your Clipper card, or show a Muni Passport, then proceed downstairs to the platform. To go west, choose "Outbound"; to go east, choose "Downtown." Electronic signs show which

streetcar is about to arrive. Doors open automatically to allow passengers to enter. In the event they don't open at a street-level or low-level platform stop, push on the low bar beside the exit.

Stops above ground are indicated by an orange-and-brown metal flag, or by a yellow band around a pole, marked "Muni" or "Car Stop."

Lines J, K, L, M, N, and T all use Breda cars, which have a

distinctive silver-and-red look. The F line streetcar runs only along Market Street, with vintage streetcars from all over the world. Streetcars are also known as Light Rail Vehicles (LRVs).

DIRECTORY

Muni Information

Tel 331 (inside SF);
(415) 701-2311 (outside SF);
TTY: (415) 701-2323
w sfmta.com

Muni Passports

Hyde and Beach Public Transit Kiosk
Hyde & Beach Sts. **Map** 4 F1.

Visitor Information Center
Lower level, Hallidie Plaza,
Market and Powell sts.
Map 5 B5. **Tel** 391-2000.
w sftravel.com

Sightseeing by Bus and Streetcar

Popular routes are outlined on the map below. Historic streetcars run on the E and F lines along Market Street to the Wharves. The N line streetcar runs above ground from the Ferry Building to CalTrain depot. More information is available from Muni or the city's Visitor Information Center. For more bus and streetcar routes, see the map on the inside back cover of this guide.

F line streetcar approaching the Ferry Building

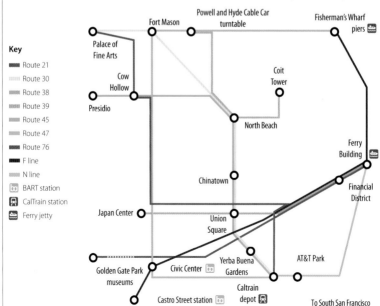

Key
- Route 21
- Route 30
- Route 38
- Route 39
- Route 45
- Route 47
- Route 76
- F line
- N line
- BART station
- CalTrain station
- Ferry jetty

Fort Mason

Powell and Hyde Cable Car turntable

Fisherman's Wharf piers

Palace of Fine Arts

Cow Hollow

Presidio

Coit Tower

North Beach

Ferry Building

Chinatown

Financial District

Japan Center

Union Square

Golden Gate Park museums

Civic Center

Yerba Buena Gardens

AT&T Park

Castro Street station

Caltrain depot

To South San Francisco

Traveling by Cable Car

As the only "moving national monument" in the United States, San Francisco's cable cars are world-famous *(see pp106–7)* and every visitor will want to ride one at least once. The cable car service runs from 6.30am to 12.30am daily. There is a flat fare of $7 for each journey, with a discount for seniors and the disabled after 9pm and before 7am. Although this is a great way to experience the city, buses and streetcars *(see pp282–3)* are often a more practical option.

Using the Cable Cars

Cable cars run along three routes. The Powell–Hyde line is the most popular. Starting at the Powell and Market turntable *(see p119)*, it skirts Union Square and climbs Nob Hill providing good views of Chinatown. It continues past the Cable Car Museum *(see p105)*, crosses Lombard Street *(see p88)*, then descends Hyde Street to the turntable near Aquatic Park *(see pp174–5)*. The Powell–Mason line also begins at Powell and Market streets and follows the same route to the Cable Car Barn. From there, it passes by North Beach and ends at Bay Street. Sit facing east on the Powell lines and on your journey you will see

some of the city's best-known sights. The California line runs from the base of Market Street, at the Embarcadero, along California Street. It passes through part of the Financial District and Chinatown. At Nob Hill the Powell lines cross the California line, so passengers can transfer between lines. If you have a one-way ticket you will need to purchase another, but those with a Muni Passport have an unlimited number of cable-car rides. The California line then continues over Nob Hill, ending at Van Ness Avenue. For each of the three lines, the return trip follows the outward route, so riders are able to catch views from the other side of the car.

Commuters like to use cable cars too, so avoid traveling during rush hours if possible (7–9am and 4–7pm Mon–Fri). Whatever time you travel, though, you are much more likely to get a seat if you board the cable car at the end of the line you have chosen.

Tickets

If you have not already purchased a Muni Passport *(see p282)*, you can buy a ticket ($7) or a one-day pass ($17) from the conductor. Tickets are collected once you board. Muni passes, souvenir tickets, and maps are available at kiosks at Powell and Market streets and at Hyde and Beach streets, or at the city Visitor Information Center *(see p283)*.

Cable-Car Stops

To catch a cable car you can line up at either end of a line or wait at a stop. Stand on the sidewalk and wave to alert the gripman. Do not board until the car has come to a complete stop and be prepared to jump on quickly. Stops are marked by maroon signs that display the outline

Recognizing Your Cable Car

Currently 40 cable cars operate on the city's three lines. Each car seats 29 to 34 passengers and, depending on the type of car, can accommodate an additional 20 to 40 people standing.

On the front, back and sides of every cable car is the name of the line: Powell–Hyde, Powell–Mason, or California Street. The number of the cable car is also displayed. California Street cars are easy to identify because they have a driver's cab at both ends. Cars on the two Powell lines have only one cab.

The conductor and gripman are generally friendly and helpful, so ask one of them if you are not sure which line to take to reach your destination.

Bell

Grab handle

Line board

Car number

Running board (holds up to eight passengers)

Headlight

Bell

Destination board

POWELL & HYDE Sts.

13

SAN FRANCISCO MUNICIPAL RAILWAY

Side seating

Running board

Gate

Sightseeing by Cable Car

The city's hills present no problem to cable cars. They tackle precipitous slopes effortlessly, passing sights and areas popular with tourists. The most thrilling descent is the final stretch of the Powell–Hyde line.

Key

—— California line
—— Powell–Hyde line
—— Powell–Mason line
◒ Turntable/crossing
○ Terminus
▦ Cable Car Barn

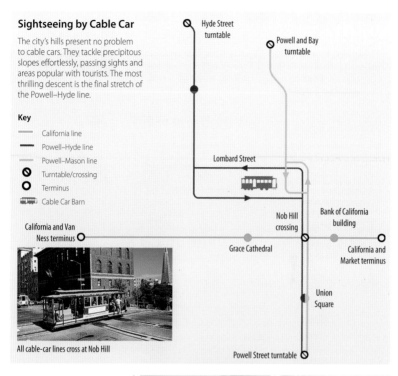

Hyde Street turntable
Powell and Bay turntable
Lombard Street
California and Van Ness terminus
Nob Hill crossing
Bank of California building
Grace Cathedral
California and Market terminus
Union Square
Powell Street turntable

All cable-car lines cross at Nob Hill

of a cable car in white, or by a yellow line painted on the road. On weekends, the stops at Powell and Market, and at Fisherman's Wharf, are typically very crowded – be prepared to wait at least 30 minutes.

Traveling Safely in a Cable Car

If there is not a crowd, you can choose whether to sit or stand inside, sit outside on a bench or stand on an end. More adventurous passengers may prefer to hang onto a pole while standing on a side running board.

Wherever you find a place, be sure to hold on tight. Do not get in the way of the gripman; he needs a lot of room to operate the grip lever. This off-limits area is marked by yellow lines on the floor. Use caution while on board. Passing other cable cars is exciting, but be extremely careful not to lean out too far, because they get very close to one another. Be vigilant when

boarding or getting off a car. Often cable cars stop at an intersection so that you have to get on or off between the car and other vehicles, and this can be dangerous. All passengers must get off at the end of the line. If you wish to make a return trip, you must wait for the car to be turned around on the turntable, or switched to the return line, before boarding again.

Passengers riding on a cable car's running board

DIRECTORY

Useful Numbers

Cable Car Barn
1201 Mason St.
Map 5 B3.
Museum **Tel** (415) 474-1887.

Muni Information
Tel 701-3000.
Ⓦ sfmta.com
Cable-car information, fares, Muni Passports.

Traveling by BART

The San Francisco Peninsula and the East Bay are linked by BART (Bay Area Rapid Transit). This is a 103 mile (165 km) rapid transit system with a fleet of high-speed, wheelchair-accessible trains. BART is an easy and efficient way of getting to both Bay airports.

The BART logo

Taking a Trip by BART

1 BART trains run 4am–midnight Mon–Fri, 6am–midnight Sat, 8am–midnight Sun. BART stops at four stations beneath Market Street – Civic Center, Powell, Montgomery, and Embarcadero. All trains from Daly City stop at city-center stations before heading for the East Bay through a 4-mile (6-km) underwater tunnel. Transfers in the East Bay are possible only at two stations: MacArthur and Oakland City Center – 12th Street.

KEY

— Richmond–Daly City/Millbrae

- - - Millbrae–Bay Point

— Fremont–Daly City

- - - Fremont–Richmond

— Pleasanton–Daly City

2 BART tickets are issued by machines. Rates are posted near the machines inside BART stations. Clipper cards (see p282) are also valid on BART services.

4 The value inserted is shown here. To buy a round-trip ticket, insert twice the amount for a one-way fare.

5 Tickets (below) are magnetically coded with the value, which is then printed on the ticket.

Insert ticket into barrier this way   **Magnetic strip**

8 All trains display their final destination – westbound to San Francisco/Daly City, for example; or eastbound to Oakland, Richmond, Bay Point, or Fremont. Train doors open automatically. Platforms are marked with the end of the line in the direction in which the train is traveling.

3 Insert coins or bills here. Machines will accept coins and notes, and most will also take debit/credit cards. The machines can give up to $10 in change.

6 Your ticket is issued here. Each person traveling should have his or her own ticket, or Clipper card.

7 To gain access to the platforms, you must run your ticket through a turnstile or use your Clipper card. The fare for your trip is automatically deducted from the ticket/card value. Before you leave the station, you must re-insert your ticket in the turnstile. If any value remains, your ticket will be returned as the turnstile opens.

9 BART stations have personnel on hand to answer questions and assist passengers with the machines. For further information, visit www.bart.gov or telephone 989-BART (989-2278).

Ferries and Bay Trips

Though the city provides various transport options, ferries are still a favorite way to get around. They shuttle to and from the cities of San Francisco and Oakland *(see pp166–7)*, as well as the smaller towns of Tiburon and Sausalito *(see p163)*. For locals and visitors alike, it is one of the best ways to appreciate the beauty of the Bay Area. Grab a snack or a drink from the concession stand, and bask in resplendent views of the bridges Angel Island and Alcatraz.

Ferry Services

Bay Area residents adore their ferries. During the week, commuters use them to avoid traffic on the bridges, and at weekends suburban families leave their cars behind and hop on for jaunts to the city.

Ferries do not have audio tours to identify the sights along the coastline, but they are less expensive than sight-seeing cruises (the trip from San Francisco to Sausalito is $11.25 each way). Food and drinks are available on board. Note that ferries carry only foot passengers and bicycles, not motor vehicles.

Golden Gate Ferry services depart from the Ferry Building, on the Embarcadero, which is a destination in its own right *(see p114)*, housing food shops, a weekly farmers' market, and several restaurants. The **Blue and Gold Fleet** docks at nearby Fisherman's Wharf *(see pp80–81)*.

Bay Trips

Bay sightseeing cruises from Fisherman's Wharf are operated by Blue and Gold Fleet and **Red and White Fleet**. Destinations include Angel Island and towns on the north shore of the Bay *(see pp162–3)*. There are also combined boat and bus tours to visit San Francisco and Muir Woods *(see p162)*. Tours cost $31–$100.

Many Bay trips pass near Alcatraz *(see pp84–7)*, but only **Alcatraz Cruises** sells tickets and tours to The Rock.

Hornblower Dining Yachts offers weekend brunches and dinners from Wednesdays to Sundays on its charter cruises (call to check timings). **Oceanic Society Expeditions** arranges nautical environmental safaris with an onboard naturalist to the Farallon Islands, 25 miles (40 km) offshore. These safaris often spot whales on the way to the islands from March through May. There are also whale-watching expeditions off San Francisco's west coast (from $120 per person, *see p260*).

Check with individual operators for schedules and seasonal variations.

Popular Ferries and Bay Trips

Vallejo

Larkspur

Tiburon

Sausalito

Alcatraz Island

Fisherman's Wharf piers

Ferry Building piers

Alameda

Bay trip vessel

KEY

— Bay trips

— Alcatraz Island (Alcatraz Cruises)

— Sausalito ferry

— Tiburon ferry

— Larkspur ferry

— Vallejo ferry

— East Bay ferry

Driving in San Francisco

Congestion, a shortage of parking areas (and their high prices), and strictly enforced parking laws discourage many visitors from driving in San Francisco. Speed limits vary, but the maximum is 35 mph (56 km/h) within the city. Many streets are one-way, with traffic lights at most corners in the city center.

Car Rental

You must be at least 25 years old with a valid driving license (a US or International Driver's License is best) to rent a car. All agencies require a major credit card or a large cash deposit. Damage and liability insurance is recommended. Always return the car with a full tank of gas to avoid the inflated gas prices charged by the rental agency. Many agencies now offer the option of pre-paying for a tank of gas at lower-than-average gas prices, which is well worth doing if you know you'll use at least a tank of gas. It is less expensive to rent a car at the airport: rental taxes are $2 a day more in the city.

Traffic Signs

Colorful signs and symbols point the way to the main tourist areas, such as Chinatown (a lantern); Fisherman's Wharf (a crab); North Beach (outline of Italy). "Stop" and "Do Not Enter" signs are red and white. "Caution" and

"Yield" signs are yellow and black. "One Way" signs are black and white. If there is no oncoming traffic, drivers may turn right at a red light. Otherwise, red lights mean stop and amber lights mean proceed with caution.

Parking

Parking meters operate 8am to 6pm Monday to Saturday, except on national holidays, when parking is free. Most meters have short time limits, usually of 1 hour. City-center parking garages cost $15 to $30 a day, and most accept cash or credit cards.

Curbs are color-coded: red means stopping is prohibited; yellow is loading zones; green allows 10 minutes' parking, while white permits 5 minutes during business hours. Blue curbs are reserved for the disabled. Some parking spaces are tow-away zones: check signs for information. By law you must curb your wheels when parking on steep hills. Turn wheels into the road when facing uphill and toward the curb when facing downhill.

Penalties

If you park your car at an out-of-order meter, expect to get a parking ticket. Blocking bus stops, fire hydrants, driveways, garages, and wheelchair ramps will also incur a fine, as will running a red light. For details of traffic regulations, contact the **Department of Parking and Transportation**. If you receive a ticket, you are expected to pay the fine or appear in court. After five parking tickets, a "Denver Boot" may be clamped to the wheel, immobilizing the car. This is

removed when the fines are paid. If your car has been towed away, call the **Police Department Towed Vehicle Information** line. You'll need to go either to the city's Department of Parking and Transportation or to **Auto Return**, depending on whether a private towing company or the municipal towing service has towed your car. Expect to pay a towing and storage fee. For rental cars, you'll need to show the contract before the car will be released. Cars taken to the city lot face an additional parking ticket.

Driving Outside the City

No toll payment is required to leave the city via either the Bay Bridge or the Golden Gate Bridge, but you will need to pay coming back in. Speed limits on highways in and out of San Francisco are 55 mph to 70 mph (88 km/h to 112 km/h). During rush hour, cars with 3 or more occupants can use the carpool lane, avoiding both traffic and tolls. Further east, north, and south, only two occupants are needed. It is legal to drive in the carpool lane when it's not rush hour, but not to avoid the bridge tolls. Those caught using the carpool lane illegally face steep fines.

Driving across the city's landmark, the Golden Gate Bridge *(see pp64–7)*

San Francisco's Taxis

Taxis in San Francisco operate 24 hours a day. Taxis can be hard to find, especially in the outer areas, but the drivers are generally helpful and friendly. Many drivers are veterans eager to share their knowledge of the streets. Taxis are licensed and regulated, so you can always expect courtesy, efficient service, and a set price. The guidelines below will help you find a taxi, get an idea of the fare, and understand the regulations.

Inside a Green Cab with a hybrid engine *(see p280)*

Taking a Taxi

Cabs have a rooftop sign that is illuminated when the vehicle is vacant. The various company liveries are red, white, and blue; yellow; yellow and orange; and green. All taxis display the company name and telephone number, plus the cab number.

To catch a cab, wait at a taxi stand, call and request a pick-up, or try to hail a vacant cab.

When you request a pickup, give your exact address and name. You are expected to meet the cab on the street, but the dispatcher will typically call with an automated message when the driver is outside. If you wait more than 15 minutes, call again. Requests for cabs to the airport usually get a quick response. Passengers ride in the back seat, which may or may not have seat belts. The meter is on the dashboard. Note the company and cab number or the driver's name and number. Tell the driver your destination and the cross-street, if possible. The driver should get you there in the shortest amount of time. Traffic congestion can slow the best drivers down, so it may be better to pay the fare, get out, and walk the final few blocks. Taxi drivers do not carry much cash, so be prepared to pay by credit card, or with bills of $20 or smaller. Add a 10 to 15 percent tip and hand it to the driver before you get out of the cab. The driver will write a receipt on request. Check you have all your belongings before you get out. If you have left something in a cab, call the cab company and give them the cab number or driver's name.

Fares

Fares are posted inside the cab. There is a flat fee (around $3.50) for the first mile (1.6 km). This increases by about $2.25 for each additional mile (1.6 km), or 45 cents a minute while waiting outside an address or in traffic delays. The average fare from San Francisco airport to the city center is $45. Fares from the Ferry Building to the west coast ocean beaches are about $30. These fares are estimates only, and they do not include any additional charges such as time spent waiting in heavy traffic, or a tip for the driver.

Regulations

Taxi drivers must carry with them photographic identification and a permit to drive a taxi, called a medallion. Following legislation in 2010, all taxi cabs are now non-smoking. If you need to complain about a taxi driver, call the **Police Department Taxicab Complaint Line**.

DIRECTORY

Taxi Companies

Big Dog City Cab
Tel 920-0700.

DeSoto Cab
Tel (877) 691-2170.

Green Cab
Tel 626-4733.

Luxor Cab
Tel 282-4141.

Yellow Cab
Tel 333-3333.

Information

Police Department Taxicab Complaint Line
Tel 701-4400.

Driver number	Company name	Official taxi license	Company phone number

A San Francisco taxi in yellow livery

STREET FINDER

The map references given with all sights, restaurants, hotels, shops, and entertainment venues described in this book refer to the maps in this section. A complete index of the street names and all the places of interest marked on the maps follows on pages 301–8. The key map below shows the area of San Francisco covered by

the *Street Finder* only. This includes the sightseeing areas (which are color-coded) as well as the whole of central San Francisco, with the main districts where restaurants, hotels, and entertainment sites are located. Because the city center is so packed with sights, there is a large-scale map of this area on pages 5 and 6.

Key to Street Finder

- Major sight
- Places of interest
- Other building
- CalTrain station
- BART station
- Bus terminal
- Streetcar station
- Cable-car terminal
- Ferry boarding point
- Tourist information office
- Hospital with emergency unit
- Police station
- Church
- Synagogue
- Mosque
- Buddhist temple
- Hindu temple
- Golf course
- Railroad line
- Freeway
- Pedestrian street
- Cable-car line

Scale of Maps
1–4 and 7–11

| 0 meters | 500 |
| 0 yards | 500 |

Scale of Maps 5 & 6

| 0 meters | 500 |
| 0 yards | 500 |

Sausalito, Larkspur

Alcatraz Island

PIER 27

PIER 23

PIER 19

PIER 17

PIER 15

Exploratorium

PIER 9

PIER 7

San Francisco Bay

PIER 5

PIER 3

Oakland, Alameda

PIER 1

FRONT STREET

DAVIS STREET

THE EMBARCADERO

JACKSON STREET

WASHINGTON ST

DRUMM

World Trade Center

PIER 2

Ferry Building

BATTERY

MARITIME PLAZA

EMBARCADERO PLAZA PARK

CLAY

Embarcadero Center

JUSTIN HERMAN PLAZA

SACRAMENTO ST

DAVIS ST

Hyatt Regency Hotel

STEUART STREET

SAN FRANCISCO OAKLAND BAY BRIDGE

FRONT STREET

STREET

Embarcadero

Pacific Coast Stock Exchange

Amtrak Terminal Ticket Office

MISSION STREET

SPEAR STREET

MAIN STREET

Rincon Center

<< 333

PIER 24

STEVENSON ST

Montgomery St

MINNA STREET

BEALE

FREMONT

HOWARD

Folsom

PIER 26

Greyhound Bus Depot

1ST

<< 700

Transbay Terminal

FOLSOM STREET

STREET

ELKHART ST

390 >>

PIER 28

TEHAMA STREET

CLEMENTINA ST

GROTE

PIER 30

Cartoon Art Museum

2ND

MALDEN AL

GUY PL

LANSING ST

<< 460

STREET

PIER 32

Pacific Telephone Building

ESSEX ST

Museum of Modern Art

HAWTHORNE STREET

DOW PL

1ST STREET

Center for the Arts

Brannan

PIER 34

3RD

Moscone Convention Center

HAMPTON PL

VERONICA PL

DOW PL

BRYANT

RINCON

BRANNAN STREET

THE EMBARCADERO

PIER 36

FOLSOM

300>>

STREET

<< 665

HARRISON

STILLMAN ST

DE BOOM ST

PIER 38

Street Finder Index

General Index

Acknowledgments

Dorling Kindersley would like to thank the many people whose help and assistance contributed to the preparation of this book.

Main Contributors

Jamie Jensen grew up in Los Angeles and moved to San Francisco to study architecture at the University of California at Berkeley, where he still has his home. His other credits include *Built to Last*, an authorized biography of the Grateful Dead, and numerous travel guides including the *Rough Guide to California*. His most recent project is *Road Trip: USA*, a practical travel guide to the "old roads" across America.

Barry Parr was born in the San Francisco Bay Area, and studied English literature at the University of California at Berkeley, and at Cambridge University. He has written and edited travel guides, and writes for many magazines

Additional Photography

Lisa M. Cope, John Heseltine, Trevor Hill, Neil Lukas, Andrew McKinney, Rough Guides/Nelson Hancock, Rough Guides/Angus Osborn, Ian O'Leary, Robert Vente, Peter Wilson.

Additional Illustrations

James A. Allington, Annabelle Brend, Craig Draper, Steve Gyapay, Kevin Jones Associates, Simon Roulston, Sue Sharples, Paul Williams, Ann Winterbotham.

Cartography

Aennifer Skelley, Jane Hugill, Phil Rose, Rachel Hawtin.

Index

Indexing Specialists, 202 Church Road, Hove, East Sussex, UK.

Design and Editorial

Mardoe Blacker Publishing Limited
Managing Editor Alan Ross
Managing Art Editor Simon Blacker
Project Secretary Cindy Edler
Dorling Kindersley Limited
Managing Editors Douglas Amrine, Carolyn Ryden
Managing Art Editor Stephen Knowlden
US Editor Mary Ann Lynch
Map Coordinators Simon Farbrother, David Pugh
Production Hilary Stephens
Maps Lovell Johns Ltd., Oxford UK
Street Finder Maps based upon digital data, adapted with permission from original survey by ETAK INC 1984–1994.

Revisions Team Namrata Adhwaryu, Tora Agarwala, Asad Ali, Hansa Babra, Shruti Bahl, Meghna Baruah, Sreemoyee Basu, Marta Bescos, Subhashree Bharati, Subhadeep Biswas, Michael Blacker, Dawn Brend, Laaren Brown, Maxine Cass, Aaron Chamberlin, Kelly Chamberlin, Neha Chander, Peter Cieply, Sherry Collins, Lisa M. Cope, Imogen Corke, Melissa Corrigan, Caroline Elliker, Alice Fewery, Emer FitzGerald, Jo Gardner, Emily Green, Fay Franklin, Kyra Freestar, Sally

Hibbard, Paul Hines, Katie Hogg, Rose Hudson, Claire Jones, Heather Jones, Bharti Karakoti, Rupanki Arora Kaushik, Sumita Khatwani, Rahul Kumar, Esther Labi, Maite Lantaron, Celeste LeCompte, Hayley Maher, Nicola Malone, Alison McGill, Joanne Miller, Karen Misuraca, Sonal Modha, Adam Moore, Mary Ormandy, Rakesh Kumar Pal, Catherine Palmi, Susie Peachey, Helen Peters, Marianne Petrou, Andrea Pinnington, Schchida Nand Pradhan, Mani Ramaswamy, Lucy Richards, Kat Rosa, Steve Rowling, Dan Rubin, Sands Publishing Solutions, Anuroop Sanwalia, Azeem Siddiqui, Rituraj Singh, Mary Sutherland, Hollie Teague, Nikky Twyman, Conrad van Dyk, Deepika Verma, Lauren Viera, Ros Walford, Amy Westerwelt, Hugo Wilkinson.

Special Assistance

Marcia Eymann and Abby Wasserman at The Oakland Museum of California, Stacia Fink at the Foundation for San Francisco's Architectural Heritage, Richard Fishman, Debbie Freedon at the Legion of Honor, Michael Lampen at Grace Cathedral, Dan Mohn, Chief Engineer of Golden Gate Bridge, Dr. John R. Nudds at Manchester University Museum, Richard Ogar at Bancroft Library, Peppers, Riggio Café, Royal Thai Restaurant, Scott Sack at the Golden Gate National Recreation Area, Sandra Farish Sloan and Jennifer Small at the San Francisco Museum of Modern Art, Stella Pastry and Cafe, Stephen Marcos Landscapes, Dawn Stranne at the San Francisco Convention and Visitors Bureau, The Little Cafe, Carl Wilmington.

Research Assistance

Christine Bartholomew, Jennifer Bermon, Cathy Elliott, Kirsten Whatley, Jon Williams, Michael Wrenn.

Photography Permissions

Dorling Kindersley would like to thank the following for their kind permission to photograph at their establishments: Asian Art Museum, Cable Car Barn Museum, California Academy of Sciences, Cha Cha Cha, Chinese Historical Society, City Hall, Coit Tower, Columbarium, Crocker Galleria, Ernie's, The Exploratorium, Fort Mason Center, Fortune Cookie Factory, Foundation for San Francisco's Architectural Heritage (Haas-Lilienthal House), Golden Gate National Recreation Area (Alcatraz), Gump's, Hyatt Regency Hotel, Kong Chow Temple, Kuleto's, MH de Young Memorial Museum, Mission Dolores, Nordstrom, The Oakland Museum of California, Presidio Museum, Rincon Annexe, Saints Peter and Paul Church, San Francisco History Room, San Francisco Main Library, San Francisco National Historical Park, Sheraton Palace Hotel, St. Mary's Cathedral, Temple Emanu-El, Tosca, USS *Pampanito*, Veteran's Building, Wells Fargo History Room.

Picture Credits

Key: a = above; b = below/bottom; c = center; f = far; l = left; r = right; t = top.

Works of art have been reproduced with the permission of the following copyright holders:

The Publishers are grateful to the following museums, companies and picture libraries for permission to reproduce their photographs:

21st Amendment Brewery: 224tc. **Acquerello:** 216bc. **Alamy Images:** Aerial Archives 49cr; Agencja Fotograficzna Caro 233br; Arcaid Images 35crb; BANANA PANCAKE 184–5; Patrick Batchelder 131br; Danita Delimont/Darrell Gulin 145; David Taylor Photography 96; DB Images/Jeremy Graham 138br; Eagle Visions Photography/Craig Lovell 172; Michele Falzone 67br; Robert Holmes 102tc; Brian Jannsen 68; Victor Korchenko 126bl; Nikreates 129tl; Douglas Peebles Photography, 219c; Prisma Bildagentur AG/Malherbe Marcel 150–51; Emily Riddell 223bc; Robert Harding Picture Library Ltd. 219tl; Roberto Soncin Gerometta 218cla; **Roger Allen Lee:** 188c; **Allsport:** Otto Greule, 52c; **Archive Photos:** 34bc, 104bl; **Armstrong Redwoods State Reserve:** 190c; **Attaché Communications:** Phil Gosney for Amtrak 278bl. **AWL Images:** Gavin Hellier 43tr.
Bancroft Library, University of California, Berkeley: 24cla/ clb/br, 24-25c, 25cla/br, 26br, 28clb, 29crb, 148c; **Morton Beebe:** 181tr; **Berkeley Convention and Visitors Bureau:** 164tl; **Blackbird Inn/Foursisters.com:** 212bl; **Simon Blacker:** 41tl, 192tr; **Boudin:** 222bl; **Bridgeman Art Library:** *The Thinker (Le Penseur)*, by Auguste Rodin (1840–1917), Musée Rodin, Paris 158tr; **Marilyn Blaisdell Collection:** 29cra. **California Academy of Sciences:** 152–3 all; Caroline Kopp 147cr; Dong Lin 38br, Susan Middleton 37cla; **California Historical Society, San Francisco:** 29b, 30cla, 31crb, 48crb, 148b; **Camera Press:** Gary Freedman 34tr; **Carolyn Cassady:** 34tl, 88bc; **Center for Urban Education about Sustainable Agriculture:** 269cra; **Cephas Picture Library:** Mick Rock 195br; **Chateau Tivoli Bed and Breakfast:** 208cra; **CityPASS:** 266crb; **Club Fugazi:** Charles Zukow Associates/Rick Markovich 89tc; **Corbis:** 8-9; Morton Beebe 181br; 45bl, 200tr; Jan Butchofsky-Houser 129br, 180cla; Richard Cummins 10cla; Gerald French 201t, 206–7; Lowell Georgia 127br; Robert Holmes 40bc, 194br, 195tl, 223tr, 249cra; Catherine Karnow 183tr; Latitude/Jean-Pierre Lescourret 108; Jean-Pierre Lescourret 275tl; Craig Lovell 47br; Charles O'Rear 194cl; Proehl Studios 136clb; Reuters Newmedia Inc 247bl; Royalty free 182cla; San Francisco Chronicle/Deanne Fitzmaurice 45tc; Michael T Sedam 75br; **Culver Pictures, Inc:** 33tl.
Dreamstime.com: Card76 13tr; Cecoffman 176cl; Kobby Dagan 78; Elf0724 12cra; F8grapher 11t; Prochasson Frederic 5tr; Jewhyte 1; Srongkrod Kuakoon 267tr; Pius Lee 4cb; Chee-onn Leong 5cl; Maislam 233tl; Fabrizio Mariani 93br; Meinzahn 10br; Photoquest 12tl; Rglinsky 288bl; Tanyabird777 202br; TasFoto 175tc; Dmitry Vinogradov 264-265; Lawrence Weslowski Jr 51bl, 232br. **Embarcadero Center:** Donna Ewald/Peter Clute/Vic Reyna/Ed Rogers: 72crb; **Exploratorium, www. exploratorium.edu:** Photo courtesy of 94–5 all. **The Fairmont San Francisco Hotel:** 215tc; Ferry Building Marketplace: Rien Van Rijthiven 111crb; **The Fine Arts Museums of San Francisco:** *Sailboat on the Seine*, c.1874, by Claude Monet, gift of Bruno and Sadie Adrian, 38cla; *Saint John the Baptist*, by Matti Preti, 40cla; High chest, museum purchase, gift of Mr. and Mrs. Robert A. Magowan, 146tr; *Saint Wenceslaus, Patron Saint of Bohemia*, after a model by Johann Gottlieb Kirchner (b.1706), hard-paste porcelain, museum purchase, Roscoe and Margaret Oakes Income Fund, 158bl; *Waterlilies*, c.1914–17, by Claude Monet, oil on canvas, Mildred Anna Williams Collection, 158cl; *Old Woman*, c.1618, by Georges de la Tour, Roscoe and Margaret Oakes Collection, 159cla; *The Impresario, (Pierre Duc-arre)*, c.1877, by Edgar Degas, oil on paper board, 159bl; **Fog City:** Ellipses PR / Cesar Rubio 11br.
Gallery of California, Oakland Museum of California, 2012: Arlen Ness, Harley Davidson, QuickNess, 1972 produced, customized in 1984 168bl; **Steven Gerlick:** 107bl; **Gather Restaurant/Fortune Public Relations:** 229t; **Getty Images:** Flickr/Can Balcioglu 2-3, /fuminana 54-5, /Michael Kitromilides 156-7, / vns24@yahoo.com 58, /William Storage 36; Mitchell Funk 132; Roy Giles 80cla; Lonely Planet Images/ Thomas Winz 124; News/Justin Sullivan 44crb; Robert Harding World Imagery/Yadid Levy 279tr; RB 131bl; George Rose 220cl; Donna Santisi 34c; Stone 52bc; Stringer / JOSH EDELSON 180bc; Justin Sullivan 272tr; UpperCut Images/ Robert Houser 160; **The Girl & the Fig:** Steven Krause 229br; **GoCar:** 281ca; **GLBT History Museum:** Daniel Nicoletta 138c; **Golden Gate Bridge Highway and Transportation District:** 64–5 all, 66tl/bl, 66–7tc, 67tr; **Golden Gate National Recreation Area:** Don Denevi Collection 67clb, 82cl, 84clb, 85clb/br; **Stephen D. Gross, G-WIZ G&P:** 190bl.
Robert Holmes Photography: Markham Johnson 39bl, 51cr. **Ine Tours:** 235cr; **The Image Works:** Lisa Law, 131cr; **iStockphoto.com:** Canbalci 110tr; Spondylolithesis 50br. **Joie de Vivre Hotels:** 210tr, 213tr; **JP Morgan Chase:** 272bl. Courtesy of Landmark Theatres: 248tr; **Lawrence Hall of Science, University of California:** Peg Skorpinskin 164br; **Lengendary Napa Valley:** 193bc; **Courtesy Levi Strauss & Co., San Francisco:** 137c. **Andrew Mckinney Photography:** 5tr, 26cla, 30bc, 31bc, 32bl, 33tc/cra, 34br, 49cb, 51ca, 53bl, 57cra, 66br, 72bl, 171bl, 173ca, 186cl/bl, 187tr/br, 188bl, 189tl, 191br, 193tl/tr, 198br, 199bl, 202tr, 203tl/tr; **Alain Mclaughlan:** 276br; **Magnes Museum Permanent Collections:** 19th-century blue velvet embroidery brocade robe, 165tc; **Magnum Photos:** Michael K. Nichols, 35bl; **Mark Hopkins Inter-Continental Hotel:** 104tc, 208bl; **The Mexican Museum:** 41bc; **Michael Mina Restaurant:** 225bl; **Mineta San José International Airport:** 277bc; **Monk's Kettle:** 228tl; **Museo Italoamericano:** *Muto*, 1985, by Mimmo Paladino, aquatint and sugarlift etching,

gift of Pasquale Lannetti, 39tl; *Meta III*, 1985, by Italo Scanga, oil and lacquer on wood, gift of Alan Shepp, 75bl; **Museum of the City of San Francisco:** Richard Hansen, 21br, 30clb, 30–31cl, 31tc/clb.
Napa Valley Visitors Bureau: 192cb; **Peter Newark's American Pictures:** 4t, 25bl, 27tl/crb/bl/br; 28bl, 85bl, 107crb; **N.H.P.A.:** David Middle-ton 196bl; John Shaw 205cr; **NOPA:** 226tr; **Bob von Normann:** 191tl.
Oakland Convention Bureau: 167tr; Oakland International Airport: 277tr; Courtesy The Oakland Museum History Department: 21bl, 25cra, 26cra/clb, 27cra, 28cla, 29tr, 31cra, 32cl, 33crb; Oakland Museum of California: 169tl; Phyllis Diebenkorn, Trustee, Ocean Park No.107, 1978, Richard Diebenkorn 168cl; Matthew Millman Photography 168tr, 169cr; Jeff Warrin 169br; Orchard Garden Hotel: 209b, 214bc.
Pacific Union Railroad Company: 29tl; Pier 39 Corporation: 249tl; www.photographersdirect.com: Justin Bailie 198tl, 200cla, 201br; Ann Purcell Travel Journalism, 200br; Nancy Warner 182bc, 183br; Picturepoint: 85tl; Precita Eyes Mural Arts and Visitors Centre: *Balloon Journey* © 2008 Precita Eyes Muralists, by Kristen Foskett 142crb; Hillcrest Elementary School © 2007 Precita Eyes Muralists 142cb; *Oakland, Stop the Violence* © 2007 Precita Eyes Muralists. Directed by Joshua Stevenson. Designed and painted by AYPAL youth (Asian Pacific Islander Youth Promoting Advocacy and Leadership) including Recy, Marcus and many others. Acrylic paint on Tyvek 142b; Presidio of San Francisco: NPS staff 61tl. Queen Anne Hotel: 209tr.
Red and White Fleet: 287tl; Rex Features: B. Ward, 35tl; San Francisco Arts Commission Gallery: 128tc; San Francisco Blues Festival: 247tl; San Francisco Cable Car Museum: 28br, 107tl; San Francisco Comedy Celebration Day: 248cl; San Francisco Convention and Visitors Bureau: 42bc, 50cra/bl, 52cra, 53cr, 163b, 248bl, 266cra, 278cra; San Francisco Fire Department: 270clb; San Francisco Maritime National Historical Park: 267bl; San Francisco Municipal Transportation Agency: 268tl, 282ca/br, 283tl/cr, 285crb; San Francisco Museum of Modern Art: *Back View*, 1977, by Philip Guston, oil on canvas, gift of the artist, 39crb; *Orange Sweater*, 1955, by Elmer Bischoff, oil on canvas, gift of Mr. and Mrs. Mark Schorer, 117crb; Henrik Kam 120tr; *No 14*, 1960, by Mark Rothko, 120c; *Country Dog Gentlemen*, 1972, by Roy De Forest, polymer on canvas, gift of the Hamilton-Wells Collection, 121br; *Lesende* (Reading) (1994) © Gerhard Richter 121cr; *Melodious Double Stops*, 1980, by Richard Shaw, porcelain with decal overglaze, purchased with funds from the National Endowment for the Arts and Frank

O. Hamilton, Byron Meyer and Mrs. Peter Schlesinger, 121clb; *'92 Chaise*, 1985–92, by Holt, Hinshaw, Pfau, Jones Architecture, steel, plastic, rubber and ponyhide, Accessions Committee Fund, 122br; Steelblue 121clb; *Les Femmes D'Alger (Woman of Algiers)*, 1955, by Pablo Picasso, oil on canvas, Albert M. Bender Collection, gift of Albert M. Bender in memory of Caroline Walter, 122cl; *Cave, Tsankawee, New Mexico*, 1988, by Linda Connor, gelatin silver print, fractional gift of Thomas and Shirley Ross Davis, 123br; *Graphite To Taste*, 1989, by Gail Fredell, steel, gift of Shirley Ross Davis, 123c; *Michael Jackson and Bubbles*, 1988, by Jeff Koons, porcelain, purchased through the Marian and Bernard Messenger Fund, 123tc; San Francisco Opera: 126clb; San Francisco Public Library, San Francisco History Center: 24bl, 30bl/br, 31bl, 33clb/bl, 34cra/bl, 44cl, 82c, 85tr, 104crb, 148tr; San Francisco War Memorial & Performing Arts Center: 249bl; San Francisco Zoo: 162tl; San Jose Convention and Visitors Bureau: 170t/c, 171t; Science Photo Library: Peter Menzel, 20tr; David Parker, 20cl, 21tr/cr; SF Green Cab, LLC: 280cla, 289cla; SoMa StrEat Food Park: 227bl; Mark Snyder Photography: 234tl; Sonoma Valley Visitors Bureau: Bob Nixon, 220tr, 197cr; Spectrum Color Library: 189br; STA Travel Group: 268cr. Tahoe North Visitors and Convention Bureau: 198tr; Deacon Chapin, 199tr.
University of California, Berkeley: *Within*, 1969, by Alexander Lieberman, gift of the artist, University Art Museum, 179b.
Vision Bank: Michael Freeman193cra.
Walgreen Co.: 271ca; Wells Fargo Bank History Room: 23b, 26-7c, 27tc, 112br; Val Wilmer: 32crb.
Yellow Cab Cooperative: Lunchana 289bl; Yerba Buena Center for the Arts Galleries: 39br; Ken Friedman 116tr; Yerba Buena Center of the Arts Theater/Margaret Jenkins Dance Company: 117tl.

Front Endpapers: Alamy Images: Danita Delimont/Darrell Gulin Lcla; David Taylor Photography Rcrb; Brian Jannsen Rtl; Corbis: Latitude/ Jean-Pierre Lescourret Rbc; Getty Images: Flickr/Phoenix Wang Rcra; Flickr/vns24@yahoo.com Ltr; Mitchell Funk Lbr; Lonely Planet Images/Thomas Winz Lbl.

Sheet Map Cover: Getty Images: Mitchell Funk.
Cover: Front main and spine – Getty Images: Mitchell Funk. Back – 123rf.com: Susan Patricia Leonard.

All other pictures Dorling Kindersley.
See www.dkimages.com for further information.

Special Editions of DK Travel Guides

DK Travel Guides can be purchased in bulk quantities at discounted prices for use in promotions or as premiums. We are also able to offer special editions and personalized jackets, corporate imprints, and excerpts from all of our books, tailored specifically to meet your own needs.

To find out more, please contact:
in the United States **specialsales@dk.com**
in the UK **travelguides@uk.dk.com**
in Canada DK Special Sales at **specialmarkets@dk.com**
in Australia **penguincorporatesales@penguinrandomhouse.com.au**

San Francisco
Transportation Routes

Key

PH ‑ ‑ ‑ Cable car line

18 ‑‑‑ Bus route

18 Bus terminus

N ‑‑‑ Muni Metro surface

N ‑·‑·‑ Muni Metro subway

N● Metro terminus

— CalTrain line

CalTrain station

Streetcar station

BART station

Coach terminus

Ferry boarding point

0 kilometers 1

0 miles 0.5

Marin Headlands

76

Golden Gate
Bridge

Fort Point
Lookout

San Francisco

MASON STREET
29
DOYLE DRIVE
28-76
29
29
28

PRESIDIO

The Presidio

Mountain
Lake

PRESIDIO
HEIGHTS

43

41-45

3-43
2-43

33

44

1

CALIFORNIA ST 1-2
2-33

Lincoln
Park

18

SEACLIFF

Legion
of Honor

18

1

CALIFORNIA STREET

29

2

CLEMENT STREET

1

2

GEARY BLVD 38

18-38

1

38

GEARY BOULEVARD

ARGUELLO BLVD

43

38

38

BALBOA ST 31

2-38

RICHMOND

31

44

BALBOA ST

31

33

5

MASONIC AVE

31-38

2

BALBOA ST

29

21

43

45

OUTER RICHMOND

31

FULTON ST

5-21

HAYES STREET

5

FULTON ST

5

28

de Young
Museum

44

California
Academy
of Sciences

STANYAN ST

HAIGHT
ASHBURY

7-33-43

7

7

43

33

Golden Gate Park

29

28-29

Stow
Lake

7

LINCOLN WAY

7

N

LINCOLN WAY

44

PARNASSUS AVE 6-43

6-43-44

LINCOLN WAY
29

7

7

N

28

JUDAH STREET

N

JUDAH STREET

44

SUNSET BOULEVARD

23RD AVENUE

22ND AVENUE

19TH AVENUE

9TH AVENUE

6

43-44

K-L-M-T

OUTER
SUNSET

INNER
SUNSET

TWIN
PEAKS

7

NORIEGA ST

7

NORIEGA ST

28

LAGUNA HONDA BLVD

29

Sunset
Reservoir

48

6

Forest Hill

48

QUINTARA ST

28

48

44

PORTOLA DRIVE

43

48

44

PARKSIDE

29

28

He closed his eyes. The words beat as rain. He replied.

She went twice through the list, and backwards, and chose at random, station or code words, but he was always sudden in answer, and never wrong.

She slapped the list on the desk.

"O, hell!" she said. "Now look what I have got to do. Why am I such a fool?"

"No," he said, and got up. "It is wrong to think in such a manner. And I was far more wrong. This money is yours as examiner. I passed because of you. At seven-fifteen tonight there will be time and place for other privilege. You cannot forget I only worship?"

She turned her back, hands clasped between the flowers.

"Very well," she said. "Seven-fifteen, tonight. But this time you will have no fear. I will see to it. Vutthi will meet you and bring you to me. The thousand rupees are mine without a receipt?"

"Without!"

"All I promised, I will pay," she said. "I am waiting for you. Don't be late!"

He went out and Gond took him back to the office. There were many pieces of paper, two of them important, and he settled them on the telephone with promise of money, which, of course, gave him a hold for the future. Nothing happened without money, but when money passed, other matters came into view, and favours came back, as they must.

It was the only way to be.

At seven, the paperwork was finished, and he called a taxi, giving Shiva's address. He stopped a few hundred yards away, and walked in darkness. Near the house, Vutthi's white braids shone, and she took his hand with a shake to tell him nothing was loose, and led through the garden to a gallery door, in, to the warm scent, and up the stairs of pink carpet, to the white door.

Shiva, in a white voile sari, opened, and shut, and leaned against the panels, and pushed herself off, and went to the brass table, and lifted the bottle.

"Whiskey I got for you!" she whispered. "Yes?"

"I don't drink," he said. "I will drink the beauty of you, nothing less. They can't bottle you!"

"You make one shamefully wrong!" she sai[ ] cushion. "First, I want to ask a big favour. [ ] thing for me?"

"I can do things for many people," he said. [ ]

"I have a house. It was an aunt of mine. [ ] The tenant held on to the lease. He pays th[ ] years ago. But I have found he employs wome[ ]

"A whoreshop?"

"Exactly. But my aunt was a sainted wo[ ] like. I do not like. How should I get rid of [ ] times the rent if he goes away!"

"But why should he go away? Why not [ ] forty percent of the gross? Cash? Every week[ ]

"But a dream!"

"You think so? Give me the address!"

She wrote, and looked so frowningly at hi[ ]

"I don't believe you!" she said. "You are ha[ ]

"On what? All you have to do is say nothi[ ] am right. In cash. Will you believe me i[ ] week?"

"I will believe you!"

"Good. Off with everything and let me see [ ]

"But you are treating me like an idol!"

"Why not? Aren't you? You deny you a[ ] Different from the common? Why are y[ ] Minister? Is everybody? If he goes away, y[ ] you? If he writes letters, you correct his l[ ] You think it isn't known? You are his br[ ] Doesn't everybody know? Don't you? For wh[ ]

She turned away.

"It is what a secretary is for," she said.

"Good. And at the Mashoba? Extra money[ ]

"It is necessary!"

"To keep going here? You should put a n[ ] Minister!"

"Tell me how!"

"Very simple. When I come back from Bom[ ]

"Vutthi will meet!"

"Good. Put a screw. Better than promise of [ ]

the business school here. I have a certificate. And seven years in insurance. And I wish to work for you. You have been so kind to Gond. It is my duty!"

"Whatever you earn now, you will earn double with me. Gond will take you to Seripur tomorrow. He will tell Babuji my wishes. You will make yourself as comfortable as possible until the men come to build the office. I shall be there on Friday. Gond, find out times of arrival, last flight from Bombay. Meet me. I shall come back here. I shall stay here tonight. Pick me up at six o'clock tomorrow morning. How did you buy that suit?"

"Khusti bought it for me. She also bought the driver's suit and boots and helmet. She is the best sister. I will pay back!"

"No need," she said, the small, small voice. "He needed. I had money. He got!"

Prem counted notes.

"You must accept this," he said. "You are both in my employ. I am responsible. You cannot deny?"

"But it was also my love," she said. "Can you repay?"

Prem picked up the notes.

"You are right," he said. "Gond, you will take this money, and buy with a brother's love whatever you think Khusti would most like. You understand? No denial. How is Khusti to get to Seripur? There is no bus service, is there? Where do you live?"

"In my father's place in the tyre market," Gond said. "Behind. We are wishing to go away. We would like to find a place. We save!"

"But my father is a hard man," Khusti said. "He takes everything. He tears my clothes!"

"Find a good place," Prem said. "I will pay the first three months. Gond, you pick the best of your friends. Without a mouth. He will take Khusti to Seripur in the morning, and back at night. If Babuji wants something, he will get it. I will pay. Pick twenty of the friends you trust. They shall each have a Ganesh. Only yours will be black. You will form a company. I will arrange the details. Khusti will control the books. You will deal only with Dal. If you find somebody buying gas or anything else in another place, he is finished. Understood?"

Sideways nod.

"Khusti," he said. "If you are like your brother, your life is sweetened by all you hope for. Gond will see to it. I shall guarantee. But we have no mouths!"

"None," she said. "I have ears and eyes, but no mouth!"

"Enough," he said. "Why does your father tear your clothes?"

"He wishes to make me a bed-girl. I will not. For this we save. We think of you. You are Krishna!"

"No, no, no!" he said. "Please. I am ordinary. I hope never anything more. Gond, you will not take your sister back to the tyre market. Tomorrow, if you can't find a place, she will stay here until you do. I will pay. She will not go back to the tyre market. As a brother, you will see to it. I shall stay here. Come at six o'clock. Miss Khusti, until Friday!"

She and Gond gave him *namaste* in both palms to forehead.

"Good night, Premji!" she whispered. "We have flowers in our prayers!"

CHAPTER 7

Delhi airport was a ghost of sleepy ones, and porters hid. When anybody needed a porter, they reappeared but they had another price. Gond solved. Prem waited in the line, saw a face, disbelieved, but she was there.

Miss Turlo.

He went to her, and asked.

"Yes," she said, tall. "The Minister instructed me to take notes. So I am here. You object?"

"Never," he said. "I have first appointment thirty minutes after we touch down. You come?"

"Of course. It is what I am sent to do!"

The tall one, in a beautiful blind of clean breath.

She had a seat apart, and he made no effort to be with her. But he had a further idea about the Minister. If that one could dare to think that a Miss Turlo might restrict his area of activity, then she, and the Minister, would learn.

He slept until they touched down.

Das had a car for him. Miss Turlo was elsewhere.

"Go here," he told the driver. "Wait for me!"

They stopped at the dock gates. A havildar wanted to make unwonted enquiries, but a note assured entrance. They stopped outside Godown Number Fourteen, a large place, and a watchman came, but he gave him a note, and the side door was opened.

The place was full. Of everything. He looked into his mind. Engines. Spares. Bodies, doors, every part of a car. Dials, small things, anything anybody wanted, all here. And by the thousand. Radios, every kind. In the tens of thousands. Spare parts for radios, by the thousands and thousands. A warehouse, ready for quick sales, but one look and he decided no knock-downs, but only full price.

He was in the third aisle, and Miss Turlo came in heel-click.

"I am only making a note," she said, high, in that space. "I don't wish to disturb!"

"Take notes," he said. "You don't disturb. You will help. I have an idea what is here. Do you?"

"I am only told to see and report," she said. "There is a great deal here. Yes?"

"A great deal," he said. "Of no value. I have wasted my time!"

"You can't say that!" she said. "There is no much!"

"Unsaleable," he said. "Who will buy? At what price? I think I must withdraw. I do myself great harm. Nothing here is worth real money. Very few things will realise a price!"

"But the Minister believes there are crores of rupees here!" she said.

"Rupees of what? Who will buy? Advertise? What is here? Contraband? Extra from Customs? What is the value? Shall I tell you? Or do you, intelligent girl, do you *know?*"

She looked about the quiet place, full of packing cases and crates, and nodded.

"I think I do," she said. "Outdated?"

"Exactly. Who wants it? Tell me. How do we *sell*. To who?"

"It is all worthless?"

"I appeal to you. What do you say of articles taken in contraband of ten, fifteen years ago?"

"Contraband?"

"Why are they here?"

She looked about, hands in pockets of the long blue overcoat.

"Possibly," she said. "Possibly. We have to think again?"

"Of course. What else?"

"I didn't know it was so dead!"

"What is more dead than manufactories of fifteen or more years ago?"

"I begin to see how you think."

"How else *is* there to think? Who is going to buy this rubbish? Outside, in the villages? Very well. Why should I be asked to waste my time? I am very sickened!"

"I think the Minister is most anxious for it all to be taken off the department's hands. It is causing very much worry, you see?"

"Telephone to him. Tell him what I say. It is mostly junkish stuff. I can sell it only in lots. If he *wants* me to sell. But I won't do it without his word *directly* to you. Or else I go back immediately to Delhi!"

"Wait, now, please, Mr. Prem!" she said. "I know this is a very important matter from the Minister's point of view. We *must* have it out of the way. It's why he sent me. I will phone the office from the gate. Please wait!"

He watched her almost running down the aisle. She had long legs, pale-brown hair, Anglo-Indian skin, coffee and creamy, everything he liked. He saw a telephone on the table by the door, almost hidden under paper and old ledgers, higgle-piggle. The number Dal had given replied, and he asked for four trucks to be sent to Godown Fourteen on the east wharf, and the same trucks to go loaded to Dal's showroom in Delhi, and come back for more.

"How many trucks have you got?"

"You will have ten five-tonners? I have twelve more altogether."

"Send them all, with ten porters. Special money I pay."

"They will be there. One hour. How about the gate?"

"They will be passed. Ministry permit. Get more!"

"Ah!"

He tore off the covers of some of the items, finding toothbrushes, cosmetics, whiskey by the hundred crates, brandy, gin, champagne, a lot of other stuff, and then a sofa, in soft leather, that folded down to make a double bed. There were twenty. Ten would come to him, and two more for Gond and Khusti. He put one down and it kept its promise. It was firm, but soft. Bedding filled other big boxes. Gas stoves, refrigerators, kitchenware, household stuff, it was all there. There was so much. All the labels were torn off, and stencils had been painted out. But he saw enough to guess it was an aid-shipment side-tracked, and he thought he knew why the Minister worried. Found, it could be laid at his door. The Opposition would create an uproar. He might have to resign. Then there was threat of criminal prosecution. All sorts of curious thinking developed. Miss Turlo might have a hand in it. A lot of implications were in the cases of drugs and medicaments. Her father was a physician, and her mother was something to do with hospitals. He knew her facts from birth.

He heard her coming back, the heel-click of boots that made her inches higher, and stilting.

"Yes!" she said, a bit excited. "He says sell at any price. Simply liquidate everything. If you can save him a few cases of whiskey and some cigars, it is very well done. And you will bring the cash to him, and he will give you twenty-five, not twenty percent. If that is perfectly satisfactory?"

"Yes. It is satisfactory. But how shall I trust you?"

She frowned, and turned to him, full in the eyes.

"Trust?" she said. "What do you mean, *trust?*"

"You could have called anybody, police or Customs. How do I know? I could never prove I was working for the Minister, or anybody else. It would be denied. What proof? I have a letter. A forgery? You are here to catch a fellow trying to take advantage. How do I know?"

"It's ridiculous!" she whispered, afraid. "It is so *ridiculous!*"

"Not!" he said. "Think of my position if police break in, now. What am I to say? Everything can be denied. What is my defence?"

"No," she said, blank. "It's impossible. Everything is properly structured. Sell for what you can. That is the final word. I am witness. Also, that you have twenty-five percent. To be paid before I go back to Delhi!"

"And what will you get?"

"I might have a present," she said. "A sari length?"

"It's all?"

"He's not open-handed!"

"Supposing I said twenty-five thousand rupees, cash in the hand? To stay here and take note that everything is taken away Supposing?"

"Too much a dream!"

"No dream. *Notes.*"

She threw back the coat and lifted her head and neck.

"It is so hot!" she said. "This morning terribly cold. Now, *hot!*"

"Take off," he said, and tugged the sleeve, walking her down toward the bed in shadow. "I want to see you in the middle of *that*."

She looked at the shiny leather.

"O!" she said. "What a beauty of a thing!"

"You would like one? It will be delivered to your place. Not a word said anywhere."

She put an open palm on it, pressed.

"I can't believe it!" she said. "It's wonderful leather. *Real!*"

"It will go to your place. Give me the address. But I want to see you in the middle of this one. Naked!"

"Oh, I couldn't!"

"Take off. Twenty-five thousand. In the hand!"

"Somebody will come!"

"You will come!"

"No. I mean, somebody will come in!"

"Nobody. I have the key. Take off. The middle of the bed!"

"I have never been. I am truly virgin!"

"The sweet better. I have never known a virgin of twenty-seven. You were playing with yourself?"

"Oh, no!"

"But now you will take off all, and play, and I will watch!"

"Somebody's coming in!"

"No chance. Off. Middle of the bed. Naked!"

"You are cruel. I could walk out. Complain to the Minister!"

"Twenty-five thousand rupees!"

She let the overcoat drop from her arms. Slowly, she pulled down the zip of her dress. She never looked at him. The dress came off. She stood in bodice and little pants, like a swim suit.

"You want more?" she whispered. "It is awful!"

"It is beautiful. I didn't know you held such a wonder. Off!"

She took off the bodice. Her teats were small, but full, and his fingers squeezed, and the nipples were long, pink. She pushed hands flat into the pants' waist, and took them down to her ankles, and stepped out.

She fell on the bed, face down.

"Be soon," she whispered. "Be quick. Whatever you want, take. But not very long!"

He took not very long and she was not such a virgin, but very good, and enjoying, and pushing to him, and making nice little sounds, and becoming beautiful suddenly. She passed a hand, and raised the left knee, both as if to feel the leather.

"There is no bathroom here?" she asked.

"At the end, just past the table with the telephone."

"Excuse me," she said, and picked up her clothes, and ran, tall, creamy-coffee, brown hair flopping, but she had a black nuptial, so there was dye work somewhere, pretty business for somebody, and he wondered if there was profit in opening a place only to dye the nuptial.

He went down to the telephone and called Das.

"Ah, Prem? So happy to hear you!"

"Come to Godown Fourteen. How many five-tonners did you get?"

"I can get all you want. Up to thirty. Full maintenance!"

"Come here without loud show at two-thirty. I will meet at the gate!"

"How many five-tonners!"

"At least thirty, for several hours every day, into Bombay, and then to Delhi. You have the warehouses. Empty them. We need them. Is Bhoomijai still in business?"

"Bring him? He is bigger than the rest together. Listening?"

"Yes, both. It is a question of crores. Cash!"

"Your only worry will be finding boxes to carry. Cash is *there!*"

"Bring him, I like the idea of Bhoomijai!"

Dal's men thumped the door just after Miss Turlo came out, dressed, cool, knowing nothing, showing less, and started to clear the desk, trying to keep her shining head from the dust.

He took the man down the main aisle to the engine crates.

"A lot of work," he said. "You need at least twenty men to keep the line moving. I think you will get ten engines on each truck. You will take them to Dal, direct, to Delhi."

"He sent a telegram to give special help. This load will take at least four, perhaps five journeys. I can get more trucks?"

"No. Trucks spaced at intervals will not be a convoy. A convoy can be stopped!"

"Your head is hard. The drivers will have money?"

"For themselves, and to give away!"

"Four times the normal rate?"

"Certainly. Take your own from that. Special present at the end. No slip-ups!"

The man waved his hands.

"Where there is money, no slips!" he said. "Delhi and return less than two days, day and night drivers?"

"Dal will send trucks from Delhi today for the rest. Fly to Delhi, and fly back. I want to find out if I can trust you. I must leave on Thursday. Count this, and give me a receipt. There, at the desk. Good?"

"Very lovely," the man said, counting the wad with wet fingers and a thumb that looked as if it had been squashed wide by a press. "I shall be back before you go. You can be sure to depend. Dalji has always depended. Thirty years!"

"You know Gupta Das, here?"

"Import, export, shipping, transport, Customs agent, and God knows what? Of course. Who doesn't? I am always working with him or his managers. Ask them about Mehta Roy. I am first in my line!"

The man's good fire was in his eyes.

"Harijan?" Prem said, to the far corner.

Roy nodded downwards.

"Good, again," Prem said, quietly. "I am also. Also few know. We will work together? There should be mutual—I shall say once more—*mutual* benefit? We understand?"

Roy took the tears with his fingers.

"I have heard courage from a brother," he said. "Now I have more. I shall help!"

"Good. Load up!"

The men came in, and from the way they set about the stack they were no novices, and they were getting sixteen crates in the trucks, with higher sideboards, twenty. When they left, at intervals of thirty minutes, there were one hundred engine crates left, and fifty crates of spares, and hundreds of tyres in sets, and he put hand to forehead to pray he would find whole bodies of cars and trucks in all the rest piled behind.

Miss Turlo made notes, head on one side, to the neck, it seemed, in the river.

"What were those boxes?" she asked.

"I think dolls from Japan," he said. "They will be junk on the Delhi market. A good price, do we care?"

"How much?"

"If the luck comes to us, perhaps half a lakh. Depends on the dealer. Ready sale to children? In the villages, of course."

"I would like one!"

"Should I open a whole crate for one? One missing from a crate, what does the merchant think? Somebody is cheating? In other crates, how many more? No. A deal is a deal. Be satisfied with your bed. It will remind you?"

"I would like a doll to remind me!"

"You shall have. With the bed. And remember. I am in Office Number Eleven. And you are having twenty-five thousand rupees. It's not enough?"

"Believe when I see!"

"Where will you stay tonight?"

"The Western."

"You should be staying only at the Taj Mahal. You are entitled. I say you will be at the Taj. I will tell the Minister. How *can* somebody, acting so importantly for his department, stay at a lodging house? Telephone the Taj, now. We want two doubles. I will give him personally the account!"

"He will think we slept?"

"I will deny!"

She laughed, and took off the telephone.

"Until when?" she asked.

"Thursday morning!"

"He will *know* we slept!"

"Very well!"

"He will phone my father. There will be hell!"

"With the cash, and his cigars and whiskey, who will he phone? Take whiskey and cigars for your father. What will be hell?"

She laughed again. He was liking her.

"It was what the Minister told me, that first time," she said. "That young fellow will go a long way. If he attends to his business. The moment he is outside, the vultures will eat him. He meant politics!"

"I will never be. Believe me, I have seen enough. I know them all. Except for a few, I spit. But the few will never be any good. Too many against!"

"My father says so. He says he doesn't know why he goes on saving people to live on in such a muck-rake of a world. It is sickening to be civilized!"

"But your father wants the drugs and medicines in this consignment?"

"The Minister promised there would be a chance!"

"You are here only because of that?"

"Don't look at me in such a way, please? Well, yes, I suppose. It is possible?"

"If the proper price is paid? Drugs and medicines are very high today. True loyalty to the Minister. I must get competitive price. Telephone the Minister. Ask what I am to do. Telephone your father. Ask what he is prepared to pay. Cash. Before delivery. Or I will get my price here, and the Minister will receive it!"

"It is worth what?"

He turned the wad of paper to her.

"I have been through with medical catalogue," he said. "The price of each is beside entry. The total is below. You see it?"

She pushed a fist in her cheek, and her eyes were broken eggs.

"But not so *much!*" she cried.

"It is an entire base hospital. Beds, equipment, surgery, drugs, medicines, everything. How much?"

"But not all that!"

"Exactly. That's less than half price. I get it cash, or no sale, and I can sell it for more!"

"I can phone my father?"

"Phone him. Tell him to get his transport here. All expenses are his. But he will produce that sum, cash, or the entire consignment is on the market at three times the price. Call him!"

"He could never get so much!"

"To sell for three times? Four, five times? Call him. Call the Minister!"

He went out in the sun, and another truck went out for Delhi.

Down at the main gate, he spread the notes, and told them about Mr. Das coming at two-thirty. Everybody made the sideways nod. All in order.

Back at the godown, all smiles.

"He will fly with the money," she said. "He says it is cheap. But he wants to be sure of the drugs?"

"There are no drugs," he said. "There are cases of medicaments, but no drugs. It is the American way. They lock everything up!"

"But it is why he is bringing all that money!" she squeaked.

"He still has a bargain. And you get twenty-five thousand. Plus a percentage of what he pays. Of course? Do you work for nothing?"

She put down the pencil, and clasped hands behind her neck.

"Ah, Prem!" she said, in the glad voice. "Such a beautiful day. How much do you think?"

"Not less than another twenty-five thousand? And you will tell everybody?"

"Not a small word. Never. Will you always let me work with you? Yes? I will work. I can tell you many things. Fifty thousand rupees? How wonderful. Prem, you are a beautiful man!"

CHAPTER 8

Das brought Bhoomijai in the evening.

Fat, and frowning because of his money, Bhoomijai looked down the list, scratching inside his shirt, and slipping his eyes to Miss Turlo with almost a splash of saliva.

"How much you are asking, and let us be clear, I am paying only very below current market price," he said. "I know the reason for hurried sale!"

"Share with me," Prem said. "Miss Turlo, you have worked long enough. You may please go home!"

"She lives here?" Bhoomijai asked, looking at the shining brown-haired figure in blue, going in and out of overhead lights, away. "I would employ her. Highest salary!"

"Not free. I am employer. What *is* reason?"

"MISA, of course," Das said. "They are already starting arrests. But not Bhoomijai. He is beyond them!"

"What is MISA? Have I missed?"

"Maintenance of Internal Security Act," Das said. "It came into full effect last night. There are hundreds of arrests. Smugglers, hoarders, traders in foreign currency, all in danger. But not Bhoomijaiji. He knows great deal. Too much, eh, Bhoomijaiji?"

"Completely ridiculous, of course. I have more to say than any informer. About everybody. Nothing will come to me!"

The scratch of personal cheques, the whispered promise of counted notes, and a small clink of gold coin all seemed in the air, noisier than the truck starting its engine.

"It's not the reason for this sale," Prem said. "These godowns are the department's. They are needed for consignments of American grain. These goods can be disposed. They are no longer required for the department. I shall sell to highest buyer. All out, Wednesday night!"

"You asking what?"

Prem wrote the figure.

Bhoomijai looked, and pushed the paper off the table.

"A triumph of absurdity!" he said. "Who could think of it? You are young in business!"

Prem picked up the paper.

"I have Mudji Chagan coming in the morning," he said. "Jhem Patel in the afternoon. Between the three of you I shall have my price!"

"I shall telephone them," Bhoomijai said, sitting back. "We shall arrange a price, and you can take it or leave!"

"*This* price," Prem said. "*Cash*. Not one paisa less. *Now* telephone!"

"You are putting up my back. An entirely inexperienced paper-pusher speaking such a fashion to me? Das, put sense into this fellow!"

"Well, a diplomacy would be wiser, yes," Das said, almost creeping. "We don't want to upset Bhoomijaiji, do we? This is why I got him to come here, isn't it?"

"Listen, the last time I talk," Prem said. "The price is *that*. Telephone where you like. You know your competitors would go any lengths beating you in lucrative bargains. Over that price you could sell five times. Are you teaching me basis of business? I passed many years ago!"

"I am disliking your tone and manner!" Bhoomijai said, staring the mudsplashes into black points. "I could put you behind bars!"

"*Put*. One more word, I don't do business with you. We are understanding what I say?"

"Wait a little!" Das said, hands out, seeing himself sadly losing fat commission. "We are knowing you are Ministry man. Where is your authority?"

Prem slowly took the Minister's letter from his breast pocket, presenting with a slapped hand.

Bhoomijai read, and looked, pushing chin under ear at the side, a shiny stare.

Das read.

"Well, it seems you have firm ground," he said. "If the price—?"

"The original price is on that paper," Prem said. "I have prospectives. Don't worry. I shall sell for one crore more, easily. I report to the Minister, morning and night. He knows where enquiries come. He is in position to cause great trouble!"

Das looked along the aisle to the dark doorway, and his eyes went sideways down to Bhoomijai.

"It would be bad time for complications," he said, almost to himself. "Very bad. Police. Customs. Income Tax?"

Bhoomijai pushed from the chair, and hit the table with his thick stick, and again, savage, and turned, stick up, ready to hit.

"I could have people to inflict certain hurts on you!" he shouted. "Who are you to talk in low fashion to me?"

"That remark costs you one crore more," Prem said. "That is two crores over the blanket price I offered. For madness and unseemly behaviour, there is always penalty!"

"If you were always in Bombay, I would destroy you piece by piece!" Bhoomijai said. "But you are a Delhi *desi*. Beyond my reach!"

"*Desi?*" Prem said. "People not speaking good English? Very well. I am *desi*. Even so, I am better than any Bombay *prick!*"

"O, now, now!" Das said, fists to his ears, shut-eyed at the roof. "How did we come to this? Business, business. Nothing more. Who is worried with Delhi or Bombay?"

"I, for one, am not!" Prem said. "I fly to Delhi on Thursday, and I report to the Minister, cash in the barrel. No argument or insults will prevent. This merchandise, you know what it is worth? The price you pay me can be swollen three or four times. If you don't, others will. Alacrity is the soul of business!"

Das picked up the list.

"Let us examine!" he said, softly. "Nothing lost in verifying. Many richly fat entries. Nothing but profit in the market!"

Bhoomijai rested on the stick to get up.

"I would like a glass of milk and a thick piece of saffron cake," he said, in a long groan. "I am very hungry. It is always very abrasing to my temper, you see. Find somebody to go!"

"I will," Prem said. "Pursue your examination. Milk and cake!"

He went out to the gate, and asked the havildar, and one of the men said he would go. He gave a note, and the man ran.

He passed more notes for taking.

"If police, or any others coming in, let me know," he said. "I am here till Wednesday night, or early Thursday. Many trucks will come from Delhi. Others will come from Das, here, in Bombay. Work with me, you are always right side. Always something healthy to put in the pocket!"

He pointed to the telephone, and a smile of permission let him dial Taj Mahal, and a miracle, it answered. He asked for Miss Turlo, and the receiver clacked.

"Miss Turlo? It is Prem!"

"O, Mr. Prem. I am so glad. My father is here, and wishing so much to see you!"

"I have got Bhoomijai and Gupta Das nosing the goods. I will be at least an hour. How did he find you?"

"I called him this morning after you told me Taj. We shall stay until you are here. The grill is always open!"

"I hope you are?"

"For you, yes. Come soon!"

He waited for the man to run in, breathless, with the package and bottle, and he gave another note.

He went back to the godown, and saw the two on the east side, prodding and poking, looking at the list, and ticking.

"Cake and milk!" he shouted. "Come and get!"

Bhoomijai waddled like a big goose, flat foot, dab-dab on the inside of the shoe as if every step hurt. The big belly shook side to side, and he breathed little sniffs, and his eyes were cowpats, with black viper spots, shiny. He tore the package, and bit a double mouthful from the cake, and drank and drank the milk, and swallowed, and made an air noise.

"How much I owe?" he asked.

"Hospitality," Prem said.

"My valuers will be here. Five o'clock, too early?"

"Earlier? I finish on Wednesday. Prospectives here tomorrow. Four o'clock?"

"Five o'clock. I shall know more the value."

"You know now. It is the same price, plus two crores!"

"Please say little!" Das said, arms out, in address to some god. "Everything is too good for imperceptibles. Are we so ludicrous advertising sign, and touched the boy to slow down, keep out of direct lights, find a way through small lanes of stalls, to the other side of Malwan Khan's sheds. Shadows still moved at work. He tapped the seat to stop, and got out, and the boy shut the motor. The blue truck was not there, or hiding. Just then Bedwa came, no higher than a child, from behind a cloth stall, and turned his head, and went back toward the shed's greenish light, and the lathis followed, and became part of the dark.

Prem went into the shed's space, puddled with fat scourings from the complexion cream mixers, and looked for the sad, sullen face of Ghal, always tired, always in half a yawn, always pointing to somebody else, or running to a machine, any excuse not to talk, not to say he was Malwan's only assistant, a graduate in chemistry, but earning no more than Malwan would pay, about a twentieth of his worth in wages alone, but at least five times more than he would earn outside as a Harijan.

"Ghal," he shouted, in the stink of boiling fat. "Where are you?"

He came from the room piled to the roof with cream jars, and tubes, and packaging, and stood, staring, tired, not part, not wanting.

"Listen, now," Prem said. "There will be changes from tonight. Can you take charge here? All departments? Without advice or supervision? Of any kind?"

Ghal nodded. Nothing changed in his eyes.

"I am in charge now," he said, and swallowed a yawn. "What difference?"

"You will be responsible. To me. Your salary is ten times. From tonight. All profits, monthly, split half, to the rupee. We speak between four eyes. Remember. I also have other friends!"

He looked toward the tall line of lathis in shadow beyond the doorway.

"I have no mouth," Ghal said, in light, as though other thoughts burned.

"Work tonight and tomorrow as if no change was, except that all the people here will earn five times more," Prem said. "Have you seen me?"

"I have never seen you!"

"Did you hear words?"

"I hear the machines!"

They put hands together, and bowed, hands to forehead, and Prem went out, with Bedwa and the lathis behind.

"Malwan Khan's house," he said. "Ten times ordinary rate for the lathis. He will go in the Jumna. Look for buried money. Do not touch his women and children. Let them take all they want, and burn the house. But save the paper. For me."

CHAPTER 3

"Prem, we have spoken for almost thirty minutes and you have told me nothing, and I want to know *why!*" the Minister said, from the window, back to the room. "You understand me? I want to *know!*"

Prem bowed low, hands to forehead.

"If I knew what the Ministerji wanted to know, I would tell," he said, above a whisper. "So far, questions about the police. In my lowly place I know them. By their names. But talking, or going home, or any small friendship? Impossible, as I have said. How possible?"

"It could be flogged out of you?"

"If it is not in my mouth, how is it in my body?"

"A flogging is not pleasant!"

"I would find it in my lowly duty to accept to be flogged, if it would assure the Ministerji that I am Prem Naran, humble and faithful and smallest and most devoted servant!"

"I could take away your position?"

"To crush the ant from its way? What is any ant?"

"You don't speak as a messenger, or a porter," the Minister said, pushing the curtain aside. "Are you a member of a political party?"

"I have no party, Ministerji. I shall never have. I know politicians. I have no vote. I have no wish. Why should I?"

The Minister looked at the file on the desk.

"You were pupil of the Lord Reading School for three years," he said. "After, at the Normal in Lucknow. Then the Rajagopalachari at Vaipur. Why all the chopping and changing?"

"I was an orphan. My father—I called him—Mr. Raybould. Where he went to teach, I went to learn. He put me in here as a runner. He died. I became junior messenger. I earned promotion.

I have always served. Truly. As he taught. He was a wonderful man. To me. To everybody. If I meet a Raybould boy now, we think of him. O, yes, we cry!"

"He was against Independence?"

"He was persecuted because he *supported* the Gandhi-Nehru-Maulvi Pasha movement. How many times he was in prison? How many English wore the Gandhi cap? How many wove their own? He did. I did. And how many wear them today? Or weave their own?"

"No necessity," the Minister said. "What we wanted, we were given. How many railway officials do you know?"

"We send many consignments to Government offices and State Legislatures," Prem said, keeping heat from his voice. "I know them all. All transport. All lines. All time-tables. All officials. Railways. Roads. Air. Everybody. Anywhere. I don't need a book. Why should I? For these years, I am here. Every day I hear the times, when, how, what, how much. Should I neglect my job?"

"You are well taught," the Minister said, looking at a corner of the desk.

"I was first always in English. Then mathematics, and bookkeeping. Then business, and organisation."

"You were very young," the Minister said, looking in the other room, at E.E.D. in a black sari, a marvel of quiet.

"If the tree has sap it will rise. Make sure of the sap. It is the juice!"

"It seems to me that you could be useful," the Minister said. "I could crush you in a moment. Remember that. I shall think. There may be small jobs you can perform. I shall consider. Where is the Mashoba?"

"I have heard of it from others, Ministerji. I have never been there. It is far beyond my small place. I have said I have no mouth?"

"Go," the Minister said, and fell, not sat, in his big black leather chair. "I shall call you!"

Prem went out, low from the waist, both hands to forehead, though in reaching the far door, he passed close to E.E.D.'s desk, and he took the small, warm, sandalled foot, and pressed, and it stayed in his hand, and he exulted, and opened the door, and stood in the corridor, and breathed hard, thinking of the Guru, and Mr. Raybould, and himself, but there seemed no real link.

He cycled back to the office, and made short work of mail collections, and filling members' boxes with letters and notices, and then watching the sweeper empty the waste-baskets ready for Bedwa. The Houses were in recess, but the staff were still busy, and the drafting clerks worked almost day and night, trying to build paragraphs in English, and then Hindi, and every word an argument of shaken fists, a catfight in each comma, riots over a full stop.

He wanted to push them all out and do both by himself, without one single bead on the brow. They were all lawyers or failed B.A.'s and they haggled for the sake, only to prove how profound their knowledge of legalities, what scholarship in languages, how many saints on a pin's head, what number of tones in the length of the sitar. The foolishness, Mr. Raybould often said, of urbs. Every second they are having to make sure they are themselves by knowing. They know, therefore they are. They do not know, they are not. They are burning constantly on the ghats of fear, leaping in their frightfat, spitting sour little globs of tension, and covering with courteous behaviour, a skin that an argument will tear, provoking screams, pouts, refusals to speak, and then flowers, and exaggerations of sorrow. But still the ghats burn.

At ten to three the gate havildar called to report a waiting scootercab. Prem collected mail and registered packets, and got in, and the boy started, and stopped at the main mail office. Prem got receipts for the packages dropped the mail, and walked out.

"Such a small time for such a lot!" the boy said.

"They know who I am. I don't have any queuing to do!"

"My sister has to wait for many hours every day. To weigh the letters. Then to buy the stamps. Then to make sure the weight and the stamps are both correct. Hours she is waiting. She could burn everything. But what can she do? Where would she find another job?"

"She speaks English?"

"Who gets work without English?"

"What does she do? How old?"

"Twenty-four. A secretary. Firebird Insurance."

"What tribe or sect is your father?"

"Of the tribe of tyre repairers. Of the sect of the hungry. It is what my sister says. Who speaks of this? We say we are Maronites. She went to school with them. What other way?"

From the boy's back, he saw, and heard.

They were of the Great Family.

"How much do you pay for this scooter per day or week?" Prem asked, and pointed to the turn. "Here. Go to Dal's."

"I pay for petrol, and I give my father half of the fares," the boy said. "I give my mother one half of mine. My father got it in a traffic wreck. His friends in the market repaired it. We all stole pieces—"

"Where did you get the licence?"

The boy laughed.

"I have not got one," he said. "If I am stopped, I pay. What can I do?"

"You must have one. How can you drive decently if you are stopped by any policeman? I shall get it."

"You are son of Krishna?"

"We are brothers. Enough? Wait here. Keep a look for me, steady!"

He went in the wide doors of the showroom, and Dal saw him through the plate glass of his office, and swung bare feet high off the desk, and came, fat, big, laughing, black.

"O, Prem, my both eyes and ears!" he shouted, and threw out his arms to embrace, but the turning police trucks outside brought a dance out of the way.

"Bedwa brought the box," he whispered.

Dal nodded, staring, aware.

"Where is it?"

"In a tool chest in the garage outside. Why?"

"Get it for me. No time. Go!"

Dal turned on heelless slippers, heavy, ponderous, and the mauve underlip quivered in a thickness like liver, but he moved swift as a scorpion, out to the big garage at the back. Prem made a movement of the hand on the window to catch the boy's eye, and pointed to the back. The scootercab started, and he ran to the garage in time to see Dal lift the blue box out in a clatter of tools.